Town Born

EARLY AMERICAN STUDIES

Series editors: Daniel K. Richter, Kathleen M. Brown, and David Waldstreicher

Exploring neglected aspects of our colonial, revolutionary, and early national history and culture, Early American Studies reinterprets familiar themes and events in fresh ways. Interdisciplinary in character, and with a special emphasis on the period from about 1600 to 1850, the series is published in partnership with the McNeil Center for Early American Studies.

A complete list of books in the series is available from the publisher.

Town Born

*The Political Economy
of New England
from Its Founding
to the Revolution*

Barry Levy

PENN

UNIVERSITY OF PENNSYLVANIA PRESS

PHILADELPHIA

Published by
University of Pennsylvania Press
Philadelphia, Pennsylvania 19104-4112

Printed in the United States of America on acid-free paper
10 9 8 7 6 5 4 3 2 1

Library of Congress Cataloging-in-Publication Data

Levy, Barry.
    Town born : the political economy of New England from its founding to the Revolution / Barry Levy.
        p.   cm.— (Early American studies)
    Includes bibliographical references and index.
    ISBN 978-0-8122-4177-8 (hardcover : alk. paper)
    1. New England—Economic conditions.   2. New England—Politics and government—To 1775.   3. Cities and towns—New England—History.   4. Land settlement—New England—History.   5. Power (Social sciences)—New England—History.   6. City and town life—New England—History.   7. New England—Social conditions.   I. Title.
    HC107.A11L48   2010
    330.974'02—dc22

                                                                          2009016456

CONTENTS

PART III
Town People

INTRODUCTION

IN 1760, SOME fifteen years before the American Revolution, the young John Adams witnessed and became fascinated with, though somewhat frightened by, the exuberance of autonomous workers at play. Taking a break from his legal studies, Adams "rode to the Iron works landing" in Weymouth, Massachusetts, "to see a vessel launched." These happy affairs symbolized the viability of the New England economy, the skill and cooperation of the empowered workers, and—assuming the ship floated—the profitable completion of a long job. Afterward, the workers and town folk celebrated nearby at Thayer's tavern: "The rabble filled the house," noted Adams, and "every room, kitchen, chamber was crowded with people." He observed "negroes with a fiddle" and "young fellows and girls dancing in the chamber as if they would kick the floor thro." The scene was untamed and joyous. Adams spent "the whole afternoon in gazing and listening." "Fiddling and dancing, in a chamber full of young fellows and girls, a wild rabble of both sexes, and all ages in the lower room, singing, dancing, fiddling, drinking flip and toddy, and drams—this is the riot and reveling of taverns and of Thayer's frolics."[1] As an intellectual worker Adams was both with, and apart from, the male and female mechanics in the scene, yet he admired them and spent the whole day. These workers had many natural advantages: they were young, well paid, drunk, and animated by music. Yet much of their frolic stemmed from their political power. At least on this Tuesday evening, New England town democracy seemed to agree with its practitioners.

Early American workers rarely frolicked gloriously around their completed work. In Virginia, slaves did not celebrate the tobacco harvest. In Pennsylvania, workers drank their rum during the wheat harvest, not after it. Elsewhere, in "townless" America, many people lived in secular heaven, or hell, with a clear, often intimate, view of the other condition. Outside of New England, as Allan Kulikoff has shown, white males had more good farmland than was available anywhere else and little political interference blocking their enjoyment of it. They came to own remarkably large farms and enjoyed an equality of condition among themselves unknown elsewhere.[2] Because land was so readily available, however, labor was in short supply, wages were relatively high, and well-paid wage earners were quick to buy land. In these conditions, in order to produce staple export crops like rice, wheat, and tobacco, the privileged landowners in colony after colony constructed societies that violently stripped labor of human value and laborers of political power. Their main invention was racial slavery, in which white farmers treated Africans and their descendants like beasts of burden and allowed them virtually no rights. This brutal and violent labor regime dominated South Carolina, Virginia, North Carolina, and Maryland, and even important sections of New Jersey, New York, and Rhode Island.[3]

In much of the middle colonies, especially Pennsylvania, farmers came to rely less on African or Indian slaves than floods of white indentured servants and redemptioners who were obliged to work for a number of years in exchange for their passage to the land of fine farms and promised opportunity. Although the fate of these bond servants requires more study, crime statistics and tax lists show that by 1750 Pennsylvania was also becoming a society in which forms of coercive labor were becoming plentiful and hard to escape, and many farmers employed servants, slaves, and hirelings on their broad acreage.[4]

Massachusetts proved an important exception to this common American social organization. By the mid-eighteenth century, the average New England farm family occupied a remarkably small farm on marginal land with only an acre or two of tillage. New Englanders did not have farms about which poor European peasants dreamed. Few pictures of them remain. Yet in Massachusetts slavery was rare, labor was respected, and despite the pressure of a growing population on tiny landholdings, social and political restiveness was remarkably exceptional, while consumption of luxurious English goods was widespread.[5]

The explanation for New England's distinctive and far more equitable and egalitarian, yet productive, order was less the challenge of its stony farmland than its unusual political organization: the political economy of the town. From settlement the English settlers divided their New England colonies into towns and insisted that no one could settle anywhere else. Each town was incorporated, and the town corporation (sometimes dominated initially by land speculators) owned the land and sold it, reserving some to lure needed artisans or to form into a common. By the early eighteenth century, although towns differed dramatically in population and degree of economic development, they had a nearly uniform political organization. The political organization of the Atlantic port of Boston, concentrated on the Shawmut peninsula, was identical to that of decentralized rural Hadley. Town meetings were sovereign, gathering three or four times a year to set public policy. Smallholders and male laborers voted and held sway. In the March meeting they usually chose up to seven selectmen and many lesser officers to run the town between meetings and one to four deputies, depending on population, to send to the legislature, called the General Court. Towns collected almost all the revenue for the New England colonies and collected revenue for themselves to maintain the town: to keep a minister (an imperative of being a town); to build roads and other public infrastructure; to support the poor; and to maintain a free school (another imperative of being a town, except in Rhode Island). In this system the town born, who had large numbers of children, quickly found themselves with rather small landholdings, but they retained the ability to use political power to develop the local economy while keeping outsiders from cheapening the value of their labor power or stealing their resources. Each town formed its native-born residents into a hard-working and skilled town labor force to create wealth—and occasionally to celebrate their achievements.

New England's male workers exercised more political power and enjoyed greater equality than almost any other producers in the Atlantic world. Their position was due entirely to the town's political economy. The town maintained at least three conditions that encouraged equity. First, the town was more or less democratic, so the white men who did the work also made or heavily influenced economic policy to protect the value of their labor and develop town resources for their own benefit. Second, New Englanders believed the town should have considerable power when intervening in households to encourage workers' productivity, and they used this power to build esteem for laborers. They subordinated families to the needs of the town, creating a town labor force. Third, towns supported schools that not only enhanced the value of labor by making white workers literate and numerate but also traumatized children, forcing the formation of male work groups based partly on disassociation and controlled violence. This severe socialization made New Englanders effective at doing the worst work available, the men becoming mariners and soldiers, and women capable of having many babies, producing textiles and livestock, and suffering their sons' deaths in early adulthood at sea. Massachusetts was a "Christian Sparta," as Samuel Adams described it. These traits were not only cultural or religious but, thanks to the town, embedded in material practice. The town meeting met three and four times a year, and the selectmen and other officers they chose carried out their will; family visiting and oversight and intervention in families was frequent and consequential; the towns spent money on schoolmasters and schools that were scenes of violence and trauma.

The town political economy created a large region in America where labor earned respect, relative equity ruled, workers exercised political power despite doing the most arduous and dangerous tasks, and the burdens and horrors of work were absorbed by the citizens themselves. This social order served as a basis for assertions of American equality and liberty. Historians have long wondered why respect for work and workers, equity, and idealism dramatically entered early America amid its emphasis on privileged property holders and degraded, often enslaved, workers. How could the American Revolution and its values of equality and liberty have been conceived and voiced first in a slave society?

Focusing on Virginia, which produced some of the greatest revolutionary leaders, Edmund Morgan in *American Slavery, American Freedom* argued that racial slavery and liberty were connected in a paradoxical, yet symbiotic, relationship.[6] In a preindustrial world where almost all labor was done by humans, the existence of racially defined slavery allowed white men to conceive of a republican society of mutual dignity and white privilege and assert republicanism supported by labor from an eternally inferior black working class that was tightly controlled and politically oppressed.

This book provides an additional response to that question: New Englanders, while exhibiting elements of the racism that pervaded America society and a robust xenophobia of their own concoction, nonetheless exceptionally, and often painfully, created a society in early America that modeled and spread equity and respect for labor and laborers. The mechanism for this labor system was a political economy centered on the town. New England had town labor systems, not family labor systems. The town labor force was composed of men and women over the age of six who did often dangerous productive work and competed well with other New World labor regimes economically. From age twenty-one, most men exercised political power. While lagging in farming, New Englanders fed themselves, made some of their own clothes, and could build and sail ships better than anyone. These achievements grew from the town political economies.

The democracy of the New England town and the town itself have received substantial attention and boundless homage, though not lately. Most
recently, with a few notable exceptions, the most sophisticated historians
have judged that town meeting democracy did not really do anything of
importance and that New England towns were so various that even the con-
cept of the town is a useless abstraction.[7] In the 1960s and 1970s, Edward
M. Cook, Kenneth Lockridge, and Michael Zuckerman questioned whether
smallholders and laborers actually had political power, or whether towns were
actually oligarchies. These historians' intensive and systematic research led
them to disagree on significant points, especially about the historical and
intellectual context and meaning of towns' democratic expression, but all
supported the position that smallholders and laborers in virtually every town
had a large share of the power, that deference of smallholders to their social
betters was limited, and that New England town democracy, if imperfect and
of debatable cultural meaning, was real. Their work remains among the most
important literature in early American studies. Despite the issues raised by
these works and their demonstration of a potent and unusual form of laborers' democracy in early America, interest in New England town democracy
then collapsed.[8]

Some historians concluded that democracy had little meaningful impact
on anything that really mattered. Just as Cook, Lockridge, and Zuckerman
were preparing, defending, or publishing their works, other historians crafted
persuasive naturalistic and deterministic frameworks to explain the development of the New England family and the New England economy without
virtually any reference to the town. In 1970, John Demos led the way in
demonstrating that the New England family was less a matter of law and
political context than natural processes and material forces. Birth intervals,
life spans, work routines, and times of weaning grew more interesting than
town elections in determining the structure and fate of a family. Important
issues of gender finally got long overdue attention, creating the construct of
the patriarchal New England household based on land, the psychology of
gender formation, long life spans, and religion. The patriarchal family seemed
so strong and certain in its operation that it rendered town institutions mere
expressions of those families and their long-lived, controlling fathers.[9]

The New England economy, Bernard Bailyn demonstrated, grew despite
town governments, for it was ultimately the Boston merchants who designed
the trade links to the West Indies in the 1640s that saved New England from
economic obscurity. The merchants designed those patterns in the face of

almost ruinous town and provincial interference.[10] Insofar as towns created economies, those economies failed. Recently, Daniel Vickers and Allan Kulikoff have written large, impressive books purporting to explain wide areas of New England and provincial economic and familial development without any reference to politics. Margaret Ellen Newell and Stephen Innes, while establishing the contribution of politics to Massachusetts economic growth, fail to confront the dominant narrative or bring politics to the local and personal level.[11] Because historians judge by default that town meeting democracy had no impact on family and economic life, they logically conclude that it did not matter, so local democracy is unworthy of their attention. In extracting politics from their social and economic narratives, these historians stand apart from an illuminating trend among English historians of the early modern period who over the past twenty years have decidedly put the politics back into social and economic history and have insisted that even peasants had political lives of importance.[12]

In Massachusetts, town meeting democracy obviously had a significant impact on people's economic and social lives. To take but one example, the Boston town meeting and others diverted the massive post-1760 immigration, which Bernard Bailyn has called the great eighteenth-century *Volkerwanderung*. After the end of the French and Indian War, North America emerged as a powerful magnet attracting people on the periphery of Britain and Europe. Bailyn estimates that approximately 221,500 immigrants arrived in the North American colonies between 1760 and 1775. This unprecedented surge of newcomers represented about 10 percent of the total population of the colonies in 1775. As Bailyn put it, "an average of about 15,000 people were arriving annually, which is triple the average of the years before 1760 and close to the total estimated population of the town of Boston in this period."[13]

Boston and other New England towns actually received only a few stragglers from this massive immigration. In his careful study of a register of English and Scottish immigrants to North America from 1773 to 1775, Bailyn discovered that a paltry 77 of 9,364 emigrants from Britain (less than 1 percent of the total) landed in any New England port. In this four-year span, the whole of New England, which was expanding as fast as other regions, got almost as many emigrants as did Grenada, while New York attracted twenty-five times as many (1,954), Philadelphia eighteen times as many (1,414, not counting the numerous Irish and German immigrants), and Virginia and Maryland forty times as many (3,102). Even Nova Scotia got ten times as many immigrants (758) as New England did.[14] What forces repelled these hopeful travelers from the New England region?

Environmental explanations fall short in this case. To be sure, immigrants may have judged that New England's economy offered limited prospects; it had a large and growing population, and it lacked open, attractive farmland. These conditions explain why fewer immigrants entered New England harbors, but not their near-total absence. The region's economy had need of many skilled laborers, so why were strangers unwelcome? In truth, if New England had been like other regions politically, many immigrants, their potential employers, and their merchant transporters would have found the region a viable destination. As Bailyn's analysis of the English and Scottish emigrant registers shows, some 60 percent of the 1773–75 emigrants were young males from southeastern England with artisan skills.[15] These men were not seeking farms. New England had many industries suited for them; especially shipbuilding, which underwent rapid expansion just before the American Revolution. The shipyards lining the Merrimack River launched seventy-two vessels in 1766 alone. According to one contemporary source, colonial American shipbuilders built 64,685 tons of shipping between 1769 and 1771; New Englanders built 44,173 of these tons (68 percent). Shipbuilders sold from £40,000 to £80,000 worth of American shipping annually to England, capturing about 30 percent of the domestic English market in commercial ships. The large ocean-going vessel and its rigging was, arguably, the most sophisticated and expensive commodity of the age.[16] Ship construction required not only shipwrights and carpenters but many other artisans such as block makers, caulkers, blacksmiths, and sawyers. The industry offered substantial employment to less-skilled workers such as loggers and carters. Many young English artisans might have found the New England industry attractive, with its high wages. Shipbuilding entrepreneurs may well have desired to lower labor costs by luring foreign workers to their busy yards.

To protect their wages and social value, however, New England workers chose to shut the doors to the massive influx of servants from Britain and Europe. Blocking outsiders was an established custom, so they merely enforced laws that had long deterred immigrants and their movers and sellers. They stopped vessels at Boston's harbor islands and inspected every immigrant for smallpox; they made every immigrant and captain post bond; they hired house searchers in Boston to uncover outsiders who had not entered legally; they made every immigrant get the selectmen's permission to open a business. In sum, they banished immigrants from their midst. If an immigrant overcame these restrictions and entered Boston legally, he or she could not move to a neighboring town without facing similar scrutiny and harassment.

In erecting these barriers, the town meetings retained the power of town-born workers in local labor markets, even if their power inconvenienced some entrepreneurs by raising labor costs. The absence of significant immigration into New England was a political phenomenon. Unlike many other early American working folk, New Englanders had the political means to enforce their will. No wonder the crowd rollicked at Thayer's tavern.

It is instructive to compare recent work on New England labor and family history with Richard Morris's classic *Government and Labor in Early America* (1946). Virtually every page of Morris's book is about law and political decisions; he assumes that workers' status and their share of the wealth they created was always largely determined by their political power as revealed in laws and court cases. Morris wrote at a time of strong labor unions and clear demonstrations of the government's effectiveness in the economy during the New Deal and World War II. Morris thought that political power determined the position of labor. However, neoliberal economic thought argues that governmental regulations are futile and counterproductive. Labor markets work best without interference, or so the thinking goes; intervention leads only to the creation of informal enterprises and economic stagnation.[17] Today labor unions are weak, and money flows into academia from proponents of deregulation and privatization. It is necessary to be reminded that historical reality is not subject to the fashions of ideology and power, though it would be illegitimate, in a book that emphasizes human agency and contingency, to argue that historians simply have absorbed and reflected in their works the most remunerative ideologies of their day.

Other matters have deterred historians from studying towns. During the initial period of enthusiasm for local community studies in the 1970s, historians discovered that New England towns varied nearly endlessly in regard to origin, size, demography, industry, and distributions of wealth and power.[18] Many scholars concluded that no prototypical New England town existed. Studying towns individually or collectively seemed an exercise in myth construction, not a valuable analytic undertaking.[19] While the facts document towns' diversity, they suggest the importance of the uniformity of town political organization in Massachusetts and other New England colonies in creating and containing that diversity. Urban seaport towns and inland rural towns had the same political organization; all were ruled by a town meeting and the selectmen they chose. Every town was under the political sway of its white male laborers and smallholders, whatever its size and economic base. The universality of town democracy kept Massachusetts, despite its diversity, relatively peaceful and unified politically, even during the American Revolution. Massachusetts avoided the near civil wars of New York and Pennsylvania, because in Massachusetts many of the poor and most male workers were already empowered politically.[20]

Modern historians are not the first to question whether New England had a unified culture, or what—if anything—held Massachusetts society together, given its obviously fractured and diverse culture, not to mention the variety of its towns. Mere geographical location was not enough; myths and other forms of mental magic work only in retrospect. The existence of a divided Massachusetts culture was the theme of Benjamin Colman's Election Day sermon, "The Blessing of Zebulun and Issachar," which he gave on November 19, 1719, to the Deputies of the Massachusetts General Court. Colman boldly wrestled with the socioeconomic rift already apparent between rural dwellers and coastal urbanites. By 1719 Boston was a busy metropolis, a shipbuilding and mercantile center, and Massachusetts was a wealthy colony with a major trade to the West Indies. Yet the colony was suffering from a lack of currency, and the fiat money in circulation was due to retire in tax payments. Less than a year later Colman's brother, the merchant John Colman, was arrested for libel after publishing *The Distressed State of Boston*. Political strife was evident.[21]

In giving an election sermon intended to promote unity, the minister was confident and thus candid and confrontational. Colman chose as his text Moses's last blessing of the tribes of Israel, specifically his blessing of the tribes of Zebulun and Issachar. Zebulun, as Colman noted, "was a tribe of merchants and mariners," and Issachar was employed in "tillage and feeding cattle." Colman highlighted these tribes' different lives and vastly different levels of wealth. The rift in ancient Israel reflected the differences obvious in the audience sitting in full view whom Colman addressed: the homespun-wearing farmers from towns like Deerfield and Brookfield, and the far wealthier Boston and Salem deputies resplendent in the latest London fashions.

The minister of the wealthy Brattle Street Church in Boston, Colman began by highlighting differences and sources of tension and envy. Colman argued that occupation eclipsed proximity and kinship: "How near in blood were Zebulun and Issachar, and even their lots adjoining too, and yet the one situated and made for traffic by sea, and if occasion for war; the other for pasturage and peace." Colman noted that Zebulun was at least twice as wealthy as rusticated Issachar (probably an underestimation of the disparities in his audience). Colman compared them to Jacob and Esau, brothers with different talents and appearances, rivals for their father's bounty, siblings with no love for each other. It was a provocative analogy, for hairy Esau was certainly the rural men in the audience and sly Jacob the urban men whose intelligence and providence gained them all of Esau's inheritance. Esau, like the farmers, got a pittance. As an urban man, Colman doubtless provoked the farmers in the audience by arguing that the Zebulun tribe had more experience of world affairs, took more risks, and possessed more martial prowess. He granted only that Issachar had fewer worries and slept more soundly.

After openly admitting the differences and distributing the insults, Colman proceeded to argue for unity. He contended that, despite their distinct functions, interests, talents, and rewards, Zebulun and Issachar actually composed a single society under God. Colman claimed that Massachusetts was economically and socially similar to ancient Israel. The Massachusetts clergy had long argued that the Massachusetts settlers and their society displaced the Jews and Israel in divine time as the chosen people, so it was reassuring to hear, as another proof of their special place in God's drama, that Massachusetts society, like ancient Israel, had two major tribes. It could hardly be a coincidence that the two societies turned out so similarly structured. As Colman emphasized, this exalted place in history carried responsibilities as well as blessings, especially supporting the clergy and the college with generous amounts of tax money. Implicitly, farmers had to accept their lesser share of wealth and lesser importance in the holy society while being responsible citizens.[22] Yet the question remained unanswered: did the excitement of being unequal stars in a world drama of divine contract and redemption, being the current holders of Israel's contract with God, reconcile Zebulun and Issachar to their unequal lots in life and to each other?

Yet there was clearly more than the filament of a historical myth holding together people with such disparate amounts of wealth and such distinct kinds of work and knowledge. Despite being more convincing about the differences than about unifying experiences in Massachusetts society, Colman implicitly addressed links between the tribes that did not need to be discussed so explicitly because they were obvious to all. What was largely left unsaid was what could be seen and experienced in the room. Colman addressed some ninety-three deputies of the ruling Great and General Court. They were not chosen by a mathematical formula but by towns, one or two to a town depending on its population, though Boston could have as many as four. Colman knew that the colony was ruled by its rural residents chosen by town meetings of middling farmers, artisans, and laborers. Among other things, they had the power to assess and proportion taxes. In the year he spoke, the General Court had authorized some £8,520 in taxes and determined that Boston pay £1,299, 16 percent of the total.[23] Although he was much wealthier than most of the deputies he addressed, Colman admitted by his very presence that they had power over him, which certainly lessened their envy. He could dress better than they did, but they could tax every piece of clothing off his body.

Colman also knew that seafarers and farmers were tribes because in Massachusetts men tended to remain in the town where they were born. The colony was composed of tribes of seafarers and farmers with distinctive patterns of mobility or intermarriage between tribes and towns. Massachusetts had an unusual political and familial order based on town government with every citizen and every estate under the jurisdiction of a town, itself ruled by a town meeting composed of its male working inhabitants.

Although the towns differed in size, economic base, and wealth, they all shared a political economy and a distinctive labor regime that was uncommon in the British Empire. Each town, whether a wealthy seaport or poor livestock-grazing center, limited who could enter the town to work for long periods; each town oversaw families and the economy through a town meeting in which all white male inhabitants had a say; each town developed a labor force by way of its public schools and stern discipline. Only the other New England colonies—New Hampshire, Connecticut, and more arguably Rhode Island—were similarly organized and had political economies and labor regimes based on the town and workers' power. It was the town political economy and the organization of labor by town that made New England a unified culture. All this Colman did not have to say because it was obvious and, in any case, not prudent to advertise too boldly.

It is essential therefore to analyze the political economy of New England towns. Political economy encompasses the interaction between political power and wealth creation and distribution, particularly how a labor system was formed and sustained. Historians have looked at New England towns in a variety of ways: as survivals of age-old English customs, as centers of consensus and peace, as traditional communities in transition to modernity, as centers of sustainable agricultural practices. Historians need first to understand that they were chiefly political economies and labor systems. Almost all New England towns chose to limit immigration, making local entrepreneurs depend primarily on local labor and placing extra costs on imported labor. By restricting the labor market, the town forced wages higher and kept rents lower. They invested in the reproduction of labor through schools and discipline. In order to become economically effective, towns demanded hard work from all their citizens. By valuing labor and by policing their borders, New England towns gave working people unusual political power and extensive responsibilities. This political economy made Massachusetts distinctive, dangerous, and unified, despite its occupational and religious diversity. New England was more than a geographic region and a set of abstract ideals, myths, or conceits, or even a diverse people held together by their shared belief in God. New England was defined by its towns' political economies, the merriment at Thayer's tavern.

Because this book emphasizes human contingency, it tells stories as well as presenting quantitative evidence to prove its points. It reinterprets Massachusetts history in light of the town political economy. It concentrates on complicated stories chiefly from nine towns: Boston, Dedham, Ipswich, Marblehead, Salem, Scituate, Taunton, and Watertown in Massachusetts, and New London and Stonington in Connecticut. The political economy of New England towns is a paradigm developed from these stories and related quantitative analyses. Towns were constantly changing. For example, Scituate began as a totally open town with weak institutions, but developed into an almost iconic closed New England town in the late seventeenth century as it became a shipbuilding center. Although these nine towns were among the most influential in the region, they were just 2 percent of all New England towns and just some 3 percent of those in Massachusetts. Nonetheless, the reinterpretations asserted in this book aspire not only to unsettle but also to replace previous interpretations. The real gaps that remain between this narrative and the immense body of available evidence should provoke other historians to tell more stories about New England's political economy and society with the politics left in.

When the politics are put back into history, many essential questions arise. Where did the town come from? How did it affect the economic development of Massachusetts and New England? How did its political economies impact the lives of families and people? The first part of this book examines the origins and development of the Massachusetts town labor system and political economy. Part II tells how the towns' political structures and the state of Massachusetts teamed with entrepreneurs and workers to create a powerful export economy that also won workers' affection and aggressive loyalty. Part III revisits the New England family, with the town and the town labor force not simply as a backdrop but as a major force in family security, happiness, and grief. The epilogue discusses Massachusetts taxation and what happened to the powerful political economies of the towns in the nineteenth century.

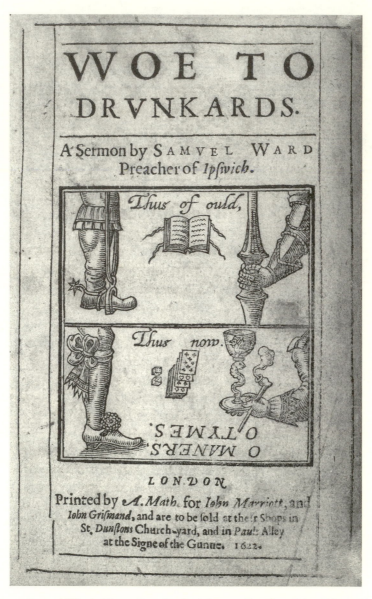

Figure 1. Samuel Ward, *Woe to Drunkards: A Sermon* (London: John Grismand, 1627). Samuel Ward, town preacher in Ipswich, England, was the brother of Reverend Nathaniel Ward, a clerical leader in early Massachusetts and preacher in Ipswich, Massachusetts. Their father, John Ward, had preached in Haverhill, Massachusetts, and in Bury St. Edmunds, Suffolk, England. This 1627 sermon shows that English Puritans were long concerned about religious and social declension and that they considered puritan reform masculine and militant, and returns to traditional culture feminine and limp. Courtesy of the Huntington Library.

PART I

Foundations

CHAPTER ONE

Political Economy

Blessed is he that considereth of the poor, the Lord will deliver him in the time of trouble.
  Psalm 41, KJV

WHEN THE PRINCIPAL inhabitants of Swallowfield met together in a town meeting for the first time, they defined themselves as "a society or common doing of a multitude of free men collected together and united by common accord and covenants among themselves." They agreed to hold more meetings, "to the end we may the better and more quietly live together in good love and amity, to the praise of God and for the better serving of her Majestie." They assented to twenty-six articles, including a pledge to dissuade young couples who could not afford a house from marrying; a pledge to take all their servants to church on the Sabbath; and an agreement "that every man shall be forbidden to keep inmates, and whosoever doth keep any inmates, to complain on them to the justice."[1]

This town meeting, with its twin commitments to concord and reform, took place not in seventeenth-century New England but in the southern English county of Berkshire in 1596, just before the founding of British colonies in mainland North America. A generation later, similar meetings were held in New England towns an ocean away. Indeed, the Swallowfield farmers' stress on amity and fellowship as well as the meeting format sound remarkably like the communal chords struck in the first meeting in Dedham, Massachusetts, so well described by Kenneth Lockridge, held just thirty years later.[2]

However, as the English historian Patrick Collinson remarks, "the purpose of the Swallowfield meeting was not sociable, but administrative and corrective, with a special emphasis on remedies for problems arising from the dearth and hard times prevailing in one of the most arduous decades ordinary working people . . . have ever had to endure: poverty, bastardy, petty theft, disorderly drunkenness, insubordination."[3] Whether in England or Massachusetts, local leaders wanted to incorporate loving relations among neighbors into their new institutions, but not as an end in itself. Their plans had another purpose: they saw a united town polity as a way to solve economic and social problems righteously. And, despite their rhetoric of harmony, they often adopted polarizing and provocative policies. They were economic reformers exercising state power, not traditionalist communitarians.

Colonial American historians have treated New England towns as traditional villages, emphasizing their peasant background and communal orientation, and building narratives of declension and modernization from these simple beginnings. There are grave dangers, however, in confusing customary peasant villages with innovative New England towns.[4] When Winthrop's fleet sailed for America in 1630, these socially stable, even static, peasant villages, if they had ever existed, had virtually vanished from the English landscape. According to the consensus of recent historiography, English society and local government had undergone a profound transformation in the half-century before the Puritans embarked for Massachusetts Bay. In particular, parishes had been changed by state formation. Though many signs of good neighborliness and festivity survived from the past, villages and towns had been largely remodeled. New England's leaders, often drawn from the vanguard Keith Wrightson called "the thrusting bearers of innovation" in England, brought a fundamental commitment to reform in local government.[5]

The prevailing historical narrative—New England's origins in communitarian towns and their more or less rapid abandonment of customary practices and communal values for the morally dubious but seductive attractions of liberal individualism and the dynamic, simultaneously destructive and creative forces unleashed by nascent capitalism—overestimates the importance of tradition and community in the colonists' minds while neglecting their passion for the righteous rearrangement of economics and power. These two dimensions of social life, the political and legal configuration of legitimate authority and the organization of property, labor, and exchange, were self-evidently intertwined, so this account adopts the historical term "political economy."[6] New England towns were established by ardent social and political reformers who had combated poverty and disorder at home by remodeling rural parishes and market towns and brought their new notions of positive government and a godly social order with them. The revolutionary transformation of England and the founding of New England were interrelated in substance as well as sequence, as early modern societies were deliberately reshaped across the transatlantic world.

English Origins of New Englanders and their Reformed Towns

To make Massachusetts towns, the colonists transplanted refashioned rural governments like that of Swallowfield, as well as reformed city governments like those of Dorchester, Ipswich, Salisbury, and Norwich. Propertied groups in both urban and rural places had transformed them during the Reformation and nearly completed the job under the guidance of the humanistic reformers who informed the expanding Tudor and Stuart state. Many of Massachusetts's founders, especially the colony's leaders, were town dwellers, and a substantial proportion of early immigrants came from market towns as well as larger cities in southern England. In the early modern period, however, town and countryside were closely linked, as people circulated among farming villages, market centers, and urban areas. Even London grew primarily by the influx of newcomers from the countryside rather than natural increase. All English cities, with the partial exception of the densely packed City of London within the medieval walls, had households with vegetable gardens and yards teeming with poultry, milk cows, and pigsties, as well as piles of wood and hay. Market towns, like villages, were surrounded by fields cultivated by their residents. By today's standards, early modern cities would appear rustic and disheveled. At the same time, even relatively small places were organized with town charters, electing officials and exercising a significant degree of local autonomy. Like the residents of rural parishes, town dwellers relied on their local governments to address social problems they considered serious.

Most of those who colonized New England came from southern England, where the transformation of political economies was most advanced. Studies by Virginia DeJohn Anderson, Roger Thompson, David Cressy, Timothy H. Breen, and Stephen Foster have consistently found that the majority of adult males who brought their families to Massachusetts were artisans, merchants, and professionals; only about one in five were farmers. For example, in a study of 273 Massachusetts-bound men who left from the ports of Great Yarmouth and Sandwich (based on a list that identified their occupations), Breen and Foster concluded that "the 1637 group was made up mainly of families headed by urban tradesmen somewhere in mid-career." Urban backgrounds were even more common among the men who governed New England. A study of 102 men who arrived between 1620 and 1633 and became colonial leaders (deputies, assistants, governors, and ministers) shows that about half (at least 49 men) came from towns with more than 2,000 inhabitants; two-thirds (14 of 22) of those who became assistants and judges came from towns of equivalent or larger size. Rulers drawn from gentry families, such as John Winthrop, lived in country houses but were only a generation removed from trade; Winthrop's father came from a clothier household in London.[7]

Many Massachusetts clergymen had held positions in towns, most frequently lectureships, and many of the clerical emigrants were renowned urban reformers. The city was a productive place for Puritan preachers. In rural parishes, regular clergymen often had to put up with poor pay and interference from bishops and local gentry. Well-connected laymen, who controlled the land whose taxes funded parish churches, kept the tithes for themselves and gave small salaries to country vicars. Anglican bishops often demanded conformity to the Anglican liturgy whatever the minister's objections. Urban parishes and corporations, in contrast, supported and controlled lectureships, which required ministers to preach the Word rather than preside over disputed rituals and ceremonies. Clergymen in cities and towns enjoyed large, literate, and responsive audiences. Rural residents routinely absented themselves from church services, and listeners were often indifferent to preaching. In urban centers, newcomers found church attendance a useful path toward belonging, and apprentices, artisans, and shopkeepers who were striving to succeed appreciated the Puritans' emphasis on humanistic ethics and self-discipline. In study of thirty-seven emigrant clergymen from greater East Anglia, Roger Thompson found that eleven were urban lecturers, including the renowned Massachusetts preachers John Cotton, Thomas Shepherd, John Wheelwright, John Wilson, and Thomas Hooker.[8]

The majority of Massachusetts colonists, wherever they had lived just before they departed, came from rural places in southern England not far from towns and cities. Even today, the ancestral homes of many early New England families remain rural, despite the recent intrusion of suburban houses and noisy highways. Southern England contained not only the capital and numerous large towns but also the most fertile chalk and clay farmland in the country. Gentry and yeomen in the region often grew wealthy by supplying meat, grain, and other foodstuffs to the cities, especially London, and reinvested their profits in agricultural improvements. Many Massachusetts settlers came from East Anglia, especially the Stour Valley on the Essex-Suffolk border. The cultivated landscape of Dedham vale, now designated an "area of outstanding natural beauty," was made famous by the paintings of John Constable. His *The Dedham Vale* (1802), which hangs in the Victoria and Albert Museum in London, evokes rural serenity. The pleasant valleys of southern and eastern England, dotted with ancient villages, open arable and pasturelands, deep green hedgerows, and small copses of woods, were home to thousands of early New England colonists.[9]

The towns that these emigrants transplanted to New England were recently reformed rather than traditional models of local governance. Between 1530 and 1630, the Tudor and Stuart governments transformed medieval parishes into modern governmental units devoted to controlling and reshaping the political economy. What was brought to Massachusetts was a newly rationalized parish in which Christian humanistic ideas developed in nearby cities were imposed on both market town and countryside for the benefit of both order and prosperity. The 1535 survey of all church lands in England (called the *Valor Ecclesiasticus*) counted 8,800 parishes. The parish had become a more active institution after 1215, when church leaders made the laity responsible for raising money to maintain the church building, to provide liturgical objects, and to pay the clergy for some services. In discharging these tasks, localities began to organize themselves for broader purposes. In rural and urban parishes alike, the laity raised funds, elected leaders, and negotiated with higher authorities. The churchwardens received gifts from wealthy locals, rented and sold parish-owned property, and held entertainments such as church ales. Rural parishes distributed parish-owned sheep and pigs among farmers' flocks for tending. Some parishes sponsored religious plays and processionals on the fifty-odd devotional holidays during the year to celebrate their local saints, glorify God, and attract visitors. Wealthy aristocrats and seasonal laborers seldom served as churchwardens to administer these tasks, but many people between these social poles did. Participation in parish government tended toward inclusiveness; in some dioceses laborers and even women commonly served as churchwardens. From these activities grew commitments to local governance, local economies, and local identities. By working together, the laity produced the church-building boom that gave the landscape its characteristic rhythm of church spires, each within sight of one or two others. Embellished with high towers, sonorous bells, and finely carved rood screens, newly erected or refurbished parish churches became self-created symbols of local success in fulfilling divine responsibilities.[10]

The English reformation that took place in the mid-sixteenth century abruptly shifted the center of gravity of the parish from sacred to more secular affairs. Many people resisted the Protestant government's suppression of their lively religious rituals, which some interpreted as an attack on their local identities. In northern and western England, including York, Lincoln, and Exeter, mass protests and uprisings were met with armed force. Those who founded Massachusetts were not among these recalcitrant traditionalists. Thomas Cromwell and other Tudor politicians, often spurred by people in the villages, transformed the rural parish not only by removing its core of religious festivity and ritual but also by making it into the administrative unit of what has been called the "parish state." In 1538, Cromwell secured a parliamentary act demanding that every parish in England, which by then numbered about 9,000, keep a register of every birth, marriage, and death, laying the foundations for "political arithmetic." As historical demographers gratefully observe, "it is probable that no other country possesses such a considerable number of registers of fair quality from such an early date." The state increasingly intruded into the parishes to supply money for its military machine. As the historian Eamon Duffy quipped after reviewing all the new demands for money for war, and lesser outlays for religious articles, in the parish books of Morebath, Devon: "The English Reformation also established the rule of thumb that anything given to the glory of God was liable to end up, sooner rather than later, being confiscated by the Crown and turned into a gun or a soldier's coat."[11]

The state transformed the parish most dramatically through the passage and implementation of the Elizabethan Poor Laws, especially those of 1598 and 1601. The parliamentary legislation placed the power and responsibility for handling the country's growing number of poor folk on the parish. Every parish was required to appoint at least two overseers of the poor to raise and distribute money to relieve all the parish's poor. The vestry and overseers were responsible for identifying the deserving poor, who were made impotent by age, disease, or accident, and differentiating them from the poor who were inclined to idleness or incorrigibly corrupt and deserving of punishment. They were also charged with extending new forms of assistance to the laboring poor, worthy people who stood in need of jobs, better wages, and education. In order to encourage industriousness and the accumulation of wealth, the overseers were to bind out poor children as apprentices and put the recalcitrant poor into workhouses. The act gave parish constables the right to seize vagabonds, give them a whipping, and then order their return to their place of birth or settlement. Each parish was to establish a poor rate, a compulsory tax, to fund these responsibilities, and was authorized to take property with the permission of the court when taxpayers failed to pay their due. With the rates came the responsibility of the parish to police newcomers who worked for or lodged with villagers in order to avoid harboring growing numbers of poor folk who would raise the tax burden. Implicitly, each parish had the responsibility of creating enough wealth to help the poor and supply employment at decent wages to the needy. As the historian Paul Slack concludes, "There is no doubt that the Poor-Relief Act of 1598 gave power as well as responsibility to the parishes."[12]

These measures were not imposed from the center on villages and towns, but grew in a partnership between the center and localities that were wrestling with worrisome social changes. The sixteenth century was a time not only of religious strife and state formation but also of profound economic shifts and disturbing social problems. By the second quarter of the seventeenth century, when the great Puritan migration to America occurred, the English population had more than doubled in a little over a century, rising from about 2.3 million in 1524 to 5.3 million in 1656. Prices, pushed by rising demand, increased dramatically, but wages failed to keep pace. The ratio of prices to wages was the worst it ever had been (or would be) in recorded English history. According to the index compiled by C. H. Phelps-Brown and S. V. Hopkins, the cost of a basketful of consumer goods in southern England rose sixfold between 1500 and the 1640s. Real wages declined sharply, with the nadir coming in the 1620s. Begging became common as even casual laboring jobs were hard to find. Thousands of youth wandered about looking for work or charity. In rural areas propertyless people faced starvation, especially in the 1590s when harvest failures were followed by high bread prices. They flocked into urban alleys where they drained resources and terrified the authorities, who lacked the armed police forces of modern cities. Those who had a more secure niche in town or country described the wandering poor as vagrants, rogues, and criminals—a subculture of shiftless and masterless men who constituted a threat to order. The 1620s and early 1630s were marked by a major depression in the textile industry, which had furnished employment to many men and women in towns and rural villages. Repeated harvest failures and outbreaks of the plague that followed periods of dearth in the 1590s, 1625, 1626, 1631, and 1637–1638 exacerbated the plight of the poor.[13]

Many people in the cities and towns, as well as in the capital, sought to use state power to address these problems. Puritans and their allies, and even many of their foes, believed that what some deplored as the desecration of the parish was a necessary and righteous use of public authority in order to produce a godly and productive political economy that promised to make England into a just and blessed land. Puritans were frequently among these urban reformers; indeed, many were in the leadership. Those who think of Puritans as self-righteous and stiff-necked and city dwellers as tolerant and resilient may be surprised at this association. Yet many seventeenth-century English people, including pious Protestants, conceived of the best possible human society as having an urban form. As Margo Todd has shown, Puritans were deeply influenced by the Northern Renaissance and humanist thinkers such as Erasmus who, informed by the wisdom of the Ancients such as Cicero, saw the city as the locus of civilization. Foxe in his *Book of Martyrs* referred to Colchester, a garrison town in the Colne valley, as "a city upon a hill." John Winthrop was repeating a familiar trope when he proclaimed en route to Massachusetts aboard the *Arabella*: "We must consider that wee shall be as a Citty upon a Hill, the eies of all people are uppon us." Many historians have examined Winthrop's belief that Massachusetts would become a model society, but few have taken seriously the governor's dream that this forested landscape would soon become a new Colchester, Salisbury, Norwich, or Dorchester.[14]

English cities and market towns became incorporated during the sixteenth and seventeenth centuries. Middling artisans and merchants gained greater political and legal freedom from their gentry and ecclesiastical rulers and more control over their own lives. A new form of civility and confidence developed in these towns. Men who had completed apprenticeships, who were the sons of full citizens, or who had purchased rights and liberties earned the title "freeman" at adulthood. After taking an oath affirming his loyalty and acknowledging his public responsibility, a man gained liberty to work, vote, and in some cases, govern his town. Trained in households and shops, schools, and guilds, freemen were usually literate, informed by humanistic thought, and active participants in politics—in their own eyes, at least, as civilized as any country gent.

By using constables and town watches to patrol the walls and corporal punishment and fines to reform and deter deviants, the leaders of incorporated towns and cities encouraged urban property holders to define who they were by excluding those who did not belong and exposing unacceptable conduct. By preaching God's Word eloquently and persistently, Puritan ministers instructed city dwellers that they might control the impulses within themselves and, perhaps, in others, and thereby promote good order and godliness. Protestant preachers spoke as though each person's disposition to sinful or virtuous conduct was affected by his or her neighbor's. The Puritans' sense of mutual responsibility was rooted in the presumption that although each person is answerable directly to God, people live in society, thus sin is contagious—but so might virtue be. Additionally, preachers constantly reminded them that the whole city would be held accountable by God for every sin. Protestant ministers helped secular reformers control urban life with a system of law and punishment, social legislation, new civic institutions, and pulpit persuasion.

Tangible as well as spiritual rewards would accompany the cleansing of a city from sin. Plagues, fires, famines, depressions, and riots frequently shattered early modern cities and market towns. Men and women were convinced by rational thought and direct experience that good order is imperative in a world with limited wealth and great potential for social conflict. The fragility of the physical environment offered an object lesson in the precariousness of order. Interpreting the sensible evidence in relation to such biblical precedents as Sodom and Gomorrah, Puritan ministers predicted that sinful conduct would unleash imminent, divinely sanctioned destruction. Since England was the new Israel, they explained, only godliness protected any city against God's fury. "Doubtless, we belonging to godly cities, and being for our parts members thereof, shall escape . . . many dangers, and remain a quiet habitation," proclaimed Robert Jenison, master of Mary Magdalene Hospital and Protestant lecturer in Newcastle upon Tyne. When King Charles I and Archbishop Laud largely rejected key components of the reform movement and began to quash Puritan town ministers in the 1630s, many frightened folk decided to move to America in order to maintain the momentum of urban reform and to avoid divine fury. "God begins to ship away his Noahs, which prophesied and foretold that destruction was near," remarked Thomas Hooker in 1631, "and God makes account that New England shall be a refuge for his Noahs and his Lots, a rock and a shelter for his righteous ones to run unto; and those that were vexed to see the ungodly lives of the people in this wicked land, shall there be safe."[15]

Many of New England's ministers had previously worked to create godly cities in England. Thomas Hooker, the founder and leading minister of Connecticut, preached in Chelmsford, a major market town in Essex, from 1626 to 1629, when he left for Amsterdam. Nathaniel Ward, who became the pastor of Ipswich, Massachusetts, came from a family of urban preachers and reformers. Samuel Ward, his brother, preached in Ipswich, England, where the corporation elected him town preacher in 1602 and he remained for thirty years. Samuel Ward wrote several tracts filled with Christian humanistic thought advocating cooperation between ministers and magistrates in the construction of godly cities whose economic growth guaranteed equity and harmony. Nathaniel Ward's father, John Ward, preached in Bury St. Edmunds, the county town of West Suffolk, which took pride in its ruined abbey's association with the Magna Carta. Peter Thatcher, whose son became pastor of Dedham, Massachusetts, had preached in Salisbury, Wiltshire, a town of some seven thousand people and a hotbed of urban reform. John Davenport, the first minister and founder of New Haven colony, was the son of the mayor of Coventry, England, and had preached in London, where he had heroically attended to the spiritual needs of families devastated by the plague. John Cotton had been pastor in the port town of Boston, Lincolnshire. Although not an emigrant, John White was a founder of the Massachusetts Bay Company and recruited capital and talent for the colony. The leader of Dorchester's social and economic reformation, White coordinated a total overhaul of the Dorset shire town's political economy after a devastating fire on August 6, 1613. David Underdown, whose history vividly re-creates these developments, argues that the reform program realized in Dorchester was prototypical of Puritan designs for godly towns in England and America.[16] Urban energies, visions of redeemed polities, and concrete programs of social as well as religious reform, rather than ancient village traditions, informed the political economy of Massachusetts and New England towns.

An Exemplary Program of Social and Moral Reform

Southern English townspeople responded to their perceived problems with a host of innovative measures, instituting a full-scale reform program that they carried into colonial Massachusetts. The goal was to dignify and improve labor by creating a prosperous, full employment economy and by reforming the consciences of laborers and holders of wealth. Authorities protected town-

born labor from outside competition by restricting in-migration; they publicly punished unproductive town-born laborers; they used a newly invented
institution, the Bridewell (or house of work and correction), to punish, train,
and discipline labor; they emphasized schooling and apprenticeship for all;
they gave and encouraged charity; they encouraged wealth creation and investment in social betterment; they intruded into families on the slightest
pretext; and they focused their attention and punishment upon youth, children, and the households in which they lodged. Authorities emphasized a
rhetoric of community and solidarity, but their actions were confrontational
and even coercive in pursuit of a reformed political economy.

In 1631, just as John Winthrop and the passengers of his fleet were beginning to organize Massachusetts, the mayor's court in Norwich, a city known
for its Puritan domination and the home of many who soon emigrated to
New England, was beating or whipping 35 town-born and 35 outside-born
adults and youth each year. On December 28, 1631, for example, the Norwich
mayor's court recorded, "Richard Gymon apprentice with Thomas Symond
for running away and begging is ordered to be punished in Bridewell and
sent home to his master."[17] Begging was absent from early New England, but
the Norwich court's actions resembled the coercive labor regime of Massachusetts—even though New England had a shortage of labor and relatively
high wages, while Norwich faced a surfeit of youth and distressingly low
wages.

The novel regime evinced in Norwich combined punishments, restrictions on in-migration, economic regulation, education, economic development, and charity. A successful textile town whose workers produced the
"new draperies," a lighter and increasingly popular form of woolen fabric,
Norwich attracted more youth than it could handle, a prevalent problem in
southeastern England. In order to protect the town born and limit the
amount of money needed to support the poor, Norwich constables sent outside youth who were not enrolled as apprentices away with a pass to their
hometowns. They whipped those who they thought looked suspiciously
like vagrants, who had repeatedly visited Norwich, or who had run away
from masters and mistresses. They also supervised the town's own youth
and adults, in order to suppress idleness and moral offenses and to increase
productivity. For example, in November 1631, the court ordered that Dennys
Powle, an apprentice with John Beavis of St. Michael's parish, be "whipped
at the post" for running away and "michery"—a combination of petty thiev-
ing, lying, and complaining. In the same month, the authorities whipped

Alice Belton at the post for michery and beat Agnes Furnys for begging and wandering. None of these actions exemplified traditional good neighborly ideals; instead, they represented new ideas and strategies for reform.[18]

In addition to correcting disorderly behavior and idleness, the authorities required that all town-born youth live under a demanding master or mistress. The authorities forbade single men and women, even those of adult age, from living without a master, "living at their own hand," or even living with lenient parents. On January 20, 1631, for example, the Norwich mayoralty court ordered that Ursula Hobson and Anne Patten be retained in service within ten days or be sent to Bridewell. The Bridewell was a stone building in the middle of Norwich (now devoted to shoppers and tourists) that served as a prison, punishment center, and workhouse, an idea that started among Puritans in sixteenth-century London and spread to other towns and rural parishes. Until they found places in service or were sent from the city, master-less youth were set to work vigorously in the Bridewell, beating hemp or doing other menial tasks under strict supervision enforced by corporal punishment. The Bridewell also served as a job placement agency, inducing the unemployed to accept any position that offered them an escape. On April 16, 1631, for example, the court noted that "Sara Stubbs lately committed to Bridewell is now retained with John Cooper from this day for a year, and is to have for her wages 26s 8d to be paid quarterly and a pair of hose at the end of the year." The authorities also freed young men from the Bridewell if they agreed to join the army.[19]

If town officials deemed any Norwich household a nursery of idleness, they banned children and youth from living there with nary a worrying that they were disrupting parent-child relationships. In June 1631, the mayoralty court, observing that "Alice Dennys and Elizabeth Dennys, daughters of Robert Dennys of St. Peters, live with their father," decided that the household supplied only enough work for one daughter. Fearing that at least one daughter would become idle, it decreed that "Elizabeth hath time to provide her a service within fourteen days or otherwise she is committed to Bridewell."[20] The officials' unconcern for the parties' wishes in the matter signified that they regarded this unproductive household as a potential source of moral disorder that justified intrusive and coercive correction.

However harsh, these interventions and punishments were part of an idealistic plan to dignify labor and reform the poor. Similar plans were carried out in many other cities, towns, and rural villages, especially those under the control of zealous Protestants who followed the strictures of civic humanism.

Norwich was the first English town to make a detailed census of the poor in 1570 in hopes of collecting the facts necessary to eliminate unworthy recipients of charity and to discover the causes of poverty. This sophisticated, systematic effort to assist the poor continued in the 1630s. When a bad harvest threatened the poor with starvation, the mayoralty court ordered, in order to prevent beggary, that "the alderman in their several wards do cause the overseers of every parish to take view of the poor, and to certify the number of their several households and what they earn weekly, and which of them are able to work and do want work, and what the aged and impotent poor stand in need of, to the end their wants may be supplied." After this detailed survey, they doubled the poor rate, the tax paid for public support of the town's poor.[21]

The authorities adopted new forms of assistance that went beyond long-established modes of charity. Using funds bequeathed to the town by the rich for the benefit of the poor, the court reimbursed clothiers for losses if they supplied work to the poor as wool combers and hosiers and ordered "that a knitting school dame shall be provided in every parish where there is not one already to set children and other poor to work."[22] The city sought to alleviate hunger by giving bread to the poor who were too infirm to work and offering subsidies to the able-bodied. At times of scarcity, the court ordered that no malt be used for beer and no flour be used for fancy pastries instead of bread. The authorities then bought bread from the bakers and sold it to the poor at a lower price. The whole town became mobilized to help the poor and eliminate poverty.

Norwich had long supported a children's "hospital," a residence for poor and orphaned male children too young to be bound out to work. The facility was overcrowded, though its capacity had been enlarged from thirty to ninety over two decades. On June 1, 1631, as the people of Boston in Massachusetts were clearing ground for planting, the mayor and alderman of Norwich announced that departures had created room for new admissions. Twelve children applied for seven openings. No parish could recommend a candidate to the hospital unless it guaranteed him employment at age fifteen.[23] A few hospital children attended Oxford and Cambridge on scholarships furnished by the taxpayers and became Puritan clergymen and urban reformers.

The city's chronic overpopulation and underemployment made it impossible to find places for all needy children in public institutions, so the Norwich court gave financial incentives to masters who took them as apprentices. In February 1632, the mayoralty court noted, "it is thought fit as heretofore that William Steward shall have ten pounds lent him at Christmas next because he hath taken a poor boy in St. Symonds parish to be his apprentice." Some members of the city corporation did not appreciate the aggressive campaign in this war on poverty to place poor children in families. Robert Carter earned notoriety for criticizing the mayor's policy and the prominent clergyman John Spendlove, saying "Spendlove for all his great looks shall not put children upon us."[24] The underlying idea was not to accept poverty as an inevitable part of life but to eliminate it by creating conditions that rewarded hard work, and by training and disciplining everybody to work steadily and skillfully. Economic growth and individual improvement were the reformers' twinned goals.

This campaign against poverty developed among a people accustomed to interference in personal life, for there was little separation between the household and the workplace and even less privacy. The city government flowed from the town's guilds, whose officers regularly decided which households could take how many apprentices and which households produced goods of acceptable quality. Much of the agenda of the mayoralty court involved mediating disputes between guilds, punishing members on behalf of the guilds, and fining men and women for violating the rules regulating the weaving of woolens. Each weaver had his or her cloth mark registered with the mayoralty court. The court readily acted to prevent overproduction of cloth and other commodities in order to avert the excessive lowering of prices. In 1630, for example, it announced that the town's weavers "shall forbear and leave weaving of all manner clothes, stuffs, and lace made of worsted yarn . . . from the fifteenth day of this instant August for one month according to an ancient ordinance in that behalf made." Economic regulation was long accepted in principle, and during the early seventeenth century local authorities practiced it more systematically. During economic downturns, the Norwich court removed journeymen from the city in order to stabilize wages and privilege the town born. On May 14, 1631, for example, the court declared that "John Crowder a journeyman brewer lately taken into service by Nathaniel Browne is ordered to depart this city before Tuesday next otherwise he standeth committed to Bridewell." Whether he liked it or not, Nathaniel Browne did not have freedom to hire and retain whomever he wanted.[25]

The reform movement spread to rural parishes across southern England. Keith Wrightson and David Levine have carefully and skillfully reconstructed the early modern parish of Terling, Essex, showing how godly Protestants helped fracture its once festive and forgiving culture as unrelenting reformers demanded order, industry, piety, and productivity. Lying thirty-eight miles east of London on the river Ter, the parish was blessed with fine clay soil and proximity to many market towns. Its economy was almost wholly agricultural. An area of ancient enclosures, its large farms produced wheat and barley, and the larger farmers did well, employing many wage laborers, rebuilding their homes, and often buying the land of smaller farmers with their profits. Laborers and smallholders fared poorly in the face of inflation and stagnant wages, as well as competition from migrants who flooded into the parish. In 1524, laborers composed about a quarter of the people on Terling's tax lists, but by 1671, while the number of yeomen and large renters remained the same, laborers comprised half of those on the tax lists, and their real wages had steadily declined.[26]

In response, the wealthy farmers embraced the poor laws and strengthened the local state in order to feed and support the increasing number of poor. Many farmers became Puritans or godly Protestants, supported a series of evangelical parish ministers, and participated actively in town government. For example, they formed the Henry Smith foundation (named after the benefactor who bequeathed the starting capital), administered by parish officers and funded by the largesse of a parishioner, to provide clothing and food to needy workers. At the same time, they sought to reform the poor. Their stress on literacy led them to hold classes in the church building. They took vigorous action in local courts against alehouses, idleness, illegitimacy, and fornication. In addition to punishing bastard-bearers, they prosecuted married couples whose "early babies" (born within eight months after the marriage) revealed they had premarital sexual intercourse. Equally important, they sought to expel in-migrants and forbade parish residents from providing them with housing. By 1620, the reformers were enjoying significant successes. However, as Wrightson and Levine point out, the campaign waged by parish notables and well-to-do-farmers to treat poverty as a social disease was more coercive and less communitarian than historians had previously recognized. For example, recipients of the Henry Smith foundation were compelled to wear "HS" on their clothes to identify them as objects of charity lest they spend too much time in an alehouse or engage in sports on Sunday.[27]

Rural parishes across the arable regions of southeastern England and in scattered locations in the more pastoral Midlands and mixed farming areas elsewhere used a potent combination of public intervention and evangelical preaching to increase productivity and reform the poor. By 1630, nearly half the parishes of Essex County, England, had ministers of broadly Puritan sympathies and instituted active reform programs. In the southeast, rural parishes adopted forms of charity similar to those in the cities and market towns. The vestrymen of Braughing, Hertfordshire, bestowed £1 on each poor maid of the parish who married, but this bridal gift depended on her virtue, which was demonstrated by not giving birth for at least nine months after the wedding. Rural parishes sought to make the children of the poor productive, not only when they were orphaned but also when their parents lacked sufficient resources to employ them profitably. In rural Constantine, Cornwall, in 1596, the vestry placed out some sixty poor boys and girls among some fifty parish households, where they were to remain until the age of twenty-four. Each household had to provide their young servants with clothing and food, though households in need of support got it from the parish. The program was virtually mandatory: a household could opt out of the charity, but had to pay a shilling a week into the parish fund. In the Cotswold village of North Nibley, Gloucestershire, the vestry ordered a census in 1604 of all children in the parish fit to be bound apprentice "and that now live pilfering and stealing in every corner."[28]

Once parishes had set the poor rate, many defended their village boundaries and their pocketbooks against poor not their own, including disciplining employers and landlords who took in newcomers. These programs resembled the ways Norwich policed its labor market. In the rural village of Boxford, Suffolk, the vestry agreed in 1608 to allow lodgers from outside the parish only with the consent of six property-holding inhabitants. Landlords were required to put up bonds indemnifying the town for any public expense caused by their lodgers, especially in case of illness or unemployment. Similarly, as reported by the historian Steve Hindle, "in 1598, the Constantine vestry compelled all landlords to maintain lodgers and their prospective families at their own expense: in 1650, it insisted that irresponsible landlords should be rated for the poor 'not according to their ability' but 'according to the damage and charge' which they 'bring the parish unto by their folly'."[29]

The transformation of the parish into a vehicle of state-sponsored social and economic reform was not universally accepted or uniformly adopted. Many rural parishes refused to enact a poor rate and continued to allow nearly unrestricted begging. In one of the best recent histories of the poor law, Paul Slack estimates that only a quarter of parishes in Essex and in Shropshire, a sparsely populated county in the northwest Midlands, had imposed involuntary taxes to support the poor by 1660. Many English folk resisted the legal control of alehouses and the suppression of sports and festivities.[30]

Puritans had no monopoly on reform measures that were designed to increase wealth and productivity. Civic reform was first suggested by humanists such as Juan Luis Vives, who hoped to apply the wisdom of the ancients, exemplified by Cicero and Seneca, to contemporary problems. Sir Thomas More's *Utopia* (1516) contributed to the idea that poverty was not natural and inevitable but a product of corruption in politics and society. Many English people thought reform a practical necessity given the pressing problems of low wages, unemployment, and vagrancy personified in the wandering poor. Many Anglican leaders shared these new ideas about order, reform, and charity with the Puritans. In 1630, the Privy Council of Charles I with the support of Archbishop Laud (who were at that moment taking powerful measures against Puritan clergy and congregations) were distributing questionnaires throughout England in an effort to enforce the collection of poor rates, the regulation of alehouses, and compulsory church attendance. As Margo Todd has pointed out, Puritans and Anglicans differed not about reform or the work ethic but about whether reform should seek to change each individual conscience, as the Puritans wanted, or, as the Laud faction demanded, focus on obedience to hierarchy and superiors.[31]

Still, if not all reformers were Puritans, virtually all Puritans were reformers, supporting a social agenda that encompassed the elimination of poverty and the remodeling of the political economy. These enthusiastic Protestants were propelled by both fear and idealism. Their idealism was anchored in a widespread belief that human beings informed by the Word of God could create a just society, with a full employment economy and ever-increasing wealth, and eliminate poverty and civil humiliation. When John White proposed establishing a municipal brew house in Dorchester to support a school for the poor, he argued for the plan by adducing the axiom of "knowledge causing piety, piety breeding industry, and industry procuring plenty."[32]

Some Puritans feared that the stalling of their reform movement by Archbishop Laud would bring social disorder and divine displeasure, causing devastating fires and plagues that might even culminate in the destruction of England. Catastrophes were common enough experiences to lend concreteness to people's imagination of disaster and shape their apprehension of the future. For example, in the 1620s a third of the population of Norwich had died of plague within a few months. Such traumatizing events colored people's response to social chaos as well, making moral reform a vitally important way of dealing with disaster and sorrow. For example, in Salisbury following the outbreak of plague in 1627, the Puritan reformer Henry Sherfield persuaded the aldermen to adopt a thorough program of practical measures to stave off disease and spiritual efforts to please a punishing God. Paul Slack quotes his words to epitomize the Puritan approach to reform: "I well know that no good thing can be effected without the hand and blessing of God and it is he that worketh both the will and the deed. Yet I do also know that we must use all the good ways and means which God shall discover unto us to bring to pass even what God hath determined to do."[33] In a deft fusion of divine disposing and human proposing, Puritans used moral and political economic reform to cope both psychologically and practically with intense fear and explosive social problems.

Reformed Towns in Colonial Massachusetts

The founders of Massachusetts adopted the innovative, activist, and state-infused form of local governance that was central to the reform agenda, rather than reverting to a more consensual and communal model, as many previous historical narratives implied. The town records of Boston, Dedham, and Watertown demonstrate that, while living in a new world that was sparsely populated and had a scarcity rather than a surplus of labor, Massachusetts colonists followed policies nearly identical to those of English innovators—indeed, in the colony reformers had a free hand, rather than having to struggle against established authorities. They created town governments that restricted their labor pools to the town born and interfered freely and provocatively in households. Local governments played active roles in economic development, controlling access to resources, regulating the poor, and subsidizing the enterprising, all in order to nurture a godly commonwealth.

Early Massachusetts was full of places for workers. As Daniel Vickers and others have explained, the founding families had only a meager supply of labor. New England was populated primarily by relatively young couples with young children, most of whom were toddlers. Nonetheless, the land seemed to offer inexhaustible resources, and the colony had lofty economic ambitions. In order to build farms with both crops and livestock, colonists tackled the enormous tasks of clearing the forest, fencing fields, planting English grasses, and constructing barns to store grain and hay. They accepted the fact that for a generation their livestock would be poorly tended and barely fed. Foraging cattle, hungry horses, and roving pigs routinely broke through the colonists' feeble fences and ate the colonists' and neighboring Indians' crops. So enamored were the colony's leaders of their model of villages under godly rulers that the least ethnocentric among their ministers thought they could not show the native people any more love than by placing them in "praying towns" modeled on English parishes. But attempting to enslave the native inhabitants en masse was unworkable as well as unthinkable; so was solving the colony's labor problem through importing slaves from Africa or the West Indies. Puritan leaders could not risk relying on an alien labor force because they aspired to build a city of God in which all who were allowed to enter would be offered means for redemption.[34]

Colonists imposed the same godly rules upon themselves. Massachusetts towns persistently emphasized planned and shared economic efforts. Although the colony and its towns left many economic matters to the market, governing bodies regulated key elements of production, distribution, and consumption. Massachusetts leaders initially attempted to pass legislation setting wages, but those proposals failed when they collided with the expansive labor market. Yet many prices were set locally. In Boston the price of bread was fixed by law from 1635 to at least 1739. In 1729 a penny loaf was to be three ounces, a penny wheaten loaf five ounces, and a penny household loaf seven ounces. To facilitate enforcement, the town's bakers were required "to mark their bread which they bake for sale with the first letters of their sir names." Following the procedures used by the English state in case widespread harvest failure led to dearth, Boston used public money to open a granary to store grain and flour that could be sold at low prices to the poorer inhabitants. In 1716, for example, the Boston selectmen "ordered that the crier be employed to cry the grain at the granary vizt. Wheat at 6d, and Indian [corn] at 3 shillings per bushel to be sold on Tuesdays and Fridays in the forenoon and that Mr. Griggs be directed to sell only to the inhabitants of this town, not exceeding two bushels to one family." The colony's General Court authorized regulations to ensure that merchants in the port city could not enrich themselves by depriving its inhabitants of essential foodstuffs. During times of shortage, Boston selectmen limited the exportation of grain from the colony, demanded that merchants sell part of their supply at reasonable cost, and required import merchants to sell stipulated amounts of grain to the town bakers.[35]

The Boston town meeting carefully regulated chimney sweeping and carting to maintain quality and fair wages, for these services contributed materially to the health and security of the densely built town. In 1708, Boston selectmen concluded that chimney sweeping was being done poorly, "for the most part performed by careless and unfaithful slaves." They had good reason to fear disastrous fires. The town meeting "voted that the town will take it into their own hands to provide chimney-sweepers." The selectmen granted a monopoly to one or two men who were held responsible for the quality of the work performed. In 1738 Mr. Huiship ran the business with five employees. The town banned the use of other sweepers on penalty of large fines. As Boston grew larger and its trade expanded, the town meeting grew less liberal in its economic policies and passed many additional regulations. By 1723, the town demanded that all porters—who were often Indian, Negro, or mulatto—be approved by the selectmen and that each porter be backed by a bond of at least £50 that was forfeited on bad behavior. The town meeting demanded that the offending porter go directly to the house of correction and "receive the discipline of the house and remain six days." By 1738, the Boston town meeting made carting a monopoly, authorizing twelve men to perform the job, issuing them official badges inscribed with a pine tree, and fixing their wages: "for housing and porterage of salt—two shillings per ton." Businesses had to use authorized porters. The town expected them to work hard and to refrain from "profane cursing and swearing, drunkenness, gaming, fighting, quarrelling and other rude and disorderly carriage on the dock and wharves or in any of the streets of the town of which common porters have been too notoriously guilty."[36] The porters remained notorious for disorderly behavior. Colonists and their children often made laws stricter to battle persistent sin and hardly stopped their campaigns in the face of unregenerate human nature.

The people in the outlying towns of Dedham and Watertown acted collectively to promote and regulate major aspects of their economies as well. Watertown organized the common herding of livestock on lands belonging to individual farmers as well as undivided land reserved by the town. By 1670, the Watertown selectmen assigned all cattle to one of four herds, each with a separate herdsmen and permissible route and grazing area, for six-month periods. The selectmen specified, for example, "that the third herd shall begin at widow Thatchers and soe to drive along to Henry Brits and John Biskews and to Thomas Straights and Charles Stearns and then to turn in the left hand and to feed all the land from the path to the white house and to the fourth end of Mr. Mayhew's plain and the middle of the great pond."

During the summer and fall, when the fields were full of crops that needed protection from foraging animals and farmers were busy with planting, haying, and harvest, all cows and oxen had to be enrolled in a town herd. Farmers might hire a private herdsman, but still had to pay their share of the public service. By 1651, the selectmen charged Solomon Johnson, who rented a house and land in Watertown for seven years, with caring for all the "dry" cattle during the summer; "wet" cows were kept where they could readily be milked by their owners. Dedham had similar arrangements by 1652 for cattle and by 1667 for sheep.[37]

Rural towns assisted individual entrepreneurs in the construction and maintenance of mills because they provided vital services to households. In 1636, the Dedham selectmen gave Abraham Shaw sixty acres of land to erect a water-powered mill to grind corn. He would be allowed to run it for his own profit and to sell it, but the town had the right of first refusal. The town assisted with the mill's construction, ordering "that every man that hath lot with us shall assist to bring the millstones from Watertown mill by land unto the boating place near Mr. Haynes, his farm." Ensuring adequate service remained a public responsibility. The mill was in part a public entity. By 1650, people were complaining about the "insufficient performance of the work of the mill" and asked the town to encourage the building of an additional mill, but consensus was hard to gain, so the current miller Nathaniel Whiting enjoyed his monopoly for another decade. In time, public demands spurred action, as the town meeting decided to grant liberty to Daniel Pond and Ezra Morse "to undertake the erecting of a new mill." Whiting and his allies responded by offering a plan "to supply the town sufficiently by grinding for them," but a committee who "attended . . . heard and considered" his proposals turned them down. By 1655, fifteen years after the first public complaint, Dedham had two mills on the same stream and three owners who squabbled about the flow of water. The town also granted subsidies and monopolies to businessmen who erected a sawmill and a fulling mill.[38]

Defending the Dignity of Labor

Significantly, while towns allowed and regulated entrepreneurship, they controlled the supply and value of labor tightly. Their labor policy stemmed from the towns' obsessive and consistent policing of their boundaries to maintain clearly defined identities in their own eyes and in the sight of God.

Each Massachusetts town was to be a godly commonwealth that carefully controlled those who belonged there and deliberately decided who was allowed to enter in order to enhance the material and spiritual welfare of all its residents. The colonists recalled the chaos caused by the surplus of youth and the wandering poor in England and the degradation of labor that resulted. To avoid these corrupting conditions, towns sought to offer the means of redemption—education, hard work, a decent livelihood, discipline, and the hearing of the Word—to all those within their boundaries.

New Englanders became obsessed with defining and policing boundaries. Town officials perambulated their bounds annually in cooperation with neighboring towns. Authorities exercised constant oversight and control over the admission of new inhabitants. The founders of Dedham, Massachusetts, stated in the town covenant their determination "That we shall by all means labour to keepe off from us all such, as are contrary minded. And receive only such unto us as be such as may be probably of one harte, with us as that we eitheir knowe or may well and truly be informed to walk in peaceable conversation with all meekness of spirit for the edification of each other in the knowledge and faith of the Lord Jesus: and the mutual encouragement unto all temporal comforts in all things: seeking the good of each other out of all which may be derived true peace."[39] The language may seem communitarian, but the policies and practices it justified focused on the exclusion of those regarded as likely to disrupt the peace or diminish the material advantages of town residents rather than on their mutual aid and encouragement, though any deviant or disruptive conduct was certainly subject to correction. The covenant constituted a positive assertion of political power to generate and maintain a well-paid and disciplined work force. In sum, Massachusetts towns adopted the reform policies that had emerged in the godly towns of England from which so many colonists came.

As in England's incorporated cities and innovative parishes, boundaries were carefully controlled and the movement of labor deliberately restricted. An unregulated labor market was not allowed to develop regionally or even colony-wide. Boston, Watertown, and Dedham records from 1635 to 1739 show more than a thousand instances in which town meetings and selectmen controlled, directed, and developed labor. Officials stopped and inspected laborers at the border of their towns; ejected outside laborers; told employers to get rid of them; fined men and women for hiring, harboring, and hiding outsiders; collected bonds from employers and sponsors to cover any public expenses that might arise from allowable outsiders; inspected the labor of every family; educated, trained, and coached workers; told town-born youth where they might labor; and reformed poor workers by reducing their freedom. The towns subordinated families and individuals to these purposes with a powerful and sophisticated machinery of control. These policies were similar to those that masters had exercised in England's reformed towns and parishes. In Massachusetts, freedom to hire and freedom to work without regulation did not exist. Dignifying and developing work was too sacred to be left to individuals or to the whims of an unrestricted labor market.

In order to implement this policy, the towns had to curtail some economic rights of individual residents. This imperative was obvious in the initial stages of economic development, when improving land and exploiting natural resources were essential undertakings, but the policy continued to be practiced—sometimes with even greater vigor—through the eighteenth century, after these urban and rural economies had matured. In Dedham, Watertown, and Boston, residents initially could sell their land to outsiders only with the consent of the selectmen. A Boston town meeting affirmed in 1635: "noe shall sell their houses or allotments to any newcomers, but with the consent and allowance of those that are appointed allotters." Dedham stipulated: "no person soe admitted and having lott with us shall at any time hereafter alienate, bargain, sell set over or assign the sayd lott or any parcel thereunto belonging unto any person whatsoever not being of our society for the term of one whole year or more except it be unto such as the major part of our said whole company shall approve of." In June 1636, the Boston town meeting voided Richard Fairbank's and Isaac Gulleymore's sales of houses to strangers and fined each man two pounds; in September it voided three other sales. In Dedham, Peter Woodward requested permission to sell some of his land to a stranger, Peter Bent, but the selectmen ruled, "Peter Bent is not allowed to purchase land in Dedham." Property holders later gained the right to sell to whomever they wanted, but the buyers still had to gain the town's consent to live and work on the land they had purchased.[40] Not until after the American Revolution did ownership of land in a town warrant the rights of inhabitancy without town approval.

Town members could not hire and house laborers from outside the town without obtaining permission from the town and in many cases filing bonds on their workers' behalf. Historians have often depicted the cruelty of New England's warning-out policies: towns often rejected the poor and sent them away. Here, as in seventeenth-century England, localities' refusal to accept needy people as residents saved their budgets while hurting the poor who lived outside the town. But, unlike the situation in many English cities, the poor did not appear in Massachusetts public records simply because they were wandering about desperately seeking food, shelter, and employment. In a striking number of cases, they appeared in the town records because they had been hired to work by a householder or farmers. These were not placeless and unemployed, but unwelcome competitors with town-born labor. Others had rented land from town residents. New England towns' enforcement of residence rules by warning out strangers was as much a matter of disciplining and regulating householders, employers, and landlords who belonged to the town as it was of rejecting the wandering poor.

Dedham, Watertown, and Boston wrote laws directed at controlling their own townspeople's appetite for hiring and harboring laborers and tenants from elsewhere instead of utilizing local working people. In 1636, the Boston town meeting "ordered that no townsman shall entertain any strangers into their houses for above fourteen days without leave from those that are appointed to order the town's business." In 1647, the meeting ordered that "no inhabitant shall entertain man or woman from any other town or country as a sojourner or inmate with an intent to reside here, but shall give notice thereof to the selectmen of the town for their approbation within eight days after their coming to the town under penalty of twenty shillings." In 1662, it passed an ordinance establishing a fearsome fine of a pound a night for entertaining unreported strangers. These policies became stricter and the penalties harsher over time, as Bostonians were determined to maintain control over the supply of labor even though many strangers passed through the seaport. These laws were hard to enforce, and were ignored during emergencies such as King Philip's War when towns surrounding Boston were destroyed and desperate refugees flooded into the seaport. However, enforcement was constantly renewed, thanks to its popularity among the working population, and was effective enough to shape residents' marriage and migration patterns. Dedham and Watertown passed similar laws, and all three localities renewed them repeatedly through the eighteenth century.[41] Because workers and tenants were often scarce in these towns, many households found hiring outsiders enticing. Town residents knew that they themselves needed policing in order to limit the town budget and maintain its wage structures. The renewal of these restrictive laws by the town meeting demonstrates that the town folk generally, not just its leaders, supported coercive policies against open hiring even though many households tried to ignore the law on occasion.

Town residents could hire outside laborers if they got the approval of the selectmen and offered a bond to pay for all the damages and expenses that might arise while these workers lived in the town. Bonds for young children were set as low as £5, but for adults they averaged £10. Unless a household had the means to post a bond, they could not hire outside labor. The net result was to make the labor of strangers more, rather than less, costly than local labor. In Boston, the town meeting required bonds for all incoming businessmen and -women who hoped to open a shop or ply a trade. When the newcomer could not afford a bond, he or she needed to recruit wealthy local men and women to provide collateral and implicitly stand as sponsor. This policy assured the town that if the newcomer's shop failed, creditors had relief. In addition, sea captains and merchants had to offer a bond for every passenger they brought from abroad (except for slaves, whom they might keep or sell). The costs could be daunting. In 1736, Captain James Williams, Greshom Keyes, and Josiah Flagg had to offer a bond of £1,100 to bring 43 Irish passengers into Boston.[42] No wonder Boston failed to attract immigrants until well into the nineteenth century; the seaport was notoriously unwelcoming of strangers who sought to stay.

The selectmen and town meeting reserved the right to accept or reject strangers, whether bonded or not, and exercised their own discretion to enforce their definitions of the public good. In 1715, William Cutlove, a London distiller, crossed the Atlantic only to be told by the Boston selectmen "to depart inasmuch as more of that employment is not needful in this town." On the other hand, about a year earlier the selectmen embraced James Pitson, a newcomer from London, who petitioned the selectmen to "sell cyder as a retailor at his house which he hires of Colonel Ballintinee in Marshall's Lane in Boston." The selectmen approved, "so long as he sell cider only, he being a stranger comes well recommended, the motive to this is that the skillful management of cider may prove a common benefit." Selectively admitting newcomers helped the selectmen and the town meeting direct economic development. Towns recruited in-migrants to fulfill a perceived economic and social need.[43] Through these policies, Massachusetts and other New England colonies helped develop such vital industries as textile manufacturing and shipbuilding.

Towns made regulating labor a centerpiece of their policy. Despite the time and trouble that meaningful enforcement entailed, labor regulation defined the identity of the region and the place of individuals within it. In Boston by 1664, "for the more convenient . . . dispatch of merchants affairs or any other relating to strangers and our inhabitants," the town meeting hired a ringer to strike a bell "at 11 of the clock every working day to give notice . . . to all persons concerned that they may assemble in the room under the townhouse for the space of one hour" so that employers could register the outsiders they had hired. Selectmen frequently fined and warned those who used outside labor without permission, and over time they redoubled their efforts and raised the penalties violators incurred. Periods of relative relaxation alternated with regimes of strict enforcement. The temptation to hire outside labor and the resulting pressure to regulate it were greatest in Boston. By 1700, the town had become the busiest North American Atlantic port in the English empire and offered many entrepreneurial opportunities that attracted outsiders and made their labor contributions invaluable. The small scale of the city, still confined to the peninsula and joined to the mainland only by the "neck," which might be awash at high tide, facilitated the detection of strangers, though the wharves lined with warehouses and piled with goods were notoriously porous borders. A fear of Irish infestation increased policing drastically in the 1720s.[44] Supervision in Dedham and Watertown also varied, but was often draconian.

No liberalizing trend toward deregulating the labor market is visible in seventeenth- or eighteenth-century Massachusetts. In contrast, in many seventeenth-century English cities new industries developed outside the walls. With the Restoration, Puritan civic reformers were dislodged from positions of public leadership. Guild-like labor regulation declined drastically by 1680 and then collapsed completely.[45] However, in eighteenth-century Massachusetts, the towns continued to play an active role in shaping the political economy. Though people never stopped bringing outsiders into their houses as renters and laborers, the selectmen never stopped watching and disciplining the strange workers and their local hosts, as town meetings continually authorized them to do. By instituting and developing the reform-oriented policies and practices of the incorporated towns and parishes of seventeenth-century England and carrying them out consistently in a society in which they did not encounter concerted political opposition, Massachusetts and other New England colonies created political economies and labor regimes noticeably different from those in England or the other American colonies.

Towns Intervene to Regulate Household Labor

Careful examination of towns' interventions into households that hired outside labor illuminates the workings of the political economy and its impact on families. Many households desired to bring in labor, and often two, three, or more households conspired to keep a worker in town. In 1662, Boston selectmen complained about strangers "shifting from house to house, which unless timely prevented as it hath already been to our detriment so it threatens further mischief and charge unto us." To solve the problem, the town imposed a pound-a-night penalty for harboring a laborer already banished by the town fathers. The practice of sharing a worker among households continued nonetheless. In 1667, the town fined Steven Brace "for setting up his calling of felt maker without liberty from the selectmen." Soon after, the town fined his many customers and supporters—James Landon, Joseph Davies, John White, and Clement Sammon—"for entertaining and employing Steven Brace contrary to a town order." In Watertown in 1685, the selectmen ordered Joseph Hastings to "clear his house of an inmate that had sheltered himself there." The constable reported that the young man had left that household, "but he was now sheltered at Mr. Nevinson's." In Dedham in 1695, the selectmen observed that a number of families had lodged James Bringo, a Negro, and ordered "that our inhabitants be forbidden to entertain him."[46] Multiple families harbored workers not out of kindness but for labor and profit. As Puritans knew, sin was everywhere, even within.

Significantly, selectmen distrusted and devalued family ties when identifying and banishing outsiders. In Watertown in 1682, the selectmen faced a complaint "that George Lorrance had taken his wife's brother into his family." Constables told Lorrance "that the said selectmen doth not allow him to entertain his wife's brother unless . . . he give in security to the selectmen to save the town harmless." When Lorrance declined, the selectmen fined him and banished his wife's brother. In 1701, the Dedham selectmen told John Starr, who was identified as an impotent person, "to forthwith depart out of this town of Dedham and that his brother Comfort Starr is disallowed to entertain John Starr." The town did not take Christian brotherhood or neighborliness literally. In 1736, Boston selectmen forced "Mr. Richard Avery to attend next Wednesday in order to give security for his daughter who came a passenger with Captain Crocker from London." The suspicious selectmen did not presume that a father would support his own daughter in difficulty without the incentive of a formal bond. In 1678 Dorchester selectmen refused to allow John Brown, who was born in Dorchester, to reestablish residency there "to be a help to his father and mother."[47] The town protected itself, rather than the family, and they defined who belonged to the town in a strict legalistic fashion: a town member was so by law, not by blood.

The selectmen showed no special consideration to widows who hired outside workers. These female household heads often needed labor, since they had buried their husbands and were left with young children under foot or alone with grown children long gone. Taking in lodgers or renters might enable them to maintain their households without putting out most of their children to others or resorting to poor relief. Yet in many cases, towns denied them the right to hire or rent to strangers. In 1692, Watertown selectmen forbade "the widow Underwood" from taking into her house "Benanuell Davis with his family." In 1694, they told Widow Page to eject her inmate John Heredine and ordered Mrs. Hopper "not to entertain Henry Reiner without sufficient bond be given by persons responsible to save the town harmless." Widows often could not afford bonds. In 1704, Watertown selectmen coupled charity with close supervision: they gave Widow Parry "liberty to set up a small house upon some piece of the town's common land that the selectmen shall appoint, and . . . not to take any inmates without the town's leave."[48]

Why did selectmen deny many households the right to use outside labor for more than two weeks? A major reason was to prevent outside laborers from becoming a burden to the town treasury should they be disabled by illness or accident. The determination "to save the town harmless" was not a mere expression of prejudice against strangers but a matter of substantial financial import. In 1691, Watertown selectmen discovered that the hired man Mrs. Shareman paid "to carry on her husbandry" developed a leg infection that led to gangrene. James Gibson had lived in the town for a year, so the town by secular and divine law had to pay for two doctors and months of food and shelter and then was obliged to support a one-legged farm worker for the rest of his life.[49] New Englanders regarded their towns as subject to divine surveillance and judgment, so those who belonged within them deserved to be given the means of life and redemption no matter what the cost. Towns asked those members who took in labor from the outside to assume these costs themselves.

Equally important, the policy of boundary maintenance aimed to protect the wages and dignity of town-born labor. In 1718, George King of Charlestown, a mast maker, asked the Boston selectmen for "liberty to exercise his trade in this town." Without asking for a bond, they "voted . . . their disallowance of his said request"; evidently they decided there were already enough mast makers in Boston. In some cases, officials specified what kind of work an outsider had to do or what skills he had to possess in order to remain in town. In 1665, the Boston selectmen decided that "John Hubbert hath not liberty to abide to continue in the town unless he serve three years to perfect him in the trade of a joiner."[50] By excluding outsiders or un-qualified workers, the town helped make town-born labor more valuable. Additionally, by restricting outside renters or tenants, the policy helped maintained low rents for the town born.

Like the godly towns and parishes of England, Massachusetts towns paid careful attention to the mental and spiritual development of town-born workers. Most towns mandated educational systems to develop the talents of their children and youth. Yet direct interventions into families were frequent, regardless of whether children were being taught to read. Since neither Mas-sachusetts as a whole nor its individual towns could promiscuously recruit labor, it was vital to extract as much work as possible from the laborers they had. The records of Boston, Watertown, and Dedham from 1630 to 1739 contain 134 cases in which town authorities intervened in families to ensure the present and future productivity of youthful labor. They often removed children from their parents' households and placed them in other households where they would be more usefully employed, properly trained, and effec-tively disciplined. Town officials cared little for the claims of family love or children's need to stay with parents.[51] They also disregarded the values of neighborliness, consent, and consensus; then, as now, nothing was more pro-vocative than the state taking children away from their parents and kin. The numbers found in town meeting records are probably underestimates, for in Boston and elsewhere some removals of children were handled by magistrates and overseers of the poor as well. All three towns developed workhouses or Bridewells in the seventeenth century, well before any economic crisis dic-tated them. To Massachusetts colonists, workhouses were simply part of the tool box needed to produce civility and productive labor.

By the early eighteenth century, the Boston town meeting organized house-by-house inspections of all the families in town, paying special atten-tion to poor children. On January 31, 1715, for example, "the justices and selectmen" agreed "to visit the families . . . to inspect disorderly persons, new-comers, and the circumstances of the poor and education of their chil-dren." Town officials and Quarterly Court judges acted together to maintain good order in Boston, conducting annual inspection sweeps from the 1680s through at least the 1730s. In 1734, fifty men visited all the families in eight Boston wards in teams that included a justice, a tax assessor, an overseer of the poor, and a selectman.[52] Here was a concrete demonstration of the power wielded by the "parish state." Inspection day ended with a meeting of these

officials to discuss the state of the town and consider remedial measures. No
doubt the magistrates moved many children to new homes as a consequence
of the fearful inspection day.

In Massachusetts, magistrates and selectmen by law had wide authority
and a positive duty to intervene in and rearrange households. The General
Court demanded that town selectmen "see that parents train up their children in learning, labour, and employments; if not, upon the presentment of
the grand jury, or other information of neglect, the said townsmen are subject
to fine." Selectmen were compelled to interfere; inaction or a plea of ignorance was not an option. Selectmen could "impose fines upon such parents
as refuse to give the account of their children's education." In other words,
all parents had to explain how they were raising their children, what they
could read, and what employments they pursued. The selectmen had the
right with the cooperation of two judges to "put for apprentice such children
whose parents are not able and fit to bring them up."[53] Parents did not have
to commit crimes, abuse their children, or even be impoverished to lose their
children; they simply had to forfeit the confidence of a majority of the selectmen and two judges. Selectmen exercised powers similar to those that English
godly towns and rural parishes once had wielded over the apprentices and
their host families in the trades. Parents' rights to their own children's labor,
if they existed at all, were tenuous and conditional.

In most cases, the selectmen who deemed a family unfit would negotiate
with them about removing a child or two, with the threat of court action
looming in the background. These discussions were often a condition of the
town offering aid to a needy family. In 1656, the Watertown selectmen decided that Mrs. Phillips was doing a poor job of raising her "loose living"
son Jonathan. The town threatened her with court action "except she undertake for her son as to have him under government or otherwise to dispose of
him to some such place or way that may." In Boston in 1656, the selectmen
decided that "the son of Goodwife Sammon living without a calling, that if
she dispose not of him in some way of employ before the next meeting that
then the townsmen will dispose of him to some service according to law."
Similar interventions had been carried out in the city of Norwich and in rural
parishes as remote as Constantine, Cornwall, in the 1630s, but in Massachusetts they continued through the eighteenth century. Sometimes many families received notice that their idle and poorly educated children must be
moved. In 1709, the Watertown selectmen noted "that there are several families within said town that are needy and suffering: and that have great families

of children that are not provided for as to food or rainment as they ought to be, neither are they educated or brought to the public worship of God, whereby they are like to be filled with nothing but ignorance and irreligion: which families are Thomas Corahs, Charles Chadwick and Daniel Magregor." The selectmen appointed committees to visit these families "to order each family to dispose of most of their children to such families as the selectmen shall approve of and that if they shall refuse so to do that the selectmen will dispose of them as the law doth oblige and expect with them."[54]

In most cases, parents submitted and spread their children among other households. However, some resisted public intervention. In Watertown, Obadiah Coolidge admitted to the selectmen on March 24, 1727, that due to sickness in his household "he was not able to support his family." The selectmen strongly advised him "to put out his children into some good religious families where his children might have good care taken of them, and to do it forthwith, to prevent them the trouble thereof." However, by the next meeting less than three weeks later, Coolidge had "not complied with their advice to put out his children." The selectmen ordered "that the said Obadiah Coolidge's wife and children and household goods be forthwith removed to the dwelling house of the widow Rachel Goddard of said town, there to continue under the care of the said widow and her son Ebenezer until further order from the selectmen." Rachel Goddard was Coolidge's mother-in-law. About a month later, the selectmen observed that their order had not been carried out. It was clear by May 30, 1727, that Coolidge and his wife were determined to keep their family intact. In August, Coolidge's wife petitioned the Watertown selectmen to "receife her household goods which were lodged per order of the selectmen at the house of her mother Rachel Goddard in order to remove with her husband to Marlborough, there being some probable prospect of their living together there and gaining a comfortable maintenance." The selectmen complied, though a number of Coolidge's children had already been placed out.[55] Most families accepted the authority of the selectmen and surrendered their children. The alternative was to find a place or settlement in another town, which was itself a serious challenge.

The decisive action against Obadiah Coolidge was part of a crackdown on idle children and inefficient households in Watertown. In 1727, Watertown compelled the movement of children from poor to rich households by posting a notice ordering poor families to put out their children to "such religious families where both body and soul may be taken good care of" and threatening sanctions for disobedience. They also organized a pauper auction just before planting time. The notice told "such persons that have a desire to take children or servants, to meet with the above said select men at their meeting on the first Monday of April next at the dwelling house of Mr. Thomas Learned innholder in said town at three of the clock in the afternoon of said day."[56] The legal and financial obstacles that wealthier households faced in obtaining outside laborers no doubt increased their appetite for the labor of the children of their town's poorer households. The policy of defending the town's boundaries contributed to the policy of intervening in "problem families." This strategy of exercising control over both strangers and residents and the political economy it advanced presumably helped poor children in Watertown to have an instructive and productive, if not a loving, childhood.

After they reached adulthood, many youth continued to face town oversight and control of their labor. In 1636, the Massachusetts General Court "ordered that all towns shall take care to order and dispose of all single persons and inmates within their town to service, or otherwise, and if any be grieved at the order of a town, the parties to have liberty to appeal to the governor and council, or the courts."[57] Any young person, unless he or she was married or could sustain a household of his or her own, had to live under the supervision of an older man or mature woman. This restriction was identical to laws in godly English towns and rural parishes restricting youth and single adults from "living at their own hand." In seventeenth-century Norwich, the mayoralty court placed single youths in the Bridewell until they got a place in service. In New England these laws were more often enforced against males, whereas in Norwich 80 percent of those identified as "solitary livers" were female. The historian Paul Griffiths speculates that in Norwich authorities suspected that young women living alone were prostitutes, for only such a trade could sustain them among low wages.[58] In Massachusetts, higher wages meant that young men could live on their own and exercise their healthy lusts unless regulated by law.

From 1650 to 1683, Dedham and Watertown systematically enforced the act by holding special sessions of the town board to ensure that every bachelor accepted a year-long residence in an approved household. Young men were given some choice in the matter: Watertown selectmen recorded in March 1657, "it is ordered that Jonathan Phillips, Joshua Barsum, Samuel Benjamin, John Knapp have liberty to provide themselves to covenant with some honest masters for a year, between this and Cambridge Court, and in the mean time, to give a weekly account in writing of every days work into the hands of the selectmen."[59] These young men earned their own wages, but their productivity and habits were closely supervised by the selectmen in the short term and by a fatherly or motherly head of household in the longer term.

In Dedham, a special annual meeting oversaw the placement of "young persons in such families in the town as is the most suitable for their good." For example, five young men were granted their "desire to sojourn" in specific households "so long as they demean themselves orderly." Amos Fisher was allowed "to sojourn at his father's house," while some of the others shared surnames and perhaps kin ties with their hosts. Most young men left their father's house for work elsewhere, but stayed in town. The system balanced autonomy and control. A young man could leave a poor household or one where his labor could not be effectively utilized. He could seek the best wages possible in town, which made both moral and economic sense. The selectmen rejected some requests: "Whereas William Dean have desired to sojourn at the house of Ester Fisher upon complaint and proof of his ill behavior, the selectmen declare they do not allow him to sojourn there."[60] The selectmen thought Dean needed sterner discipline than that provided by a female. In Boston, young unmarried adults were not assigned to service or residence in specific households, but they were expected to work and, most often, to live with their masters. Boston required the town born to complete adequate apprenticeships, even if they worked for their fathers. Finally, all these towns cited adults for idleness and placed them under receivership and guardianship. In Massachusetts no one was free to labor as he or she wanted, no one was free to use labor as he or she wanted, and no one was free not to labor. Everybody who belonged to the town labored and hired labor under moral and legal oversight.

In Massachusetts, labor was constructed by towns that operated throughout the seventeenth and eighteenth centuries in much the same ways that godly English towns and rural parishes had operated in the early seventeenth century. Town political economies protected the value of labor by shielding local workers from competition from outsiders; they demanded that employers prefer town-born labor by making them pay extra and assume the risks of hiring strangers; they provided education and discipline so children would learn to work productively. Town restrictions made labor valuable and ensured the dignity of local laborers. Outsiders and strangers suffered from exclusion, as did enslaved Africans and Indians, but those English men and women who were recognized as belonging to the town were assured that public policies and religiously sanctioned practices were designed to ensure that their labor led to advancement and marriage and, for men, active citizenship, and that their children, provided that they worked, would never be degraded. The implementation of Protestant social reforms guided by civic humanism, especially the diffusion of political power to smallholders, allowed the colony to develop a society that valued labor and minimized slavery. In other American regions, where markets in labor and land were allowed to develop without such restrictive regulations and orderly processes, bound servitude and then chattel slavery developed as major institutions.[61] In Massachusetts, where the cities and towns interfered with entrepreneurs' ability to accumulate the labor they wanted, laboring men and producers retained their dignity. By imposing their urban vision on the forests, by restricting the power of employers and the mobility of workers, Puritan towns created enough justice to make plausible the illusion that the American landscape generated freedom, rough equality, and social redemption.

The historical significance of the transplantation and continuation of the reform strategies of godly English cities and parishes across seacoast and inland Massachusetts is far-reaching. The question of whether "community" flourished or declined is of lesser import. Now, as in the colonial period, "community" is a rhetorical trope that may be made to serve many masters and stand for various interests. Complex organizations from box stores to universities call themselves communities and offer narratives about their ability to facilitate the pursuit of happiness or other worthwhile ends among their "associates." Still, the point is promoting consumption or intellectual production. New Englanders developed a unique, resilient, and persistent political economy. Thanks to towns' protection of their labor and the development of its productivity, Massachusetts workers with the liberty to work in their own town enjoyed relatively good wages, and rents remained relatively low.[62] By historical standards, compared to slavery or bound labor, this policy did not require much coercion or violence, though it demanded self-discipline, and violence was hardly absent. The repeated renewal of laws restricting outsiders and their employers shows that common men long supported the public protection of their own and their children's labor from outsiders, including slaves, and from an open market in wage labor. This labor system, which was rooted in the reform-oriented parishes and cities of early modern England, grew in Massachusetts into a political economy that made New England a distinctive region with a social trajectory all its own.

CHAPTER TWO

Stripes

Stripes, or whipping, is a correction fit and proper in some cases, where the offence is accompanied with childish or brutish folly, with rude filthiness, or with stubborn insolency, with beastly cruelty, or with idle vagrancy, or for faults of like nature. But when stripes are due: it is ordered, that not above forty stripes shall be inflicted at one time; Deut 25:3.
Laws of New Haven Colony, 1644

IN HIS JOURNAL, John Winthrop described punishments for misbehavior more frequently than sermons inculcating proper conduct. Inflicting punishment and studying its effective application were a significant part of his responsibilities as governor. During the voyage to Massachusetts, he made two overly pugnacious young men "walk upon the deck till night with their hands bound behind them." When Winthrop detected a teenaged servant overcharging a child, he ordered the servant's hands "to be tied up to a bar and hanged a basket with stones about his neck and so he stood 2 hours." Once in Massachusetts, his task shifted from simply controlling youth to making them work productively. Consequently, his interest turned to the whip and the noose. At the whipping post, Winthrop marveled, Mary Oliver "stood without tying and bare her punishment with a masculine spirit, glorying in her suffering." At the scaffold, William Hatchet, convicted of bestiality, screamed when authorities cut the throat of the cow the boy had buggered. Winthrop argued in court, as well as in his journal, that magistrates should have wide discretionary power to determine punishments in noncapital cases.[1]

It is disturbing to witness the lurid preoccupations of "the forgotten founding father."[2] In his eyes, dramatic punishments, alongside good preaching and shrewd legal constructions, were a necessary and rational means of creating a new kind of labor force composed of children who behaved like obedient servants and of obedient servants who were treated almost like children. The Puritans were unique among early Americans in unabashedly and publicly whipping and terrorizing not only cultural outsiders, such as Native Americans and Africans, but their own people—their own countrymen and women, their own children, the people whom they loved. They literally whipped their colonies' labor pool into shape. It was in the service of this new socioeconomic order that Winthrop studied punishment so carefully. New Englanders created the most egalitarian labor regime in early America, so the governor's horrifying devotion to punishment as an art and science was also a blessing.

Christian humanism provided a lofty set of principles for English reformers, but creating a workable society on that basis in New England was a difficult assignment. In the 1630s, Massachusetts colonists faced a major economic and cultural crisis. Coming to a place with vast material resources, bringing with them ambitious ideas about economic relations in a godly commonwealth, they faced a crippling labor shortage. With the ethical and political tools at their disposal, they cooperatively fashioned a novel labor force by amalgamating the colonists' children and other English youth into a subordinated laboring class whom they treated harshly, yet justly. In the other British colonial regions, property-holders spared their own children from the most menial and burdensome work and from the most violent suppressions of self-assertion and pleasure; they inflicted all these oppressions on imported outsiders, either indentured servants or, increasingly, enslaved Africans. They treated the outsiders brutally and relegated them to a permanently demeaned, degraded, and marginalized lower caste.[3]

Such evil doings were not gratuitous. In a preindustrial economy, lacking any sources of power beyond animal and human muscles, production usually required many workers who were driven by violence as well as hunger.[4] Productivity almost never increased, given the lack of technological innovations. Wealth was limited. In order for the privileged to flourish and enjoy the leisure to pursue culture, the great majority of people in Europe had to settle for low wages and political powerlessness. Early modern societies were clearly hierarchical. Elites oppressed the poor violently in order to control them.

In England, daily violence was limited because the lower orders composed a vast surplus labor pool, growing ever larger in the early seventeenth century. Workers and children could often be tamed with threats of unemployment and starvation. Although the whip was used privately and publicly, corporal punishment was directed mostly against vagrants and criminals. Disobedient servants could be replaced with willing ones, and wages remained low.[5] Many Puritans bemoaned the increasing powerlessness of laborers in the 1630s. In Massachusetts, labor issues were complicated by Christian ethics and by some Puritan leaders' desire to improve the status of manual labor. When considering emigration from England, John Winthrop deemed unemployment and declining wages excellent reasons for leaving: "The land grows weary of her inhabitants, soe as man whoe is the most preatious of all creatures, is here more vile and base, then the earth we tread upon."[6] Winthrop wanted all people to be appreciated for their work, and he certainly thought that the common people should be more valuable on the market than land.

Labor in America was in much shorter supply than in Europe, a fact all the more frustrating because of the continent's ample but relatively undeveloped land resources. Native Americans seldom worked for the colonists voluntarily, and the survivors remained highly susceptible to European germs. The English surplus labor pool was an ocean away. Even when English laborers could be imported, they resisted perpetual subordination. Cheap land was available for laborers in America, and colonial societies competed for the limited supply of immigrant laborers. American elites tended to grow even more brutal than their English and European counterparts in the effort to accumulate and control servants.[7]

By the end of the seventeenth century, experiments in relatively nonviolent labor systems in Anglo-America had largely failed, and many colonial elites turned to slavery to obtain adequate labor power. In the Chesapeake, the English initially established a labor regime composed of indentured servants. Tobacco planters and their merchant allies lured thousands of young English workers by offering them relatively short terms of servitude followed by high wages and access to fertile lands. Many servants died from disease and malnutrition, but perhaps a third survived and became yeomen; a few even became gentle folk.[8] The planters shrewdly avoided repelling these youth by establishing a legal system that offered some justice to servants and by avoiding tawdry and repellent public lashings, though they left masters free to exercise violence in private. However, in the 1690s the demand for labor in the expanding Chesapeake tobacco lands, fed by the labor needs of ex-servants, exceeded the supply of importable British workers. At the same time, tobacco lands became less available, more expensive, and less profitable. Instead of abandoning tobacco for less labor-intensive crops, Chesapeake planters turned to African slaves. Knowing that slaves could only be supplied, retained, and made to work by means of torture and terrorism, Chesapeake planters grew ever more violent and racist, enacting brutal slave codes.[9] Though the tobacco planters had previously avoided rituals of public whipping, their private behavior was less gentle, and by 1700 they had adopted kidnapping, murder, and terror as their prime labor control methods. These colonies used less public violence than the Puritans but allowed enormous violence in households and on ships bringing over Africans.

In Massachusetts, people attempted to ensure that violence was exercised by the state rather than by individuals, to determine punishments by law rather than arbitrarily, and to administer the system rationally in order to reform people and to create an ethically and economically effective labor system. In the cause of rationalizing state violence, the townsmen served as enforcers, jurymen, indicters, perpetrators, and occasionally victims. As a consequence of the state's monopoly of force, seventeenth-century Massachusetts had the most open legal violence; its reputation for the whipping post and stocks was well deserved. Yet eventually it became less violent than virtually every other American colonial society.[10] New England inculcated self-discipline in its hard-working children.

The Economic and Ethical Riddles of Massachusetts' Labor Shortage

In Puritan New England, the labor shortage had ethical as well as economic dimensions. Many Puritan leaders harbored seemingly incompatible economic and ethical expectations. "I doubt not but we will rayse good profit not only by our fishing trade (which is sufficiently knowne)," wrote Richard Saltonstall from Massachusetts in February 1631, "but by hempe, flaxe, pitch, tarr, pottashes, sope ashes, masts, pipe staves, clapboards (and iron as we hope)." However, Saltonstall noted, "without hands nothing can be done, nor any thing with any great profit until multitudes of people make labour cheape." John Winthrop sought to ensure that economic development would be compatible with an inclusive Christian society, and diligently defended the colony's need to "keepe off whatsoever appears to tend to our ruin or damage" and therefore "to lawfully refuse to receive such whose dispositions suite not with ours and whose society (we know) will be hurtful to us."[11] Getting enough workers, reforming them, and integrating them into a civic community of saints was a monumental task—perhaps even an impossible undertaking.

In the 1630s, to be sure, thousands of English people immigrated to Massachusetts in what became known as the Great Puritan Migration. But most of these colonists were members of relatively wealthy young families, with many dependents and few working-age persons. The depth and complexity of the Massachusetts labor shortage is suggested by comparison of the ages, sex, and family connections of 3,415 emigrants who left England between 1634 and 1636 on thirty-five ships bound for Virginia and Massachusetts. Only 31 percent of the Massachusetts-bound passengers were men between the ages of fifteen and thirty-five—in their prime working years, at least for physical labors requiring brute strength rather than skill. The rest of the Massachusetts emigrants were older men; young, pregnant, or middle-aged women; and very young children. These families typically paid for their own passage, were inspired by the Holy Spirit, were literate, had craft skills, had capital from selling their life accumulations in England, and promised a virtuous, familial society.[12] Yet they posed an immediate economic problem because they lacked the sheer muscle power required to transform the Indians' lands into a commodity-producing economy. In Massachusetts labor was so scarce that few salable commodities were produced. The colony's livestock, which more established families sold to newcomers, were poorly supervised and relatively unprofitable. A major source of the difficulty is that small children were expected to look after large animals. In 1640, Winthrop wrote a memorandum about a young girl who, after falling asleep in the woods, lost seven cows; she ran away and hid, expecting to be beaten by her master and mistress. Even with strict discipline, children did not make the most productive workers.[13]

Early Massachusetts lacked the Virginians' brawn and ethical laxity. The Virginia-bound vessels were filled with men between the ages of fifteen and thirty-five; three-quarters of the passengers fell into this highly productive group. The young men were mostly indentured servants who paid for their passage by agreeing to sign a contract whereby each would work for an American planter for three or four years, while being adequately fed and clothed. English merchants sold their contracts to tobacco planters along the rivers that flowed into Chesapeake Bay. The young men were starved for food and females, guzzled alcohol when they could get it, spat out oaths, and shivered with cold; many got sick, and a considerable proportion died. Many historians have disliked these disorderly, unfortunate immigrants. Nevertheless, these youthful laborers had the raw strength required to produce tons of tobacco as servants, wage laborers, and planters.[14]

Making the labor situation more perplexing in Massachusetts were the moral sensitivities of the founding families and their civic leaders. Many Massachusetts colonists arrived in flight from the same youth that they would desperately need as workers. The colony refused to embrace the most affordable, short-term strategy to solve the labor shortage: the enticement of British youth from the lower sort with accommodating terms of employment. In rural England, farm laborers were usually hired as servants for the year. Children typically left home at age fourteen for service or apprenticeship. In the early seventeenth century, a surplus of home-leaving youth created unemployment, harsh competition, and social unrest, low wages, and violence, especially in the bustling towns of southeastern England.[15] While Chesapeake planters sought to harvest surplus youth for their muscle power, Puritan householders feared and loathed these masterless folk—unless they could reform them.

Puritans believed that the unreformed Anglican church's emphasis on ceremonies, instead of plain sermons, strong discipline, and literacy, ill prepared these young men and women for independence, much less to face the judgment of God. Puritans told tales of English maypoles, cockfights, drunken brawls, and lewd women with exposed breasts who had enticed and endangered their own and their children's souls. Puritan parents wanted to keep their children near home and under the influence of godly masters, ministers, and magistrates. New England offered a refuge of land, ministry, and political independence where strict institutions might develop a reformed social order.[16]

Some colonists hoped to construct a viable economy by employing their own children instead of the profane youth they left on the English docks. The Reverend Francis Higginson promised New Englanders that their numerous young children would help produce New World crops. Higginson reported in 1630 that the local Indians had cleared thousands of acres and had developed an agriculture centered on maize, called Indian corn, that allowed small children to contribute by almost playfully forming mounds around the newly planted seeds. "Little children of five years old," wrote the minister, "may by setting corn one month be able to get their own maintenance abundantly." The settlers never achieved this imagined self-sufficiency; they were correct to worry about the heavy burden of young dependents. Hundred-foot trees, rocky soil, and icy winds crushed five-year-olds' vaunted playtime productivity. Colonists wanted to believe any version of the minister's tall tale, however. In 1634, William Wood had to disillusion potential emigrants, warning that "whereas it hath been formerly reported that boys of ten or twelve years of age might do much more than get their living, that cannot be, for he must have more than a boy's head and no less than a man's strength that intends to live comfortably."[17]

Until their toddlers grew to men and women, the settlers needed adolescent and adult workers. Ironically, the very people whom the settlers hoped to escape, they now desired, attracted, and unintentionally empowered. Thanks to the wealth of the godly immigrants, in the 1630s and for many decades thereafter, skilled and unskilled workers in Massachusetts got the highest wages in the British Empire. Despite many attempts to regulate wages, Governor Winthrop reported that by 1633, "the scarcity of workmen had caused them to rayse their wages to an excessive rate, so as a carpenter would have 3s the day, a labourour 2s 6d and etc."[18] English workers got, at best, about a shilling a day. Massachusetts wages were at least one and a half times those in England, and Massachusetts labor costs exceeded those of any other contemporary colony.[19]

The high cost of labor threatened the colony's economy. The West Indian historian Hilary Beckles has argued that the cost of white indentured servants in the 1630s in the Caribbean and Virginia was about £1.6 a year, plus food, clothing, and shelter. With the costs of subsistence included, and accounting for losses by disease and running away, a servant in Virginia cost perhaps £8 annually. Once freed after three or four years, these servants became laborers earning from £10 to £15 a year. In comparison, at two and a half shillings a day, Massachusetts common laborers cost from £20 to £35 annually, more than double the costs of labor in Virginia or the Caribbean.[20] The New England economy could not immediately produce any staple crop like tobacco or sugar that yielded a profit despite such high labor costs.

Thanks to high wages, Massachusetts attracted many young servants and laborers by the mid-1630s. In *New England's Prospect*, William Wood relayed that it was "generally reported" that in Massachusetts "servants and poor men grow rich, and the masters and gentry grow poor." In the new Israel, money was cascading from the pious top to the profane bottom of the social scale. Most telling was the dramatic bankruptcy of John Winthrop himself, a godly member of the English gentry, who bought and developed Massachusetts acreage with cattle, got no profit, paid excessively high wages, took out loans, and went broke. With his permission, the court whipped and cut off the ears of his hapless manager, James Luxford, for this and other misfortunes.[21]

In 1635, among 1,413 passengers on English vessels that arrived in Massachusetts, over a third were neither married to, nor children of, other emigrants on the ships. These young people often received high wages supplied by the life savings of labor-starved families. Though a minority of all the colonists, these young, single workers (or young men who had left their wives in England) composed a substantial fraction of the most valuable laborers: men between the ages of fifteen and thirty-five years. Among the 734 emigrants in this age group, 496, or 68 percent, were neither married to other passengers nor the children of families on board ship. These youth were especially common on the ships from London, where word of Massachusetts' alluring wages and healthy climate spread through inns and taverns. For example, the passenger list of the ship *Elizabeth* in 1635 showed that thirty-four of seventy-three passengers, or 47 percent, traveled alone, rather than as a child or servant with a household group. The largest of the nine household groups on the *Elizabeth* was headed by forty-year-old Clement Bates, a tailor. He traveled with his wife Ann, age forty; five children, from age fourteen to age two; and two male servants. Listed after the Bates were four "tanners of Saint Alphage, Cripplegate": William Holdred, age twenty-five; Roger Preston, age twenty-one; Daniel Bradley, age twenty; and Isaac Stedman. Most of the unattached passengers on the *Elizabeth* were young males. Among the forty-eight males on the *Elizabeth*, thirty-one, or 65 percent, were detached from any household on board, and these men averaged twenty-two years of age—in their prime years for performing physically demanding labor.[22]

The influx of young workers, while essential to the immediate sustenance of the colony, posed both economic and ethical problems. By the mid-1630s, as wages soared, Massachusetts' labor and productivity problems alarmed sophisticated men and women. Their concerns are worth considering. In 1636, John Winthrop's sister, Lucy Downing, wrote from England expressing the view "that many good people here, and some that understand New England reasonable well, both by sight and relations of friends that are able to judge, they do much fear the country cannot afford subsistence for many people, and that if you were not supplied of incomes from hence your lives would be very miserable."[23] Such English Puritans saw the Massachusetts economy as a bubble. Capital investment came from religious emigrants and benefactors, but the capital created no commodities that could be sold for English or European goods or money. Instead, the capital went to laborers who for inflated wages built houses and cleared and fenced fields for a subsistence economy of saints. Only the continuous arrival and expenditures of religiously motivated and relatively moneyed English families and the contributions of well-wishers in England paid these workers' exorbitant wages and kept the colony afloat. Many believed that the bubble would eventually burst.

John Winthrop understood the situation from a public as well as personal perspective. His journal is full of illustrative examples. In 1642, Winthrop told the story of "one Richard _____ servant to one _____ Williams of Dorchester, being come out of service, fell to work at his own hand and took great wages above others, and would not work but for ready money." "In a year, or little more," noted Winthrop, "he had scraped together about 25 pounds, and then returned with his prey into England, speaking evil of the country by the way." In England, his friends, who were opposed to Puritans, "eased him of his money, so he knew no better way but to return to New England again to repair his loss in that place which he had so much disparaged." In this story, Winthrop emphasized the ironic twist that the scoffing laborer had to return to the colony he ridiculed. Yet Winthrop must have been aware how the story revealed the sad weaknesses of his own society and economy. The laborer took his £25 back to England because the money he accumulated would only be wasted in New England to buy goods at inflated prices. The high cost of labor forced New England farmers to raise the prices of foodstuffs and other necessities. Cattle raised in New England were selling in the mid-1630s at the same price as cattle raised in Wales and transported across England and the Atlantic Ocean to the Boston market.[24] Rampant inflation made it easier for the man to speak critically of New England. The money the laborer received did not come from the profits on commodities made in Massachusetts; it came from the life savings of religious families who had emigrated to New England. These young families needed labor desperately, so they dispersed their savings to young laborers rather than investing them in profitable enterprises. This was not a recipe for economic development.

Meanwhile, the prosperity of young workers threatened the moral viability of the colony in the eyes of its major shareholders—middling Puritan colonists. Puritan fathers and mothers thought it difficult to keep their own sons and daughters working at home contentedly when next door or even in their own lofts a growing fraternity of upwardly mobile bachelors, often dressed in the latest London fashions, lolled in unprecedented money, leisure, and power. In December 1635, Nathaniel Ward, the minister of Ipswich, Massachusetts, wrote to John Winthrop, Jr., expressing his and many other pious families' alarm and disgust: "Our thoughts and fears grow very sad to see such multitudes of idle and profane young men, servants, and others with whom we must leave our children, for whose sake and safety we came over." Unless the profane youth were curbed, Ward threatened to leave and promised a large exodus: "If it be not remedied we and many others must not only say with grief we have made an ill change, even from the snare to the pit, but must mediate some safer refuge, if God will afford it." Ward's threat to abandon the colony was real; at that time, before the Puritan Revolution, Lord Saye and Sele was recruiting Massachusetts colonists for his Caribbean colony on Providence Island with the argument that New England would never develop a viable economy.[25]

Puritans were unable to agree on the best solution to this labor and moral crisis. Saltonstall and other entrepreneurs wanted to attract more young laborers and servants of the meaner sort. They deemphasized the emerging town labor system and the discipline needed to sustain it and favored a freer labor market. Ward's letter suggests this solution was politically unpopular among the settled townsmen. Over a decade later, Winthrop's brother-in-law proposed making a just war against the Narragansett Indians in order to capture them and exchange them in the West Indies for African slaves.[26]

Other Puritan leaders thought a family labor system could be fashioned in America, but only with drastic reformation of the household through the imposition of state power and the judicious use of violence. In 1637, John White, an experienced English reformer and supporter of Massachusetts colonization, wrote a searching letter to John Winthrop that opened White's "heart so boldly" that he desired Winthrop "to burne my letter when you have perused it." White believed that the family labor system, which he championed, was failing in New England. Only the money brought by new arrivals and sent by English Puritans was keeping the colony alive. White thought increased productivity was essential to prevent economic disaster. He believed that the most moral solution was the draconian education of Massachusetts youth: "A great part of your body hath been unaccustomed to laborious courses who will hardly be brought unto them in their age, all the hope is in training up the youth in time." Their parents were beyond reform, but a new work ethic could be inculcated in the children. "You have the low country's pattern for industry," White lamented; "I wish I could present you any other for family discipline."[27] In light of the cruel and insulting implications of his argument, it is not surprising that White wanted the letter burned after reading. In time New Englanders adopted town labor systems that subordinated production in individual households to more collective forms of labor. More immediately, they used state-sponsored public violence to curb youth and set them to work.

In the spring of 1636, Hugh Peter, minister of Salem, demanded that authorities "take order for employment of people (especially women and children in the winter time) for he feared idleness would be the ruin of both church and commonwealth."[28] To leaders like White and Peter, the key to making family labor work was to override traditional English familial limits on callousness in order to take vigorous measures to employ everyone, especially the colonists' children, more intensively than they had been worked before. Middling English people's conventional reliance on the labor of the abundant lower orders needed to be erased. Winthrop and other leaders boldly adopted these suggestions and fashioned a new labor system in the towns of Massachusetts.

Legal and Legislative Solutions

With the support of most propertied colonists, Governor Winthrop used the law to shape a well-paid but strictly controlled labor force. Following their purge of religious radicals during the antinomian crisis, Winthrop and other discipline-minded leaders assumed command, and Massachusetts soon became the Anglo-American leader in the public whipping of youth.[29] The magistrates sought to repel intractable British youth and to compel the available children and potentially docile servants to carry the burden of production. At the same time, the magistrates sought to delay youths' accession to the power and privileges the labor market would normally give them. Though a whole host of legal and spiritual remedies were fashioned to construct this new order, whipping and coercion were essential ingredients.

Between 1635 and 1660 Winthrop and other leaders relied upon the law and official, rationalized violence to cut the knots tied by the labor shortage and the colony's moral ambitions. First, they curbed servants. Servants contracted to work for a term of years in exchange for passage to America. Upon signing or marking their contracts in England, few servants—or, for that matter, their masters—anticipated the high wages that would be paid to free labor in Massachusetts. A servant in Massachusetts enjoyed unusual economic power. He was no longer floating in a vast pool of surplus labor, as in England, nor did he sink into servitude among the impoverished majority of Virginians. In Massachusetts, surrounded by needful, rich, and relatively unproductive households, a young servant's labor and strength could lead quickly to independence, wealth, status, and leisure.

Some servants used their economic clout to negotiate and renegotiate advantageous contracts. The Plymouth court reported, for example, that in 1639 Job Cole not only paid for the passage of his servant Thomas Gray to America but "also promiseth that if the said Thomas Gray approve himself well and faithful in his service, the said Job will remit him a year or two of his term." Given the temptation to abscond and earn high wages, Cole decided to shorten Gray's contract in return for his compliance. The brute power of the laborer in an unregulated market was clear in the 1639 renegotiations between Thomas Prince and William Honeywell. Honeywell was to serve Prince "until June next, and some further time which he should also serve for absenting himself divers times from his service." Honeywell had apparently sold his own labor when he should have been working for his master. However, Prince had just taken some land on the south side of the town of Plymouth and he needed Honeywell's muscle to develop the property by "setting, planting, and weeding the acres." The new deal was that if Honeywell worked hard for Prince "and not loyter or work with any other man except it be . . . by licence from Mr. Prince," Prince agreed to release "the said William Honeywell all the term he should have served him." Additionally, Prince agreed to give Honeywell "half the crop at harvest for his pains." After this year-long contract expired, Prince agreed that "the said William is to have . . . 25 acres of land." The twenty-five acres was part of the original contract, but in the 1639 renegotiations the once derelict Honeywell gained remission of all labor time he owed Prince and got half the yield of his future servile labor.[30]

It was psychologically difficult and morally trying to remain a servant in Massachusetts. The high wages possible outside a contract signed in ignorance of such unusual conditions made freedom ever more tantalizing, servitude ever more onerous, and stern masters ever more eager to extend servitudes instead of paying market wages. The situation caused emotional and social instability. Winthrop reported that at least one servant with a long contract, haunted by the phantom of high-wage freedom, committed suicide. Some servants ran away; many others behaved badly. Mary Dudley, John Winthrop's daughter, complained in 1636 that her maid, once dutiful, had "got such a head and is grown so insolent, that her carriage towards us, especially myself, is insufferable." Dudley noted that "if I bid her doe a thing, she will bid me to doe it myself." Because Dudley was pregnant and could not find another maid, she accepted the girl's derelictions for months.[31]

To some colonists, maintaining servitude in Massachusetts seemed impossible. Writing to Sir Simonds d'Ewes in 1633, the Reverend John Eliot suggested that the English aristocrat bring no normal servants to Massachusetts, "for if they be either rich and workful they will desire freedom." Servants like these would leave or extract high wages. Instead, Eliot suggested d'Ewes bring servants "fit to attend a gentleman that are not fit for labor." Governor Winthrop grew to hate young menials whose ambitions made a mockery of the pious Christian households and neighborhoods he had envisioned. He seemed unduly gleeful that two servants, who wanted higher wages and waded into the bay to gather oysters for sale soon drowned in a high tide. "It was an evident judgment of God upon them, for they were wicked persons," proclaimed the governor. "One of them, a little before being reproved for lewdness, and put in mind of hell, answered that if hell were 10 times hotter, he had rather be there, then he would serve his master."[32]

The legal repression of arrogant servants increased sharply after 1635. In 1630, the court prohibited any servant from trading commodities without his or her master's license—a sign that servants were getting or stealing money. In September 1634, the court ordered that no servant might obtain land in any town "till he hath approved his faithfulness to his master during the tyme of his service." The law made moral character and fulfillment of the original service contract, not money, the key to land acquisition. In 1636 the Massachusetts court ordered "that no servant shall be set free, or have any lot, until he have served out the time covenanted, under penalty of such fine as the Quarterly Court shall inflict, unless they see cause to remit the same." This law criminalized shortening terms and by implication renegotiating contracts to accommodate the high-wage labor market. The new law forbidding the renegotiating of previous labor contracts was enforced against masters as well as men. For example, in June 1639, the Massachusetts court fined both Captain Stoughton and Ralfe Allen forty shillings "for releasing his man

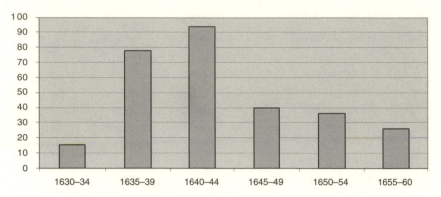

Figure 2. Number of free-living servants publicly whipped in New England, 1630–1660. Sources: Records of the Governor and Company of Massachusetts Bay; Records of the Court of Assistants of The Colony of the Massachusetts Bay, 1630–1692; Records of the Colony of New Plymouth in New England, 1620–1692; Public Records of the Colony of Connecticut, 1636–1776; Records of the Colony and Plantation of New Haven, 1649–1769; Records and Files of the Quarterly Courts of Essex County, Massachusetts.

before expiration of his time." Trading servants' terms for effort and loyalty was now illegal.[33]

Enter the Whip

From 1635 to 1645, Massachusetts, Plymouth, Connecticut, and New Haven authorities shattered servants' vaulting ambitions by extending terms to punish bad behavior and by publicly whipping and humiliating servants. After 1635, New Englanders commonly witnessed the lashing of a proud servant after town meeting or a religious lecture. The full fury of the crackdown on ambitious, rebellious, and free-living servants peaked between 1639 and 1642 (Figure 2). Public whipping ebbed only after authorities erected a strict New England labor regime and deterred ambitious servants from immigrating, and after both existing servants and children had internalized the new rules, accepting stern discipline with the promise of high wages and access to resources in the future.

The favorite instrument of magistrates and juries was the public whipping. From 1630 to 1660, Massachusetts magistrates whipped considerably more youth than Chesapeake tobacco lords did, at least officially. Authorities in Essex County, Massachusetts, could affirm that they whipped five to twelve times as many children and servants as any single county in the Chesapeake colonies. Judges ordered the whipping of only five servants in the Maryland Provincial Court in St. Mary's between 1637 and 1650, and of only two servants in the county court of Accomack-Northampton, Virginia, from 1632 to 1640.[34] In contrast, Essex County authorities whipped no fewer than twenty-five children and servants during a comparable nine-year period (1640 to 1648). From 1630 to 1660, the four Puritan colonies (New Haven, Connecticut, Massachusetts, and Plymouth) whipped no less than 289 people, chiefly children and servants. Though women were among those brought to the whipping post, 80 percent of those whipped and hanged (227) were male. In 1639, a banner year for the lash, magistrates flogged no less than thirty-one—almost three a month. From 1635 to 1660, scarcely a month went by without the whipping of a child or servant before a large crowd.[35]

Massachusetts magistrates perceived youth as out of control. Many indulged in sexual play, including fornication, masturbation, sodomy, and bestiality. Sexual offenses provoked 35 percent of the whippings. However, before 1650 more servants earned a whipping for slothful and disobedient behavior: idleness, stubbornness, night walking, refusal to take directions. Workplace faults dominated. On March 5, 1644, for example, the Connecticut Court ordered that "Susan Coles, for her rebellious carriedge toward her mistress is to be sent to the house of correction and be kept to hard labor and coarse dyet, to be brought forth the next lecture day to be publicly corrected and so to be corrected weekly until order be given to the contrary." Many servants and children stole, ran away, and spoke disrespectfully to masters and mistresses. In 1641, for example, the Essex court demanded that "William Wilson, servant to Captain Robert Bridges, is whipped at a lecture day or town meeting for cursing his master." In New England's biblically based legal order, masters enjoyed the same authority as parents. When children or servants disobeyed the fifth commandment, "Honor thy father and mother," they risked a public whipping or worse.[36]

Punishment was meant to be an exemplary spectacle. The marshal tied the victim to the post—in Boston, a cannon—and delivered up to forty stripes in full view of the crowd. While some sinners showed stoic courage, many groveled in pain and shame before the crowd. Some staved off the whip by showing contrition. On June 4, 1634, the Plymouth Court noted: "Dorothy Temple for uncleaness and bringing forth a male bastard is censured to be whipt twice, but she fainting in the execution of the first, the other was not executed." Some accepted years of unpaid labor in place of ten or twenty minutes of public whipping. In order to avoid a single public whipping, Charles Thurston in 1646 agreed to toil as a servant for two more years. The bloody dramas disgusted some humble colonists. A woman accused of heresy in New Haven in 1646, "being asked by Mrs. Moore whether she saw the persons whipped for their unnatural filthiness about a month since, she answered no, but they were cruelly whipped and that her sonn said he had rather fall into the hands of Turks and hath rather be hanged then fall into their hands." Apparently many English folk were not reconciled to such shows. In 1656, the Essex County Court presented an Andover servant, William Young, "for abusive speeches in wishing them all hanged who instituted whipping, and saying that he thought they must have been a company of rude debauched fellows."[37]

New England Puritans' use of public and rational violence to reform youth and manage labor differed from the policies in both the Chesapeake and New Netherlands. New Englanders wielded the most public penal violence in early America. Yet from an English perspective, this practice was a continuation of innovations made by Puritan urban reformers. As Paul Griffiths has shown, in Norwich, England, between 1580 and 1645 the Mayor's Court ordered to be whipped 2,039 men and 1,086 women—about forty-nine floggings a year. Norwich's typical year of flogging easily topped New England's most bloody single year. The penal regime in Norwich was similar to that in Massachusetts. The court brought convicted young folk to the marketplace on Saturday to be whipped for their own reformation and for the edification of the crowd. Some differences arose from the distinct economic situations in the two places. In Norwich, wages were low and many youth were looking for work, lounging about in despair, begging, and stealing. Norwich authorities sought to reform these youth with public violence. In Massachusetts, servants and youth encountered a labor market that favored them. Authorities sought to curb the arrogance and festivity of youth in order to reconcile their own view of an orderly society with the power of these laborers. They sought to make youth a humbling stage of life in which people would learn responsibility, morality, and self-discipline. A typical case was that in 1641 of "Benjamin Hammon, John Hardy's man," who was "fined £5 and whipped for disobeying his master, and bound to good behavior for one year." Norwich servants did not have £5 to offer the state. The point was to humble Hammon for the good of his soul, not to take his money from him. Massachusetts and Connecticut magistrates quickly built houses of correction to train wayward youth in how to labor and to pray. In doing so, they copied the Bridewells in English cities. Yet, the New England authorities rarely assigned servants to these institutions, a routine sentence in Norwich. The labor shortage in Massachusetts demanded that servants stay with their masters and work. Remarkably, despite our own expectations that a public whipping would mark a man or woman for life, several colonists who had been whipped as servants grew up to be respected town officials. For example, Simon Bird, who ran from his master the year he came over and got whipped, later became a constable and owned property worth over £200. The fact that he had been publicly whipped did not mar his reputation, as it would have in New Netherlands.[38]

Under the duress of the labor shortage, Massachusetts authorities had reason to compel as much work as possible from their own children. They threatened and inflicted violence on their progeny in much the same way as they did their servants. Indeed, in the mid-1640s Massachusetts passed legislation, based on biblical precedent, making children's disobedience a more serious crime than servants' disobedience. Massachusetts was unusual in terrorizing their own beloved children, although servants were whipped more often. Disobedient children were publicly whipped with great fanfare—no doubt as a lesson to overindulgent parents as well. In 1640, the Essex County Court sentenced "James Smith jr, to be severely whipped for filching and stealing and disobedience and stubbornness to his parents." In 1657, the Essex Court noted that "James White, jr. confessed that his father struck him for some faults and he held up an andiron at him, and when his father asked him what he would do, said he should know by and by." The court ordered the son to be whipped publicly; in threatening violence, the father was acting within his prerogatives. In 1635, the Massachusetts court "ordered that John Pease shall be whipped and bound to good behavior, for striking his mother, Mrs. Weston and deriding of her." In 1643, John Winthrop reported, "there was a piece of justice executed at New Haven, which, being the first in that kind, is not unworthy to be recorded; Mr. Malbon, one of the magistrates there, had a daughter about ____ years of age, which was openly whipped, her father joining in the sentence."[39] Whipping colonists' children publicly was common in New England, but the governor was delighted by this new wrinkle: the father joining with the other magistrates on stage in the public flogging of his own child. This spectacular act dramatized the way state violence permeated the whole society.

Moderating Physical Correction

Massachusetts tried to organize violence into a rational system to reform individuals, which meant both demanding and moderating its applications. Violence was easier to start than stop or moderate, physically or psychologically. By 1639, Winthrop and some other leaders realized that the violence against children and youth they had sanctioned had gone too far and had become a threat to their Christian community and English decency. The public beating of so many servants legitimated outrageous private beatings. Some masters became grotesquely abusive. In the mid-1640s, Governor Winthrop and others attempted to moderate the violence by defining permissible cruelty and by identifying and punishing overly sadistic violators with almost as much fanfare as they did rebellious youth and children.[40]

In 1639, a Cambridge grammar school (the forerunner of Harvard College) attracted the sons of Puritan gentry with its rigorous educational methods. Its able headmaster, Nathaniel Eaton, echoed in philosophy and action the crackdown under way on proud children and servants. However, Eaton's sadistic excesses unintentionally parodied the magistrates' policy and embarrassed and shocked authorities, as well as hurting children. After a disagreement, Eaton beat his usher (teaching assistant) Nathaniel Briscoe viciously, yet methodically, for two hours. Only the intervention of the minister Thomas Shepherd stopped the attack. John Winthrop described it vividly: Eaton "caused his man to fetch him a cudgel, which was a walnut tree plant, big enough to have killed a horse, and a yard in length, and taking his two men with him, he went up to Briscoe, and caused his men to hold him, till he had given him two hundred stripes about the head and shoulders, etc. And so kept him under blows (with some two or three short intermissions) about the space of two hours." Upon being "asked, why he used such cruelty to Briscoe, his usher, and to other [of] his scholars (for it was testified by another of his ushers and divers of his scholars, that he would give them between twenty and thirty stripes at time . . .), his answer was that he had this rule, that he would not give over correcting till he had subdued the party to his will." Eaton's excesses were a dark reminder that the crackdown could lead to destructive acts and negative publicity. On September 9, 1639, the Massachusetts court "ordered that Mr. Eaton should be discharged from keeping of schools with us without license; and Mr. Eaton is fined by the country £66 17s 4d, which fine is respited till the next court, unless he remove the meanwhile." The court also ordered Eaton to pay the nearly dead Briscoe £30 in damages.[41]

After the Eaton case, Massachusetts courts examined and punished other abuses of workers by masters. Many of these cases were difficult to decide, for the authorities and jurors understood that the labor system required some violence. It was often difficult to tell how much violence was used, let alone whether it was justified. In December 1639, Marmaduke Pierce of Salem was put on trial for murdering his apprentice. The inquest jury had found the boy's skull fractured and his body emaciated. The trial jury agreed the boy had been undisciplined and that Pierce had used "unreasonable correction." However, before dying the boy had given contradictory testimony about whether his fracture was caused by his master's measuring yard, his master's broomstick, or by chance fall of a branch. In a capital case, evidence had to be clear. Pierce was acquitted.[42]

In 1644, Winthrop devoted considerable space in his *Journal* to the case of William Franklin, a Newbury farmer, and his servant, Nathaniel Sewell, a London street urchin collected and shipped to New England on the *Seabridge* in a charity scheme. Nathaniel Sewell was clearly a lazy and shiftless lad bred in London's slums. In order to transform him into a good servant, Franklin, according to Winthrop, "used him with continual rigor and unmerciful correction, and exposed him many times to much cold and wet in the winter season." Some corrective acts were obviously sadistic and depraved, such as "hanging him in the chimney." Despite his exertions, Franklin failed to improve the boy significantly. As the law prescribed, he decided to bring the boy before a magistrate in Boston for a hearing and likely public whipping. To accommodate the lad on the journey, Franklin tied Sewell "upon an horse, and so brought him (sometimes sitting and sometimes hanging down) to Boston." Along the way, the boy called "much for water," but Franklin "would give him none, though he came close by it. . . . The boy was near dead when he came to Boston, and died within a few hours after."

Was this murder? Some saints thought not. After all, the master was trying to reform an incorrigible child, not to hurt him. In the general plan, there was no overt intent to harm. The pain was inflicted for a worthy goal. The immediate cause of death, the trip from Newbury to Boston, was a lawful act of transporting an accused criminal to court. Winthrop argued that Franklin had killed Sewell by degrees, doing violence to him and ignoring his needs and illnesses over a long period of time. Although Franklin's overt purpose was to reform Sewell, his regimen was "evil because it arose from distemper of passion." In this case, the master's anger spurred him to exceed the reasonable use of force with his charge, with fatal consequences to both. Winthrop found support for his opinion in Exodus and Deuteronomy: as Winthrop put it, that "if a master strike his servant with a rod, which is a lawful action, and he die under his hand (as this servant did), he was to die for it." Though some objected and Franklin maintained his innocence, the jury and court agreed with Winthrop. Franklin became the first person hanged in Massachusetts for homicidal correction.[43]

The Franklin case established that even when physical correction was required, the corrector stood fully liable for homicidal consequences. For servants, a forty-stripe maximum generally became the rule, enacted explicitly into law in New Haven. The biblical reference was to Deuteronomy 15:3: "Forty stripes he may give him, he shall not exceed; lest, if he should exceed, and beat him above these with many stripes, then thy brother should be dishonoured before thine eyes." Ideally, punishment changed a "wicked man" into a "brother," but excessive punishment dehumanized the criminal and prevented his reintegration into society.[44] The biblical rule helped Massachusetts people regard even sinful and then tortured children, servants, and slaves as fellow human beings, and it gave them an ancient and godly maximum for inflicting pain on children.

Authorities regulated not only the number of stripes but other details of punishment. For example, in 1682, the Essex Court judged that Phillip Fowler was justified in punishing his servant, Richard Parker, but "they did not approve of the manner of punishment given in hanging him up by the heels as butchers do beasts for the slaughter." The court cautioned Fowler and made him pay costs. In September 1673, the Essex County court fined Nathaniel Wells for verbally abusing his servants by calling one "base rogue" and "French dog."[45]

By the mid-1640s, many servants, their neighbors, or their families complained to the authorities about abusive masters. Some servants found relief. However, forty stripes a day still licensed masters, parents, and school teachers to inflict much pain in order to gain obedience. For example, in 1681 an Irish maid, Joan Sullivan, complained about her master and mistress, the Maules of Salem. Several witnesses corroborated her sad story. John Flint deposed "that being in Thomas Maule's shop, he heard a great cry in the house and looking in saw Naomi Maule beating and thumping her Irish servant maid on the head in a very violent manner and also kicking her." Hannah Sibley deposed that "she saw Joan as she came from Mr. Gedney's to make her complaint, and her face was bloody and swollen about as large as a child's fist. There was also a wound on her face, which she said her master did with his horsewhip." Strengthening the maid's case was authorities' and the public's dislike of Thomas Maule, an aggressive and litigious Quaker shopkeeper. As one witness noted, "he is known to be a great liar and a contentious person amongst his neighbours, reviling and backbiting of them."

Yet, despite the hubbub, the Maules' abuse of Sullivan never violated Massachusetts law. Witnesses proved that Joan Sullivan was a Catholic girl stubbornly faithful to the mass and reluctant to hear Protestant sermons. She had lied occasionally. The Maules kept their punishments within the legal limit. Even Joan Sullivan unwittingly supported the Maules' legality by testifying that "my master Maule hath some times stuck me at least 30 or 40 blows at a time" with a horsewhip. John Flint, a sixteen-year-old servant in Maule's house, testified that "he had seen his master beat Joane unreasonably with a maunatee [horsewhip] at least thirty or forty stripes." The servants thought forty blows hideous and unreasonable. Yet, showing an almost Talmudic precision unusual to Quakers, Maule never hit the maid more than forty stripes a day. Because Sullivan was disobedient and in need of reform, Maule kept roughly within biblical limit, and Sullivan did not die of her injuries, the judges deemed Maule's methods legal and dismissed the case.[46]

In order to ensure that masters visited only "moderate" violence upon servants and children, officials became expert on reading children's bodies for signs of excessive, illegal punishment. When the servant Tobias Taylor came to him with complaints about his master in 1682, the grand juryman Jacob Perkins, Sr., went to work with the expertise common to television crime-scene dramas. He noticed that Taylor's wrists were "very much waled and swollen by the cord which he tied him when he whipped him, hanging by the hands with his legs tied straddling as he could not stir." The extra swelling meant that the master had not simply tied the boy to a post, but had suspended him in the air while whipping him like a side of meat, a sign of immoderate and inhumane punishment. Perkins got two other men to join him in inspecting "the boy's naked body and saw many long red marks sixteen hours after the whipping."[47] Thanks to his experience, Perkins saw foul play.

Children also became experts on beatings, and some became accustomed to trauma. A servant, Elizabeth Herren, cleared her mistress, Elizabeth Woodberry, from charges of beating her excessively by testifying in 1664 that

Woodberry "never struck her but two blows in her life, and these might have been given to a child of two years. She offered to strike her once at Mistress Gardner's house, but said Elizabeth kept it off with her hand."[48] Murdering servants and children was outlawed in a labor regime that relied on rational doses of corporal punishment and public humiliation, but the new regime produced people like Elizabeth Herren, who thought taking and giving blows without tears was normal.

This dulling of sensibilities was one price of fashioning a relatively egalitarian labor system in Anglo-America. Lacking an adequate supply of labor, the magistrates used the rod, among other instruments of authority, to meld servants and children together into a working class. Laborers were dignified by being recognized as members of the body politic, not defined as a caste apart, in return for their diligent obedience. To a greater extent than elsewhere in America, Massachusetts landowners avoided reliance upon slavery or any permanently demeaned lower order. They gained sufficient productivity by working their children callously like servants, while often educating their servants like children. They jumbled the two into a single subordinated and controlled class. This is not to say that they repressed important distinctions between children and servants. Nor is it to argue that race and gender, whether that of their own children or of servants, made little difference. However, as formed by lawful violence in the first decades, the menial class in Massachusetts consisted primarily of youth, both children and servants, many of whom would graduate after many years of instruction and subordination into privileged adult status. Violent compulsion was seen as necessary to make all servants and all children take their place in preparation for adult life.

The melding and humbling of servants and children had compelling religious as well as economic motives. Governor John Winthrop's ideal was a family in which children and servants joined together into a single modest workforce under godly patriarchal control. In the new Israel, pride was to be suppressed; all citizens were to be humble "servants of God." Indeed, there was not a greater honor or title. The most prestigious elders or ministers were often referred to as "servants of God," which meant that they humbled themselves and worked diligently and tirelessly for God their master. Humble work that ignored worldly social status was a sign of salvation.

In 1634, Governor Winthrop wrote in his journal about his fourteen-year-old son Stephen's triumphant spiritual journey from pride to servitude. Constant listening to ministers, especially John Cotton, caused Stephen to struggle, as he must, with his conviction of unworthiness. "For diverse months he was held under such affliction of mind, as he could not be brought to apprehend any comfort in God, being much humbled and broken for his sins (though he had been a dutiful child, and not given up to the lusts of youth)." The adolescent "went mourning and languishing daily." "He came at length to be freed from his temptations and to find comfort in Gods promises," rejoiced Winthrop, "and so being received into the congregation upon good proof of his understanding in the things of God." Confirming Stephen's change of heart, the governor saw daily evidence of his conversion in his diligent labor: "he went on cheerfully in a Christian course, falling daily to labor as a servant." Stephen accepted menial labor—chopping wood, fixing fences, paddling canoes—even though, socially, he was a gentleman's son.[49]

Winthrop insisted that his niece, who boarded in his household, dress in a way that rendered her nearly indistinguishable from the servants. Writing in 1635 to her father in England, Mary Downing remarked, "for my habit, it is mean for the most, as many servants." She distinguished herself from them only by a linen headband, "which is the most allowable and commendable dressing here." Her mother wanted her to dress more finely, but she found all mother's fashion hints unacceptable, "for they gave great offense, and, seeing it hath pleased the Lord to bring me hither amongst His people, I would not willingly do anything amongst them that should be displeasing unto them."[50]

Massachusetts society was the Winthrop household writ large. In England children and servants were visibly differentiated by their diet, clothes, lodging, and work. In their dress, labor, and living, as well as the punishments to which they were subjected, children and servants were treated more similarly in Massachusetts than anywhere else. The blurring of boundaries between children and servants is evident even in the colony's laws. In 1654, for example, the preamble to a law passed by the General Court designed to suppress unruly workers declared: "Foreasmuch as it appears by too much experience that divers children and servants doe behave themselves too disrespectively, disobediently, and disorderly towards their parents, masters, and governors, to the disturbance of families, and discouragement of such parents and governors." The law stated that a parent or master could complain to a magistrate about a child or servant, and the authorities would then whip the child or servant "not exceeding ten stripes for one offence." Significantly, no distinction was made between children and servants: both were considered the core of the troublesome workforce, and both were liable to be whipped.[51]

In the household, the servants and children were placed together below the master and mistress. They lodged and ate together. In 1657, Nathaniel Shipley, an orphan who hired himself to work around Wenham, told Jacob Parker's wife that "he lodged at Mr. Fiske's house with his children in the upper room and pitied them for lying so cold." Fiske, the minister, claimed that Shipley was lying about his children's discomfort, but nobody thought the idea of a servant lodging with the minister's children in the loft implausible; the issue was the heat in the room. In 1681, Abraham Briggs praised the generous treatment a Salem shopkeeper gave his servants. Briggs observed the shopkeeper and his wife at dinner or supper and noted that, after they "had finished, their servants and children sat down to the same diet." What was remarkable to the observer was not that the servants and children ate together, or that they ate separately from the master and mistress, but that both groups had the same food.[52]

Conflating servile and filial roles, servants in New England often called their masters and mistresses "father" and "mother." In a 1675 court case involving the contested estate of Thomas Lowthrop, Bethiah Lowthrop claimed that Sarah Gott, a servant of Lowthrop, had been adopted, citing among the evidence that Gott called the Lowthrops "father and mother." But "as for her calling them father and mother," noted the plaintiff, Ezekiel Cheever's wife, "it is no more but what is ordinarily done to . . . servants." She noted that another Lowthrop servant, who had left the household with little attachment, used the same form of address. The blending of servitude and childhood in status as well as nomenclature became a tradition in New England. In 1797, at the age of nine, Asa Sheldon left his mother and landless father in Lynnfield to serve the Parkers as a farm servant. David Parker and his wife were about forty years of age and had in their household their only son David, about eighteen years, and two daughters, Polly and Sally, "who were a few years younger." As Sheldon remembered, "Mrs. Parker told me to call her 'mother,' and certainly she acted the part of a mother to me."[53]

Masters and mistresses might correct their children and servants, but children—even adult children—could neither correct the household servants nor expect obedience from them. Even in the absence of a master, authority never explicitly or implicitly devolved upon the natural child, no matter his age. In 1655, Jonathan Wade went to England and left his affairs in the hands of his wife, his son, and his servant William Deane. Deane had a fine reputa-

tion for hard work and, according to his mistress, was "ready and forward
. . . in that which was good, in asking her children questions out of the
scriptures and herself also." Yet Deane refused to obey the son, Jonathan
Wade, Jr., or to accept him as a substitute for his absent master. When Wade
reproved Deane for a minor act of neglect around the farm, Deane furiously
grabbed the son's cane "with one hand, and with the other took an axe and
held it up" against Wade's face and declared "he would not be commanded
by him." When Wade, Jr., charged Deane with being an unruly servant,
Deane countersued, winning court costs and damages. The court accepted
Deane's surly defiance and regarded the servant and the adult child as social
equals.[54]

In the weekly meeting for worship, male children and servants by law
mingled together in a conspicuous section of the meeting house. The courts
had often complained about "much disorder and rudeness in youth in many
congregations in time of the worship of God, whereby sin and profaneness is
greatly increased." As a remedy for their rough-housing and jabbering during
holy sermons, the court ordered that "the selectmen do appoint such place
or places in the meeting house for children or youth to sit in where they may
be most together and in publick view, and that the officers of the churches,
or selectmen, do appoint some grave and sober person or persons to take a
particular care of and inspection over them." Incorrigible disturbers were to
be "whipt with ten stripes." In Watertown, as in many other towns, the town
folk built a gallery for male children and servants. On January 18, 1669, the
selectmen agreed to "take their turns every man his day to sit upon the gallery
to look to the youths that they may prevent miscarriages in the time of public
exercises in the Lords Day and also that the two constables shall be desired
to take their turns there also."[55] Interestingly, female children and servants
were allowed to disperse themselves throughout the female sections of the
meeting house. Girls may have been less trouble; perhaps, if seated together,
the congregation's male gaze might have been too often directed at the chorus
of nubile women. Male children and servants shared similar status as a potentially troublesome class. These humiliating, although effective, arrangements
lasted for over a century. Lucy Larcom remembered that as a child in Beverly,
Massachusetts, she thought the biblical phrase "going up into Galilee" referred to "clattering up the uncarpeted stairs in the meeting-house porch as
the boys did, with their squeaking brogans, looking as restless as imprisoned
monkeys after they had got into those conspicuous seats." "Imprisoned monkeys" expresses the discomfort inflicted on the young male New England

workforce, whether children or servants, who were perceived as a perennial threat to order.[56]

There were important distinctions between servants and children in a household. After sixteen years of labor children got land or dowries from the parental estate, while servants usually got freedom and a small payment, as well as the liberty to earn relatively high wages in their adopted town. Parents certainly gave more love and affection to their children than they did to their servants. Yet for a fourteen-year-old under family government, the differing rewards that lay a decade ahead might have seemed so distant as to be almost meaningless. Both servants and children faced years of subordination, menial work, and physical correction at a time of youthful energy and lust. In Virginia black and white servants often ran away together, but in New England children and servants ran away together. For example, the Essex County Court in September 1655 reported, "Thomas Moore and Hackaliah Bridges, one for running away from his master, and the other from his father, were fined." The court did not think it strange that two members of the subordinate class should sin together. In the early years, New England authorities were vigilant against spaces in their society where servants and children could meet together to enjoy life without proper adult supervision. In New Haven in 1650, authorities uncovered the Meekes' house where late at night children and servants met to roast meat (some stolen), drink alcohol, and dance wildly until dawn. They fined the adult hosts and whipped the servants and children, "for who can be secure, of his children or servants, or goods, if this be allowed."[57]

Children and Servants Retaliate

The most powerful combination of enraged servants and children arose later: the fourteen hard-working teenage girls of Salem—servants and children—who in 1691–1692 cooperated wickedly in telling a story of witches to set the colony on its ears and have many adults executed for the pains some inflicted on the girls themselves. As Susan Amussen has insightfully pointed out, violence was used not only by the state to impose its behavioral rules but also by powerless people to attempt to uphold their own values. She observes that in seventeenth-century England, witchcraft or the impersonation of the witch was often used by poor women to threaten fellow villagers who refused to give them alms.[58] In New England there were many witchcraft stories, but the most celebrated witchcraft cases were initiated not by scorned widows, but by possessed children. Children and servants—or orphaned children working as servants—discovered that they could use the story of Satan's afflictions to express their distress and temporarily relieve their misery as the colony's drudges. When we examine these incidents from the point of view of the overburdened children who proclaimed themselves oppressed by witches, New England's witchcraft crazes become less mysterious. The witchcraft story was a way children could express to their masters and mistresses that they were in grave trouble. Some of the stories were about deep traumas; many were about too much work and too little play. Satan and the witches provided a way to negotiate the labor of children and evaluate their virtue. Once they had seized the upper hand, the children killed with the cooperation of the courts.

The situation is clearest in a less notorious but carefully documented case. John Goodwin, a pious brick mason in late seventeenth-century Boston, had six children. "Of these children," noted Cotton Mather, "all but the elder, who works with his father at his calling, and the youngest, who lives yet upon the breast of its mother, have labored under the direful effects of a stupendous witchcraft." The great minister's 1689 account is remarkable for its humanity, close observation, and unintended humor. The central fact is that although these children belonged to a wealthy household, "their parents also kept them to a continual employment which did more than deliver them from temptation of idleness and as young as they were, they took delight in it."[59] But it appears that their delight had limitations.

The affliction began when the eldest daughter accused an Irish servant girl of stealing some linen. Here servant and child divided. The Irish girl's widowed mother had a reputation as a witch, and she took offense at the accusation and "bestowed very bad language upon the girl."[60] Seeing the servant and the eldest Goodwin daughter as essentially equal household workers, the Goodwins did nothing. In response, the daughter became visited by strange fits. These fits grew and spread among the children, convincing Mather and John Goodwin that Widow Glover had severely afflicted the children. From a modern perspective, it does not take a clinical psychologist to see that the children were acting out their distress at being overworked, at being preached to endlessly and never listened to, of being prevented from moving their bodies. They were using their fertile imaginations and their culture's images of evil to rehearse the fears, delights, and dreads of childhood. From a commonsense point of view, these children's afflictions were healthy. They used the story of satanic possession to gain the power to play, which their elders interpreted as demonic visitations. Thanks to Satan, the children were allowed to depart from their false selves as good little workers and become passionate, willful children.

Even Cotton Mather observed what was from his point of view a notable incongruity. "The variety of their tortures increased continually . . . though about nine or ten at night, they always had a release from their miseries and ate and slept all night for the most part." If the children were tormented by hysteria or other anxieties, as some historians have argued, they would hardly have eaten with gusto and slept punctually like sated teenagers day after day. Much of the affliction involved miming and improvisational theater. "They would bark at one another like dogs and again purr like so many cats. They would sometimes complain they were in a red hot oven, sweating and panting at the same time unreasonably. Anon they would say cold water was thrown upon them at which they would shiver very much." One child even creatively imitated being "roasted on an invisible spit." Their playful afflictions had a physicality so at odds with their normal routine that Mather was astonished. "Yea, they would fly like geese," noted Mather; "and be carried with an incredible swiftness through the air, having but just their toes now and then upon the ground, and their arms waved like the wings of a bird."[61] The vision of children flapping their arms, cackling, and running around a late seventeenth-century Boston residence while the colony's greatest minister looked on with dread and astonishment presents a wonderful tableau.

Thanks to the Satan story, the children were allowed to stop working and to express their hostilities and even their love of chaos. Mather thought it was the witch's work that "if any small mischief happened to be done, where they were; as to tearing or dirtying a garment; the falling of a cup, the breaking of a glass, or the like, they would rejoice extremely, and fall into a pleasure and laughter very extraordinary." This joy in destruction was rare for the working children of Boston, where order and productivity were so hard-earned, though today anybody who has been to summer camp or school cafeteria has experienced the same delight at dropped trays. These children found satanic permission to express contempt for authority. "Nothing would so discompose them," noted Mather, "as a religious exercise." Inspired by the unholy spirit, the children discovered a way to frustrate their intellectual patrons, a way they have seemingly passed down to many modern students. As Mather described it, "these two worthy ministers Mr. Fisk and Mr. Thatcher, bestowing some gracious counsels on the boy, when they then found at a neighbor's house, he immediately lost his hearing, so that he heard not one word, but just the last word of what they said."[62]

Not all the play was frolicsome and wholesomely cathartic. Released from work and restraint, with an attentive audience, one girl engaged in more deep and complex play. Remarkably, defining the girl as troubled rather than as possessed by evil, Mather took one daughter home to observe her carefully and facilitate her recovery. The Goodwin girl used the opportunity to confront her dread of childhood mortality, which was quite common in Boston. "The demons having once again seized her, they made her pretend to be dying; and dying truly we feared at last she was; she lay, she tossed, she pull'd just like one dying, and urged hard for someone to dye with her, seeming loth to die alone. She argued concerning death, in strains that quite amazed us; and concluded, that though she was loth to dye, yet if God said she must, she must, adding something about the state of the country, which we wondered at."[63] Here was a girl using her culture's religious ideas and sense of civil unity to confront death, while her teacher looked on. Only Satan's story made Mather stop and listen to the child who had learned so much from him.

An important feature of the story of the Goodwins' children's affliction is Cotton Mather's participation in the children's play. He displayed an element of respect and love that was rare in the harsh Massachusetts labor system. His patient, empathic attentiveness probably explains why they were "cured." Most of the time Mather appeared merely to observe the children's antics with keen attention. However, as an intellectually if not physically playful man, Mather could not help but get involved. He discovered that the possessed children could not read orthodox Protestant Christian material easily but could readily read heretical Quaker tracts and Catholic prayers in his vast library, which he opened to these rampaging, bewitched children. The idea of the game was that the children invested with Satan could not confront truly godly material without pain and dread, but could easily read unsound material. Once Mather caught the theme (and it is unclear who invented the game), he could not help but expose the children to many authors he disliked. They became the final judges of what was true and false, though in an inverted way. They read his cues perfectly. He was clearly delighted when the children as Satan's agents could happily read his enemies' work. He was equally delighted when they could not read his material or that of his friends. "I shall therefore add," he noted, "that my grandfather Cotton's catechism called Milk for Babes and the Assemblies Catechism would bring hideous convulsions on the child if she looked into them; tho she had once learn't them with all the love that could be."[64] Perhaps Mather flapped his arms and cackled.

Mather was unconsciously following the prescriptions of a latter-day child psychologist, D. W. Winnicott, who argued that therapy is about play between the therapist and the patient, which forges real emotional connections beneath the deadening outer surfaces of propriety. Winnicott would draw a squiggle, and give it to the child who would add to it. They would discuss and add to their mutual creation, forming an inner attachment along the way. As Winnicott defined it in 1971, "psychotherapy takes place in the overlap of two areas of playing, that of the patient and that of the therapist. Psychotherapy has to do with two people playing together. The corollary of this is that where playing is not possible then the work done by the therapist is directed toward bringing the patient from a state of not being able to play into a state of being able to play." The witchcraft story among the children began the play, not Mather. Witchcraft became a kind of squiggle between Mather and the children, where both could exchange their real emotions: the children's fear of death, their need for exuberance, their need to be listened to, especially their need for freedom from work; and Mather's need to be validated, his childlike love of science, his playfulness, and his deep love for children. The children were cured to the extent that they enjoyed a society in which play was possible.[65] Yet, if the witchcraft story was the artistic form through which the children and Mather could connect in play, there were victims. The authorities hanged the old Irish woman, Widow Glover, as a witch.[66]

Hard work was also at the root of the possession of Elizabeth Knapp, the sixteen-year-old servant of the Groton minister, Samuel Willard. For three months in 1671–1672, Elizabeth acted strangely: having fits, barking like a dog, speaking rudely in a gruff voice to the minister. Soon the minister and town physician agreed that Knapp was possessed, though no local witch was convicted of the crime. No one played with Knapp; Willard was not Cotton Mather. Eventually Knapp confessed that she was struggling with Satan, who was tempting her. Historians have found deep psychological problems in Knapp: a split personality, or a deep ambivalence about the female role in Massachusetts. Yet, two and a half years after her recovery, Elizabeth Knapp married; she subsequently became the mother of at least six children. She showed no deep or lifelong pathology.[67] Knapp used the story of Satan, which she got from her minister, as a way to help her cope with being overburdened by work, but it backfired on her.

Knapp's satanic fantasies and temptations related chiefly to her unremitting labors. Women worked as servants from the age of four or five until they married, usually in their mid-twenties. They took care of children, cleaned, prepared meals, emptied chamber pots, weeded gardens, spun, wove, knitted, sewed clothes, and tended animals. They worked inside dark and cold houses. Their chief break from routine was listening to lengthy sermons on Sundays, which spoke often of Satan. As Samuel Willard related Knapp's story, she discovered that the devil came to her while she was working and offered her a sort of alternative service. According to Knapp's confession, she spent some three years negotiating with Satan, who offered her a better job at better pay. As she put it, "the devil had oftentimes appeared to her, presenting the treaty of a covenant and proffering largely to her: viz. Such things as suited her youthful fancy, money, silks, fine clothes, ease from labor to show her the whole world, etc."[68] Satan was a kind of union organizer, though the union he represented was illegal.

At first, Knapp turned him down, using the imaginary dialogue to express her desires but also confirming her Christian rejection of Satan's worldly temptations. However, in the Willard household, her work seemed endless, so Satan became more persuasive. "She seldom went out of one room into another, but he appeared to her urging of her" to defect to a more indulgent master. Satan tempted her to murder the Willards' children whom she had to drudge for, "especially the youngest, tempting her to throw it into the fire, on the heath, into the oven." In a barely concealed threat, Knapp confessed to her master "that once he put a bill-hook into her hand to murder myself."[69] Knapp battled constantly with an imagined Satan who represented all her suppressed desires and the anger aroused by her impossible work situation and insensitive overseers.

What is pathetic is how little she wanted in such a situation in exchange for her soul. Once Satan almost got Knapp to sign his book with an offer "to bring her in chips for the fire." The covenant Satan urged upon her was a modest indentured service contract. She told Willard once that she had agreed to enter a seven-year contract with the Devil: "in year one she was to be faithful in this service, and then in the other six he would serve her and make her a witch." Remarkably, even when giving away her immortal soul, Knapp expected to work as a menial for one year before she got six years of power and then an eternity of torment. Knapp was unable to imagine an

alternative world. She grew up being subjected to hard labor that even privileged children had to do and surrounded with stories about the combat between Christ and Satan. Later she offered Willard a sensible interpretation of
her plight, which historians, following Willard, have been reluctant to believe. "She then declared as much, that the occasion of it was her discontent,
that the devil had sometimes appeared to her; that her condition displeased
her; her labor was burdensome to her, she was neither content to be at home
nor abroad; and had oftentimes strong persuasions to practice in witchcraft."
Knapp did receive rapt attention from Willard and other ministers, who got
her to confess her fantasies and her fears that the Devil had tempted her.
Willard never interacted with her as Mather did with the Goodwin children;
he often bullied her, and at best he called her an "object of pity."[70] It is not
clear how she cured herself of her discontent beyond her remarkably astute
self-analysis. But his prolonged examination freed her temporarily from her
onerous work routine and made her aware of how much she hated the unremitting labor she was expected to perform. Knapp was the daughter of a
selectman in Groton. She was a child-servant, the key to the Massachusetts
labor system.

Knapp's story resembles that told by the girls of Salem, who also spent
their time working in dark houses. Strikingly, the witchcraft stories allowed
these female servant-children to express their position in the household in a
way that attracted the attention of her master and mistress. It also gave them
power and leisure. The story they told made perfect, if perverse, sense. Satan
was a man who tried to seduce the servants and had sexual relations with a
woman who hit the servants. In most New England households, the middle-
aged master was implicitly if not explicitly attracted to his female servants.
To the servant maids, he represented desirable money and power as well as
fearful sexual violation. He slept with the servant's mistress, who often beat
them and stuck them with pins. In the Salem version, the story of Satan,
who inspired middle-aged women to afflict young girls with corporal punishment and who had sexual intercourse with middle-aged male devils, arose
largely from contested power relations within the workplace and was cast in
terms of the stories about Satan the girls had heard in church.[71]

The active involvement of enraged children and servants in the persecution of witches was the price of exploiting children's labor so intensely instead
of creating an outside class of servile drudges. What stories would the slaves
of the other colonies have told if anybody had listened to them; if they found
a medium welcome to the adults in power that enabled them to protest the

madness inflicted upon them? Yet their masters and mistresses were not their parents and relatives. Their silence is more disturbing and horrifying than the theatrical and sometimes homicidal discontent of the Massachusetts children who fought back so playfully and imaginatively.

From Punishment to Discipline

In the mid-1630s, the life savings and material needs of religious English families briefly made Massachusetts an ideal labor market for workers. It had the highest wages available in the British Empire. Young men and women arrived and prospered. The Massachusetts authorities realized quickly, however, that such highly paid and empowered young folk would soon destroy their fledgling labor system along with their religious society. They also realized that they had to increase the productivity of all young people in order to survive economically. Starting around 1635, they crushed servants' and laborers' ambitions with law and rod in public spectacles of pain and imposed their own version of servitude: long terms, deep obedience to the master and mistress, familial trappings, hard work, literacy, moral education, future opportunity for wealth, harsh physical correction, and integration into a Puritan commonwealth. They adopted many measures of the godly English towns from which they came to the American wilderness.

In pursuit of control over labor, authorities consistently acted violently. Their measures were particularly repulsive in the eyes of proud and brave British youth, who largely ceased coming over after 1635, and they remain repugnant today. Yet, their measures did create a distinctive labor system in New England that never deteriorated into slavery—though slavery existed as a secondary labor institution in this region. By melding servants and children into one laboring class, propertied Massachusetts folk wounded themselves emotionally but took the souls of all laborers seriously and developed a labor system that was far more egalitarian and gave far more dignity to the laborer than other early American economic systems, which typically distanced leisured, pampered children from menial slaves. Far from transplanting the English household, the Puritan leaders developed a new kind of labor force for New England, more democratic, productive, and pained.

CHAPTER THREE

Settlement

IN 1845, NATHANIEL Hawthorne returned to his native Salem from Concord. In 1846, he obtained a position at the Salem Custom House, the subject of the opening of his most famous novel, *The Scarlet Letter*. In that introductory sketch, he puzzled about why the town of Salem had "a hold on my affections." Speaking of the present, he remarked, "the spell survived, and just as powerfully as if the natal spot were an earthly paradise . . . no matter that the place is joyless for him; that he is weary of the old wooden houses, the mud and dust, the dead level of site and sentiment, the chill east wind, and the chillest of social atmospheres." Hawthorne concluded, "the sentiment is probably assignable to the deep and aged roots which my family has struck into the soil." Hawthornes had lived in Salem "now nearly two centuries and a quarter," and "this long connection of family with one spot, as its place of birth and burial, creates a kindred between the human being and the locality, quite independent of any charm in the scenery or moral circumstances that surround him."[1]

The haunting power of Salem pervades Hawthorne's romances, as the curse in *The House of the Seven Gables* so powerfully attests. Hawthorne articulated the spiritual, psychological, and ethical dimensions of being both inspired and disturbed by a sense of place. Yet the phenomenon had a mundane, material, and historical side that informed all of these themes. After all, identity is also defined by "kindred," a word that in Hawthorne's use links family to place. Whatever its spiritual and aesthetic aura, the town, far more than the family, provided New Englanders with the basic social welfare, economic viability, and security that underlay quests for individual identity like that of Hawthorne.

In Essex County, Massachusetts, the Hawthornes' deep loyalty to their native town was shared by many other patrilineages, groups composed by generation after generation of fathers and sons that can be loosely called clans. A surprisingly large number of Essex County families devoted themselves to a single town or two within the county, spurning most of the twenty-five other townships, including those adjacent to the town of choice. Among seventeen male Hawthornes who had probates in Essex County between 1677 and 1837, twelve lived in Salem, three in Lynn, and one in Hamilton. They inhabited no other Essex County town. The Archers surpassed them in town concentration. No less than twenty-three Archer males had wills or administrations probated in Essex County between 1694 and 1839, and every single Archer male for 150 years had died a resident of Salem. Like the Hawthornes, the Archer males were chiefly mariners and merchants. Salem was home to some thirty-nine patrilineages, comprising in total 366 men, who acted much like the Hawthornes and Archers: over two centuries, at least 60 percent of their male adults in Essex County dwelt in that seaport town.[2]

Essex County towns were remarkably adhesive, given their economic foundations in seafaring. The Dollibeers treated Marblehead, the town adjacent to Salem, as their "center of the universe." Among the adult male Dollibeers who died in Essex County between 1683 and 1838, nearly eight out of ten (twenty-two of twenty-eight) lived in Marblehead. The Dollibeers, too, were chiefly fisherman and mariners. Yet until 1806, after some two centuries in Massachusetts, no Dollibeer male ever settled legally in adjacent Salem. On the other hand, not a single Hawthorne or Archer ever bothered to move a few miles from Salem and adopt the neighboring seafaring town of Marblehead. And for two hundred years and more, not a single one of the myriad Dollibeer, Hawthorne, or Archer males permanently resided in Beverly, a small port town across the bay.

Rural towns also held locally committed clans. For example, among adult male members of the Ayars family who lived and died in Essex County between 1650 and 1840, not less than 70 percent (thirty-five of forty-nine) had their wills or administrations probated in Haverhill. Most were farmers and tanners. Only one Ayar ever lived in Andover, the adjacent rural town. The Abbots were equally loyal to Andover. Among adult male Abbots who lived and died in Essex County between 1630 and 1840, again 70 percent (sixty-two of ninety) remained in Andover; the sole Abbot who gained residence in neighboring Haverhill died in 1798. Town boundaries were not merely administrative divisions signified by markers on the road; they defined familial and economic relations as much as geography.

People's devotion to one town and their depreciation of their neighboring towns were often expressed in popular culture. In this respect, New Englanders resembled the English; one British historian has called this trait "local xenophobia."[3] In the late eighteenth century, a Marblehead sea captain, "Flood" Ireson, refused to help a distressed vessel filled with fellow Marbleheaders in a storm. When Ireson got back to Marblehead, the women tarred and feathered him for his negligence and cowardice and carted him through the town in a ritual shaming. The act inspired a poem by John Greenleaf Whittier based on these well-known schoolboy verses memorializing the event:

> Old Flood Ireson for his hord hort
> Was torred and feathered and carried in a cart
> Old Flood Ireson for leaving the wreck
> Was torred and feathered all up to his neck
> Old Flood Ireson for his great sin
> Was torred and feathered all up to his chin
> Old Flood Ireson for his bad behavior
> Was torred and feathered and carried to Salem.

Being "carried to Salem" was the final indignity for Ireson, as bad as the dishonor of being tarred and feathered.[4] For their part, Salemites had no great respect for the neighboring Marbleheaders. The Salem minister William Bentley believed that these neighboring towns had fostered two distinct physical types; he regarded the difference as the result of inbreeding, an impression supported by the statistical analysis of marriage patterns. In 1812, after attending a militia muster, Bentley noted: "It is observed that the Marblehead men are more muscular and stocky than those of Salem, but those of Salem are taller, better formed, and appear to greater advantage . . . by stocky, a common and vulgar name is intended, shorter, thicker, and stronger frame." In terms that had clear connotations of status, the Salem tribe was tall, lean, and elegant, while the Marblehead tribe was short, hairy, and awkward.[5]

Nothing in the current historical scholarship explains the persistent loyalty so many people had to such separate, yet similar, Massachusetts towns. Generally, the fact itself is denied. For example, in her book on geographic mobility in England and New England, Alison Games reported that after coming to Massachusetts in the seventeenth century many immigrants jumped from one town to another, so that in the mid-seventeenth century persistence rates in Massachusetts were no greater than those in the Chesapeake. She concludes that "whatever the puritans rejected about English culture, it was not the endemic patterns of migration that demarcated points in the life cycle as fully as did sacraments and hiring fairs."[6] This observation may well apply to the immigrant generation, but this liberal individualist construction of the past fails to recognize that migration could suddenly slow down or follow different patterns once political economic circumstances encouraged people to stay in a single town or to find similar towns that welcomed them. Absent in the work of many scholars is any recognition of the personal impact of local political economies in New England.

Those historians who have noted a subculture of immobility in Massachusetts explain the pattern through the repressive and neurotic interplay between fathers and sons. Articulated in classic form by Philip Greven, this explanation starts with the fact that parents lived a long time, on average, and argues that fathers controlled their sons' labor by refusing to grant them land until relatively late in life; as a result, many men had to remain in their towns of birth to acquire land at all. This treatment, it is inferred, emasculated Massachusetts men, making them timid and conservative.[7] Chapter 9 on Dedham refutes this shibboleth by showing that sons' wages were sufficiently high and rents and land prices sufficiently low to make paternal control ineffective and immaterial. Moreover, the irrelevance of this explanation to patterns of immobility and town adhesiveness can be demonstrated from wider patterns as well as through detailed town studies.

An analysis of probates and surnames in Essex County from 1630 to 1840 shows that maritime towns, in which land ownership and long-lived fathers were atypical, had as many, if not more, adhesive families than did rural towns in which landownership and long-lived fathers were often found. The Hawthornes, the Archers, and the Dollibeers were maritime families. Whether sons remained in these towns had nothing to do with powerful patriarchs and everything to do with economic opportunities available to the town born. In a study of 301 relatively uncommon surnames, including 4,893 males whose probates were registered in Essex County between 1630 and 1840, the top town of residence for each surname that appeared in a town at least twice held on average 65 percent of the males with that surname for over two hundred years. Among landed families, in which most males were farmers, the top town held 60 percent of the males, and among maritime families the top town held over 67 percent of the males in the county with the same surname.[8] By this measure the most adhesive towns in Essex County were Marblehead and Salem, both ports in which most males were mariners and fishermen and relatively few were farmers. Marblehead, where there was little land to be had and many fathers died young in accidents at sea and epidemics in foreign ports, had the largest number of families or surnames in which 70 percent or more of the men in the county with that surname continued to live in that town until death. Indeed, Marblehead remains one of the most xenophobic towns in Massachusetts.[9] Contrary to received wisdom, Essex County mariners lived and died in the same town as their ancestors more often than did Essex County farmers.

What kept men in the town of their birth and ancestry was not so much paternal power over land as settlement in a town itself. Strangely, historians have considered the support afforded individuals through patriarchal kinship, but have neglected to consider towns themselves as guarantors of their welfare. The town provided the most effective social insurance people needed to thrive in an uncertain and punishing world. Settlement in a town provided men with privileges they could get nowhere else: protection of their labor environment and wages; free education for their children; access to such vital resources as common land, timber, and water; subsistence in poverty, disaster, disease, and the debility of old age; participation in self-government; and access to town improvement projects and public employment. Informal sources of security were attached to town membership as well. A person's birth town usually contained relatives who did not want to see a kinsman or his family in the almshouse or on the poor rolls. Extended kin-groups and towns often became synonymous in their support.

Nathaniel Hawthorne's ambivalent attachment to Salem illustrates a creative individualist's need for security and services that a small nuclear-family household could not provide but a New England town did. Fortunately, Hawthorne's education and rise to prominence did not depend on his father but on the patronage of a local kinsman. Hawthorne's father, also named Nathaniel, was a Salem sea captain. At the age of thirty-three, he died of yellow fever in Surinam. The young Nathaniel was then four years old. The captain left his widow, Elizabeth, and four children a paltry estate of $296. Hawthorne's mother took the children to her brother, Richard Manning.

Another Salemite, he owned the Boston and Salem stage coach line and supported Nathaniel and his siblings. He sent Nathaniel to grammar school and then to Bowdoin College. Manning's stage coach business and accompanying tavern depended on his good graces with the Salem authorities. His support of his nephew was typical of what was given to relatives in Salem; although the amount and character of assistance depended on the family's means, it was customarily given in accordance with the locality's unspoken rules.

After college, Hawthorne returned to the Mannings' home in Salem. He lived without a visible occupation and wrote his first stories in the attic room of the modest house on Herbert Street. His main source of income was the Massachusetts Democratic Party, for which he wrote hack pieces. The local party got him a salaried place in the custom houses of Boston and Salem, signifying the town's appreciation of his work. His authorship enhanced his reputation and the reputation of Salem itself as a cultural center—at least until he libeled the town in the sketch that prefaced *The Scarlet Letter*. Significantly, Hawthorne also married a locally born woman, Sophia Peabody. While delineating the most robust forms of American individualism and becoming one of America's most brilliantly articulate self-created men, Hawthorne depended materially on the customs and loyalties and even the laws of his native city-state, Salem.[10]

Settlement and the security and psychological support that accompanied it were achieved by being born in or accepted by a town. It is important to remember that in the seventeenth and eighteenth centuries, people could not buy health insurance, unemployment insurance, disability insurance, or even fire insurance; there was no system of pensions or retirement, or tenure. People had to rely on their own accumulated property, their savings, and ultimately on family, neighbors, or just plain luck.

Town Settlement and Political Economies

The crucial importance of settlement in a town or parish arose when England adopted what is known as the "old poor law" in 1601. After the Reformation and the dissolution of the monasteries, the English government and people could no longer rely on the church and informal charity to take care of the poor. With a rising and increasingly mobile population, authorities judged that the poor required care lest their disorderliness and misery destroy society.

The solution was to make use of England's some 9,000 parishes and require each parish to take care of its own poor. The state stipulated that each parish keep reliable birth, marriage, and death records so that a person's settlement could be determined. Each parish was required to raise money by means of a "poor rate" in order to provide relief to its indigent residents. A parish was responsible for all people born in that parish who had not obtained a legal settlement elsewhere.

Settlement laws and their application were of vital importance to individuals and society in both England and Massachusetts. However, the rules differed subtly but meaningfully in the two places. In England, a settlement was obtained initially through a person's father and then, for married women, through a husband (as was the case in New England). Newcomers could obtain legal settlement in a parish by renting land of a certain value, serving a full apprenticeship, or working for a year as a servant there. As Keith Snell has shown, because new legal settlements were hard for laborers to obtain, many English people lived in parishes in which they were not legally settled and had a "home parish" elsewhere where they had to go for relief. In many English places there was little overlap between those who actually resided there and those who were legally settled there. The English settlement laws stimulated geographic mobility, because host towns need not be responsible for the welfare of new short-term laborers.[11]

Massachusetts lawmakers avoided this arrangement, which divided a town's population into two groups, those legally settled and those merely resident. Yet lawmakers still relied on settlement to provide the rights and privileges of belonging. In 1639, the Massachusetts General Court decided that all persons residing in a place for just three months without legal challenge by the selectman were in essence settled there. The length of probation increased over time, but in general settlements were rapidly obtained.[12] To avoid being held responsible for growing numbers of poor people or people they did not want, New Englanders had to be vigilant and wary of outsiders. After three months, unless something was done, a stranger became entitled to a lifetime of public assistance.

Yet this difference in law, while important, was less significant than the political and economic differences between England and New England. Accepting somebody as legally settled was in part an economic decision, for it would potentially affect the labor market, the amount of capital in the town, and the burdens on the poor tax. Labor markets, prices, and taxes were of great concern then, as they are now. Who made these decisions mattered, for those with the power to do so shaped the political economy of the parish or town. Here the differences between England and New England by 1700 were striking. In England most parishes had only a few landholders, who held the important political offices such as justice of the peace and who made the essential economic decisions. These gentry and wealthy yeomen decided how much labor was needed in the parish and whether new laborers were to be accepted as resident or as legally settled. Their interest was in keeping labor cheap and abundant locally without having to pay taxes to support unemployed or underemployed laborers when distress came.[13] In New England there were many landholders in each town. More important, decisions about whose settlement was to be accepted and whose was to be challenged were made by the selectmen, who were themselves elected annually by the town meetings, composed of virtually all the white male inhabitants of a town. In New England the townspeople had a substantial amount of power in deciding the economic shape of the town, including its labor pool. It was often in the townsfolk's interest to limit the size of the labor pool, although a rapidly growing labor pool might be needed to accommodate new industries. In New England, the people's distinctive ability to decide who was legally settled created a lively politics of settlement in each town and intensified local xenophobia.

An excellent way to study this process and to gauge the social differences between eighteenth-century England and Massachusetts, flowing from differing political economies at the local level, is to study marriage and geographic mobility from a parish or town perspective. Thanks to the excellent marriage and birth records for seventeenth- and eighteenth-century England and Massachusetts (themselves evidence of the importance of legal settlement), it is possible to measure how easily men and women moved between various localities and what effects, if any, Massachusetts towns' democratic control of legal settlement had on individual lives. To compare patterns of settlement, marriage, and migration in England and New England between 1650 and 1790, I studied four English parishes—two in the northwest and two in the southeast—and four Massachusetts towns—including both seaports and inland agricultural communities. This comparison of marriage and local political economies illuminates their effects on the intimate lives of working folk in the British Empire during the eighteenth century.[14]

This study shows how important the matter of settlement was, how pervasively it shaped mobility patterns in New England, and how profoundly New England differed from England. In Massachusetts, young people's choice of a spouse was often heavily influenced by a town's policy toward accepting outsiders as permanent settlers. The many problems in existing surveys of exogamy were avoided by examining birth records for forty years prior to each marriage to see whether a bride or groom was actually born in the town or parish in which they married.[15] Additionally, the birth registers were examined for two decades following each marriage to see how many children a couple had in the parish or town in which they married, a fairly reliable indicator of whether they actually lived in the parish, village, or town in which they were married and for how long they remained there. Focusing on those parishes and towns for which reliable registers are available narrowed the scope of the study somewhat, but significantly enhanced the reliability of the findings. When possible, court and town records were examined to study the local authorities' response to each marriage. Massachusetts towns often "warned out" or rejected people as inhabitants after they married in the town. This additional information illuminates the lives of common folk: how mobile they were; where, if anywhere, they belonged; how they balanced legal settlement and employment opportunities; and how vitally they were affected by local arrangements of economic power.

Massachusetts towns had a distinctive pattern in regard to marriage, settlement, and childbearing. People married outsiders or across town boundaries in Massachusetts almost as often as they did in England, but most of the people born in any Massachusetts town usually had one or both parents who had also been born in the town. In sum, town-born males had advantages in their hometowns and labored under disadvantages in other towns. This pattern is not evident in the English parishes, particularly those in southeastern England. Massachusetts males in rural areas and women in seaports tended to have their children in their towns of birth. In these communities, families with strong local roots challenged the right of outsiders to intrude on their privileges.

The proportions of husbands from outside the parish, village, or town were similar in these English and Massachusetts locations (Table 1). In Massachusetts, however, men who had been born outside the town usually left with their brides and had their children elsewhere. For example, from 1650 to 1800, outside males produced only 13 percent of Watertown's children, while during these years outside males produced 69 percent of Hollesley's. An exception was Marblehead, which tended to welcome male outsiders because they were needed to replace native mariners who died at sea. Yet 56 percent of Marblehead's children came from marriages between two native-born

TABLE 1. MARRIAGES AND THEIR CHILDREN IN EIGHT MASSACHUSETTS TOWNS AND ENGLISH PARISHES, C. 1650–1790

	Marriages								Children							
	Native marriage (both man and woman town born)		Male outsider with native woman		Female outsider with native man		Both outsiders		Parish-born children of two town-born parents		Parish-born children with one town-born parent		Parish-born children of males born outside parish		Parish-born children with no town-born parents	
	Per-centage	Num-ber	Per-centage	Num-ber	Per-centage	Num-ber	Per-centage	Num-ber	Per-centage	Num-ber	Per-centage	Num-ber	Per-centage	Num-ber	Per-centage	Num-ber
English Parishes																
Askham, Westmorland	37%	141	35%	132	12%	47	16%	62	57%	397	37%	258	28%	195	6%	46
Walton-le-Dale, Lancashire	23%	48	24%	49	30%	61	23%	48	21%	133	56%	363	44%	282	23%	150
Horringer, Suffolk	9%	30	33%	110	16%	53	42%	140	18%	97	55%	301	53%	289	27%	146
Hollesley, Suffolk	9%	19	24%	53	16%	35	51%	113	6%	19	48%	143	69%	204	45%	133
Massachusetts Towns																
Malden, Middlesex	47%	126	14%	38	28%	75	11%	28	54%	626	36%	413	19%	217	10%	115
Marblehead, Essex	47%	238	26%	130	12%	60	15%	73	56%	689	34%	413	34%	416	10%	128
Scituate, Plymouth	45%	223	25%	126	19%	96	11%	55	63%	738	29%	333	16%	189	8%	92
Watertown, Middlesex	43%	295	30%	208	10%	67	17%	118	73%	1,126	26%	387	13%	200	2%	30
Total		1,120		846		494		637		3,825		2,611		1,992		840

Sources: Askham Registers, Walton-le-Dale Registers, Horringer Registers, Hollesley Registers, Malden Vital Records, Marblehead Vital Records, Scituate Vital Records, Watertown Records, Watertown's Early Settlers.

Marbleheaders. Among the English parishes, only Askham in remote Westmorland (now Cumbria), in northwestern England is remotely comparable.
In Massachusetts the maintenance of families in a town and their privileged
position in relation to town resources was part of a political process that
distinguished the democratic Massachusetts towns from parishes in England
that were under the control of aristocrats, the landed gentry, and large-scale
farmers.

In the propensity of men and women to marry and raise their families
in their native town, the Massachusetts towns most closely resembled Askham, in the remote English county of Westmorland. In Table 1, Askham sits
alongside the New England towns in the greater propensity of residents to
choose locally born spouses and the higher proportion of children with locally
born parents. These surface similarities have enhanced the false impression
that the proverbial Massachusetts town was a quaint and sleepy economic
fossil of a traditional English way of life, not driven by a dynamic, modern
socioeconomic strategy.

The apparent similarity in the geographical immobility of these populations is profoundly misleading. Marblehead and Scituate, as well as other
seaports, harbored major industries, and their residents visited all parts of the
Atlantic world. At the same time, these quasi-sovereign and democratic town
meetings regulated who could settle there and sought to protect and enhance
the welfare of the town born by their public policies. Nothing similar was
happening in England, where local political authority was in the hands of a
few gentry families and wealthy yeoman farmers. The differences become
clear when the local political economies and marriage and child-producing
patterns of these English and Massachusetts communities are sketched and
compared.

Askham, Westmorland

This picturesque village had some 360 residents in 2001. Located in the part
of present-day Cumbria that was formerly Westmorland, Askham adjoins
the river Lowther. In the late seventeenth and eighteenth centuries, most
people in the parish were relatively poor. Most of the land was owned by the
Sandford family, who lived in Askham Hall. In 1724, the Earl of Lonsdale of
the Lowther family from across the river bought the Sandford estate. Lonsdale used the profits from this estate, as well as income from many other

manors and from court, to build the fantastical Lowther Castle in 1806 and St. Peter's church in 1832, both designed by Sir Robert Smirke, the architect of the British Museum. William Wordsworth, the poet, came from and often visited this area; his father worked as an agent for the Lowther family. The majority of Askham residents were tenant farmers and farm laborers. The farmers enjoyed customary leases. The estate had to offer a relatively secure form of tenure in order to retain farmers because the land was remote and hilly and the climate cold and windy (wind farms have recently been set up in the vicinity). Most farmers grew some grain for subsistence on arable patches, and raised sheep and cattle for subsistence and sale. With such marginal farms, it was also difficult to attract and retain wage labor. The parish's relative poverty convinced the more powerful families to allow many poor families to stay in the village and marry locally during the period 1650–1790.[16]

Among the 382 Askham marriages studied, 141 (37 percent) were between people both born in Askham. These marriages produced 397 children, a majority (57 percent) of the total born between 1650 and 1810. Marriages between women born in Askham and men born outside the parish were almost as common (132), but produced substantially fewer of the parish's children (149, or 21 percent). Many Askham women married men from outside the parish and then moved elsewhere. Still, the parish seemed hospitable to many outside males willing to settle there. In this way, Askham differed from the rural Massachusetts towns studied, where the town meeting restricted outside men's access to town resources. In contrast, Askham's endogamy—the pattern of natives marrying natives—and the fact that locally born couples were the main source of children born in the town resemble patterns in many New England towns.

Marriages between a man and woman who both came from outside the parish were less common. These sixty-two marriages produced only forty-six children (7 percent of all those born in the parish), indicating that most of these couples left fairly quickly. Marriages between men born in Askham and women born outside the parish were, surprisingly, less common than those between two outsiders. Perhaps it was difficult to persuade a woman to come and live among people she did not know in obscure poverty in a windswept, upland village whose land was more suitable for pastoral than arable farming. Only forty-seven (12 percent) of the marriages were of this type, and they produced 109 children (15 percent of the total). The population of Askham was highly inbred: a majority of the children born in the parish had both a mother and a father who had been born in the parish, and almost all the children born in the parish (93 percent) had at least one parent who had been born in the parish.

In Askham, this pattern of endogamy and local adhesion came from long-term economic conditions and landowners', tenants', and laborers' strategic adjustment to these realities. The Lowthers and Sandfords usually gave tenants leases for three lives. Tenants paid a steep fine (fee) to obtain such a lease and could enter three names into the lease, usually a husband, his wife, and a child. So long as any of these three lived and held the lease, the tenant family paid a relatively low annual rent. However, if the tenant family wished to extend their hold on the land for a longer period, they had to enter more names. The landlord then would demand a steeper fine. This form of tenancy rewarded farming families' loyalty and interest in land that otherwise would not be greatly in demand. It was a useful tool for landlords in marginal agricultural situations. Clearly, the Lowthers and Sandfords were successful in keeping the estate populated. A few rural Massachusetts towns far from transportation routes and markets may have resembled Askham in attracting just enough outside labor while rewarding and retaining the locally born, but in those places a relatively large group of landowners exercised their economic power through the town meeting rather than through long-term contracts. But many Massachusetts towns had more diverse economies and rapidly growing industries. In these places, endogamy and local adhesion resulted chiefly from the exercise of local democracy to keep strangers at bay and the town born privileged.

Walton-le-Dale, Lancashire

About sixty miles south of Askham sits the parish and township of Walton-le-Dale, on the river Ribble near Preston, Lancashire, in northwestern England. In the seventeenth and early eighteenth centuries, Walton-le-Dale developed into a major textile-producing center. It was what is known as an open parish, with many large and small landowners as well as industrial proprietors. Joseph Livesey, a prominent Methodist advocate of temperance in the nineteenth century, was born in Walton-le-Dale in 1794, was orphaned, and worked as a handloom weaver in his grandparents' cellar for six shillings a week. He later became a cheese factor, printer, and publisher, dying in 1884 with an estate of £21,500. His success was atypical, but his career suggests the open entrepreneurial world of Walton-le-Dale. By 1801 its population had grown to 3,832.[17]

An analysis of 503 marriages between 1654 and 1753 indicates that many people moved rapidly into and out of growing Walton-le-Dale. The most common occupations listed for grooms were weaver and linen weaver. More marriages were contracted between two people who had not been born in Walton-le-Dale than between native couples, men from outside the parish marrying native women, and men born in the parish marrying women born elsewhere. But all four types of couples contributed almost equally to the children born in the parish, indicating that newcomers who married in Walton-le-Dale tended to stay there as often as locally born spouses did. During this hundred-year period, only 21 percent of the children born to these 503 couples had parents who had both been born in Walton-le-Dale.

Horringer and Hollesley, Suffolk

The inland village of Horringer and the seaside parish of Hollesley lie about forty miles apart in East Anglia, the homeland of many Puritans who emigrated to Massachusetts in the first half of the seventeenth century. Nearby towns have namesakes in New England: Haverhill, Ipswich, and Cambridge. Suffolk's sandy and rich loam soils are suitable to arable farming. Although smallholders had once held much of the land, enclosure and engrossment by large landowners had eliminated smallholders by the middle of the seventeenth century. Agriculture was very profitable, given the excellent quality of the land and the region's proximity to London and other towns. Speaking of the Suffolk district that included Hollesley, Arthur Young observed in 1784 that the area was dominated by a "great number of landlords the occupiers of their own lands . . . gentlemen farmers from 200 to 500£ a year, who cultivating their own property, do it with a spirit that very few leases will permit within a very few years."[18] The agricultural economy was thoroughly capitalist, dominated by wealthy yeomen farmers who relied on landless wage laborers. Farmers cultivated carrots and other crops for food and feed and bred horses, especially the famous Suffolk punch, which excelled at farm work. Horringer, near Bury St. Edmunds, was also dominated by a few large landowners and had even more fertile soil. In 1727, Horringer contained about one hundred adult males, but only eight had enough property to vote in the parliamentary elections. Property holding and political power in the

village and neighboring area was dominated by the Hervey family, who became the Earls of Bristol. Over two generations, between 1794 and the 1820s,
they built the spectacular Ickworth House, featuring a great central rotunda,
curved corridors, and flanking pavilions. Beginning in 1769, Lancelot "Capa-
bility" Brown designed the beautiful Ickworth gardens, part of which lay in
Horringer.[19]

In both Suffolk parishes the majority of people were farm laborers. Horringer was probably much like the parish of Welnetham, which lay some five
miles away, and was described in the 1790s by the Reverend S. Phillips.
The parish contained twenty-three farmers' households, holding 113 people
including servants and children, and thirty-one laborers' cottages, containing
140 people. The farmers' houses sported windows and were built of brick;
the laborer's cottages were, according to Young, "in general bad habitations;
deficient in all contrivance for warmth, and for convenience; the door very
generally opening immediately from the external air into the keeping-room,
and sometimes directly to the fire-side." Laborers worked for about a shilling
a day. During the harvest, the farmers brought in transient laborers who were
supplied with lodgings and earned twelve shillings a week.[20]

Lacking political and economic power, the laborers rarely gained settlement or stayed long in Horringer and Hollesley. The marriage analysis shows
a very mobile population. In Horringer, according to study of 333 marriages
there between 1653 and 1790, marriages between two people born in Hollesley
produced only 18 percent of the 542 children produced in Horringer by these
marriages. A significantly larger percentage of the children came from marriages in which at least one partner had not been born there. Significantly,
27 percent of all the children derived from marriages between a man and
woman neither of whom had been born in the parish. E. J. Buckatzsch,
who studied surnames in Horringer between 1550 and 1850, found substantial
population turnover: "The main conclusion appears in fact to be simply, that
throughout the three centuries surveyed, relatively large numbers of families
were leaving the parish and being replaced by others with different names. It
appears to be untrue that *at any time* between 1650 and 1850 more than a
very small minority of the inhabitants of this village were descendants of men
who had been there a hundred years earlier."[21] Mobility and impermanence
were even greater among the powerless laborers of Hollesley. Among the 220
marriages recorded in Hollesley between 1682 and 1790, marriages between
two people born in the same parish produced only 6 percent of the children
born in Hollesley. Most marriages were between people born in other par-

ishes, and these couples had 45 percent of all the children. Unless a man inherited a substantial landholding in the parish, being born in Hollesley offered him little local benefit.

Four Massachusetts Towns

Malden, Marblehead, Scituate, and Watertown were clearly different. In Massachusetts towns, marriages were far more likely to involve two locally born spouses than in England, and in these towns most children had two town-born parents, and almost all had at least one. In every town studied, well over half the children born between 1650 and 1800 had two parents who had been born in that town. In no Massachusetts town during this period did marriages between people who had both been born elsewhere produce more than one tenth of the town's children. In southeastern English rural parishes, by contrast, these outsider couples produced from a quarter to almost half the children. These patterns of endogamy and persistence have long been recognized by colonial historians and form part of the traditional image of New England. In the prevailing view, however, immobility and local intermarriage are signs of an undeveloped or backward economy, while geographic mobility is a sign of progress and modernity.[22]

This deeply entrenched assumption is misplaced. Some towns in central and western Massachusetts remained undeveloped in the eighteenth century, but none of the towns studied here can be so considered; all had been settled by English families in the early seventeenth century. Farms in Massachusetts were certainly less profitable and productive than those in Hollesley and Horringer. But this difference arose more from environmental than narrowly economic factors; the land in most of New England was too thin and stony to reward such commercially oriented agriculture. Many Massachusetts towns were far more economically diversified than either Hollesley or Horringer, even though their adult residents were far less mobile. By 1720 Scituate, a coastal town equidistant between Boston and Plymouth, was producing hundred of tons of shipping a year. In 1705, Scituate shipbuilders built at least nine vessels comprising 480 tons for investors as far away as London. In 1784 Hanover, which was set off from Scituate in the early eighteenth century, had 126 dwelling houses. Its 425 acres in tillage and 253 acres of fresh meadow supported some 367 cows and 711 goats and sheep as well as other livestock. Eleven sawmills, two tanneries, and two iron foundries were located along the river, and the Four Corners neighborhood became a prime location for shipbuilding. The tax list shows that, remarkably, 85 percent of the town's 250 adult male workers were legally settled in Hanover, suggesting that the town opened settlement to newcomers who brought vitally needed skills and capital. Similarly, in 1784 Watertown's 120 households tilled only 385 acres and pastured 314 cows. It had the usual mix of rural industries: six tanneries, four grist and sawmills, two distilleries and sugar houses, and thirty-two workshops separate from the dwelling houses.[23] Most men combined artisanal or industrial work with agriculture. Massachusetts towns were economically dynamic, yet politically and demographically quite different from parishes in England, which had a few landowners and a large population of powerless and geographically mobile workers. New England towns may have been regarded as obnoxious, or even dangerous to elite power and its ideologues, but they were not "backward."

Size certainly had something to do with the very different rates of mobility at marriage seen in England and Massachusetts. English rural parishes, especially in southeastern England, were usually—but not always—smaller in size and population than Massachusetts towns. Hollesley in Suffolk County, England, in 1801 contained 3,987 acres and 461 people, while Malden in Middlesex County, Massachusetts, in 1784 had 6,500 acres and 812 people.[24] In Malden young men and women had a significantly larger choice of potential spouses, which is part of the reason that 34 percent of the marriages in Malden were between people born in the town while only 9 percent of the marriages in Hollesley were between people born in the parish between 1650 and 1790. However, differences in size fail to explain other dramatic discrepancies. For example, during this period comparable proportions of women born in Hollesley (24 percent) and Malden (14 percent) married men born outside the parish and town, respectively. Yet while the marriages between parish-born women and newcomers produced almost a quarter of the children produced by all the marriages recorded in Hollesley, similar marriages produced less than a tenth of the children born to all the marriages recorded in Malden. While the marriages between two people born elsewhere produced almost half (45 percent) of the children born in Hollesley, such marriages produced only one tenth of the children born in Malden. In New England, couples in which the bride was not born in the locality were more likely to remain after marriage than their counterparts in England, while couples in which the groom or both partners were outsiders were less likely to remain there than their English counterparts.

In virtually all the localities studied, men born outside the parish, whether or not they married parish-born women, produced a much higher proportion of the children born in the locality in England than they did in Massachusetts. In Walton-le-Dale, Horringer, and Hollesley, grooms who had been born elsewhere fathered 44 percent, 53 percent, and an impressive 69 percent of the children born in the parish, respectively, whereas in Malden, Scituate, and Watertown these fellows fathered only 19 percent, 16 percent, and 13 percent of the children born in the town, respectively. It appears that in England men could enter a parish and have children there, while in Massachusetts it was far more difficult for strangers to do so. The relatively greater size of these localities was not the main factor involved in the higher propensity of Massachusetts men to marry and remain in the place they were born.

What kept outsiders from marrying and having children in New England towns was democratic town politics and the arrangement of settlement laws, supported by a pervasive prejudice against strangers that was no less powerful because of its informality. Local politics mattered to people's lives. At a certain point in their development, in order to preserve town resources and an advantageous labor market for town-born males, many Massachusetts towns decided in their town meetings and through their selectmen that outside men, with some exceptions, should not gain settlement or long-term residence in their towns. In England, gentry families and wealthy yeoman farmers dominated local politics; there were no town meetings. Vestry meetings, where key decisions were made, were often closed. It was in the big landowners' interest to increase the labor supply and lower wages, so outside men were welcome. At the same time, the gentry arranged national settlement laws to help them keep the costs of supporting the poor low while allowing the mobility of labor. As Keith Snell and other historians have pointed out, by the eighteenth century landowners in southeastern England were refusing to hire farm servants for year-long terms to prevent them from gaining a legal settlement in their parishes; instead, they kept farm workers for a season, or hired labor on a daily basis (Figure 3).[25]

Marblehead appears to be a striking exception to Massachusetts towns' greater hostility to outside men as permanent settlers. There newcomers were welcome, and grooms from elsewhere fathered 34 percent of the children born to couples married in the town. Yet this exception proves the rule. Marbleheaders needed male outsiders because the town's primary industries, fishing and blue water sailing, had a seemingly inexhaustible demand for

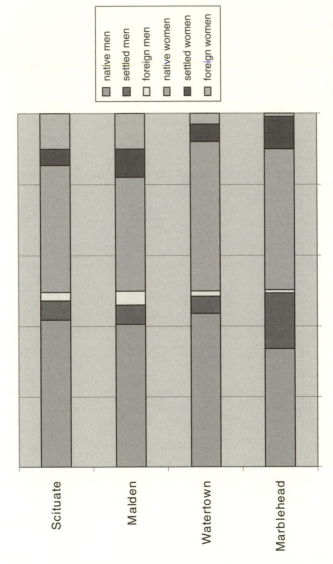

Figure 3. Proportions of children born among approximately two thousand marriages to native born, legally settled, and in-migrant men and women in four Massachusetts towns, 1650–1790. Sources: Malden Vital Records; Marblehead Vital Records; Scituate Vital Records; Watertown Records; Watertown's Early Settlers.

labor. At the same time, seafaring entailed the premature death of many of town-born males, exacerbating the labor shortage. Young widows married second and even third husbands. The distinctive conditions in seaports resulted in their adopting a different policy regarding the settlement of male strangers than that followed by rural towns.[26] Yet these maritime towns inspired as much loyalty as rural towns. They had very high rates of intermarriage among town-born people, and the children of locally born parents dominated the population. Selectmen made subtle decisions on behalf of the population they protected. Power politics produced distinctive patterns of marriage and migration.

Securing a Settlement in Watertown—Or Being Warned Out

Fortunately, numbers need not tell the whole tale. Thanks to the meticulous records kept by its town clerks during the seventeenth and eighteenth centuries and the work of the nineteenth-century genealogist, Henry Bond, who traced the early inhabitants and their descendants, it is possible to study the politics of settlement person by person in Watertown, Massachusetts. Detailed analysis of who was accepted and who rejected confirms the seriousness of town boundaries and enriches our conception of local political economies. Many historians understandably believe that "warning out" in Massachusetts was a process by which the selectmen of a town simultaneously identified and created a permanent wandering proletariat. When a poor man or woman wandered into town looking for work, the story goes, he or she was warned out before he or she could become a burden to the town. Some might even be physically removed by the constable if they refused to go. Excluding the poor is part of the story.[27] More often, selectmen warned out perfectly employable young men and women who seemed likely to marry locally, or who had already done so, and sought to benefit financially from their connections. Newcomers who remained for three months might gain legal settlement, marry, and have children, all of whom would be settled inhabitants and entitled to draw on town resources. The town often acted against male strangers. "Warning out" was where town political economies, local politics, and family politics met.

Most men understood that it was very difficult for a newcomer to marry in Watertown and settle there. Many men came to Watertown to marry, but then took their brides back to their home communities or to new towns.

Some men established settlement in Watertown in their youth and later married and had children there. Among 850 marriages recorded from 1650 to 1790, however, only ten men who had a settlement outside of Watertown married a woman who was born or settled in Watertown and then stayed or returned to Watertown to have at least two children.

Significantly, men who had married in but were not settled in Watertown and then returned to try to take advantage of their wives' relatives and connections were formally warned out. For example, in 1709 Jonathan Underwood of Cambridge came to Watertown and married Ruth Holland, a town-born woman. The Underwoods lived in Cambridge and later went to Woburn. Ruth (Holland) Underwood kept up her local connections. In 1732 she "made public confession of her sin and was received into favor" by the Watertown Church and had her son baptized there; admitting a violation of the seventh commandment forbidding fornication was often a condition for the baptism of children who had obviously been conceived through premarital sex. In 1736, the Watertown selectmen got legal notice that "one Jonathan Underwood and his wife Ruth and three children are come to reside in Watertown who came last from Woburn in the County of Middlesex the later end of April last past and now resides in the dwelling house of Captain Nathaniel Bowman of Cambridge." The next day the selectmen ordered the constable "to warn the above named Jonathan Underwood and his wife Ruth Underwood with their three children to depart forth without of Watertown and no longer to abide therein." Because Ruth Holland, although a native of Watertown, had married a stranger, she lost her settlement in the town and was unable to utilize her local connections to reestablish it. The Underwoods disappear from the Watertown records.[28]

Even far better connected women found that their kin were unable to persuade the town to accept their husbands. In 1712, Sarah Chadwick married John Pilsbury, a farm laborer who had a legal settlement in Watertown, though he had not been born there. She was already thirty-six, and by reason of her advanced age at a disadvantage in the marriage market. Sarah Chadwick's father, Charles, had owned the tavern where the selectmen often met in the 1690s, and her brother, John, was a reliable town officeholder, including serving as constable. Pilsbury and his wife moved to Lexington. In 1722 when he tried to resettle in Watertown he was discovered by the selectmen, warned out, and removed. The selectmen "ordered that the town clerk give out a warrant to the constable to warn one John Pilsbury a man which came from Lexington some time in March last past, to part out of town with his family within 14 days." Sarah Chadwick and her brothers could do nothing about it. The town trumped kin. Similarly, in 1755 Mary Saltmarsh married Abijah Hammond of Newtown. Her father, Thomas Saltmarsh, had been a sea captain and kept an inn in Watertown from 1734 to 1769. He held numerous town offices. With at least eight siblings, several of whom married and lived locally, Mary (Saltmarsh) Hammond was part of a huge extended family in the town. Like Sarah (Underwood) Chadwick, Mary kept up her local connections and had children baptized in the Watertown Church. Nevertheless, the selectmen warned them out of town in 1760 when they were "informed that one Abijah Hammond and his wife and their two children were come to reside in Watertown at the house of John Hunt, Esquire, that they came last from Newton about the tenth day of March last past." The family left.[29]

At times, the selectmen's decisions seemed cruel, though their placing the letter of the law over considerations of wealth and status is impressive. In 1728, Watertown native Deborah Cutting married Jonathan Stratton of Weston at the age of twenty-three. Her father, Ephraim Cutting, served in many town offices. The couple returned to Weston and apparently went to Hopkinton. Something disrupted the marriage: her husband may have died, deserted, or abused her. In 1738, the Watertown selectmen got word that "there is one Deborah Stratton wife of one Jonathan Stratton come to dwell in Watertown who came last from Hopkinton some time in April past and resides with her father Mr. Ephraim Cutting of said Watertown." Deborah's presence with her well-established parents seems benign, and compassion might have left this troubled family alone. However, the selectmen issued a warrant for the constable "to warn . . . Deborah Stratton forthwith to depart out of said Watertown the selectmen refusing to accept" her. The selectmen deemed it more important to protect the town resources than to help a distressed mother from an established local family. After all, Deborah (Cutting) Stratton had made her choice to marry an outsider.[30]

In some cases, the selectmen seemed to negotiate civilly with the use of the warning out sanction. In September 1765, the selectmen discovered that "one Richard Walker, last from Boston," had "come to dwell in Watertown at the house of Mr. John Hunt, esquire." The selectmen decided to warn him out. It is unlikely that they saw Richard Walker as a vagrant or miscreant. His landlord, who may also have been his employer, was among the most prominent men in Watertown. Hunt was chosen a selectman in 1747, 1752, 1754, and 1755, and represented Watertown in the Massachusetts General

Court from 1751 to 1758. Walker may well have been a promising young man. The selectmen refused to welcome him for the long term, however, because the town's well-developed resources were reserved for the town born and Walker came from beyond the town boundaries. Just a month later, on October 15, 1765, Seth Storer, the minister of the Watertown Church, married Richard Walker to Elizabeth Goddard, a town-born woman from a prominent family. The newlyweds remained in Watertown for about a year. They owned the covenant and became members of the Watertown Church, and about a year later their first-born son, Richard, was baptized there. After this, the Walkers disappeared from the town records. The warning out had been a message sent and received: Richard Walker could stay a while to marry a daughter of the town, but he could not gain a legal settlement, so he departed.[31]

A set of similar cases from the late eighteenth century shows that, as a matter of policy, town officials warned out perfectly respectable men who married local women. In 1759, the selectmen warned out Ebenezer Warner, who had come to town from Springfield. About a year later he married Elizabeth Cook, the twenty-year-old daughter of Samuel and Susannah Cook. Susannah kept school for the town, and Samuel served as a town meeting officer. But, since Ebenezer had been warned out, the newlyweds left, having no children in Watertown. This warning out was prophylactic, a way of preventing Warner from obtaining a settlement in his wife's town. In 1766, the selectmen warned out Moses Sanders from Cambridge, who was living in his future father-in-law's house; he subsequently married Sarah Goddard and left town with her. Neither of these men was poor.[32]

A few men from outside the town married in Watertown, were allowed to settle, and had children there. The warning-out system was a matter of political discretion, as the selectmen sought to better the interests of the town born who had elected them. They made exceptions to their general policy of warning out male newcomers who threatened to marry and reside in the town if those men brought substantial capital or skills that were vital to the local economy. In 1727, James Nutting of Cambridge and Mercy Barnard of Cambridge were married in Watertown. It was not unusual for people from elsewhere to marry there, for Jonas Bond, dubbed "the marrying squire," readily married couples who paid him a fee. However, Nutting and Barnard settled in Watertown and had two children born there over a period of four years. Nobody warned them out; they were recorded as inhabitants. Nutting acquired a twenty-four-acre farm and a shop. A likely explanation for Nutting's ability to cross town boundaries is his occupation: gunsmith. The selectmen may have decided that they needed one in town. Retaining an artisan whose skills were in demand was not as easy as attracting one, however; in 1731 Nutting sold his Watertown property for £450 and moved to Wrentham, another developed town.[33]

Men with valuable skills or capital could cross town boundaries more easily than mere laborers or farmers. Selectmen hoped to develop their towns economically and welcomed some artisans, entrepreneurs, and men of "enterprising character." Genealogist Henry Bond, who was born in Watertown in 1767, described Captain John Brown of Waltham in exceptional terms: "scrupulously neat in his personal habits, [he] carried finish and completeness in his dwelling, outhouses [outbuildings], and fences to the verge of extravagance." Waltham had trusted him with many town offices, voting him selectman virtually every year between 1744 and 1752 and electing him in 1748 their representative to the Massachusetts General Court. He was known as a shrewd land developer and speculator. Bond characterized him with a phrase that was common in Middlesex County: "It is impossible for Capt. John Brown to become poor." In 1761 Captain Brown moved his large family from Waltham to Weston and, as Henry Bond noted, "the prestige of his enterprising character prevented the Selectmen of that town from serving him with the customary order." Ironically, to the shock of the Weston selectmen, Captain Brown then proceeded to go bankrupt.[34]

The application of settlement law sometimes seems inconsistent to modern historians. For example, some aspects of Watertown's treatment of Susannah Holden Murch seem callous, while others seem more sympathetic. But careful analysis of the twists and turns in this case demonstrates that selectmen used settlement law to defend the town from the claims of outsiders and that town boundaries were more important than even the claims of motherhood. William Murch, a newcomer to Watertown, married Susannah Holden, a town-born woman of thirty-five, on June 24, 1734. William Murch was a laborer and church member. He went to war in 1742, serving at Castle William in Boston Harbor, and apparently beforehand he moved his family to Cambridge, from which they were warned out. In her husband's absence and in the face of Cambridge's hostility, Susannah (Holden) Murch moved with her four children back to Watertown. William Murch apparently never returned: his wife was known as Susannah Murch for years, and only "widow Murch" many decades later.

Susannah had at least five siblings in Watertown, the most prominent being Abigail Holden, who married Samuel Jenison in 1734. In 1744, the selectmen of Watertown got word that "Susannah Murch being under very poor and low circumstances having neither house or home to go to, made application to the selectmen for some relief under her difficulty." She was about forty-five and had four children. "She being very loath to be chargeable," noted the selectmen, "is desirious of doing what she can to maintain herself and child that is with her. And hopes if she could have a room she might with some small help get a livelihood." The selectmen put her into an empty house owned by Mr. Bemis and provided her with a load of wood and some meat and meal "for her present subsistence till she can take care to provide (if able) for herself."

While the selectmen decided to support Murch's request for material assistance and her aspiration to attain financial independence, they decided at the same meeting to separate her from one of her daughters. They warned out "Susannah Murch a child of William and Susannah Murch which came from Cambridge sometime in May last." Unlike the other three Murch children, little Susannah had been born in Cambridge. They decided she was a Cambridge lass and could not receive relief from Watertown even if she was living with her mother. Most probably, little Susannah could not read the warrant to leave town given or proclaimed to her by the good Watertown constable: she was two and a half years old.[35]

Susannah (Holden) Murch lived quietly in Watertown for some five years. However, in 1747, Murch ran afoul of her landlord, Mr. Brindley, and took refuge with her sister Abigail and her brother-in-law Samuel Jenison. Jenison sought assistance from the town for taking care of his sister. The selectmen decided to pay him three months' rent for her and to furnish a load of wood. Jenison then found another house for her. Again, the selectmen followed generosity with apparent callousness. In 1749, they decided "to issue a warrant to warn out of town one Lydia Murch (the daughter of William and Susannah Murch) who came from Cambridge about the middle of August last past, who resides with her mother in the dwelling house of Stephen Palmer which is in Watertown (a warrant was issued out accordingly and delivered to the constable N. Stone)." Lydia Murch had been born in Watertown in 1735. Apparently she had gained settlement in neighboring Cambridge by residence, and the Watertown selectmen took advantage of this resettlement to prevent the fourteen-year-old from sneaking across the border and living and working with her mother. Once again they treated the town boundaries as more sacred than family ties.[36]

Meanwhile, Jenison continued to pay Murch's rent, but in 1749 he again petitioned the town for assistance in doing so. This time the town meeting considered his request and "this vote was passed in the negative." Three years later, Mrs. Murch passed from being a beneficiary of the Watertown welfare system to a provider.[37] In 1752, Murch reported that Widow Mary Maddocks, who was living with her and who had long been a town problem, was ill. After investigation, the selectmen found Murch's claim to payment for her services was "not without grounds." They decided to ask Murch to continue to keep the demanding Maddocks and agreed "with Mrs. Murch that while she (Maddocks) tarryed with her and was supported by her she should receive after the rate of twenty-five shillings old tenor per week from the town." The selectmen also "agreed Mrs. Murch should have a load of wood for a requital." By 1754 the town saw Murch, then fifty-five, as an asset: a poor woman who not only did her best to support herself but also took care of other poor people who were ill. Her home became a hospital. That year, the town meeting voted affirmatively to "grant Susannah Murch a liberty to set a small building on the town's land which ly's near Isaac Sanderson's where a committee to be chosen for that end shall appoint and direct, and to enjoy said land on which said building is set during the town's pleasure." Additionally, the selectmen contributed to the construction; they "agreed that Susannah Murch have three days work about her house paid for by the town." Murch's house, located on town land, served a public purpose, not only keeping her off the poor rolls but also providing lodging for other poor townspeople.

Eight years later, in 1762, the town meeting voted affirmatively in response to Murch's request to have a garden adjoining her house. The selectmen offered a generous grant as a kind of testimonial to Murch's career in Watertown: "In as much as ye wido Murch has by the leave of the town erected a small house on the Northwest corner of said land and has by her industry subsisted herself so that she has not been chargeable to the town for years past, we are of opinion that in answer to her last request to the town that there be a small piece of land set off to said widow near her house for a garden spot and for laying firewood and etc, . . . and said land to be for the use and improvement of the said Susannah Murch during her natural life or so long as she resides or dwells in Watertown and then to revert to said town."[38] Widow Murch supported herself on the land granted to her use by the town. She was evidently caring for people who were ill and impoverished, as a number of people were warned out from her residence, including several who were already dead.

Murch left Watertown in 1777. The clerk's records note: "they signed an order on the treasurer to pay Mr. Nathan Coolidge £4:10:00 which sum he paid to help the widow Murch to Greenwich." The considerable amount offered for moving expenses suggest that by the age of seventy-eight, Murch had acquired a heavy load of possessions. Susannah Holden Murch's dealing with the town would be a heartwarming story, except for the town's insistence that at least two of her four children, aged two and fourteen, be kept from her lest they acquire or reacquire a town settlement.[39]

The application of settlement policy involved a political economic calculus, as towns and selectmen exercised discretion in their decisions. A major tendency visible in Massachusetts records is that developed towns protected the town born from outside males who sought access to town resources, especially through marriage, while accepting the arrival and settlement of outside women as marriage partners to town-born men. Although generally unprivileged, young women had the arguable advantage that, unlike young men, they could expunge any warning-out by a town if they married a settled male in a reasonable amount of time. At marriage women took on the civil status of their husbands; they became a *feme covert*, in essence losing their previous identity. This legal policy generally hurt women, but some migrants found it helpful. Consider, for example, the case of Catherine Draper: "At a Meeting of the Selectmen at the house of Capt Edward Harrington on Monday the Seventh day of Decr. 1761 They being Informed that on[e] Katherine Draper was come to reside at the house of Mathew Johnson in Watertown She came last from Deadham in the County of Suffolk her Circumstances being Such that they Refuse to admitt her to be an Inhabitant of Said town Ordered the Clerk to Issue out a warrant to warn her out of town a warrant was Issued out accordingly and given to S. Whitney and the Service done & the warrant Returned and the Caution Entered at December Sessions. Attest J Brown Town Clerk." Just two years later, the unfazed Catherine Draper married Ezekial Whitney, a town-born man aged twenty-two and a relative of the very constable who had delivered her warrant. She remained in Watertown as Mrs. Whitney for the rest of her life and had at least five children there.[40]

Patterns of Local and Long-Distance Migration

Men and women born outside the parish or town contributed far more children in most of the English parishes than did outsiders married in Massachusetts towns. However, in Massachusetts women who crossed town boundaries to marry frequently bore children in the towns where they obtained a settlement. For example, in Malden over the period from 1676 to 1790 some 36 percent of all the children born in the town had a mother who came from elsewhere, while only 19 percent of the children had a father who was a newcomer. Between 1676 and 1790, seventy-nine women came to Malden from other places and had more than one child there. About half had settled in Malden previous to marriage, and half came directly from neighboring towns. Map 1, which locates the known origins of these women, shows that most had moved from neighboring and nearby towns. This pattern of short-distance migration is rarely found among males in colonial Massachusetts.

Port towns such as Marblehead were important exceptions to this trend. Men born outside the town fathered a much higher proportion of town-born children in Marblehead than in inland towns. On the other hand, a relatively small proportion of women from outside Marblehead gave birth to children there. Most male outsiders settled in Marblehead before marriage and had probably earned a reputation as willing and able mariners. Town officials and residents agreed in the need to replenish the supply of maritime labor, so ports welcomed newcomers who were willing to go to sea. In his voluminous diaries, William Bentley often spoke highly of immigrant sailors' contributions to Salem. For example, he praised John Nesboth, known widely as "Uncle John," who was born in Aberdeen, Scotland. In the 1780s, he was captured by an American privateer and brought to Salem. After sailing out of Salem for some five years he married a local woman, and about two years later he died at Port au Prince from the West Indian flux at the age of forty-eight. "Everybody seemed to love Uncle John," noted Bentley, "and everybody was willing to trust him." Though John Nesboth's virtues had much to do with his acceptance, so too did the hungry labor and marriage markets in the port town. Bentley's younger sister married an English sailor, Charles Wooley. In 1802, "he died at Havana in the 31 year of his age with the prospects of a good voyage before him and under good and rich owners of the ship which he commanded." "In the midst of the best prospects, he has disappeared," Bentley concluded mournfully.[41]

Because Massachusetts towns were governed by a substantial majority of the adult males, many towns welcomed or denied admission to strangers based on the common perception of the local political economy and its need for labor. Towns differed in regard to how they treated outsiders, but two general patterns can be discerned: once their land and resources had been

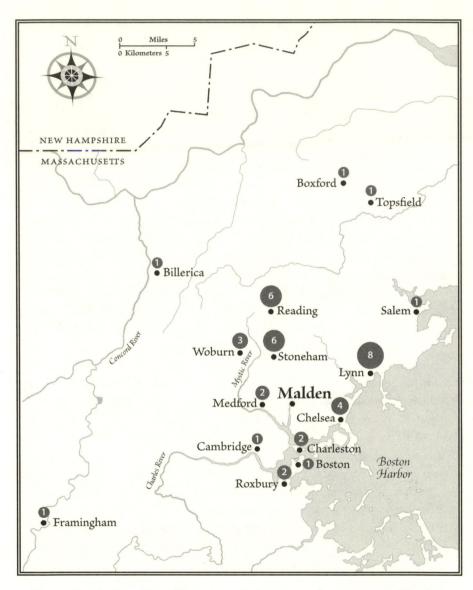

Map 1. Geographic origins of forty nonnative Malden mothers, 1650–1790. Numbers in shaded circles indicate Malden mothers from each town. Source: Malden Vital Records.

developed, most inland towns were hostile to male newcomers while welcoming women from outside the town as wives; port towns welcomed those male newcomers who were willing to risk their lives at sea.

The adhesiveness and their high endogamy rates of Massachusetts towns in comparison with parishes in England should not leave the impression that New Englanders were less geographically mobile—and thereby less "modern" and more "traditional"—than English working people. The primacy of settlement policy and local democracy in Massachusetts meant, instead, that laborers moved differently than their counterparts in rural England. Different local political economies inspired distinctive modes of work and movement, just as different bands and styles of music lend themselves to distinctive dances. English laborers tended to dance the "poor man's mill about" in response to their political and economic powerlessness that was laid down by the hegemony of the British gentry and rich yeomanry. On the other hand, the Massachusetts folk favored the "Yankee Doodle leap" laid down by the towns' relatively democratic local political economies mixed with the exhaustion of local resources and the availability of a frontier.

The consensus among social historians is that the English population in the seventeenth and eighteenth centuries was highly mobile: no more than a quarter of the population remained lifelong in their parish of birth. However, as the maintenance of regional dialects, the pervasiveness of local xenophobia, and the regional clustering of surnames suggest, most movement within the countryside occurred over short distances. According to Pamela Horn, laborers "'milled about' within a given group of villages, moving from one to the other as employment opportunities—or fancy—took them." Charles Phythian-Adams and his students have adduced convincing evidence to support the contention that England was made up of "neighborhoods," each about ten or eleven parishes in size, within which families and individuals moved freely, but rarely intruded into other regions. The frequency of movement within a distinct area consisting of ten or more parishes has made some English historians deemphasize local political or ecclesiastical boundaries in comparison to more socially meaningful organizing principles such as kinship networks.[42] The realities of English political economy make this emphasis on kin or class over parish sensible. Most English laborers had little power in any parish, given the power exercised by rich yeoman farmers and gentry, so they needed their nearby kin for support while they moved to find work. English settlement laws allowed laborers to move their residences without becoming chargeable to their new parishes so long as their stay was limited to less than a year. In such a situation, laborers were wise to keep in contact with their families and with responsive farmers and members of the gentry, while moving about within a familiar area to find what employment they could.

In Massachusetts, however, political economies were different. Since towns controlled access to economic resources and opportunities, town boundaries meant a great deal to residents. Men especially could not mill about among adjacent towns because they would be warned out soon after they crossed town borders. Laborers and their families wanted to monopolize their local advantages and protected their town's labor market from being flooded by outsiders. Thanks to the relatively inclusive town meeting, they were able to wield enough power to do so. Thus, Essex County families tended to stay in specific towns rather than circulating among adjacent communities. The Abbots remained in Andover, seldom settling in adjoining inland towns, and the Hawthornes abided in Salem, rarely moving to the neighboring port town of Marblehead. At the same time, since newly founded towns offered the privileges of legal settlement both to proprietors who organized communities and to those who devoted their labor to developing the land, Massachusetts folk could more easily abandon the security offered by their old localities and attach themselves to new and distant towns. When they moved, they ventured far, often hundreds of miles away from the town where their family had been long settled; but many migrants settled in a specific town rather than scattering across the landscape. Massachusetts people often practiced what David Jaffe has aptly called "serial town settlement," the repeated recreation of town political economies in distant places with new resources.[43]

Massachusetts men were long-distance, not short-distance, movers. Many stayed in their towns of birth, married people from the locality, and had children there. In most Massachusetts towns studied, marriages between natives produced well over half of the children born there. At the same time, the analysis also shows that Massachusetts men moved often after marriage. Figure 4 compares the contributions of different types of marriage to the natural growth of population of Scituate. Marriages between two people who had been born in Scituate produced more children than other types of marriage, and men born outside of Scituate fathered few of the children born there. However, the modal number of children produced by these native marriages was only two. The data for Watertown and other towns reveals the same phenomenon. Marriages between town-born people made the greatest

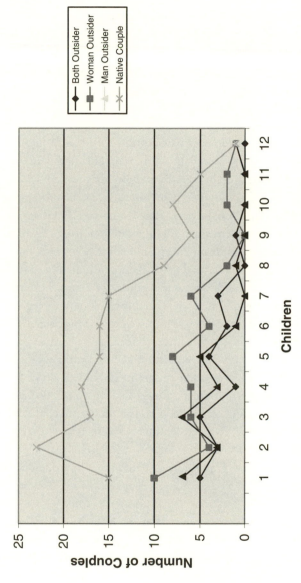

Figure 4. Number of children born to native, male stranger, female stranger, and male and female stranger couples in Scituate, 1650–1790. Source: Scituate Vital Records.

contribution to the natural increase of the population in the locality, but the numbers remained small; the modal Watertown marriage produced only two or three children. The death of a parent accounts for the truncated childbearing of some couples, but the major explanation was simply that after a time many married couples with children left their native town. This was a common experience.

Where did they go? A definitive answer would require tracing families over generations from one locality to another across New England, but there is good evidence to show that they went from long-settled towns near the coast to newly founded towns in central Massachusetts and northern New England. Upland areas in Worcester County and New Hampshire, Vermont, and Maine all grew rapidly, especially after 1760. This dramatic population increase was fueled almost exclusively by people from settled Massachusetts towns. As Bernard Bailyn has shown in his Pulitzer Prize–winning book, *Voyagers to the West*, "the New England borderland was flung outward in an enormous expansion of settlement. . . . The number of towns founded annually in New England tripled, from an average of six per year before 1760 to eighteen per year after 1760—a total of 283 between 1760 and 1776, as some 20,000 migrants moved north across the border of Massachusetts." Rapid territorial expansion also occurred in other North American regions as the threat of French and Indian power was removed by the protracted and extensive warfare of the mid-eighteenth century. However, the expansion of New England had little or nothing to do with the British migration Bailyn so thoroughly studied. Among the 9,364 emigrants he studied who left England between 1760 and the Revolution, he found that only seventy-seven settled in New England, extending to this period the finding that after the mid-seventeenth century New England tended to discourage English immigrants.[44] Nor did many German or French immigrants participate in the rapid development of New Hampshire and Maine. The expansion of New England was accomplished by the sons and daughters of settled New England families.

Local studies show the same trend. Many people whose families had long been resident in Scituate moved to Maine. In 1755 David Bryant, son of an old Scituate family, married Lydia Cudworth, who was born in Freetown, Massachusetts, about fifty miles away. After having one child in Scituate in 1758, they moved 193 miles to Bristol, Maine, where David died in 1778. Lydia then moved nine more miles to Nobleboro, Maine, where she died in 1806. Such long-distance moves were typical. Maine sources show that many founding families and later migrants came from Plymouth and Bristol counties in Massachusetts and that these families transplanted the lumbering and shipbuilding economy of places like Scituate to Maine. For example, as the historian William Hutchinson Rowe noted in his account of Yarmouth, between 1730 and 1750 the town was peopled by the Prince, Buxton, Mitchell, Seabury, Baker, Chandler, Winslow, Soule, Harris, Lewis, and York families: "Many, in fact the majority of them, were from the Plymouth colony or had Pilgrim blood in their veins, hailing from such well-known towns as Kingston, Duxbury, Marshfield, and even Plymouth itself." For example, Joseph Chandler, a blacksmith who contributed to the shipbuilding industry in North Yarmouth, came from Duxbury, where his grandfather had arrived from Leiden in 1630. Joseph moved "down east" when he was fifty; he was accompanied by his sons Zechariah, Judah, and Edmund.[45]

An annotated list of 179 people living in about forty families in Castine, Maine, in 1796 shows the significant contribution of people from Massachusetts to one of the district's northernmost towns, located over 250 miles from the border. Among those on the list born before 1770, thirteen of thirty-three had been born in Massachusetts. The rest had been born in Maine or New Hampshire, except for one person from Rhode Island, one from New Brunswick, Canada, and one from Perth, Scotland. Mark and Abigail Hatch moved from the shipbuilding towns of Scituate and Marshfield to Castine. Both were fifty years old in 1796. They had moved north soon after their marriage, for their first child, Mark, was born in Castine in 1771 and they had many more children there. They continued to live in Castine until they died in the 1830s. William Turner, who was thirty-seven in 1796, had come from Pembroke, Massachusetts, a shipbuilding town carved from Scituate.

Several founding families came from Essex County, Massachusetts. Some historians might have counted the Rea family among the strolling poor, but they were more mobile than they were impoverished. Benjamin Rea was born in Beverly in 1751 and married in neighboring Danvers in 1774 to Lydia Putnam. Their first child, Benjamin, was born in Danvers in 1775, but they soon moved sixty miles west to Lunenburg and then Fitchburg in Worcester County, relatively new towns, where they had Hannah in 1778 and John in 1780. The Reas then returned east to Essex County; their daughters Lucy and Nancy were born in Newbury between 1782 and 1784. The family had moved 227 miles northeast to Deer Isle on picturesque Penobscot Bay in Maine by the time their daughter Sally was born in 1786. They then moved twenty miles further north to the town of Penobscot, where they had Polly, Cynthia, and Oliver between 1790 and 1795. Finally they moved ten miles south to Castine, where they had Emma. The Reas moved relatively long distances, rather than milling about like English families. They had ventured at least 383 miles and tried out several new towns before settling in Castine.[46]

Watertown sent many sons and daughters west to Worcester County and north to New Hampshire and Maine. As Henry Bond noted, "descendants from the early settlers of Watertown, are not less numerous in Worcester County. As evidence of this, see the histories of Framingham, Shrewsbury, Worcester, Rutland, and Spencer." Bond's own family provides many good examples of serial town founding as families moved long distances to new towns from one generation to another. Josiah Bond, a justice of the peace in Watertown, had a son named Josiah in 1696. The younger Josiah moved forty-one miles southwest to Sutton in Worcester County; he became a leader in the town, which was incorporated in 1714. His son Henry, born in Sutton in 1741, was an early settler of Royalston, sixty-six miles northwest in Worcester County, which was incorporated in 1765. Henry became a selectman in the new town. About 1785, at age forty-four, he moved fifty-one miles north to Grafton, Vermont, where he became a selectman, town clerk, and justice of the peace. He then moved thirty-five miles north to Shrewsbury, Vermont, and in 1816, at the age of seventy-five, he moved, probably with a child's family, 381 miles west to Genesee County, New York, where he lived until his death in 1828 at the age of eighty-seven. This Henry Bond had lived in five towns and moved 533 miles. The genealogist Henry Bond was born in Watertown. Shortly after his birth, his family moved 173 miles north to Livermore, Maine. Henry's father had purchased land and several mills there and became a deacon of the first church and the town's second schoolmaster before he died at the age of thirty-five. Henry's mother Hannah remarried, and he went to Dartmouth College and became a physician. After living for a while in Philadelphia, he retired to Watertown and became its historian.[47]

These moves had common motives. According to William Bentley, some well-to-do Salem families decided in 1798 to relocate inland in order to avert the premature deaths that maritime careers entailed. Mr. G. Ropes "purchased a farm in Orford, New Hampshire on the Connecticut River." "The nearest route he gives me," noted Bentley, "is the following: from Salem to Topsfield, Haverhill, Plaistow, Hamstead, Chester, Pembroke, Concord, Boscawen, Salisbury, New Chester, Bridgewater, Plymouth, Rumney to Orford and then 7½ miles to the ferry on the Connecticut near Pratt's farm. The whole distance being 137½ miles from Salem." Bentley observed that three Salem families, all of mariners, would be on one farm when Ropes arrived. In 1734, fifty-eight unpretentious Marbleheaders bought land in New Hampshire, forming New Marblehead township (now Windham, Maine), for largely economic reasons.[48]

Many of these moves were focused on the development of the economic resources to be found in new locations. Many farmers who moved north temporarily abandoned commercial farming for subsistence farming, but they quickly developed a vibrant lumbering and shipbuilding economy. In new Maine and New Hampshire towns, the first nonresidential structure, after a garrison house to defend against attacks by the indigenous Abenakis, was often a sawmill. As the historian Charles Clark observed, "lumbering, including the cutting of masts, spars, logs, and firewood, the sawing of boards and timbers, and the 'riving' or 'cleaving' of clapboards and shingles, was a major feature of the economy of all the northern country towns throughout the eighteenth century." The inland towns supported the shipbuilding and the export mast and lumber trade of ports like Portsmouth and Portland. In 1780, a Dr. Calef reported to English authorities that the settlements along Penobscot River and Bay contained "more than 200 saw-mills when the rebellion broke out."[49]

The institution of the town played a key role in this process of economic development. The state government granted or sold land to a group of proprietors who were given a limited time to develop it, attracting a critical mass of new settlers and establishing a church and a school. The town form of political economy worked in the north because it enabled entrepreneurs to recruit a willing and able labor force. Many proprietors implemented the same strategies used previously in Scituate to lure workers and to develop resources: defining a mammoth commons on which settlers were allowed to cut trees at will so long as they used the town sawmill and sold the timber to local shipbuilders. The shipbuilding industry was dependent on rural residents who used their ox teams to move masts and large logs from the forest. Legal settlement in a town was a requirement for participation in the burgeoning lumbering industry. As one New Hampshire town proclaimed, "none but settled inhabitants shall make use of wood or common, nor that no inhabitant shall employ any about wood work but of the settled inhabitants."[50]

The salience of the town's policies and practices regarding settlement and its assertive control and active management of the local economy explain why Massachusetts folk often stayed in one town, ignoring or even disdaining neighboring towns and their citizens, then venturing hundreds of miles into risky territory to settle a new town with their neighbors. This political economy is the only explanation for Massachusetts's paradoxical mobility and immobility, its dance of staying put and then leaping.[51] Settlement policies ensured that the town born received privileged access to resources and employment as well as security in disability or old age; these benefits kept them home. Unless they had a scarce and valuable skill or large amounts of capital, neighboring towns would resist them as intruders and diluters of the town labor pool. Short-distance moves were uncomfortable. Yet they might be welcomed tens or hundreds of miles away by proprietors of new towns, whether or not they or their fathers were among the founders. The new towns could provide them with a settlement, which promised the security and support that a nuclear family and an extended kin group could not. As legally settled inhabitants of a new town, they could ensure that their children would be educated, that they would be entitled to public support in case of misfortune, and that they would have a political say in the future of their new town, including its economic structure. As the primary institution that regulated settlement and economic development, the town did not curtail risk-taking and individualism among middling folk, as some historians have argued, but supported and furthered venturesome undertakings.

Town Localism After the Revolution

Massachusetts sustained the importance of town settlement well after the American Revolution, as evidenced by the state's 1784 state tax assessment. In that year, Massachusetts towns reported individually their total assets. Among them were the "ratable polls" in the town, the "unratable polls supported by the town," and the "unratable polls unsupported by the town."[52] Since about a third of all taxes assessed on a household were paid according to the number of polls it held, polls were counted carefully. The 1784 tax list allows us to assess the degree to which Massachusetts remained a place were men worked chiefly in the town where they had settlement or whether people easily crossed town boundaries to work in other places, as they did in eighteenth-century England and in nineteenth-century America.

To analyze this data, I studied 161 Massachusetts towns with some 53,000 adult males, several of which were in the district of Maine.[53] In 1784, 89 percent of all these men worked in the same town, where they were recognized as legal inhabitants. What is most remarkable is that adherence to a settled workforce is as apparent in many long-settled and economically developed towns as it is in newly founded communities. For example, in Newburyport, Essex County, 95 percent of over nine hundred working men were settled in the town; only fifty-one men who worked in Newburyport were inhabitants elsewhere. Newburyport's economy demanded a considerable amount of labor: officials reported that it had 7,176 tons of vessels. The political exertions of the town meeting ensured that men who were born or accepted as legal inhabitants monopolized employment there. Similarly, Cambridge in Middlesex County had 467 male workers, of whom only twenty-two (5 percent) were outsiders. Aside from Harvard College, whose fellows were "unratable polls supported by the town," the town contained three grist or sawmills, twelve tan or slaughter houses, and seventy-seven shops separate from dwelling houses. It was surrounded by populous towns like Watertown, yet drew few workers from them. Boston was no exception. In 1784, the city reported 393 unsupported polls, but these unsettled workers composed only 12 percent of all the polls and the number of unsupported polls fell in 1786 to only fifty.[54] Clearly, town boundaries continued to mean a great deal even in densely populated, economically developed places. As late as 1784, Massachusetts was a place where belonging to a town was of vital importance.

During the last years of Nathaniel Hawthorne's life, as his biographer Edwin Haviland Miller discovered by reading his wife Sophia's notebooks, "Hawthorne dwelled obsessively on the poorhouse, much to the distress of his vulnerable wife. He informed Ticknor that he expected to 'die in the almshouse'."[55] Though it may be unseemly to dwell on the terrors of impoverishment, old age, and death experienced by a great individualist, it is significant that Hawthorne came to rest on the town and its welfare institutions and expressed a shameful fear that he might need their support. The town and its privileges had sustained and supported Hawthorne's individualism well beyond anything his nuclear family or career could do. As this study of settlement demonstrates, for middling Yankees the town bolstered men's political and economic power and provided them with privileged access to resources as well as a kind of social insurance. Massachusetts people stayed in the same town for generations, then moved hundreds of miles to found new settlements where they would also find support and security. For at least a century and a half, the political economies of New England towns oddly promoted the dignity of common labor by creating virtually autonomous worker enclaves and by so doing, nurtured lively, productive, and expansionist growth.

Figure 5. *The Launching of the Ship Fame,* 1802, oil on canvas, by George Ropes
(1788–1819). In Massachusetts coastal great towns and rural shipbuilding centers, ship
launchings were memorable holidays involving nearly the whole population.
Courtesy of the Peabody Essex Museum, Salem, Massachusetts.

PART II

Development

CHAPTER FOUR

Political Fabric

IN HIS 1654 history of Massachusetts, Edward Johnson boasted that the residents of Rowley "were the first people that set upon making of cloth in this Western World."[1] Although Johnson failed to recognize Native American weaving, which utilized a variety of local materials and flourished well before European contact, his declaration's ethnocentrism is intentional. The colonists were willing to eat maize as the natives did, but refused to dress like them. To maintain their identity, they needed to wear European cloth. Many historians have written well about the importance of fashion in creating colonial identities.[2] However, in the case of Massachusetts' identity, cloth production was arguably more important than cloth consumption or fashion—making mattered more than wearing. In order to create the cloth they needed, Massachusetts people applied the politics of reformed godly towns in England to the problem of a severe cloth shortage and the mobilization of labor. Because they succeeded, they created not just an abundance of sheep and textiles or enough self-made cloth to continue their identities as Europeans but also a new and dangerous political identity as an independent, distinctive, and equitable people within the English empire.

In some sense, cloth manufacture in Massachusetts was an unsurprising development. New England immigrants came largely from textile-producing districts. Indeed, as one historian discovered, a quarter of all adult males who came to New England between 1620 and 1640 possessed specific cloth-making skills.[3] Nevertheless, for about a decade, New Englanders allowed their textile skills to remain dormant. So long as Charles I and Archbishop Laud continued to dismiss Puritan ministers and interrupt urban reform movements in England's great textile towns and districts, colonists with textile skills in America had little reason to use their cards, wheels, and looms. Each year, increasing numbers of wealthy Puritans from the English textile districts departed for New England, carrying much of their wealth in cloth. Colonists sold food and livestock to the newcomers, often in exchange for fabric. So much cloth circulated in the colony that well-paid workers' sumptuous attire provoked special legislation to stop servants and laborers from dressing in velvet gowns and silk ribbons and parading like lords and ladies through Boston.[4]

Some colonial leaders, to be sure, worried about the economic as well as moral perils of exchanging English cloth for American food and livestock. Writing from London in 1636, John Winthrop's sister Lucy Downing warned her brother that she might not emigrate because the land seemed economically unproductive and overly dependent on the newcomers' money and fabric.[5] Later that year, John White of Dorchester wrote to Winthrop about the colony's trade imbalance, especially its overpriced cloth: "I have often heard at what hard rates necessaries, for clothing especially, have been sold amongst you for which I confess I have been much grieved as that which I am certain will consume you by degrees." White urged Winthrop to create a monopoly in England for the sale of cloth among New England sympathizers in order to secure lower prices. He recommended the development of fishing to furnish a salable international commodity and insisted stricter discipline be imposed on New England's workers, especially children. Although a resourceful and daring economic reformer, White failed to imagine the colony becoming a significant producer of European textiles.[6]

While a demand for cloth and textile skills existed in Massachusetts, White understood that market dynamics could not by themselves organize these assets into a viable industry. Early modern textile production was complex and extensive, involving many commodities and skilled people in intricate networks. New England lacked many of the essential ingredients of the English industry, including capital and a strong medium of exchange. Most important, New England lacked a surplus labor pool. In England, textile producers or clothiers employed skilled smallholders and landless men and women to produce goods profitably. Economic necessity made these workers willing, obedient, and cheap.[7] In New England, by contrast, the potential laborers or their households had land, and there were relatively few workers for all there was to do. Women and children might spin and tend sheep, but they were scattered under the rule of individual fathers and husbands, and the English did not customarily overwork children. How could women and children be mobilized, if the household was the major economic and political unit, if the household rule of fathers was sacrosanct, and, if capital was lacking? In order to make enough cloth, New England required more than an "invisible hand" to produce an important textile industry: it required the political will and ability—a visible hand with a stick—to muster the settlers and the new land to produce cloth. The political economy of the towns provided an answer.

The Cloth Emergency

The cloth emergency came quickly. By the spring of 1639, the flow of immigrants fell off drastically as the English regime's anti-Puritan policies began to falter. The minister Hugh Peters urged that New Englanders be set to producing their own textiles to substitute for imports and as a way of employing idle hands in the winter: "Once again I say we must look out, we want necessary linen . . . and a voyage to the West Indies would find us winter work in cotton, etc."[8] More politicians heeded Peters's remarks as immigrants and their fabric grew even scarcer. Once the Long Parliament in England was convened in 1640, reformers were on the ascendancy, and the Commonwealth and Civil War preoccupied fervent English Protestants until 1660. In England, Puritans turned toward remodeling their own towns and cities on godly lines. "This caused all men to stay in England in expectation of a new world," wrote John Winthrop in his journal, "so as few coming to us, all foreign commodities grew scarce, and our own of no price."[9]

In the absence of new settlers arriving with cloth in hand, the shortages quickly grew painful. Reflecting the sudden stoppage of immigrants and their wealth after the Civil War began, Edward Brown of Ipswich wrote to England in 1644: "We have no want of food, though not the fullness which is with you in East Cheap (London), but we are short of clothing having had little supply for a long time and many to clothe."[10] Court records from the mid-seventeenth century indicate a sudden hoarding of cloth. In 1652, John Bourne and his wife in Salem, tailors, were fined treble restitution and forced to make a public acknowledgment for "concealing some pieces of cloth, stuff, and thread committed to them and converting them to their own use."[11] Their crime involved saving the scraps from clothing commissioned by others and making an ungainly garment from them. Servants had difficulty getting clothes at all.[12] In 1645, the preface to one of the Massachusetts acts intended to rectify the cloth shortage stated that "through the want of woolen cloths and stuffs, many poor people have suffered much cold and hardship to the impairing of some of their health and the hazarding of some of their lives." Poorer New Englanders huddled dangerously close to their hearths. The General Court reported that "such who have been able to provide for their children clothing of cotton cloth (not being able to get other) have . . . had some of their children much scorched with fire, yea, divers burnt to death."[13]

The emergency most affected the poorest and weakest citizens and therefore by Christian ethics required an immediate and effective remedy. As Winthrop put it, "these straits set our people on work to provide fish, clapboards, plank, etc., and to sow hemp and flax (which prospered very well) and to look out to the West Indies for a trade for cotton."[14] The fish, clapboards, and plank were developed as commodities to sell abroad, while the wool, hemp, flax, and imported cotton were used to make cloth for local consumption, especially to clothe the poor. Both campaigns required vigorous political action.

Public Policy Mandating Textile Production

Colonists with no way of obtaining English cloth adopted a plan to make their own and much of it involved coercion. New Englanders used the relatively democratic town and governmental structure to mandate and gain cooperation and obedience for reformed land and labor use. Making European textiles in the new world was largely a political achievement.

Between 1640 and 1660, the Massachusetts General Court passed a series of orders and sent them to the towns for implementation. These acts organized and limited land use to ensure textile production and also legitimated, encouraged, and often mandated, whatever individual fathers might think, textile work among women and children. Many of the colonists had faced similar economic emergencies in England such as bad harvests and social emergencies such as plagues and they had used the power of the magistrate to gain remedies. As the political and economic demand for textiles rose, entrepreneurs and skilled workers not only responded to town orders but acted to produce cloth on their own initiative in accord with explicit public policy.

The linen cloth and cotton blends became scarce first and were the initial focus of the government's campaign for production. Linen cloth was less sturdy than woolen cloth and decayed more rapidly after prolonged wearing. A vegetable fiber derived from hemp and flax, linen came in many weights and weaves. Household fabrics lumped together as "linens" varied widely in quality and function. Loosely woven strainer or cheesecloth, pudding bags, and flour sacks were essential in the kitchen. Linen yarn woven in a diaper pattern became table linen or toweling, while fancy weavers turned out table-cloths and napkins. Finer linen yarns were woven into sheets, pillow covers, and aprons. Rough tow yarns, woven densely, became sail canvases, bed ticking, and mattress covers. When combined with cotton, linen was an important component in the clothing worn closest to the skin. In a typical seventeenth-century inventory, men's shirts, women's shifts, and other sorts of "wearing linging" were often linen and cotton blends. Workers in the fields and at the forge especially needed this cloth.

Provincial and local governments took legislative action to spur linen production and ordered the towns to oversee the production of raw materials and survey the availability of skilled labor. The orders were simple and direct. In 1639, a Plymouth Colony order decreed, "every household within the government shall sow one rod of ground square at least with hemp or flax yearly, and some one in every town to be appointed to see the same done."[15] A year later, the Massachusetts General Court sent a similar order to its towns and requested local officials to make a survey of the available resources: "The Court taking into serious consideration the absolute necessity for the raising of the manufacture of linen cloth, etc. . . . doth require the magistrates and deputies of the several towns to acquaint the townsmen therewith and to make inquiry . . . what men and women are skillful in the braking, spinning, weaving; what means for the providing of wheels; and to consider with those skillful in that manufacture, and what course may be taken for teaching boys and girls in all towns the spinning of yarn; and to return to the next Court their several and joint advise about this thing."[16] Initiative came from the towns as well. Ipswich selectmen anticipated this proclamation by appointing a "committee for the furthering of trade" that compiled a report on house-hold production of hemp and flax.[17] The whole campaign was the act of a relatively democratic state and was initiated when the towns heard the pain of the poor.

Showing responsiveness to governmental fiats, New Englanders quickly developed a market for imported raw cotton. Cotton had been recently taken up as a textile fiber by English manufacturers. Planters in Barbados were growing excellent "sea island" (long-staple) cotton, and New Englanders' first commercial connection with the West Indies, which later became the region's major trading partner, tellingly involved the purchase of cotton for government-mandated textile manufacturing. Fustians and dimities were the most common types of cotton cloth. Fustians were heavy and tightly woven and could serve as durable outerwear, especially in the summer months when worsted wool outerwear was unbearable.[18] Dimities could be more finely woven and were often patterned or decorated; they were suitable for lining breeches and for men's waistcoats and women's petticoats. Undergarments, or "small clothes"—shifts, chemises, and drawers—could easily be rinsed out and dried, even in the winter months. When used as a liner or undergarment, the softer hand of the cotton fabric made heavy woolen twills almost painless to wear.[19]

Within about a decade of the onset of the political campaign, New England merchants imported tons of cotton from the Caribbean. The 1659 inventory of Mahalaleel Munnings's Boston warehouse shows that this merchant had obtained nine bags of raw cotton weighing nearly a ton.[20] George Curwin, a prosperous Salem merchant, had overseas connections that regularly brought in West Indian cotton. He tallied up more than a ton brought from the West Indies by his own ships over two seasons' voyages. In three account books spanning the years 1652 to 1662, Curwin entered the dispersal of raw cotton to his customers almost daily. He sold two or three bags of raw cotton each year, roughly six hundred to eight hundred pounds. His 1655–1657 ledgers debited nearly a dozen customers for regular purchases of "cotton wool." Most households purchased an average of twenty pounds of cotton each year, usually in the winter months. The seasonal cycle of farm chores influenced the production of textiles even when the fibers were available throughout the year.[21]

Scattered throughout seventeenth- and eighteenth-century account books and daybooks kept by farmers and local merchants are records of the myriad transactions that moved cotton from the docks into the homes of textile producers. Joshua Buffum, a Salem merchant, consistently debited cotton wool, generally between ten and twenty pounds at a time, to his customers' accounts. He sometimes credited accounts with cotton thread presented as payment. For example, Josiah Walcott's account reveals an active manufacturing household that produced several hundred pounds of spun thread and eighty-five yards of woven fabric in the years between 1688 and 1700. Interspersed with Wolcott's purchases of sugar and other household staples were the pounds of raw cotton that undoubtedly returned to Buffum's establishment as spun thread and woven cloth.[22]

State Supervision of the Sheep on the Commons

Also in the seventeenth century, the Massachusetts General Court and the towns began to order and organize sheep raising for the production of wool, a heavier fabric needed in New England's brutal winters. A 1645 order urged that the colony's flocks be bred carefully and that more sheep be brought from England.[23] Over more than twenty years, public policy imposed restrictions as well as incentives and mandates to promote wool production. In 1654, the Court set limits on slaughtering lambs for food and ordered a moratorium on the export of breeding animals.[24] The regulation of sheep sales outside of the colony was a necessary intervention against market freedom; New Englanders were attracted by the high prices paid for sheep in the Caribbean colonies as well as the mid-Atlantic region.[25] In order to promote the growth of flocks, Massachusetts fostered the presence of sheep on commons alongside cattle. Sheep were protected from poaching and predators: anyone who drove others' sheep from a commons "or otherwise molest such sheep" was fined. The General Court also ordered that if a dog attacked a sheep, the dog's owner had to either hang the dog or pay double damages for the attack, and after a second offense the owner had to hang his dog without delay.[26]

The Massachusetts General Court asked towns to favor sheep raising, which often required the reorganization and careful town management of grazing land. The legislature issued regular proclamations covering the division and use of pastures from the 1630s on, but these orders increased in frequency and detail after the cloth crisis hit. Towns were directed to allow liberal use of the commons by freemen developing flocks. Each order repeated a standard rationale emphasizing that cloth was essential to the continued success of the colony, the divine demand to care for the poor, the unreliability of importation, and the financial burdens that paying for imported cloth placed on the immature economy.[27]

The General Court issued its orders to the towns, so the practices that local officials adopted to implement colony-wide policies can be observed in the records kept by town meetings and selectmen. This partnership between General Court and towns was a key to successful Massachusetts textile production. Ipswich introduced a town order by saying, "Whereas the General

Court hath left it in the selectmen of every town to make orders for the clearing of the commons for the better keeping of sheep."[28] As a rule, town selectmen established the guidelines and allotments of town grazing, but always within the broad rules made by Massachusetts Bay.

Since the towns implemented colonial authorities' pronouncements, they could adjust orders serving the larger interests of the colony to their particular circumstances. All towns did not have equal access to common grazing land, and economic priorities varied. In coastal towns, sheep thrived on islands or small grassy peninsulas. These grazing lands required little fencing or protection from wolves or thieves, but their capacity was limited. After the first two decades, as their herds and flocks multiplied, many coastal towns found themselves with grazing management problems that required political intervention. The minutes of the Ipswich selectmen from 1634 to 1662 reveal the problems faced by the leaders of one of the larger coastal towns and their imaginative, if intrusive, political solutions. Although sheep were owned by individuals, Ipswich households regularly pastured their sheep as a single flock for much of the year. Most of the town's common lands were made available for grazing from March to November. Sheep were the first to move out to common pastures because they did not damage the tender spring sod; the heavy bodies of the larger animals such as cows, horses, and oxen made deep tracks and wreaked havoc in the soggy meadows. In the fall, sheep were the last grazers to leave the common because they could glean sustenance from the dying fields longer than the larger foragers. Families kept their own flocks on their home lots through the early spring lambing period, but then released their flocks for long gatherings on the commons.

Originally, in order to free town folk for other essential work, Ipswich selectmen hired one or two herdsmen to take the entire town's livestock out to the commons each day between April and November. Sheep, goats, and cows intermingled promiscuously in a "great Herd." All the grazing animals had similar needs for fresh water and grassy meadows. William Fellows, the herdsman engaged by Ipswich in January 1639, moved from house lot to house lot in the early spring collecting animals into a comic parade bound for Jeffries Neck, the first town commons. In the misty morning just a half-hour after sunrise, Fellows would drive the animals out, perhaps with the help of his dog and a child. Once out on the Neck, Fellows closed the gate constructed by order of the town across the narrow strip of land connecting it to the mainland. Throughout the day, he and his team guarded the herd against attack by stray dogs, wolves, or other predators but, more important, they prevented the grazing animals from wandering back, pushing through the gate and laying waste to town gardens and fields. At the end of the day, "not before half an hour before sunset," the herd paraded back, each animal probably turning without prompting at the correct home gate. For their pains, Fellows and the other herdsmen who were hired over the years were paid in corn and grain, and received free use of a town farm. They were fined if the herd wandered and damaged property while under their care. Fellows, one of the town's sheep shearers, must have been a competent herdsman, since no mention of his paying fines was recorded in the Ipswich meetings through the period of his tenure.[29]

Thanks to wise and intrusive government and local political involvement, the Ipswich livestock population quadrupled in less than fifteen years. With such an enormous increase, the town's original common grazing land was no longer adequate, so the selectmen divided the "great herd" and assigned them to separate grazing lands. By 1654, Jeffries Neck was so overgrazed that the selectmen allowed only the sheep flock to pasture there. Four years later, the town divided the flock and hired the family of John Payne, living on Jeffries Neck, to provide a fold and care for half of the town's sheep. Thomas Manning was contracted to oversee the rest of the flock on a new common cleared on the north side of the river.[30] Under continued pressure from the expanding livestock population, selectmen used their governmental power to extend the town's pasturage and to regulate the commons already in use. They facilitated development of new common pasture by requiring labor from each householder with a claim to common rights: "the Selectmen of this Town doth order that [of] the Inhabitants of this town one able person of a family shall work one day in May or June as they shall be ordered according to the several divisions of the town upon a day's warning."[31] The Ipswich selectmen exercised power to stay one step ahead of their prolific animal population.

Individual livestock owners had to work with the town. Access to pasturage was carefully guarded by the town government, which regularly limited individuals' use of the town's resources, especially the common pastures. For example, a freeman who possessed a claim to common grazing was not able to put all of his animals willy-nilly out to graze on town-managed land. Animals other than cows were regulated using a "cow standard" (known as "gates") and were pastured accordingly: two horses to one cow, five sheep to one cow, and so on.[32] Each commonage right was measured by the number of cows the commons could accommodate and was clearly delineated by the holder's social and economic standing in the local hierarchy. Proprietors, who were part of the original town grant, enjoyed the best and largest portions of common rights, while freemen of inferior status, latecomers who could vote and were inhabitants, were entitled to much less. Strangers were politically excluded altogether. Commonage rights most often accompanied the ownership of certain land divisions, but could be devolved upon children independently.

A Rowley farmer, Francis Lambert, kept his "gates" and acreage together when he made his will in 1648.[33] Leaving the bulk of his estate to his eldest son, John, Lambert provided a small gift for his other sons out of the profits from their brother's share. The rest of the children received movables and cash payments, but no land or common rights.[34] Nineteen years later, John Lambert died leaving his wife and two young children. In his will, proved in 1667, Lambert assigned his father's commonages equally between his children, Abigail and John. He passed the common rights (which were essentially political rights or privileges valued separately from acreage) to the children as part of their inheritance. When her mother died in 1681, Abigail Lambert became a homeless minor as well as heiress to £4 of commonage in Rowley through her father. She became the ward of her paternal uncle, Thomas Lambert. Although Thomas had never received commonage from his father, he obtained at least temporary control over the political "rights of pasture" through his niece.[35]

Another Rowley family, the Stickneys, acquired additional common rights by leasing them from the town. Entering into a lease agreement with the town in 1662, William Stickney and his son, Samuel, agreed to pay rent and to lay "dung" on land belonging to the church each year. Left to Rowley's church by the first minister, Ezekiel Rogers, the land served to defray the cost of maintaining the ministry.[36] The new pasture increased the Stickney holdings by at least eight acres. The elder Stickney died three years into the lease and left his son in control of the lease as well as his inherited commonages.[37]

Those who owned more commonages than they could use for their own animals traded, sold, or rented them to town freemen who needed them. These transactions were limited to town members only, allowing the selectmen to retain control of who used town resources and to what purpose. Town fathers seldom allowed animals from other towns, even if sponsored by a resident, to forage on their common land.[38] Yet as flocks and herds grew, the pressure for adequate pasture spawned many creative arrangements to

meet farmers' needs. One industrious Ipswich freeman, Robert Lord, capitalized on his position to solve the town's lack of pasture in an unusual way.
Lord served the public community in many capacities: as an Ipswich selectman in the 1650s, clerk to the Essex County Quarterly Court, marshal, and
town gravedigger. In 1650, he petitioned the Ipswich town meeting for control of the grass growing on the burying ground. As gravedigger, Lord felt he
had the greatest claim on that land, and subsequently the town agreed. "As
long as he continues to be employed in burying the dead," the grass was his
to use or rent, but only as long as large animals such as cows or oxen did not
desecrate the graves of the departed citizens of Ipswich.[39] As a result, some of
the burgeoning sheep flocks for the new textile industry made use of the rich
graveyard pasture. Succeeding with sheep and textiles required political savvy
and involvement.

Selectmen in the coastal town of Marblehead experienced even more
difficulties obtaining and developing adequate pasture for textile production.
Located on a rocky peninsula, Marblehead had limited meadowland available
from the beginning. By 1653, a group of Marblehead freemen complained
that the common pasture available was inadequate to the town's needs. Responsive to their constituents, town selectmen agreed. However, since there
was no additional land to improve, the selectmen decided to purchase common rights from a neighboring town on behalf of forty-four families.[40] Facing
a similar shortage, Salem town residents wrangled over restricted access to
pasturage on Winter Island.[41]

For inland towns, town fathers managed grazing for sheep by deciding
what land should be cleared and how it would be divided. Lacking isolated
islands or protected peninsulas, inland towns focused on protection and control of flocks. The need for pastures arose partly from the growth of the
textile industry and partly from the utility and versatility of the animals.
Inland towns used sheep to mend "poor land" by folding them on rough
areas where they consumed the briars, weeds, and "mangy grass." In addition
to removing the coarse vegetation and noxious weeds, their manure prepared
the soil for the cultivation of good English hay.[42] Due to the high nitrogen
content of their manure, sheep could be also used to quickly revitalize ex-
hausted or marginal soils. A contemporary observer, Sarah Knight, detailed a
Connecticut town's use of their collective sheep flock as a means to improve
land as well as produce wool for local spinners and weavers. On December
23, 1694, Knight noted that the people of Fairfield "have an abundance of
sheep, whose very dung brings them great gain; with part of which they pay

their parson's salary and they grudge that, preferring their dung before their minister. They let out their sheep so much as they agree upon for a night; the highest bidder always carries them, and they will sufficiently dung a large quantity of land before morning."[43] By melding them in unusual ways, Fairfield imaginatively solved two political obligations: the maintenance of a minister of God and the promotion of sheep and wool.

In addition to supervision and regulation of livestock pasturage, selectmen even indelicately intruded into the reproduction of the colony's flocks. Initially, rams, wethers (castrated males), adult ewes, and lambs were kept together year round except for the period when individual owners folded the animals on their home lots. As town flocks expanded, management of the pregnant ewes, yearling lambs, and rank rams required more complicated and collective arrangements. In a large promiscuous flock, individual owners could not know when—or if—their ewes had been bred. In turn, they could not accurately predict when their ewes would lamb. As lambing became more erratic, losses were more frequent. When William Fellows had first watched over the "great herd," he probably could observe and inform townsmen when breeding activity occurred. Once flocks began to number in the hundreds and then in the thousands, this was no longer possible. Beginning in 1659, Ipswich selectmen took control of the flocks' breeding habits. Their first efforts focused on better husbandry; they established and enforced a prohibition on rams running with the ewes until "a convenient season" for breeding.[44] This was smart management. Lambs born too early risked freezing in the late winter cold; those who survived had to be fed precious stocks of hay if they were weaned before spring grass became available. Lambs born too late in the spring continued to nurse after the time the flocks should be culled and separated. Late lambs also prevented farmers from washing and shearing at the optimal time. Lambing out of season disrupted the breeding cycle by delaying ewes' recovery from their pregnancies. The removal of rams allowed the town to preserve a balance in their flock's reproductive cycle and in their seasonal labor requirements as well.

Forcing Labor

With land devoted to flax and hemp and carefully regulated new pastures for grazing sheep established and managed, the Massachusetts General Court and the towns forced an already preoccupied people to make cloth. At first the legislature established a system of bounties to encourage textile production, paying three pence for every shilling's worth of fabric produced in the colony: "the cloth must be made within the jurisdiction and the yarn here spun also, and of such materials as shall be also raised within the same, or else of cotton."[45] These incentives encouraged workers to learn the requisite skills, individuals to invest in equipment, and potential employers to network for sources of fibers. The General Court paid incentives for only a little more than a year, however. Colonists produced so much cloth that taxpayers complained and the subsidy was ended.[46] A considerable number of individuals claimed sizeable bounties. For example, John Whitredge, an Ipswich neighbor of Edward Browne, collected payment for the manufacture of over eighty yards of fabric in 1647.[47]

When bounties proved too expensive to stimulate textile production on the scale the colony required, the General Court hardly ceased intervention in the economy. Instead, they turned to a cheaper means: coercion. In England, towns often forced the poor to produce textiles, but it was unusual to make such demands on middling households.[48] In 1642, as part of an act to get children to do more work, the legislature ordered selectmen to divide towns into families and provide overseers to watch children and guide each group of families in their work. The supervisors or labor overseers were instructed to ignore the prerogatives of household heads and make certain that children who were assigned to tend animals develop "some other employment as spinning upon the rock, knitting, weaving tape." Selectmen were told to take measures so that "a sufficient quantity of materials, as hemp, flax, and etc. may be raised in their towns and tools and implements provided for working out the same."[49] Then in 1656, in order to improve "as many hands as may be in spinning wool, cotton, flax, etc.," the legislature ordered that "all hands not necessarily employed on other occasions, as women, girls, and boys, shall and hereby are enjoined to spin according to their skill and ability; and that the select men in every town do consider the condition and capacity of every family, and accordingly assess them at one or more spinners." A given amount of yarn was assigned as a quota for each "spinner."[50] Essentially the General Court turned the whole colony into a Bridewell and intruded into every household, demanding that households that could spin do so or be fined.

Towns took the draconian new law seriously. The law sparked heated discussion in Salem. William Titcomb, the moderator of the meeting, spoke out against the ordinance and even claimed that its existence was only a

TABLE 2. SUMMARY OF THE 1656 IPSWICH SELECTMEN'S REPORT ON POTENTIAL
SPINNING AND YARN PRODUCTION PER YEAR

	Number of households	Percentage of households	Yearly production (weight in pounds)
A whole spinner[a]	11	14	990.0
Three-quarter spinner	9	12	607.5
One-half spinner	43	55	1,935.0
One-quarter spinner	15	19	337.5
Total households	78	100	3,870.0

[a] The assessors did not define criteria for "whole spinner," presumably an able adult with much time to devote to spinning.

Source: Ipswich Town Records, Phillips Library, Peabody Essex Museum.

rumor. Titcomb agreed there had been "much agitation" about a "spinning law" at the General Court, but denied that any such severe ordinance actually passed. After the meeting, the debate resumed at a local ordinary, where Titcomb again denied the existence of the law. Then several weavers, perhaps wanting more yarn squeezed from a coerced labor population, complained to authorities that Titcomb encouraged people to ignore the new policy. When this charge surfaced at the next town meeting, the selectmen settled the issue by fining the meeting moderator Titcomb for "lying" at a public meeting.[51]

In Ipswich, however, the leaders of town meeting applied the law enthusiastically, directing each selectman to conduct a census of textile-producing capacity in a designated section of the town. Within the divisions created by the selectmen's census, they assigned each household a production quota and compiled a town plan. Here was politically charged command and control management in the town setting at its innovative and coercive height. The Ipswich selectmen reckoned that seventy-eight resident families could produce textiles; moreover, better than half of those had the ability, time, and resources, they figured, to produce about fifty pounds of yarn a year. In their educated opinion, the selectmen projected that Ipswich could produce 3,870 pounds of finished yarn per year, or about 250 yards of fabric per year per house (Table 2).

Presumably, the selectmen assessed each household based on accepted norms, availability of tools, and individual laborers in the household, as well as their amount of spare time from other essential work. They did not allow for the right of any household to refuse participation. Spinning was defined as the work of women and children, a supposedly underused labor resource.

Under the plan of the Ipswich town fathers and by decree of the Massachusetts General Court, these women and children became part of the mandated production team irrespective of the desires of the head of household or the workers' own inclinations. Public intervention into the affairs of families was common policy in Massachusetts. In this instance, the selectmen's projected annual production not only satisfied the clothing needs of the producing households but guaranteed a surplus available to the local market.[52]

In Cambridge, the selectmen also appointed a committee "to execute the order of the General Court for the improvement of all the families within the limits of this town in spinning and clothing and each of the said persons are to see to the execution of the said order in their respective quarters of the town,"[53] but did not record whether these supervisors computed production quotas. In nearby Watertown, the selectmen aggressively rearranged one household to maintain textile production as well as to restore the peace, illustrating the close kinship that Puritans posited between industriousness and orderly domesticity. In 1656, town officials intervened in the troubled, violent household of John and Elizabeth Ball, cloth workers. They removed some of the Balls' children to the homes of other weavers and tailors and allowed the couple to separate, an unusual step in colonial Massachusetts. They told Elizabeth Ball, "it is the mind of the selectmen that she set herself to the carding of two skeins of cotton or sheep's wool and her daughter to spin it, with other business of the family and this to be her daily task, the which if she refuse she must expect to be sent to the house of correction."[54] In order to add to textile production, this anguished, mentally unstable, and periodically violent woman (who had physically threatened her husband with a knife) was ordered to work in her own household or be forced to work while in confinement.

With a legal and political system favoring sheep, flax, and cloth production, some towns used public resources to lure weavers. Competition for skilled artisans was sharp during the politically led cloth revival. In 1656, the inland town of Chelmsford admitted William Howe as a free inhabitant and granted him twenty-four acres of meadow "provided he set up his trade of weaving and performed the town's work."[55] In Ipswich, the town granted not only land but building supplies to weavers. In 1671, the town gave James Sawyer, one of at least three resident weavers, the right to fell enough trees from the common to build a little shop for his looms next to his home.[56] The town regularly granted two other weavers, Thomas Lull and Nathaniel

Fuller, the right to fell pine trees from the town's common in amounts that equaled the claims of "ancient" commoners.[57]

The Fruits of Political Economy

Did these public policies, with their incentives, family intrusions, and coercive requirements, stimulate New Englanders to produce an adequate supply of textiles? Determining the volume of textiles produced in New England as a result of the government's interventions is a difficult and complex undertaking. The colonial industry was dispersed rather than concentrated. Domestic cloth production was visible to contemporary observers in nearly every part of New England's physical and social landscape. Textile production required an elaborate infrastructure, including networks between households with a variety of resources and skills: sheep raisers and shearers, wool combers and carders, spinners, weavers, and fullers.

In order for textile production to be anywhere in New England, it had to be everywhere. Domestic cloth production became visible to contemporary observers throughout the region's physical and social landscape. On farms, shepherds cared for their flocks and women harvested flax and hemp. Fiber processing began in barns and lofts. In the garrets and great rooms, families stored distaffs laden with fine blond flax strands and baskets filled to overflowing with cotton and wool rolls until they could be spun into yarn. Housewives, their servants, and their daughters turned and treadled their spinning wheels in their dooryards or inside their great halls in colder weather. Along Boston's and Salem's docks, carters moved large bags of sea island cotton into warehouses, and wagons moved the cotton into the interior for production. In shops and garret rooms weavers worked huck-a-buck and diaper designs into cloth, surrounded by their wives and children winding quills and preparing new warps. Along the banks of New England's rivers, mill wheels chattered and turned the machinery inside the braking and fulling mills of the cloth dressers.

In an effort to estimate production, historians have counted textile-related tools in inventories. This method is misleading, for rural inventories record the possessions and products of old people. In rural New England, decedents averaged seventy years of age. Looms were portable and easily moved from the arthritic to more nimble kin. In the city of Boston, the opposite problem presents itself: the dead were often young men, sailors or sea captains who died before reaching thirty. Their bachelor lives suppress the share in the sample of households with women, children, and textile production.[58]

At the same time, many contemporary observers highlighted the unexpected achievement of New England cloth output and provide witnesses and numbers to prove that the politically charged initiative was a success. It so thrived that it permanently identified Massachusetts and other New England colonies as highly problematic political entities in the British Empire. Thomas Banister, a Boston merchant, summarized the region's achievement in a 1715 essay: "we have a very considerable manufactory already established in New England, begun in great scarcity and dearness of goods" that "put them on making buttons, stuffs, kerseys, linsey-woolseys, flannels, and etc which has decreased the importation of those provinces above £50,000 per annum."[59] Indeed, in the early eighteenth century, the English guardians of the empire grew alarmed by New England's unexpected textile productivity.

For one, English custom collectors, part of whose job was to make colonists into consumers of English cloth, counted a disturbing number of sheep. In 1718 Archibald Cummings wrote to the Board of Trade and Plantations that "there may be 100,000 weight of wool annually in this province [Massachusetts] and Rhode Island but difficult to know the exact quantity." He noted that Nantucket held 10,000 sheep alone.[60] The next year he doubled the estimate to 200,000 weight of wool annually and advised that the English draw off the wool by offering a bounty to English importers. He enclosed "a sample of wool of the country" in order to demonstrate what fine stuff it was.[61] In the same year Mr. Bridger witnessed 20,000 sheep on Nantucket and added, "it is the same at Rhode Island which breeds many thousand sheep upon Block Island about five leagues from them. Many thousands more and in the Narragansett country more yet."[62] When New Englanders tried to ship the wool by water from pasture to cloth producer, the custom officers attempted to seize it, but found that local courts blocked them.[63] Yankee juries always sided with the local smugglers and farmers.

The collectors observed that although some of this wool clip was exported to France, "the most part of it is here manufactured into shalloons, serges, stuffs, druggets, and kerseys and here consumed."[64] The custom collectors and government officials agreed that New Englanders produced enough cloth for their own needs, that they made more each year, that an infrastructure for textiles production had been developed, and that imported English fabric, despite the cold climate, was selling poorly in the region.

In 1709, Governor Joseph Dudley wrote from Boston to the Council of Trade, "I must add that the woolen trade from England is also in great measure abated, the people here clothing themselves with their own wool." Because of the vigor of the domestic Massachusetts textile industry, he predicted "the trade for the [English] woolen manufactory will every year grow less, though the people increase to a very great degree."[65] In 1719, a custom officer, Mr. Bridger, reported from Boston that "I cannot omit giving your honor an account of the growth of the woolen manufacture in this province in a great many sorts, as cloths, serges, shaloons, kerseys, all sorts of stuffs almost, and some linen, and there is scarce a country man comes to town or woman but are clothed [in their] own spinning." To make matters worse, noted Bridger, the cloth industry was a darling of the Massachusetts government and people: "every one encourages the growth and manufacture of this country, and not one person but discourages the trade from home, and says tis a pity any goods should be brought from England, they can live without."[66] In Portsmouth, New Hampshire, in 1720, the custom collector, Mr. Armstrong, reported that the northern New Englanders bought most of their textiles from southern New Englanders whose "woolen manufactory . . . they have now brought to great perfection both as to goodness and quantity, several thousand pounds worth of stuffs and druggets made in several colonies are sold in the shop at Boston."[67]

From the English point of view, the vigor of the Massachusetts textile industry was a striking and ugly development that seemed to defeat the very purpose of having colonies. Everyone in England expected that the colonies would produce and process New World commodities and send them to England for sale or re-exportation in exchange for English cloth. Not only was textile production profitable—indeed, it was the major nonagricultural industry in the mother country—but it employed, fed, and quieted the poor.[68] Massachusetts' unexpected creation of a sophisticated local textile industry amid labor shortages concerned the English managers of Atlantic trade. Members of the Council of Trade and Plantations in London may have pictured the New Englanders as simple folk who, lacking any commodities, became isolated from Atlantic markets and produced primitive cloth to cover themselves. Yet what witnesses saw contradicted such a picture. By 1670, New England was a growing commercial center with a lively trade to the West Indies in rough cloth, yet at the same time the colony produced sophisticated textiles for local consumption.

Economic documents confirm the alarmed views of imperial officials.

Consider the variety of cloth in the accounts of Christopher Leffingwell, a master weaver in Connecticut during the late seventeenth and early eighteenth centuries. He presided over a thriving workshop, trained several apprentices, and employed a journeyman full time. One account book kept between 1697 and 1714 opens a window on his workshop's production during those years. Leffingwell, his journeyman, and a set of apprentices produced fifteen different types of cloth, everything from "fine napkinning" to sail canvas. The most popular cloth he produced was "fine woolin," presumably a lighter weight, fulled fabric made from yarns produced locally. Since he distinguished between blanketing, kersey, serge, and drugget in his account book, Leffingwell's "fine woolin" cloth was most likely meant for good clothing and bed furnishings. In addition, he wove fancy table linens, pattern bed hangings and "coverlids." These items, both refined and plain, were essential to every household. The poorer homes claimed the modest wares, while wealthier households purchased the fancier goods. The bed hangings and coverlets produced in Leffingwell's shop enabled him to satisfy a diverse clientele. One set of "bed furnishings" cost £7, while another set cost less than £2. Coverlets could range from £2 to £5, depending on the complexity of the design. As the master, Leffingwell designed these pieces and did some of the weaving as well.

Leffingwell produced a broad spectrum of fabric types, especially when compared to his English counterparts. This variety allowed him to draw on the labor of his apprentices to keep the looms in motion. His journeyman employee, John Birchard, was less skilled than he. In the employment agreement, Leffingwell hired Birchard to weave "8 yds per day of such cloth as is 5d p yard." This was basic fabric, but represented hard work, especially if it was a dense woolen or linen. Leffingwell allowed Birchard to weave for himself "as a part of his wages." Birchard's February 1698 list of work done "for himself" reveals that most of his weaving was of striped and plain linen. This fabric could be used for underclothes, table linens, sheets, bed ticking, and pillow covers. Utilitarian by definition, these fabrics were in use in every seventeenth-century English home, whether in the colonies or in England.[69]

Leffingwell's account books reveal the nearly endless cloth needs of his neighbors. His Lathrop account is especially revealing of the ubiquity of textile needs and production. Between 1697 and 1703, Lathrop, probably of New London, commissioned a range of textiles for Leffingwell's shop to weave. In the first year, Leffingwell's shop produced twenty-one yards of fine woolen cloth and eight yards of linen in exchange for "fine hose yarn spun."

Over the next six years, Lathrop ordered linsey-woolsey, kersey, drugget, serge, fine linen, and woolen yardage. His orders reached 113 yards of linen, 110 yards of woolen, and 6 yards of linsey-woolsey. Lathrop also commissioned one bed "coverlid." With such a large volume of cloth produced, Lathrop may have traded his finished cloth with other families. His account was often settled with farm produce, but he also bartered linen hose yarn spun in his household by his wife, servants, or daughters. These items imply a household access to raw flax and hemp or to fibers processed by his neighbors. In other exchanges, Lathrop supplied a load of firewood, rented a pair of oxen to Leffingwell for plowing, and provided a wagonload of turnips, a field crop commonly used to feed livestock.[70]

The fabrics Leffingwell supplied Lathrop likely represented only a small part of Lathrop's household needs, for all were meant for clothing and bed furnishings. There are no references to the utilitarian fabrics essential to daily life, such as toweling, diaper or tow cloth. The fine linen Leffingwell's shop produced may have been sewn into shirts, petticoats, or even sheets, but every household needed plain goods as well. Although Lathrop acquired an adequate supply (or even a surplus), he needed more ordinary cloth to satisfy his household needs. Indeed, Lathrop may well have traded some of his finer fabrics for larger amounts of coarse cloth with a neighbor. Alternatively, his household was capable of producing yarn, so Lathrop may have commissioned fabric from vernacular weavers in the vicinity. It is clear from Leffingwell's accounts that the political initiatives and market forces had combined to make Massachusetts into a productive textile center.

In the period from 1640 to 1685, an extensive and wealthy network of weavers and clothiers developed in Suffolk County, Massachusetts. References to them can be found in Suffolk County land deeds. In the period, the records reveal some thirty-five propertied sailmakers, weavers, and clothiers working in the county. Many lived in Boston, but others dwelt prosperously in Hingham, Braintree, Dorchester, Roxbury, and Weymouth. Suffolk County clothiers included William Habberfield, Josiah Cobham (senior and junior), and Joseph Torrey. In addition, the town of Braintree had a fulling mill to finish fine cloth.[71]

Fulling itself was evidence that the textiles being produced locally were not just the simple cloth of vernacular weavers. Fulling was not necessary for all types of cloth, but it was essential for good woolen cloth. In the fulling process, newly woven cloth was washed, shrunk, and then felted or mashed. Properly dressed cloth was then napped with teasels (a plant grown by local farmers) and evenly sheared for a smooth surface. The entire process took days for each length of goods and the fabric certainly shrank, but the process made fulled cloth much more valuable and wearable. By the end of the seventeenth century, the towns of Ipswich, Watertown, Dedham, Newbury, Braintree, and Rowley all had fulling mills.[72]

The best-documented fulling mill in New England was built in Rowley by John Pearson. In 1642, Pearson was invited to remove from Salem to Rowley in order to erect a mill. Styling himself a clothier, Pearson expected to take full advantage of local residents' diligence and skill in spinning and weaving. By tradition, Pearson built his fulling mill by 1643 somewhere on the Mill River near the Bay Road, which eventually became a mill complex with sawmills, grist mills, and additional fulling mills (at least two by 1700). For the next four generations, most of the Pearson men followed the family trade and participated in the fulling mills' operation.

In 1686, Peter Cheney built what would be the third fulling mill in the town of Newbury close to the Rowley line. In his petition to the town, Cheney promised to build a fulling mill within three years of his occupation of the site. Because the town's agreement with Cheney expressly connected the operations of the two mills, the new mill was clearly meant to complement Pearson's Rowley business: Cheney "doth engage himself to full this town's cloth before any other towns and to do it upon the same terms as Mr. Pearson doth full cloth."[73] The agreement followed tough political and economic negotiations. The Newbury selectmen wanted a mill so badly that they donated the land and lumber required to build it. At the same time, they required Cheney to abide by local custom and favor town residents. The relative proximity of both mills meant that weavers of both towns could expect to get their woolens fulled at a fair price.

Until 1730, for more than forty years, the Cheney and Pearson families continued to operate their mills in the Rowley/Newbury area. In 1690, the Pearsons built at least one additional fulling mill in the area. As the various milling operations there expanded, the entire complex became known as Byfield mills. Eventually Jonathan Pearson, a grandson of the original John Pearson, gained control of the entire complex when he purchased the Cheney mill in 1694 from Peter Cheney's heir. From that point on, the Pearsons ruled the Byfield operations, retaining ownership until 1809. The mills made them rich. When he died in 1693, John Pearson left an estate of over £1,000. Benjamin Pearson, the son who inherited the Byfield mills, got even richer. When he died in 1729, his estate had grown to the value of £2,600, comparable to many of Boston's great shipwrights and merchants. A considerable volume of domestic textiles flowed through the Pearson mills, making them the source of a family fortune.

Two surviving account books from the Pearson mills document a portion of the cloth that was fulled in the original mill between 1672 and 1688. The ledgers document many local textile producers, the fruits of coercive political action. The sixteen years covered by the Pearson ledgers include over 618 individual accounts, each of which represents a fabric producer. Virtually every Rowley family (104) had an account, and another five hundred were from nearby towns. Over the period covered by the ledgers, this one Rowley mill processed approximately 65,000 yards of fine woolen cloth. This figure would be impressive enough if the Pearson mill were the only one in the area. But by the 1670s there were two others: upstream from the main Pearson mill clattered the Pearsons' second mill, while the Shatswell mill operated in nearby Ipswich.[74] Each mill meant many more producer families and much more good woolen cloth.

The Politics of Cloth in the Empire

Massachusetts producers made enough good cloth in a short time to alarm the Council of Trade and Plantations in London and the English Parliament, which spent several days debating Massachusetts textile production and crafting suppressive legislation.[75]

The New England textile industry became a focus of political debate, as did implicitly the unusual political system that produced an uninvited new world textile center. Many New England merchants, including Thomas Banister, wanted to use the textile production to scare English policy makers into capitalizing and welcoming other New England industries, particularly shipbuilding and naval stores. Unless England integrated New England into the Atlantic economy, they argued, the isolated New Englanders would produce more and more sophisticated textiles and the English would lose whatever share of the cloth market they had in New England, and perhaps in neighboring colonies. These arguments were connected to pleas to allow New Englanders a circulating medium so that even common folk could purchase English goods. They also called for English merchants to offer more lenient credit terms to colonial shopkeepers who wanted to buy English goods for distribution. They called for bounties on naval stores and more contracts for

New England ships in order to bring New England into the Empire in productive ways.

These merchants also knew that New Englanders wanted not only to be good but also to look good and that their coercively and equitably produced cloth lacked the cachet of English goods squeezed from landless wage workers. Even the most spiritual New Englander felt diminished if poorly dressed. At the end of 1709, the minister Cotton Mather noted in his diary that because he was underpaid by his congregation, "I had not cloathes fit to be worn: I was cloathed with rags (which, O Lord, I acknowledge, that such a sluggard as I am, deserve to be!), and one or two of my children are no better."[76] Apparel and personal identity, as well as personal dignity, were intimately connected. "They are proud enough to wear the best English cloth," noted Governor Joseph Dudley in 1709 to the English managers, "if chopping, sawing, and building of ships would pay for their cloth and this method would double the sale of English woolen manufactory presently."[77] John Jekyll, a customs collector, remarked in 1720 that English cloth could replace domestic cloth among almost any Yankee with cash, "for ye tradesmen and mechanical part they are very ambitious of appearing above themselves and will not be seen in anything beneath ye merchant or more substantial which is in the produce of Europe."[78] In that same year, Governor Shute told the English managers that English cloth was winning the consumer market: "I have been informed that there are some camlets and druggets made in the country and sent to some shops in Boston, but I don't observe that they are worn by any but the ordinary people."[79] New Englanders supported their own political economy, but they wanted to be dressed as finely and fashionably as their cousins in London.

By the 1730s, the English guardians of the Empire appeared to lose some of their fear of New England textile manufacturing. In 1731, Governor Jonathan Belcher reported that English cloth dominated the city market and was gaining in the countryside: "the country people who used formerly to make most of their clothing out of their own wool, don't now make a third part of what they wear, but are mostly clothed with British manufactures."[80] The next year, the Commissioners for Trade and Plantations could report to the House of Commons that "considering the excessive price of labour in New England, the merchants could afford what was imported cheaper than what was made in that country."[81] Yet, the English guardians still saw a threat. In 1732, the Commissioners of Trade reported to the English House of Lords and Commons that more manufactures "prejudicial to the trade and manufactures of Great Britain" were established "in New England, than in any other of the British colonies" and partly attributed this ominously to their "chartered governments . . . and consequently the small restraints they are under in any matters detrimental to her [England's] interest."[82]

At the same time, some New Englanders were not happy about the economic and social implications of their patterns of consumption and the consequential reduction of their textile industry.[83] An imbalance of trade in the 1720s inspired a pamphlet debate about consumption, money, and political economy. These pamphlets articulated "a labyrinth of perplexing thoughts."[84] Pamphleteer after pamphleteer concerned himself with schemes to provide currency for the New England's inconsistent economy and to solve the New England colonies' sudden imbalance of trade. Many expressed painful regrets about their fellow inhabitants' and their own unwillingness to wear domestically produced cloth, which they implied was abundant and adequate enough. Many New Englanders reviled themselves for their lack of restraint: "our gentry, yea our commonality, must be dress'd up like Nobles, nothing short of the finest broad-cloths, silks, and etc. will serve their apparel." To make matters worse, noting the versatile productivity of the colony and the colonists' desire for status, the same pamphleteer observed, "we will not employ ourselves in making our own finery; but far fetched and dear bought must be articles of our adorning."[85]

Some thought such self-flagellation was inaccurate and blamed English corruptors and politicians for the problem of English cloth consumption. Even when there was no currency to spend, many pamphleteers noted that England and its local merchant allies were essentially to blame for the widespread appearance of English cloth. They force-fed fancy English textiles to New Englanders, these writers argued, by hoarding specie and even paper money, and by paying laborers and tradesmen in the city not with cash or silver, but by what was called the "trunk trade," offering goods that consisted mostly of English cloth. The wage formula was often two-thirds goods and one-third money. John Colman wondered in 1720, "is there enough [money] to pay laborers and tradesmen, without forcing them to take goods, which they know not what to do with, except to put them on their backs, for which people are very angry, and say they go beyond their degree."[86] Though in debt and unable to pay taxes or mortgages for lack of money, New England craftsmen looked like gents. Some pamphleteers argued that the practice of forced English cloth wearing became the dominant form of wages in the cities. The perceived ebbing of sophisticated seventeenth-century textiles seemed a sign of alarming inner and outer coercive pathologies.[87]

Underlying this unease was the clear sense that the equitable and puritanical New England political economy, so dearly won, was resented by the powerful English merchants, who enjoyed command over powerless laborers at home and who thought theirs the only legitimate political economy. The cloth the New Englanders craved was the product of brutal inequalities, while the cloth they had was the product of their own peculiar town political economies with their interventionist political action. The loss of control over textiles, once so confidently held and collectively achieved, seemed to some a clever and satanic plot to confuse and defeat an equitable and productive Christian humanistic order by evil forces using political power and knowledge of New Englanders' own weaknesses.

Some writers pictured the English overlords poised to break the back of New England's town-based political economy. In other words, New England textile production made New Englanders self-aware of their unusual and dangerous identity as proponents of equity in the English empire. One anonymous pamphleteer limned an imaginary gentleman who advocated the conventional political economic order: "As for tradesmen (poor scoundrels) tis pity they should have any [dignity]; what, they must have brick houses. Must they? No, a groat a day is enough for them, and it will never be good times in our account till it comes to that."[88] In 1720, the Boston newspapers published a pirated letter home written in 1704 by Paul Dudley, part of the Anglophile elite that designed the mercantile economy, foreshadowing the hubbub surrounding the letters of Governor Thomas Hutchinson before the Revolution. Both men were Supreme Court justices with strong English ties. Dudley's letter was republished and discussed repeatedly during the currency and cloth debates: "This country will never be worth living in for lawyers and gentlemen till the charter is taken away," wrote Dudley. The charter stood for the town-based government and the political economy that created the textile industry and its disturbing and heretical productivity.

Such gents would arrange affairs, this pamphleteer concluded, to prove that well-paid laborers could not sustain an industry in the face of international poverty, even after Yankee sacrifice, political organization, and planning showed they might. Yet the pamphleteer hoped that God would help New Englanders survive such clever manipulation of their weaknesses: "We hope that He who rules in the Kingdom of Providence, will deride their secret councils, defeat their designs (though' laid as deep as hell) and clothe them with shame and confusion."[89] In a sense, that is what the homespun wearing New Englanders did to the British Empire beginning in 1775. That rebellion's foundations, both its political economy and actual production infrastructure, went back to the quiet textile triumphs of the seventeenth century, when for a time the colonists and their children had, with careful planning and coercive political choreography, spun out of imperial control into their own identity.

Speaking historiographically, the New Englanders' success in textiles also ran afoul of the modern liberal American empire. Writing in 1955, at the height of the McCarthy era, Bernard Bailyn took note of the managed textile proposals and pronounced that their collective efforts failed. He was less interested in textiles than in sustaining the narrative sweep and central economic doctrines of his magisterial book, *The New England Merchants in the Seventeenth Century*. The argument goes that after the dismal failures of collective planning as colonists ignored or languished under the legislation that sought to promote textile production, defiant individual Boston merchants following laissez-faire principles saved New England from ruin by establishing markets in the West Indies. It is a fine neoliberal tale, an *Atlas Shrugged* in periwigs. In reality, the Boston merchants' contributions, which were part of a general effort by the city, hardly need the falsified collapse of the New England textile industry in order to shine brightly.[90] Yet it would have been even more difficult for Bailyn to praise government intervention in the economy, much less labor coercion, to produce equity in 1955 than it is now.

Other historians belittled the significance of the politics of textile development by inventing false or exaggerated expectations for New Englanders, then arguing that they failed to meet these goals. By 1640, at the latest, New England leaders understood that staple commodities were essential to pay for European goods. Some historians have contended that Massachusetts leaders chose cloth as the designated export commodity. Since they failed to create a substantial export-oriented textile industry, this line of reasoning goes, cloth production in New England was a failure.[91] In fact, only a few New Englanders conceived of textile production as an export industry; most knew that English authorities would suppress it quickly. Instead, they organized textile production to clothe themselves as respectable Europeans, hoping to satisfy a basic need and to fulfill responsibilities to the poor, while freeing themselves from ruinous economic dependence on English imports. Thanks largely to an effective political system, they succeeded in reaching these goals.

The Role of Women

Yet the most spectacular consequence of the deliberate creation of the textile industry in the second half of the seventeenth century has been splendidly elucidated by Laurel Thatcher Ulrich: in New England, women dominated the craft of weaving, a skill that men virtually monopolized in Europe and, as Adrienne Hood shows, in colonial Pennsylvania.[92] Through a careful study of probate inventories and diaries, Ulrich shows that by the early eighteenth century, and perhaps earlier, "work that had once belonged to male artisans had become a part-time occupation for women and girls." Women continued to predominate among persistent spinners and weavers throughout the eighteenth century, and their production, as Ulrich shows, was both quantitatively and qualitatively impressive. They made a significant contribution to New England's ability to buy less English goods, while living and appearing nearly as well materially, as other North American colonists.[93]

Ulrich focuses throughout expertly on the household and markets, which may be why she finds herself unable to explain why male weavers disappeared in New England at the time when skilled labor supposedly became more prevalent, or why women, who took over weaving, did so as unspecialized and part-time workers. She remarks, "I cannot yet fully account for this transition, although it surely involved both the fragility of artisan weaving as a male occupation and limited opportunities for female employment in an undeveloped colonial economy."[94] The key realization that eluded Ulrich is that in New England households existed within economies shaped by town politics. By keeping outsiders or strangers from easily getting work in a town, the towns maintained labor shortages throughout the colonial period and encouraged seasonal variation in the labor of both men and women. In the seventeenth century, the political system had also demanded that women produce textiles, irrespective of the wishes of their husbands. Thus, the male jack of all trades had a female counterpart, the multitasking housewife, and their skills both differed and overlapped. In towns that lionized productivity, assigning trades like weaving—which had been reserved for men—to able and diligent women freed men to kill Indians, chop trees, and build ships. In these enclaves of engineered labor shortage, Marla Miller found that women also competed with men in tailoring with the full approval of town leaders.[95] The presence of highly productive female weavers that Ulrich found overlaps almost exactly with the extent of New England towns' political economies that limited the labor market and received political instructions from the General Court.

One historian, highlighting the inevitable superiority of laissez-faire economics, argued that the seventeenth-century political textile initiative "never proved more than a disappointment to its promoters."[96] In reality, if they had survived a century, the promoters would have found that their experiment in coercive textile politics exceeded any expectations they might have imagined. The political application of reform English urban economics to the New World in this case provided among other things: enough cloth to clothe the colonists in European style and alarm English officials; an infrastructure in textile production that reduced reliance on English textiles throughout the eighteenth century; a new identity for Massachusetts and New England in the Empire as supporting a political economy distinctively and dangerously more equitable than that in England (the idea and values of homespun coming as early as the 1720s); and the transfer of an important and hitherto masculine section of the economy into the hands of women.

CHAPTER FIVE

Of Wharves and Men

THE NEW ENGLAND ideal of the godly city included limiting outsiders, making labor more valuable, and attaching workers to the locality. In turn, city dwellers were required to attend church, to keep the Sabbath, to speak no oaths except on special occasions, to learn the Bible, and to attempt to transform their own sinful selves and their children into Christians. Equally important, they had to work at a vocation. This ideal of a locally rooted, well-disciplined labor force seemed as difficult to achieve in the New World as it had in the Old; while England had a surplus of labor and wandering poor, New England had an acute shortage of labor. In other British colonies, a cheap, desperate labor force drawn from England's floating proletariat toiled under coercive conditions. In New England, as seen, the labor of women and children could be mobilized to spin and sew clothing. But who could be induced to take up the difficult artisan trades necessary for shipbuilding and the deadly occupations essential to blue-water commerce? A literate labor force limited largely to the town born seemed unlikely to pursue maritime vocations. Yet in Boston and other port towns, godly institutions, especially a relatively democratic town meeting, created a political economy that attracted shipbuilders and mariners and trained them to handle the violent Atlantic. Families played a role in sending sons to sea, as they did in setting daughters to spin, but the town's institutions created the key associations for the building and sailing of ships. Particularly important were playful, civic-minded, sanctioned, and very rough male gangs.

Boston's labor system can be seen reflected in the childhood play of Benjamin Franklin. In 1715, in order to help their minnow fishing on the mudflats near Boston's mill pond, Franklin and a group of other Boston lads stole stones to build a wharf. The work group was composed of boys from many families—a gang of peers, not relatives. Franklin assigns himself credit for the original idea. Finding that their prime fishing spot was a "mere quagmire," he proposed to the boys "to build a wharf there fit for us to stand upon and I showed my comrades a large heap of stones, which were intended for a new house near the marsh, and which would very well fit our purpose." Leader and crew worked together; "diligently like so many emmets [ants], sometimes two or three to a stone, we brought them all away and built our little wharf." Although the adult authorities—the human representatives of God—appreciated innovation, they kept work and play (and they overlapped in this as in other cases) under close communal scrutiny, just as they thought God would. When the workmen found their missing stones in the boys' wharf they "complained," and "several of us were corrected by our fathers." Faced with the likelihood of physical punishment, Franklin "pleaded the usefulness of the work," but his father Josiah countered that "nothing was useful which was not honest." In retrospect, Franklin suggests that he showed "an early projecting public spirit." After all, Boston was a manmade city of wharves, and the construction of wharves was a matter of public concern.[1]

The Boston town meeting and the selectmen prompted and oversaw the building of the port much as their fathers nurtured and corrected young Benjamin's gang of allegedly constructive "play-fellows." From 1640 on, the town meeting encouraged local men to reconstruct Boston with wharves and voted subsidies to rich merchants turned shipbuilders. Nehemiah Bourne built the first large ship. In February 1641, the town meeting sold sixty acres of land in Braintree to "Brother Wright" at "1s 2d an acre, the which amounted to £3 10s and is to pay it in to Mr. Bourne, towards the building of a ship." The town also granted Bourne a house and adjoining land as "a place for building the ship," which was laid out under the supervision of the colony's major men, "Mr. Winthrop, Mr. William Tinge, and Captain Gibbons." Private investors, including John Winthrop, added their contributions to this venture. In 1642, the grateful authorities drew a large crowd for the launching of the two-hundred-ton *Trial*. John Cotton, their best preacher, "was desired to preach aboard her," noted Governor Winthrop, "but upon consideration that the audience would be too great for the ship, the sermon was at the meeting house."[2] Many launchings and celebrations followed.

In Boston, wharves had multiple uses, in contrast to those in most other early American places. In the Chesapeake, wharves served ships that landed English manufactures and African or West Indian slaves, and were laden with tobacco for the return voyage. An urban wharf was much more than a bare dock. Warehouses densely built on Boston's wharves accepted and stored goods for trade, but also served as centers of "manufactories." Many workshops, large and small, processed imported goods or prepared goods for export; others served the maritime industry itself. Shipwrights and their Boston-born work crews used them to collect and store the wood and iron they needed. Shipbuilders could have their vessels finished at wharves as well; a myriad of artisans with shops on or near the wharves outfitted the ships with rigging and sails.

The ship was the most sophisticated machine produced by preindustrial people. Maritime historians note that a hundred-ton vessel required two hundred trees, miles of rope, yard upon yard of canvas, gallons of naval stores made from pine resin, and a ton of iron.[3] Boston had rapidly been denuded of trees and lacked all of the other raw materials. The Shawmut peninsula was virtually an island, connected to the mainland by a narrow neck that was sometimes flooded at high tide. Materials had to arrive in Boston by water. To make matters worse, the waterfront was a sandy bog, unfit even for minnow fishing, much less for landing and storing tons of timber and iron. In order to develop a shipbuilding industry in Boston, people had to reconstruct the shore with wood and stone.

Shipbuilding was essential for the survival of Massachusetts. The English civil war that began in 1640 precipitated a crisis in the colony. When Puritan families became absorbed making England into a New Jerusalem, they stopped moving to Massachusetts. No New England product could lure English ships across the Atlantic. Colonists continued to grow and rear their own food, and they fabricated their own textiles. However, without a commodity to sell abroad and a way to deliver it, they had little money or prospects. Every Sabbath, New England ministers faced an audience of shivering penitents. Sensing their despair, the English Puritan leader Oliver Cromwell sent letters to New Englanders asking them to resettle in Ireland, and later to move to Jamaica. During the 1640s many returned to England, and others left for Providence Island in the Caribbean.[4]

New England's leaders saw shipbuilding, fishing, lumbering, and textile production as the only alternatives to failure and abandonment. Textile production clothed colonists without requiring them to send money abroad, and employed idle women and children. Though some promoters hoped textiles might serve as a commodity in trade, most knew New England–made cloth could not penetrate foreign markets. Shipbuilding, lumbering, and fishing would enable colonists to find markets in the West Indies, Spain, and other places. With their own ships, New England merchants could prosper in the Atlantic world. Governor John Winthrop wrote in 1641: "The general fear of want of foreign commodities, now our money was gone, and that things were like to go well in England, set us on work to provide shipping for own." In his journal he mentioned ships built in Boston and Salem as public efforts, laborers voluntarily keeping their wages down temporarily for the general good, and voyages successfully and profitably completed.[5]

Boston subsidized and supervised the construction of wharves as it did the building of ships. In 1641 the town granted the mudflats along Bendal's Cove to a syndicate formed by Valentine Hill and other merchants to develop the waterfront with wharves and a mill within five years. The syndicate was expected to invest at least £100 in this construction and would retain the right for nine years to take fees for the landing of merchandise and maintaining of ships on their wharves, along with the profits of the mills. The prices for wharfage would be strictly regulated by the town. Over a year later the town asked John Winthrop, Valentine Hill, and other merchants to dig out Shelter Cove for the "harbor of boats," promising financial help from the town for the project. The town meeting also directed the development of a dam and pond on the north cove facing Charlestown and projected several grist and saw mills by granting land to another syndicate led by Henry Simons. The selectmen specified in detail the reconstruction to be undertaken. The new project provided Boston with water power, mast pools, sawmills, and several bridges over the creek. In addition to the land needed to complete the project, the town gave the syndicate "three hundred acres of land at Braintree for the use and encouragement of the said mill or mills." The town promised the syndicate labor to move the earth, ordering that "the said select townsmen and their successors shall procure what free help they can (by persuasion) upon any pressing occasion of use of many hands about making the banks or trenches &c. for the better furtherance of the work to be speedily effected." The selectmen expected to include the whole local population in this project, transforming Boston into a commercial and shipbuilding center with public-private partnerships. Additionally, the town gave another syndicate led by Adam Winthrop land in Braintree to begin iron manufacturing to supply the shipbuilding industry. The town sought to protect this large investment with several fortifications and a barricade to stop ships sent by hostile foreign powers.[6]

Boston aggressively encouraged wharf-building to facilitate the growth of shipbuilding. In order to build the fourteen vessels constructed in 1702, for example, some three thousand trees as well as almost nine tons of iron had to be landed and stored, along with vast quantities of tar, hemp, masts, and sailcloth. After the hulls were completed in separate shipyards, vessels might be moved to well-placed wharves where riggers, caulkers, block makers, pump makers, mastwrights, joiners, blacksmiths, and rope makers had easy access to the vessels. Boston wharves were multiuse constructions serving public and well as private interests. Most had a complex set of owners whose property and use rights overlapped. In 1672, George Halsell testified in court that in 1646 he had built a thirty-foot wharf on Edmund Grosse's land when Grosse was at sea. He soon learned that Grosse had sold the land to John Anderson, a shipwright. "The said Anderson in my time," noted Halsell, "had the use and benefit of the said wharf. . . . And built several vessels upon the same, and pulled down and set up upon the said wharf at his pleasure, without any contradiction of me or my order." While Anderson used and modified the wharf to build ships, Halsell kept "the liberty of landing and shipping of goods upon and from the said wharf free, which was the main end of my building the same." Halsell then proceeded to sell his right in the wharf to Nathaniel Patten of Dorchester. "But," he explained, "I did not, neither could I, sell the said wharf because it stood upon the said Anderson's land, only I sold the liberty and privilege of free wharfage there as being the only right I had in the same."[7] Rights of ownership and usage intermingled. Halsell built the wharf in exchange, not for money, but for the right to use the wharf in perpetuity, and he retained the right to sell or grant that privilege to another. In the meantime, Anderson built ocean-going vessels. The wharf was not anyone's exclusive property: it belonged to John Anderson, George Halsell, and Nathaniel Patten. Because the enterprise was developed with public assistance, the wharf also belonged to the townspeople who actively oversaw the construction and use of wharves.

The Boston town meeting and its selectmen encouraged artisans to build wharves and regulated their use and the prices charged for using them. The selectmen granted at least thirty-six wharf permissions between 1640 and 1650. Boston selectmen wanted wharves built to facilitate manufacturing; so many permissions included a time limit. For example, in 1652, the selectmen gave Thomas Broughton permission to wharf "before his ground which lyeth at the ferry towards Charlestown, provided he wharf within one year and a day."[8] A prime incentive arose from the creative and unusual way Boston town meeting defined property rights within its borders. By law, coastal land grants in town included all the land visible at low tide. The selectmen and town meeting knew that coastal landowners needed to build wharves in order to enjoy and profit from their tidewater property. The selectmen made complex deals with many applicants. In 1647, they not only allowed the shipwright Benjamin Ward to wharf before his property but granted him the right to rent a large area of marsh around his wharf. He got the land and rights for two years for £3 and had to pay only £4 annually thereafter. They expected him to construct a shipyard.[9]

The town established many quasi-public wharves. In 1652, the town meeting gave John Anderson, the shipwright, liberty to wharf "before the highway which adjoineth his land on the one side and the land of John Crabtree on the other side." Building a wharf directly from a public highway was important to the town because it would expedite the movement of building materials into and out of Boston. Townspeople wanted such a network of roads and wharves built quickly, but not entirely at taxpayers' expense, especially at a time when Boston and its inhabitants lacked capital. So the town made a deal with Anderson. If he built the wharf adjoining his land on the highway, he had "liberty granted unto him for to take wharfage of strangers for goods and wood (that) shall be landed by them on the said wharf." On the other hand, since his wharf was on public land, "he hath no liberty to take wharfage of any inhabitants of the town for either goods or wood landed on that part of the wharf before the highway, provided it lies not above twenty-four hours, if it be seasonable weather for to get it away or be not the Lord's day."[10] Anderson the shipwright became a wharf owner, but he could not charge Boston's own timber merchants for their responsible use of his wharf.

The selectmen allowed some private wharf owners to charge townsfolk fees. In 1660, the town granted wharfage for twenty-one years to Captain Thomas Breedon and his associates if they erected a wharf and highway in Boston, but opened the deal to local investors by adding, "it shall be in the liberty of any inhabitants to come in as a partner in the same work within six months after the finishing the said work, they paying their equal proportion of charge." For cases in which private wharves charged townsfolk, the town set the wharfage, or fees charged for unloading merchandise.[11] These public-private partnerships played a positive role in stimulating wharf construction and spurring shipbuilding.

Wharf building transformed the city. Samuel Clough prepared in 1927 a map of Boston based on the "Book of Possessions," the original land grants, reconstructing a picture of how Boston probably looked in 1640. Most of the houses stood in central and south Boston, with only a smattering of buildings along the boggy shore in what became the North End. Virtually no wharves were visible on the map. There was no mill pond alongside the Charles River or a mill creek separating the North End from central Boston. Thirty years later, in 1663, the traveler John Josselyn described Boston as a "rich and very populous" city where "the houses are for the most part raised on sea-banks and wharfed out with great industry and cost." "Wharfing out" meant connecting adjacent wharves with boardwalks upon which shipbuilding and warehousing could take place, creating a bustling and productive structure built out over the marsh below. John Bonner's map of 1722 shows the change vividly. Although central Boston was still densely built, the North End clearly had even more houses, while the route south to Roxbury seemed pastoral by comparison, showing little growth in the number of houses from 1640. The numbers of streets had multiplied by five. The mill dam and mill pond on the Charles River are visible, along with the mill creek and the bridges over it. Most conspicuous are the wharves, especially in the North End, reaching like greedy fingers into the Atlantic. Bonner's Boston map shows at least seventy-one wharves and eleven shipyards in Boston by 1722 (Figure 6).[12]

No other early American city had so many wharves or was so fabricated.[13] From all over New England, vessels with thousands of trees and tons of iron came to these wharves. Near them, men at mills and saw pits cut the timber into keels and planking, while blacksmiths fashioned the iron into anchors and cables. The men and their families lived nearby. Children played at building wharves of their own. Their fathers and mothers looked on, correcting the delinquent and encouraging what was both honest and useful. By 1714, some ten to twenty new vessels left the Boston wharves annually. Not only did shipbuilding sustain commerce, but by the early eighteenth century shipbuilding was New England's largest industry, extending along the coastline and devouring raw materials from the interior.

"The best article they have is shipbuilding," reported Joshua Gee to the English Council of Trade and Plantations in 1721, "by which they make the greatest returns, which ships when built are sent to Portugal, Spain and other parts of Europe, and many of them are sold there." From his study of the

Figure 6. *Plan of Boston in 1722* by John Bonner. The artist made the many wharves and shipyards prominent and offered legends announcing the town's smallpox epidemics and fires. Courtesy of the I. N. Phelps Stokes Collection, Miriam and Ira D. Wallach Division of Art, Prints and Photographs, The New York Public Library, Astor, Lenox and Tilden Foundations.

register of shipping from 1698 to 1714, Bernard Bailyn showed that by 1701 Boston possessed a merchant fleet second in size only to London's. Massachusetts artisans built this fleet largely in Massachusetts towns, with the plurality of these vessels constructed in Boston. "That which hath kept this town alive the last year," noted the Boston merchant John Colman in 1720, "is the number of ships which have been built in it, which employs great part of the town." Reflecting on the success of shipbuilding in his native town, a slightly older Benjamin Franklin in 1729 recommended the same strategy for his adopted Philadelphia: "it may not be amiss to observe . . . what a great advantage it must be to us as a trading country, that has workmen and all the materials proper for that business within itself, to have *Ship-Building* as much as possible advanced: for every ship that is built here for the *English* merchants, gains the province her clear value in gold and silver, which must otherwise have been sent home for returns in her stead." He explained that shipbuilding not only attracted English capital but also made a colony's other commodities cheaper and more competitive abroad by lowering transportation costs. Colonies without ships would hire the shipbuilding colony's fleet to carry their commodities, so the potential profits seemed endless. Philadelphia did develop a shipbuilding industry, but it never rivaled Boston's; its geographical advantage on the Delaware River was outmatched by Boston's wharf-building.[14]

Masculinity Boston-Style

In Boston, groups of neighborhood men not only built wharves and ships but also sailed the ships across the Atlantic. Traditional hierarchies of wealth and status went only so far in such an enterprise; the public and political initiatives that subsidized and regulated these seafaring ventures opened opportunities to the white town-born men regardless of inherited rank. These youths erected their own hierarchies through supervised and sanctioned play. These self-made hierarchies and the skills required to compete in them were essential to the Boston economy.

In the spring of 1675, the Suffolk County Court charged and convicted nine young shipwrights—John Roberts, Samuel Browne, Samuel Adams, Robert Sears, Nathaniel Greenwood junior, Josiah Baker, Samuel Woody, James Updike, and William Parkman—"for their forcible taking John Langworthy upon a pole and by violence carrying of him from the North End of Boston as far as the town dock; which occasioned a great tumult of people; meeting there with the constable who did rescue him." When the court asked the gang of young men why they behaved so violently, they argued that they were protecting skilled laborers' privileges and upholding the city's economy. Langworthy "was an interloper," they contended, "and had never served his time to the trade of a ship carpenter and now came to work in their yard and they understood such things were usual in England." "Such things" referred to the skimmington,[15] the rough ride on the pole that the young men gave Langworthy, whose intrusion threatened to depress their wages, degrade their craft, and destroy their city's righteous political economy. The judges did not credit the young men's argument or sanction their moral vision any more or less than Josiah Franklin credited his son's explanation for his gang's theft of building stones. In this case, the town fathers did not inflict corporal punishment on the young men, but did fine each of them ten shillings, a stiff but not wounding penalty. They told the offenders to pay half to the county and half to John Langworthy himself. Langworthy received at least £4 for his humiliating role in their drama,[16] which may well have helped pay for his departure from the city and his resettlement elsewhere.

This play was rougher and more ruthless than Franklin's gang's misappropriation of building materials. These young men, all in their late teens and early twenties, publicly humiliated a peer, parading him like a bagged animal for over half a mile while the crowd jeered and hooted. Langworthy was finished in Boston; he had been symbolically castrated.[17] This act was especially severe and indelible because their shipbuilding trade demanded not only expertise but also the ability to lead. Shipbuilding and seafaring were jobs for courageous and sometimes necessarily violent men. These occupations were kindred: ships had to take skilled artisans with them on long voyages because they so often were damaged and needed repair to continue.[18] Nobody could take Langworthy's leadership and authority seriously on land or at sea. In this small town, he was remembered as a pitiful victim in an unforgettable drama. His was a story of failure and impotence. Along with his honor and his manhood, he had lost his ability to work.

Allegedly these youths acted heroically to protect the rights of Boston workers against an unworthy and dangerous outsider, which they were aware their English counterparts also did. Some historians credit them with pluck and purpose.[19] The nine men's rhetoric about stopping the interloper from ruining Boston and its trades articulated political and social views shared by the majority of Boston's citizens, who actively maintained the city's restricted labor market even during its years of rapid economic growth.

The Boston town labor policy was expressed in a petition to the General Court signed by over a hundred craftsmen in 1677, just two years after the nine forced Langworthy's ride. During King Philip's War, which devastated much of inland Massachusetts, refugee families flooded into Boston as the Indians burned their towns. The General Court persuaded Boston to relax its usual restrictive rules on accepting immigrants and refugees. By 1677 the war was over, and many Boston tradesmen impatiently wanted the restrictions renewed. Their petition proclaimed that "the frequent intruding of strangers from all parts, especially of such as are not desirably qualified . . . is very pernicious and prejudicial to the town." They denounced those who "never served any time, or not considerably for the learning of a trade," yet "by hiring or buying a servant they doe set up a trade; and many times the stranger . . . draws away much of the custom from his neighbor which hath been long settled, and in reality is much more the deserving man." The petitioners argued that these untalented, moneyed strangers would impoverish the skilled workers in town. The petitioners expressed confidence in their own selectmen's willingness to revive the city by reimposing restrictive policies, if the General Court allowed it. Boston selectmen renewed their campaigns against outside workers in the 1680s by vigorously fining employers who hired outside workers. Thanks to the dominant belief in maintaining craft exclusiveness and the craftsmen's readiness to flex their political muscles, Boston remained a restricted, or at least very selective, town.[20]

Nonetheless, the nine young men were clearly not simply harassed town laborers protecting an egalitarian social order from violation. At least two of the offenders were the privileged scions of emerging shipbuilding families who owned many of the wharves and adjoining properties that jutted out into Boston harbor. Their fathers were amassing considerable fortunes. Samuel Adams was the only surviving son of Alexander Adams, one of Boston's first shipbuilders, who was already a considerable property holder in 1675. When he died in late 1676, just a year after his son's humiliation of Langworthy, Adams possessed an estate of £514. Adams lived simply like a mechanic, but he had accumulated over £400 in real estate, including two dwelling houses and a shipyard. At the age of twenty-eight, Samuel Adams got the building yard and a house. An even more privileged perpetrator was Nathaniel Greenwood, junior. Strikingly, his father was the constable who arrested the youths as they carried Langworthy from the shipyard to the town dock.

Nathaniel Greenwood, senior, was a civic-minded shipwright who had accumulated some £1,160 by the time he died in 1684. He owned an eighth of a vessel, considerable plank timber, masts, and spars, and land in Braintree. His biggest assets, however, were houses and wharves in the North End of Boston worth £800. He served as selectman from 1681 until his death. Nathaniel Greenwood would have inherited a fortune before reaching the age of thirty had he not predeceased his father. The bulk of the Greenwood estate went to his younger brother Samuel, also a shipwright. By the time Samuel Greenwood died in 1722, the property's worth had grown to £5,047, certainly one of the largest estates in Boston. Samuel Greenwood called himself a shipwright in his will. Yet the bulk of his fortune rested in Boston real estate, which he had developed into commercial and residential rental properties. Especially valuable were his wharves decked out with a shipbuilding yard, a brew house, a blacksmith's shop, and several other buildings, worth about £1,600. Greenwood lived a life of relative luxury, with expensive furniture, gold and silver plates, and a virginal (a keyboard instrument similar to a harpsichord); two slaves waited on his family. His son, Isaac Greenwood, attended Harvard and became the college's first professor of mathematics and science.[21]

These men were not exceptional among shipbuilders. Many of the first- and second-generation Boston shipwrights did well. Boston was relatively egalitarian thanks to the decision of the town meeting to control the labor market by regulating in-migration and the use of outside labor. The 1687 tax list shows that 81 percent of the householders listed owned some property in Boston, as did over 70 percent of all white adult males. Access to property was facilitated by the town regulations preventing wealthy property holders from amassing cheap labor. They had to rely on the town labor force and its skills. The tax lists show that no households had more than four adult men, and a great majority contained only a single adult male laborer. Apprentices and slaves augmented the labor force of many artisan and wealthy households, but Boston's productivity in shipbuilding and other industries was due to a town labor force, not to the multiplication of large households full of laborers (Figure 7).

Shipwrights ranked among the wealthiest citizens. Their inventories show virtually no merchandise and little debt, suggesting that they did not engage in overseas trade. Most striking are their real estate holdings: wharves, shops, and houses along the waterfront. Many were paid in specie, which they turned into pounds of silver and gold plate, real estate, and still more

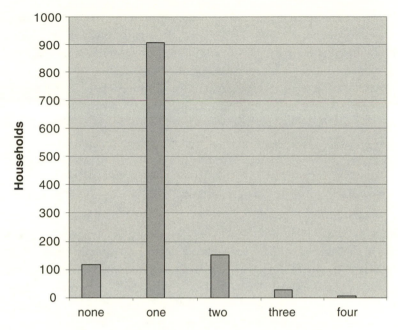

Figure 7. Adult males per household, Boston, 1687. Source: "Tax List and Schedules—1687," in *First Report of the Record Commissioners, 1876* (Boston, n.s., 1877), 91–127.

ships. Shipbuilders joined merchants and ship captains in the town's elite. The shipwright Timothy Thornton became a selectman and representative to the General Court in the 1720s. Virtually all the fourteen shipwrights whose estates were probated by 1721 served in town government, many as water bailiffs and constables. In their wills, none of these men called himself "gentlemen" or even merchant; rather, they called themselves shipwrights, ship carpenters, and occasionally mariners. The distinction was important, because a merchant or gentleman did not perform physical labor or command men directly, but stood aloof from the work of production. A merchant's or a gentleman's clean hands signified that he had the power to avoid labor. By contrast, shipwrights were mechanics; they worked with their hands as well as their brains and took pride in their origins as well as their continued participation in physical creation. They occupied an important place in the symbolic social order of Boston, standing above the less wealthy artisans and eye to eye with the equally wealthy but less physical merchants and gentlemen.

Not all the young men carrying Langworthy through the Boston streets were so privileged. Samuel Woody was the son of Richard and Francis Woody, a sergeant in the militia and a soap boiler with some real estate. While solidly middling, his son Samuel could not expect to inherit a shipyard and developed wharf property along Boston's increasingly valuable waterfront. William Parkman, John Roberts, and Robert Sears had obscure origins in the town. Samuel Browne may have been a member of the wealthy Browne family of Salem. James Updike, too, may not have been a native; town records contain no evidence of an Updike in Boston before this event.

Given their differing opportunities, what kept this crew of young workers together? Some were heirs to the Boston waterfront, others youths without visible advantages. Clearly their play had a purpose, though Langworthy himself never seemed a real threat. Greenwood and Adams probably participated in the ritual humiliation of Langworthy to create manly credibility and solidarity with their poorer peers. These assertive young men used righteous violence to protect themselves, their trade, and their city from interlopers, real or imagined, and create harmony within their own group. Whoever the leader was, the gang's theatrical act suppressed differences of class background among them, cleansing the rich boys of the suspicion that they were too privileged and effeminate to command men on shore or at sea. By poling Langworthy, they showed that they would prefer an autonomous town labor force to a debased labor force based on open immigration and an unregulated labor market, however much it might benefit them personally. This demonstration also allowed the poorer boys to show their manliness and loyalty to their wealthier peers. Here was Boston's productive, yet violent, waterfront labor system in the making, drawing workers from households of disparate wealth and forging a group of righteous, manly artisans under town oversight.

Most of the Langworthy nine became leaders. Samuel Adams became a property-holding shipwright and block maker who served Boston as a tax assessor, though he never developed his inheritance into a major shipyard. Lacking family property, Josiah Baker remained a ship carpenter. He sired a family in Boston, but often took the ferry to Charlestown, where he commanded up to £50 for his work on a vessel. John Roberts developed his own shipyard next to Nathaniel Greenwood's in the North End, paying £100 to buy it in 1685. He also invested in at least three vessels, the ketch *Mayflower* (1698), the ship *Consent* (1700), and the brig *Nevis Merchant* (1698). William Parkman married into the Adams family and displayed considerable entrepreneurial talent. He conducted a diverse shipbuilding business, and his mast-making yard was among the largest in Boston. In the summer of 1713, he took his workers to Salem to clean the bottom of the ship *Bishop*. Parkman hired the Salem innkeeper Elisha Odlin to cater the work site with food and drink. According to Odlin, Parkman and his crew ran up a tab in drinks and food of over £4 in three days. Parkman also invested in vessels himself, becoming part owner in 1710 of the twenty-ton sloop *Anna*. He died in 1730 leaving an estate of some £1,323, including £85 in masts, £56 in silver plate, and £900 in real estate. Parkman's sons followed him as sailors and shipwrights, though a gentler son, Ebenezer, attended Harvard College and became the minister at Westborough. He became well known to historians because he wrote a lengthy diary.[22]

Three of the Langworthy nine became ship captains. Robert Sears, then described as a shipwright, purchased land from Thomas Baker, blacksmith, for £34 in 1683. He married that year. He used his property to raise £60 in a mortgage agreement in 1684, of which he successfully paid by 1691. In 1690, he went to sea as first mate of the brigantine *Samuel* in the expedition against the French in Port Royal. Sears invested in shipping as well; interestingly, he and John Roberts were partners in the *Nevis Merchant* in 1698. Sears returned to the sea in his late forties, as captain of his own forty-ton sloop *Hopewell*. In 1706, at fifty-one, he became master of the one-hundred-ton ship *Charles*. Samuel Woody also became a sea captain; in 1686 he commanded the fifty-ton ship *Supply*, loaded with lumber and provisions, to Barbados. James Updike commanded the forty-ton ketch *Mary* to Nevis with fish, provisions, lumber, whale oil, hides, and tar in 1687; in 1707, at the age of fifty-two, he commanded the fifty-five-ton brig *Newport*. He bought property in South Boston from James Barton, rope-maker, in 1695. Updike continued to be a violent man. In 1691, he got into a quarrel with Paul Simons in Edward Mortimer's house. According to witnesses, Updike struck Simons several blows and kicked him with his foot. In retaliation, Simons bloodied Updike's nose. According to a witness, "Mr. Updick threatened to beat said Simons till he was cold." It had been sixteen years since Updike tied Langworthy to a pole and paraded him through Boston, but he was still quick to defend his honor.[23]

The Langworthy nine, despite their differing opportunities, knew how to command other men in perilous situations. Several fought in wars; a few had more personal quarrels. They became entrepreneurs and property holders in Boston. They raised families and drank lustily and served in political offices. Aligning themselves with others in the customs of the shipyards and the seaport, they protected the trade and the town, not their most narrowly defined class interests. Boston's town labor force was created by demonstrating worthiness and solidarity in action, not by adhering to strict guild rules and requirements, by simply gaining legal entrance into the city, or by offering obedience to patriarchs. Once legally in Boston, almost all men could play rough within the rules, if they had the character to do so. Langworthy had a right to be in Boston, as the authorities acknowledged, but he lost that right in practice by failing to protect himself from his aggressive peers. Unfortunately, somebody had to play the outsider to enable the group to cohere and prosper.[24]

An outsider could enter the town labor force and gain a privileged position only if he was successful in peer-group combat. Hector McNeill, though clearly an outsider, fought to gain acceptance as a valued member of the maritime town labor force. He arrived in Boston in 1738 as a ten-year-old in a Scots-Irish family. Like virtually all eighteenth-century immigrants, his family found entering Boston difficult. "Here we met with a very indifferent reception from the people of the country, who seem'd to have a contempt for strangers of what denomination whatsoever; more especially those who came from Ireland (whom they took for granted were all Roman Catholics)." The McNeills were Protestants. The family was quarantined on Rainsford Island in the harbor until all passengers were free of the measles that had raged aboard the vessel at sea. According to local law, the McNeills had to wait for someone in Boston to post bond to cover any losses they might inflict on the city for the next five years. Unlike Philadelphia and New York, Boston was a restricted city. Fortunately, McNeill's mother's sister had married a Boston resident who posted bond for them. When landing at Hubbard's wharf, Mr. Hubbard himself greeted the McNeill family by complaining bitterly about his financial sacrifice, asking the McNeills "why we came there; and why we did not stay in our own country." McNeill's father wept. On the long Atlantic voyage and while waiting on the island, three of his children had died of measles.[25]

Meanwhile, Hector was exchanging blows with playful Boston lads who had poured into the streets to watch a ship launching. They spotted McNeill and recognized him immediately as an outsider whom they might victimize; by beating him up, they could earn their badge of honor as protectors of the Protestant town and prospective leaders in the town labor force. They taunted and provoked him. McNeill got angry when the street boys called him "Irish!" As a Protestant, he understood Irish to mean Catholic. McNeill fought a larger boy and got the better of him. While watching the fight, adult Bostonians did not intervene, but praised the boy's mettle and adeptness. "I returned to our lodgings highly extolled by the spectators for my courage and dexterity," noted McNeill. This outsider child earned adult attention and favor in Boston because he refused to submit, but hit back powerfully and skillfully. McNeill continued his career as a fighter, a prelude to success in colonial Boston. He was soon enrolled in a Boston free public school, "the only stranger among two hundred boys." Hoping to win a share of honor and leadership by humiliating the outsider, the hostile and excited Yankee lads often attacked McNeill: "they seldom contented themselves with threshing me one at a time, but would frequently shew me foul-play, and get at me two or more at once, until they master'd me for that time." But not for long. After taking his beating from a crowd of Yankee boys quietly, he ambushed the culprits "singlely whenever an opportunity offer'd, until at last, being brought ye custom to suffer a great deal of bruising and in my turn to pay as well, they let me alone in peace." McNeill claimed that he was gentle by nature and upbringing but Boston's beatings and challenges made him brutal. "During the whole time of my boyhood in the town of Boston my life was one continued state of warfare," he explained. McNeill not only survived the fighting but shed his tender personality. Learning to turn cold in a fight enabled him to survive the town school and enter Boston's fierce town labor force.[26]

So educated, McNeill went to sea at the age of seventeen despite his loving parents' objections. Employers welcomed this strong, active, well motivated, literate, hardened, and impatient lad with a solid reputation as a tough. "I soon became much esteemed by all I sailed with, and met with great encouragement, so that in June, 1750, I was made master of a vessel in a very snug trade and constant employ." He was just twenty-two. McNeill had climbed rapidly from outsider through the forecastle to the master's cabin, a leader among men. He soon married a church deacon's daughter, validating his place in the Protestant community. In wartime, he redirected his childhood fury against Bostonian bullies to fight and murder foreigners as the master of privateers. By the time he began writing his autobiography on board the brigantine *Minerva* in 1773, he was one of Boston's most respected and noted sea captains, and he dearly loved his adopted town.[27]

McNeill's inspiring (or chilling) story, along with Franklin's boyish tale and the history of the Langworthy nine, shows that the male labor force was a club in which skill and violence in work and play superseded ancestry and wealth. Only by nurturing and disciplining a labor force that combined exclusiveness with solidarity and bent both toward assertive action could the city recruit men willing and able to go to sea in ships, one of the most arduous and dangerous forms of labor the seventeenth and eighteenth centuries offered. Seafaring was also among the most lucrative of gambles, so men bred in the rough-and-tumble milieu of the Boston waterfront thrived—as did the economy of both town and colony.

The violent and egalitarian play of Boston was tolerated, even encouraged, as a matter of deliberate policy. The Boston town meeting denied youth the theater and the playing of billiards, but encouraged frequent fighting, especially knock-downs.[28] Fierce fighting was nurtured in brutal town schools, and town authorities allowed it to spill into the streets and commons, where it reached a crescendo in the town's Pope Day festivities.

In New England, unlike many other societies, godly parents believed that their own children should do jobs that wealthy, civilized, and loving families elsewhere consigned to strangers of an inferior sort. Most societies relegated humble labor and humiliating punishments to "other" people's children. However, informed by Calvinist values that lingered well after the theology ebbed, New Englanders believed that sparing their own children hard work, physical punishment, and traumatic humiliation risked spoiling them for eternity. Responsible parents made their children work hard and start at the bottom. If they needed to be hit at a tender age to learn humility, so be it. If they responded violently, so be it, as long as they did not confront authority directly. They allowed their male children to form play gangs that fought to select leaders, to prepare for the violence they encountered at sea, and to form a defensive force against the intruding world. They learned to play rough and cold.[29]

Violent Gangs as Schools for Success

In eighteenth-century Boston and Salem, success in a neighborhood gang was necessary for entrance into the town labor force. The rough-and-tumble nature of maritime life prevailed in Salem, a town that, despite its distinct origins, developed along similar lines as Boston, manifesting an intense devotion to shipbuilding and seafaring and to the godly institutions of town meeting, church, and school. Salem, like Boston, was restricted to outsiders of the town's chosing.

The linkage of childhood trauma, education, violence, and a relatively egalitarian labor force remained in force in both towns for centuries. Salem finally outlawed corporal punishment in its public schools in 1827. The townspeople's predilection for fisticuffs is amply documented in the memoirs of its elite, who fondly recalled its traditions of controlled youth violence that reached back at least to the early eighteenth century. Robert Rantoul, Sr., the wealthy merchant and founder of the Essex Institute, noted that in the 1780s the city's youth was divided into neighborhood gangs: the "Wapping" district along the harbor, the polite "St. James" neighborhood, and the tough "Knockers' Hole" boys. The St. James boys were the sons of the wealthiest merchants and they sat out the bloodier battles on the commons, leading Rantoul to pronounce them "effeminate." The Wapping and Knockers' Hole boys fought bravely. They were the sons of sea captains, artisans, and common mariners—the middling workers of the town. Rantoul remembered "several pitched battles between the Wapping boys, in line on the commons, and the Knockers' Hole boys, in another line, under their respective leaders . . . fought with stones and other missiles."[30]

The Salem common today is a large, open park not far from the waterfront. The common has been public land since Salem's founding by fishermen from Cape Ann who sought a sheltered harbor along the Naumkeag (Eel) River. In the eighteenth century the common was used for pasturing cows and goats and as a training field for the militia. In 1801 Elias Hasket Derby, 2nd, beautified it by planting a row of stately poplars, which George Ropes, Jr., highlighted in his painting *Salem Common on Training Day* (1808). The common was not always so serene, however. Before and after the poplars were planted, gangs of ten- to thirteen-year-old Salem boys, too young to join the militia but on the verge of going to sea, staged blood-letting fights. The whole town endorsed and heartily enjoyed their twice-weekly battles.

Another distinguished Salem leader, Benjamin Browne, recalled these contests as violent, but controlled: "bruised pates and bloody noses were concomitants of those battles, for neither party were delicate in the choice of weapons or missiles." Browne added that battles between the scholars at different schools also took place on the common and that wars between the Wapping and Knockers' Hole boys often spilled into "the public streets." The gang fights were organized along military lines. "Prisoners were taken on both sides, and instead of the oath of allegiance being administered, their faces were well washed with snow, ice or frozen snowballs, sometimes cruelly applied." Browne fondly remembered the day "some twenty of the best fighting 'down-town' boys hired a large, double covered sleigh with a driver, and laid in a good stock of ammunition, viz: clubs, frozen snow balls and pieces of ice," and proceeded through the narrow streets behind the "up-towners" who were slowly pushing the mass of "down-towners" back toward Liberty Street. The strategy and investment in machinery worked, noted Browne: "here, emerging from the sleigh with shouts and yells, they attacked the 'up-towners' in the rear, who, being taken by surprise fled in all directions through yards and over fences, leaving many who were captured and trophies of victory."[31] Doubtless, his tale ignited some tired blood among the elderly gents in the Essex Institute.

The hiring of a wagon indicates adult participation. The gangs had booster clubs formed by former members who had taken their higher places in the town's social order. Rantoul and Browne noted that the authorities seemed to encourage the lads. Certainly, nobody punished them or even tried to stop them. In his view, they "seemed to enjoy the fun as much as we did." "It was considered fair sport, which every one should be willing to take as well as give." As Browne observed, "our elders, had . . . gone through the same training in their boyish days."

"Training" is a key word. Browne argued that the fights developed the port's workforce. The Wapping boys "were generally rough . . . but of good stamina, who took to the water as naturally as young ducks, and from them, grew up many of our best merchants and officers of vessels." Rantoul agreed that leadership in these boyhood brawls led to political and commercial prominence. "In the athletic recreations" (as Rantoul referred to the gang wars on the common), success "required organization and leaders. . . . The Crowninshields were generally put forward . . . the most distinguished family in the eastern section of the town, commonly called Wapping. . . . The Crowninshield boys were Benjamin W., afterwards Secretary of the Navy, Richard, who became a manufacturer, and Edward, who died young."[32]

The early Essex Institute was one of the few intellectual clubs where members told tales about their bloody street gang days: today, tourists visit the impressive mansions of these rock-throwing toughs. Beyond the comic irony, the gangs of Salem were the essential nursery of the town's commercial fleet and banking establishment. Little boys may go yachting for fun, but they do not go to sea for life and death without the prompting of adults and a fierce peer group that defines manhood in martial terms and schools them in disassociation (Figure 8).

By the time boys growing up in Salem or Boston got to be twelve, they

Figure 8. Benjamin W. Crowninshield, Secretary of the Navy (1815–1817), was born in Salem in 1772 and, like much of the Salem elite, first earned his leadership credentials as captain of the Wapping neighborhood street-fighting gang. Courtesy of the U.S. Naval Historical Center.

were well accustomed to violence and trauma. Rough sport started in dame school. Robert Rantoul went to school in 1780 at the age of four under Susannah Babbidge, who had already been teaching in Salem for some fifty years. By the time Rantoul met her she was old and fat. "She was so large," noted Rantoul, "that she could not easily perambulate her schoolroom to apply her correcting hand to the urchins, who were arrayed in the seats over the whole floor." The school was "well governed" nonetheless. "She kept at her side a cane-pole of sufficient length to reach the furthest boy in the room, and when any one was seen by her indulging in what was inconsistent with her views of propriety, he was sure to be reminded of her displeasure by a good rap." She called intractable boys to the front of the room and tied them "to her chair with a piece of yarn or pinned their clothes to hers."[33]

Punishment was as easy to avoid as it was for four-year-olds to behave consistently well. Small children were made to sit on wooden benches and listen to endless drills from *The New England Primer*. In Miss Hitty Higginson's rival Salem school, during recitations "each child was given a piece of paper to hold in both hands and directed not to drop it. . . . This was in order to keep them quiet." If the paper dropped, Hitty Higginson called to an assistant named Augusta: "Gusta, nip her, nip her." Benjamin Browne went to Babbidge's school and became a teacher's pet. He could not remember her hitting him. He did remember her beating other children, however, and doubtless experienced what psychologists call vicarious trauma. He particularly remembered in his class Lemme Perkins, who was a talented musician and whistler and also blind. To appease his teacher, Lemme "brought Mrs. B. a long stick made from a rose-bush and gave it to her, to be used instead of her cane-pole." The gift did not exempt Lemme from punishment, however: "poor Lemme somehow misbehaved himself, and got the first taste of the quality of his rod, much to the amusement and gratification of the rest of us."[34] Watching a woman beat a four-year-old blind boy with the stick he had brought her as a gift while the other children hooted and hollered was an experience Benjamin Browne could never forget.

At age seven Rantoul went to Master Watson's school to learn to write. "Here I became associated with larger boys and began to partake of the rough and tumble of life," as if Babbidge's discipline were gentle. He watched masters beat children, as well as frequent fighting among peers. "The infliction of corporal punishment in schools was a matter of daily occurrence, and upon some occasions it was administered with a cruel severity which shocked the feelings of all those accustomed to a mild parental discipline." It is important to note that daily meant each and every day. Rantoul routinely saw boys badly beaten by approved adult authority in school. He noted that "a whip, commonly called a cow-hide, was the usual instrument, and it was sometimes applied with the full strength of the master."[35]

Rantoul and Browne went on to John Southwick's school. They considered Southwick, a Quaker, a remarkably tender man. He rarely hit his older scholars, but called "the delinquent to him, and by kind persuasive words and fondling, he would invariably soften his feelings, make him to see his failing, and induce a resolution to amend." Such respite from violence was offered only to the oldest students, however. "Upon the smaller scholars he thought he could not bestow the time requisite for this result, and occasionally visited them with the rod." Browne also thought Southwick "a kind man" who "rarely used the cowhide, except as a threatened terror to delinquents, but when he did use it, he did it with no sparing hand."[36] Such a terrifying education helped boys endure and inflict violence. To become good seafarers like Hector McNeill and fine shipwrights and captains like the Langworthy nine, they learned to disassociate their emotions from their bodily sensations (to use psychological jargon), and they learned to form teams to fight one another, humiliate others, and if necessary to kill. This training, too, was the making of a town labor force on the edge of the sea.

Celebrating Belonging by Rioting in Boston

Growing up in Boston was similar to growing up in Salem. Corporal punishments in schools trained boys for fights between neighborhood gangs, in this case between the North Enders and South Enders. These fights also occurred twice a week and culminated in a pitched battle on Pope's Day, a festival celebrated every November 5 from 1690 on, commemorating the anniversary of the foiling in 1605 of the Gunpowder Plot, the attempt by Catholic infiltrators to blow up Parliament and destroy the Protestant English state.

Artisans built elaborate props: a cart of some ten to twenty feet, a large chair, an enormous wooden statue of the Pope, an oversized effigy of the Devil. They assembled what would now be recognized as a float, the Pope sitting on the chair with the Devil behind him, with a light or lantern placed in the front of the cart to allow for nighttime processions. They decorated the Pope and the Devil with garish costumes, perhaps pieced together by women. Boys wielding poles manipulated the Pope's and the Devil's grotesque, moveable heads. Littler boys in costumes ran around as the Devil's imps and climbed aboard the cart to kiss the Pope and the Devil as the parade advanced through the wharved city. Throngs of young men and boys in elaborate costumes pulled or pushed this wheeled stage from one end of town to the other, while musicians played anti-Catholic ditties and large crowds cheered the heroes through Boston's dark streets.

By the 1730s, and probably earlier, North End and South End artisans fashioned separate carts and effigies, met in the middle of town, and fought one another with "fists, stones, clubs, and other missiles," as one participant recalled. The object was to subdue the young men from the other neighborhood, grab their cart, and parade it triumphantly through the losers' own neighborhood. Deeper into the night the neighborhood artisans and their boy admirers reconciled, wheeled the surviving carts to the gate and gallows on the Neck, and burned the Pope and the Devil in a huge bonfire, symbolizing the destruction of the hateful interlopers who had dared penetrate their city. They then ate a supper together. The occasion, like Langworthy's ride, allowed young men to show their courage, artistry, and physical prowess, while symbolically protecting Boston's holy Protestant social order from evil interlopers. As one historian insightfully noted, Pope's Day riots did not signify class divisions in Boston, for all social classes attended: "The parading expressed commonly held values in communities grown slightly larger than the familiar."[37] Many historians have offered significant commentary on the political implications of these parades and fights.[38] Here I draw attention to the workaday meanings of this youthful play. The parades were expressions of the playful organization of men and boys in the process of educating themselves to be seamen and shipbuilders: to pick leaders, to undergo discipline, to construct well and artfully with wood, to express Protestant ethics and tribal loyalties, and to show the courage and prowess necessary to protect a Protestant city at home and abroad in a violent age. The parades helped make the male town work force. Each neighborhood had a Pope's Day captain. The most famous was Ebenezer Macintosh, who defeated the North End in an upset in 1764, and later led the Stamp Act riots. He was a well-established leather dresser, and his status on Pope's Day was based on his courage and leadership ability.[39]

All men of all ages participated. According to one participant, the top masters made the major effigies, but apprentices showed their prowess by making smaller versions, down to little boys who made Pope's heads from potatoes and used them to collect money. The close connections between shore and sea were obvious. As the parade began, another participant noted, the revelers organized each cart like a ship's crew and treated the city's land-lubbers as passengers: "Each *Pope* had a Captain, Lieutenant, and crew like a ship. As they passed through the streets, they civilly asked for money of the passengers, and at the doors of the houses and shops—Those who were appointed to collect money carried a small bell, which was rung by way of warning. . . . The money collected on these occasions, was expended by the crew in procuring a supper, where the combatants met to relate the feats of the day." In most years the parade and fight were well organized, though in 1764 a wheel ran over and killed a boy.[40]

The Pope's Day festivities capped the training of the town labor force in the disciplined violence needed to face enemies on the Atlantic, whether pirates or foreigners, and on land, whether the French and Indians, British troops, or political enemies at home. The battle on Pope's Day was only the highlight of Boston neighborhood gangs' calendar year of brawling. As late as 1800, Dr. Edward Reynolds remembered that the "old feud between the Southenders and Northenders, as old as the town itself . . . was the occasion of a regular battle every Thursday and Saturday afternoon" which was "not unfrequently the occasion of very serious injury to wind and limb." Twice-a-week matches made deft fighters. As another Bostonian witness noted, "Our people became veterans in this pugilistic warfare, so that when the British troops were quartered in the town, the inhabitants were invariably victorious in the frequent squabbles which occurred between them, even when the soldiers were double their number."[41]

As the cases of Hector McNeill and the Salem merchants make clear, gang violence was not only a way of forging a successful town labor force of mariners and shipbuilders but also an extension of violence in town schools between teachers and the boys and among the boys themselves. It fit with the religious notion that at birth a child was evil and required some traumatic will-breaking to begin the process of conversion. Perhaps boys set on having clerical careers and the sons of rich merchants enrolled in grammar schools were exempt from such manly brawling, but not future artisans, sailors, and shipbuilders. Far from standing aloof, many ministers participated in the fights or provided inspiration for them. John Barnard was born in Boston in 1681, six years after Langworthy's ride. He got a place in the town grammar school under the legendary Ezekial Cheever. By his own admission a top child Latinist at the age of eight, he was also "a very naughty boy. . . . You, Barnard, I know you can do well enough if you will," Cheever admonished him, "but you are so full of play that you hinder your classmates from getting their lessons; and therefore, if any of them cannot perform their duty, I shall correct you for it." Another boy got wind of this new game and purposely performed poorly, causing Barnard to be beaten several times. Barnard waited for the boy after school and then "drubbed him heartily." Barnard felt morally justified. Nonetheless, this attack was so frightening that, as Barnard later proudly remarked, "the boy never came to school any more, and so that unhappy affair ended." A few years later Barnard entered Harvard, having literally fought his way in.[42]

Barnard seemed to bridge the clerical and maritime worlds. In 1707, Governor Dudley appointed Barnard as one of the chaplains to the army on the Port Royal expedition. He experienced ambush and saw many of his friends as well as the French killed in combat. In 1709, he went to sea as a chaplain on a five-hundred-ton ship. Given his familiarity with the rigors of town youth, he gained favor among sailors. Cotton Mather in 1714 campaigned vigorously to prevent Barnard from becoming the minister of the New Brick church, an addition to his own church in the North End. Mather told Barnard he feared that most of his mariner congregants would leave him for the manlier Barnard. The group threatening to leave included several sea captains and Mr. Samuel Greenwood, the shipwright brother of Nathaniel Greenwood of the Langworthy nine. Barnard went on to become the minister at Marblehead, where he preached effectively to fishermen and mariners.[43]

Preparing to Face Death at Sea

The making of a maritime labor force was not only a matter of violent play. Boston's and Salem's rough games taught leadership, group organizations, and emotional disassociation, but blue-water sailing was riskier than ritualized combat on the town common. About 3 percent of the mariners who went to sea died each year, meaning that a man who went to sea at the age of fourteen would most likely be dead by the age of thirty-four, leaving behind a widow and orphans.[44] People expected death, especially among young children and the old, but the deaths of men in their prime and of young fathers were especially traumatic. It is inconceivable that the people of Boston or other maritime cities could have sustained such high death rates among its sons and husbands and nonetheless maintain a large, able, and propertied seagoing workforce without the play of the mind to provide a convincing explanation and effective therapy for repeated shock and trauma. Otherwise the survivors would literally go crazy, or the city's middling people would abandon its near-suicidal livelihood. Here the Calvinist idea about a crucified God and the application of this religion to the godly city of crucified adherents was crucial.

The chief clerics of Boston's shipbuilding and maritime center, the North End, were Increase Mather and his son, Cotton Mather, who were prominent among the authors of the notion that Massachusetts and Boston were of special concern to both God and the Devil. In Boston the most productive builders and most creative religious thinkers and writers faced each other on virtually every Sabbath. The Mathers' congregations were composed largely of merchants, mariners, and shipwrights and their families, although Cotton Mather noted in his diary that sailors normally disliked him. His neighbor was the shipwright Timothy Thornton. The Mathers believed that their intellectual play was as crucial to the sustenance of the city's self-sacrificing workforce as was the play of the neighborhood gangs.

As his diary and other writings show, Cotton Mather understood that his job entailed healing the souls of mariners, or at least consoling their widows and bereaved mothers. "The grievous losses and sorrows my neighbors have lately suffered by the way of the sea," he noted in his diary in April 1717, "oblige me to mediations peculiarly adapted for them." As he noted in May 1711, "here are some families in pain and fear (and with extreme reason) that their friends abroad are miscarried. I would visit them and comfort them, with pure religion, and undefiled." As early as 1698, Mather remarked that the maritime economy had made Boston a city too well acquainted with death. "In that church whereof I am the servant, I have counted the widows make about a sixth part of our communicants, and no doubt in the whole town the proportion differs not very much." The sea had claimed the lives of many young men: "The disasters on your young folks have been so multiplied, that there are few parents among us, but what will go with wounded hearts down into their graves: their daily moans are, Ah, my son cut off in his youth! My son, my son!" Mather's own son Increase died at sea in 1724.[45]

Mather believed and reassured victims and survivors that Boston's suffering, like its success, was divinely ordained. In his diary Mather repeatedly used the phrase "the widows multiply" when he heard about shipwrecks or fevers killing married men in foreign ports,[46] alluding to the words of Jeremiah 15:8: "Their widows are multiplied to me above the sand of the seas: I have brought upon them the mother of the young men a spoiler at noon day:

I have caused him to fall upon it suddenly, and terrors upon the city." In this passage God was telling the prophet Jeremiah that He was punishing Jerusalem for its disobedience. Mather believed God had created Boston as the contemporary Jerusalem, for the widows constantly multiplied and only Christ kept the city from perishing.

Mather laid out his theological interpretation of Boston's history in his 1698 lecture, "The Bostonian Ebenezer." He believed that God had chosen Boston because its people had erected churches in which inspired ministers preached God's word properly. The city's prominence was unexpected and unmerited: "the town hath indeed three elder sisters in this colony, but it hath wonderfully outgrown them all; and her mother, old Boston, in England also; yea, within a few years after the first settlement it grew to be, the Metropolis of the whole English America." In its earliest years, he recalled, "Boston was proverbially called, Lost Town, for the mean and sad circumstances of it." The town had thrived because of divine patronage, not human agency or an accident of geography: "many more than a thousand houses are to be seen on this little piece of ground, all fill'd with the undeserved favors of God." In Mather's view, Boston had been delivered from fires, epidemics, and maritime disasters by the grace of God alone, for its people's sins were sufficient to merit the city's total destruction: "Never was any town under the cope of heaven more liable to be laid in ashes, either through the carelessness, or through the wickedness of them that sleeps in it." In the catastrophes that did afflict the city, God issued warning after warning to Bostonians to repent. In Mather's view, God quarreled with Boston as He had done with Jerusalem, but Christ protected the new holy city. The ministers stood as a saving remnant, as self-sacrificing as the sailors, in the imitation of Christ: "I am very much mistaken if we are not willing to die for you too, if called unto it." He admonished Bostonians, "thou hast been lifted up to heaven; there is not a town upon earth, which, on some accounts, has more to answer for."

Listeners took seriously Mather's argument that Boston's rapid rise and preservation, despite its constant suffering, proved that theirs was a godly city, echoing the mid-seventeenth-century Puritans' vision of English towns. Probably some were moved by his dramatic account of near-catastrophes, as much as by his uplifting vision. In his diary, Mather noted that this was a rare triumphant public moment: "The Lord having helped me, beyond my expectation in preparing a discourse for the lecture, he yet more gloriously helped me in uttering of it unto a vast assembly of his people. . . . And the hearts of the inhabitants of the town were strangely moved by what was delivered among them."[47]

The mapmaker John Bonner took this vision of the godly city seriously. Bonner was a master mariner as well as a draughtsman. He owned several ships, including the brigantine *Hope* on which Reverend John William had returned from captivity in Canada following the Deerfield raid of 1704, and he made many voyages. Bonner did several plans of Boston harbor for ship-masters. In old age he worked as a pilot, guiding ships into the harbor. In addition to showing the wharves so clearly, his 1722 map contains detailed information in the legends: a list of the churches and public buildings, including schools; the dates of six "great fires" and six smallpox epidemics. These were all the components of the godly city: the word preached, education publicly provided, and a tense dialogue with a punishing God. Yet, as the map shows so clearly, by 1722 Boston had hundreds of wharves and thousands of houses. Only the gangs are left out.

Massachusetts not only built the largest American mercantile fleet, but penetrated the English market for ships. In October 1724, two years after Bonner's map was published, the master shipwrights of the River Thames petitioned the King, complaining that "great numbers of those able shipwrights brought up and employed by petitioners" were leaving for the colonies because of "the great number of ships and other vessels lately built, now building and still likely to increase to be built, in New England and other parts of America." The master shipwrights argued that the departure of their shipwrights raised the specter of "the great danger and damage that may attend the service of your Majesty in fitting out your Royal Navy on any extraordinary emergency." Parliament debated this petition in January 1725 and issued a report to the Board of Trade. On January 28, 1725, the Council of Trade and Plantations reported to the King that "we have good reason to believe, the number of shipwrights in Great Britain is diminished one half since 1710 . . . chiefly owing to the great number of ships built annually in your Majesty's Plantations: but particularly in New England." The Council recommended "laying a duty on all Plantation built ships sold in Great Britain, and afterwards employed in foreign trade" and proposed a five-shilling per ton tax on each New England ship sold in England. The measure failed to win parliamentary approval, probably because of the influence of English merchants who profited from the less expensive and faster American-built ships. As a result, by 1775 New Englanders built as much as a third of England's own mercantile fleet in addition to all of their own.[48]

New England had ample forest resources, but relatively little skilled labor to draw upon for such a vast and sophisticated industry. Yet Boston, Salem, and other ports competed with British shipbuilding towns without a comparable population. They lacked a large surplus labor pool from which entrepreneurs could recruit desperate craftsmen, mariners, and carters for little pay. The plurality of New England ships were built on, or adjoining, the Boston wharves, themselves fabricated by cooperation between the town, its workers, and its merchants during a time when the city lacked capital. Within the boundaries of Boston, men played and brawled in groups, conducted town business, and listened to word pictures of an angry, homicidal, yet loving God. Little wonder that Boston was a city in which little boys played with great energy and some risk at building wharves. The town meetings helped forge not only wharves but also a godly gang of disciplined, traumatized, and violent male workers to create wealth and equity in New England's great towns.

CHAPTER SIX

Rural Shipbuilding

AFTER 1650, BOSTON merchants invested thousands of pounds sterling in rural Massachusetts towns to develop shipbuilding and the resources it required. Boston merchants capitalized shipbuilding enterprises not only in coastal towns such as Salem, Charlestown, and Newburyport, where their investments supplemented those of local merchants, but also in inland towns that had river access to the Atlantic and good timber lands but little local capital. Between 1686 and 1713, rural shipwrights were responsible for 30 percent of all the ship tonnage built in Massachusetts. Taunton and Scituate were particularly important rural shipbuilding centers.[1]

Shipbuilding demanded enormous quantities of wood and labor. Turning standing forests into usable timber required cutters, loggers, carters, blacksmiths, sawmill operators, and workers. Much of the cargo sent to the West Indies consisted of lumber, hogsheads (large casks), and planks, all processed by rural workers. Massachusetts coopers made most of the barrels and other wooden containers for the Atlantic trade. The iron forges that supplied shipbuilders required enormous quantities of wood for fuel. Maritime historians, as noted, have estimated that building a hundred-ton vessel required two hundred trees and a ton of iron.[2] On this model, between 1698 and 1713 Massachusetts shipbuilding alone consumed about 250,000 trees. It took a virtual army of workers to cut down, transport, mill, and distribute such a mountain of timber.

Massachusetts was not a sleepy land of inefficient farmers, drowsing through long winters. If the summer belonged to haying and the autumn to the harvest, in winter many rural men awakened to work in wood. Those who had not acquired artisan skills could labor in the forests by the day or season; those with woodlots could sell lumber by the board foot. The entire enterprise was well organized and profitable, at least to the sawmill owners and timber merchants. Lumbering was not undertaken by rugged individuals armed with axes and hatchets contending with the primal forest to clear land for farming, as appears in the later romances of James Fenimore Cooper. Rather, the wages and incomes brought by cutting and selling wood sustained many long-established rural families and complemented farming. After 1650, lumbering and woodworking equaled or surpassed agriculture in economic importance across rural Massachusetts.

As shipbuilders poured capital into rural towns near rivers and the industry's demand for lumber reached far into the interior, Massachusetts towns did not free labor markets from dung-encrusted farmers' moldy restrictions on mobility and age-old customs of regulation. Just the opposite occurred. Rather than capitalist development shattering the communal traditions of static rural villages, it prompted and even provoked the formation of political economies that defended local labor and husbanded natural resources. Even where strong town governments had been lacking, the influx of Boston capital stimulated the creation of rural economies with well-organized and militant town labor systems. Taunton and Scituate were sprawling rural townships that originally had little sense of identity and whose leaders rejected religious orthodoxy.[3] When Boston money ignited a shipbuilding boom in these towns after 1650, Scituate and Taunton provincials abandoned their individualism and used Plymouth and Massachusetts law to make themselves over into strong New England towns with powerful town labor systems. Farmers and artisans in these towns did not enforce the dictates of private, patriarchal family labor or adopt free-market principles. Rather, they adopted the policies and practices that protected labor in other developed towns and added new features of their own that privileged local residents in the shipbuilding economy.

Adopting a Town Labor Protection Policy

Only twenty miles from Boston by water, the North River empties into the Massachusetts Bay at Scituate. A sand bar blocks the entrance to the river part of the year, but in the seventeenth and eighteenth centuries a large vessel could escape from the mouth of the river during high tide.[4] The North River ran far into the interior, providing access to prime timber lands filled with white oaks, the essential material for shipbuilding.

Even before 1630, John Winthrop, and the great Puritan migration, Scituate shipbuilders constructed a small fleet for Plymouth colony. After 1650, Boston capital helped the people of Scituate develop many more shipyards on the North River. After 1660, at least five new shipbuilders arrived from outside the town. Fourteen shipbuilders were active in Scituate at the end of the seventeenth century. Fifty-two Boston merchants provided about 83 percent of the capital required for the thirty-five vessels registered in 1698 (totaling 1,426 tons) that had been built in Scituate during the five previous years, pouring £5,000 into the enterprise. King William's War stimulated this flurry of activity, as Boston merchants looked beyond their own city's limited productive capacity for places to build ships to replace sunken or captured merchant vessels and warships to attack and loot enemy shipping. Among the most enthusiastic investors were Samuel Lillie, Andrew Belcher, and Benjamin Gallop. From 1696 to 1698, Lillie invested in the construction of nine vessels in Scituate; he was the sole investor in the hundred-ton ship *Providence*. In 1705, Boston merchants and mariners capitalized 340 of the 360 tons built that year in Scituate, spending about £1,000 on fourteen vessels in that year alone. With money arriving from across the bay, the sprawling town became a shipbuilding center and by far the wealthiest town in Plymouth colony (after 1691, Plymouth County, Massachusetts).[5]

Scituate, which originally encompassed fifty-three square miles, had been a New England town in name only. Formed by Plymouth colonists augmented by new immigrants from Kent, its houses and farms were dispersed, not tidily placed around a pleasant church and green. Residents suffered from uncertainty about who controlled the distribution of unsettled land, a matter that was not resolved until 1683. They not only quarreled among themselves about religion but—even worse, by New England standards—showed a talent for living with their differences peaceably. The original Scituate church, established in 1634, split over the appointment of Charles Chauncey as minister in 1641. Formerly the professor of Greek at Trinity College, Cambridge, he later became president of Harvard College. Chauncey inferred from his scriptural study that baptism could only be effectual when the child or convert was fully immersed in water. Prominent people took issue with this version of the ritual and left to form a second Congregational Church in Scituate. More outrageously, they adopted membership rules similar to those of regular Anglicans, allowing men and women who had never testified to their conversion to join in full communion so long as they behaved in a civil, moral fashion. Chauncey and his congregation deemed this laxity dangerous, and John Winthrop condemned the doctrine and its proponent, William Vassal. Yet, instead of departing to establish a religiously pure town some-where else, the losers set up a new church next to the old one, and everybody continued to live in Scituate.[6]

Even Quakers found a refuge in Scituate. Edward Wanton, who had been assigned to guard Quakers before they were hanged, became sympa-thetic to Quaker preachers. In 1661, he became a Quaker himself and fled from Boston to Scituate, where he became a shipbuilder with property along the North River and started a Friends meeting. The Quakers grew to have a strong fellowship in the town. A troop of Scituate soldiers influenced by pacifist teachings left their units during King Philip's War in 1676. From the late 1650s John Cudsworth, one of the largest landholders in Scituate and a former judge, bravely defended Quakers against persecution. Cudsworth had been a magistrate in Plymouth colony, but the Court of Assistants ejected him when he refused to enforce the harsh laws they passed against Quakers. In England, Quakers published his eloquent letter protesting against Plym-outh and Massachusetts policy. "The Antichristian persecuting spirit is very active" in New England, he wrote, and "he that will not whip and slash, banish, and persecute men that differ in matters of Religion, must not sit on the bench, nor sustain any office in the Commonwealth." He criticized his fellow magistrates' slavish obedience to Massachusetts' policies of intolerance. Although he was banned in Boston, the Scituate community repeatedly re-turned Cudsworth to the Plymouth General Court, and he later became accepted as a provincial military leader.[7]

These early shipbuilders were remarkably individualistic. The first Scitu-ate Quaker, Edward Wanton, was not a pacifist, but built warships that his sons commanded as privateers. His progeny became governors in Rhode Is-land. The shipbuilder William Barstow had settled originally in Dedham, but the town meeting chased him away because they thought him a drunk and unseemly pauper. In Scituate, Barstow was disciplined by the court for slandering the minister, Charles Chauncey, in 1647. He grew wealthy and respectable, serving in several town offices. Barstow probably began building ships around 1660, and his son continued the business. Scituate shipbuilder John Palmer, Jr., jilted Dinah Sylvester, the daughter of another North River shipbuilder, and had to pay a £20 fine for breach of promise in 1661. He supported the hated Governor Andros and served on his Council. After Andros was ousted by a local revolution in 1689, Palmer was sent prisoner to England, where he published two pamphlets in defense of the Dominion of New England. Job Randall, who built privateers on the North River, was prone to violence, being fined in 1660 for striking Edward Wanton and in 1664 for poking Jeremiah Hatch with a "ho-pole." William James, who built vessels in Scituate harbor, became locally famous in the 1690s for his daring escape in 1691 from debtor's prison in Boston. Israel Hobart, the son of the minister of neighboring Hingham's impressive Old Ship Church, arrived in Scituate in the late 1660s and built ships on the North River at what became known as Hobart's Landing. Shunning the self-effacing saltbox style of much Massachusetts domestic architecture, he built a spacious mansion and had its doorway decorated with two carved cherubs.[8]

Scituate was not yet an operating town with a normal political economy by New England standards. The people were split among three religious societies who disagreed with one another and, more shockingly, agreed to disagree. The town lacked a strong town meeting. Although it was incorporated in 1636, before 1670 it annually named only one town officer, a constable. The town initially showed no disposition to halt the flow of in-migrants. Scituate's porous borders were easily crossed by people and money. Boston entrepreneurs could operate in the town without the restrictions that a strong town government protecting local laborers might provide. Scituate appeared to be a place where contract ruled, not the civic interests of a holy town that valued labor too highly to sacrifice for profit.

Thanks to the arrival of Boston money, by 1670 the people of Scituate had to decide by action or default what kind of political economy to adopt. They could continue the policy of open borders and allow the shipbuilders to import indentured servants or slaves, or simply to employ the poor from other towns who were eager to find work. Scituate might attract capital by becoming the unregulated suburb of regulated Boston, where entrepreneurs could operate without restrictions on their labor supply or their exploitation of local resources. They could let the market dictate the cost of production and the wages of labor. But if they chose to develop a town labor force and protect public resources, they had to get busy.

The 340 tons of shipping built in Scituate in 1705 required nearly a thousand oak trees to be cut down, carted or floated to the North River, and hewed into timbers or sawed into boards. In 1705, Scituate was home to about sixty families scattered across fifty-three square miles. The workload required to build 340 tons of vessels annually was more than the town's small adult male labor force could handle. Moreover, shipbuilding-related enterprises required a wide variety of skills. Roads were built to move trees to the rivers for transportation. Livestock farmers trained oxen to move large masts and sleds of wood. Sawmills supplied the planks and boards. Iron forges turned out iron for ship construction, and yet more trees had to be cut for fuel. In a society that lacked a large pool of surplus labor, shipbuilders either had to operate within a free labor market, to develop a coerced labor force, or to rely on empowered town labor systems to supply the entire enterprise with adequate resources and reliable labor.

Surprisingly, although it remained a productive shipbuilding center and magnet for Boston money, Scituate became more, not less, economically and socially restrictive during the seventeenth century. Despite their previous rejection of Massachusetts town norms, Scituate leaders after 1670 proclaimed principles of equity and developed a strong town labor system that protected local laborers and denied access and resources to outside labor. As Boston capital poured in, town meetings flourished, public institutions were established, and a language of localism began to emerge. Residents began to define the town's boundaries and to create a privileged local labor force.

Most Scituate residents were and remained farmers. Perhaps, resenting the arrival of new workers and wealthy urban capitalists, farmers were the first to grow alarmed. In the spring of 1667, the town meeting took decisive steps toward restricting in-migration and disciplining employers in Scituate for hiring and harboring strangers. Shipbuilders seeking cheap labor brought in outsiders. The town meeting complained that these outsiders undercut the wages of town-born laborers and, when the newcomers became sick and poor, added substantially to the taxes paid by farmers. Forgetting its history of neglect, the town meeting evoked the ideology of the holy town and Christian humanism and criticized employers who lacked civic consciousness, complaining that "some persons out of their own sinister ends . . . have too aptly been harborers and entertainers of such as are strangers coming from other towns and places by which means the town cometh to be burdened and themselves many times prejudiced."[9] The town stated clearly that profit making at the town's expense was wrong and that the people of Scituate had privileges they were bound to protect. The town would not turn into an unregulated shipbuilding center.

In a whole series of moves over the decades that followed, the town meeting rejected free-labor markets. It established borders and settlement policies similar to those of Boston, Dedham, and other Massachusetts towns.

The meeting evoked the approved political economy of Massachusetts and Plymouth, grounding its actions in the "power and authority given and granted to them by the court concerning things of this nature." Residents were required to report "strangers" in their houses within five days and post bonds to cover any expenses that might arise if they fell into poverty and sickness; employers were subject to a ten-shilling fine for each week they ignored these stringent rules. Essentially, employers had to pay a premium for using outside laborers on a long-term basis. This act was aimed at keeping the costs of maintaining the sick and poor in Scituate under control and giving the town born first access to shipbuilding employment and profits from resources utilized for shipbuilding in the town. To oversee the act, the town meeting chose "Captain Cudsworth, Cornet Stetson, and Mr. Tilden," all yeomen with large landholdings. Cudsworth, who once denounced copying Boston ways, created and enforced a Boston-style political economy.[10]

Some employers continued to harbor outside laborers. In August 1682, the town meeting strengthened the restrictions on harboring strangers. Intensifying its civic rhetoric, the town meeting described those hiring outsiders as "ill-disposed persons in our town who through covetous principles aiming to increase their outward estate neither regard the condition of neither the town nor the orders thereof against such actings."[11] The new laws increased the fine from ten to fourteen shillings and promised to give one-third of the fine to whoever reported and proved the violation. It was noted that employers were abusing their right to take in apprentices and servants by offering workers contracts of only three or four months; after that, these laborers remained in town and their welfare became the responsibility of the town's ratepayers. The town thus ordered all servants to be hired for at least a year and registered with the town. The difficulty the town had enforcing its law against outsiders highlighted its determination to protect town labor in spite of the shipbuilding industry's insatiable demand for workers.

The problem of supplying an adequate local labor force was complicated by confusion over the ownership and control of the town's undivided lands. Unless the town born had the promise of land in the town, young men would leave once they were old enough to work independently of their fathers. Then shipbuilders and those who supplied them would be forced to hire "foreigners." The issue of the undivided land split the town between those who wanted to emphasize agriculture and those who wanted to accommodate shipbuilding. Uncertainty arising from overlapping public jurisdictions and private claims reigned from 1633 on without causing much conflict as long as the town remained sparsely populated. As shipbuilding expanded in Scituate, however, land became more valuable. In 1670, the General Court of Plymouth Colony, which had encouraged freemen in incorporated towns to select commissions to whom it would transfer land-granting authority, recognized a committee that was apparently resentful of the newcomers rushing into Scituate. Composed of Scituate's largest landholders and long-time leaders, including James Cudworth, Robert Stetson, John Cushing, John Bryant, and three members of the Turner family (whose progenitor had been the constable), the committee decided to reserve rights to the undivided land to those who had resided in the town as of 1647 and to their legal heirs and assigns. Latecomers would be excluded from any share. The committee then gave out generous grants, largely to themselves and their kinsmen, and decided that the undivided land would serve as a commons. Its resources would be devoted solely to agriculture and house building, rather than shipbuilding: "The rest of the undivided lands of Scituate are to remain as commons to be used by Scituate inhabitants only, for grazing and feeding their cattle and for wood for their own use. From 30 November 1674, no oak timber from the commons is to be sawn into planks, used for shipbuilding, etc. Cedar and spruce only are allowed to be transported, the spruce sawn into boards, the cedar riven into shingles." This policy would keep the forest out of the hands of shipbuilders, at least until it was divided and allotted to the proprietors and their heirs.[12]

This set of decisions immediately provoked a protest petition signed by sixty-six Scituate residents, including at least four shipbuilders. The petitioners used communalistic language, stressing the importance of unanimity for economic and spiritual growth. But their concern about those who had been excluded rings clear: "it be a dispensation so strange and dubious as is altogether beyond our apprehensions why the society of a township orderly possessed and suitably replenished with inhabitants both for numbers and quality . . . should now at once be stripped of all their privileges so long enjoyed and rendered altogether incapable of acting either for improvement or distribution either in part or in whole as a township." The commissioners, the petitioners protested, "have presumed at one stroke to cut from a right or privilege all the single persons in the town of Scituate who have lived so long in the township" even though they were not heirs of any 1647 landowner. Hard-working young men would be "exposed to unnecessary flights" or forced "to enter into servitude and bondage." The petitioners assumed that dividing society into privileged, property-holding haves and deprived, laboring have-nots was unacceptable, particularly when this distinction was drawn among longtime residents. Like the founders of the Second Church of Scituate, the petitioners assumed that stable residence and good conduct counted as membership. They remarked that the town was greatly wounded and that the shipbuilding industry had already been affected by the friction: as a result of the quarrel, some people could not "be supplied with boards for their use at Mr. Tilden's mill [Mr. Tilden was one of the petition's signers]." Economic progress was jeopardized when the town was factionalized and full of rancor.[13]

A month later, many of the same petitioners proposed a solution. In their view, all the inhabitants and their heirs should be considered proprietors with equal interests in the undivided lands, including the right to cut, transport, and sell wood outside the town. "Secondly that all the rest of the present householders of the town as also their male children, when they shall come to be settled householders in the town, as also all such servants as have already served their apprenticeship in the town, all these shall successively enjoy all other privileges . . . jointly together as the society of the township." All males accepted as inhabitants would participate in divisions of the common lands and could cut and process timber from the undivided land, but only the pre-1647 inhabitants and their descendants had a right to sell that timber to people outside the town. The new scheme would privilege shipbuilders by giving them access to the labor and wood of all those who could not transport timber from the town.[14]

In 1676, New England's rebellious natives killed at least twenty Scituate residents and burned thirteen houses, which delayed resolution of the land question. In 1683, the town meeting resolved many of these issues by making most of the undivided lands in Scituate into a perpetual timber commons. On April 5, 1683, the town meeting "doth this day freely grant to all their inhabitants the same quantity of land and in the same places that hath been since 1647 granted to any either by the court, town or committee." All the inhabitants of Scituate, duly recognized as of 1683, would all be given identical land grants. Most impressively, the town decided not to divide most of the undivided land but to hold it "as a general commons for the use of the whole inhabitants at all times successively that shall be orderly received." All current householders and freeholders were joint proprietors of this commons, "them and their male children at the age of twenty-one"; newcomers accepted as settled inhabitants enjoyed equal rights with the native-born.[15]

The commons was huge, dwarfing the famous Great Meadow of Concord. About two and a half miles across and three miles long, it contained between four thousand and five thousand acres and was larger in area than some entire Massachusetts towns. Located near settlements, the coast, and tributaries of the North River, as well as some eleven shipbuilding sites,[16] its wood was readily marketable to local sawmills, shipbuilders, and house carpenters, and for export to the West Indian market. Scituate's belatedly formed common was a bonanza for the town born.

The decision was not simply a matter of self-interest or the result of a battle between proprietors and nonproprietors. The debate turned on political economy, especially what kind of labor system Scituate would have and what kind of industry it would promote. Among the sixty-eight men who signed one or both of the protest petitions in the 1670s, no less than fifty-nine (86 percent) were deemed proprietors by the committee. Indeed, several members of the committee signed the protest petitions. At the same time, sixty-nine proprietors signed neither petition. Nor was the committee simply hostile to shipbuilders. At first the committee decided that the late-arriving Edward Wanton, the town's major shipbuilder, was entitled to only a right to use the commons, not to a share in land divisions. Soon, however, "the committee judges that Edward Wanton's children have the same privileges as one of the children of the ratable inhabitants of 1647, because Wanton is a successor of one of the inhabitants of 1647."[17] The decision made by the majority of the town in 1683 to create a large timber common meant that residents were to accommodate farming and shipbuilding in a new political economy. Instead of breaking the undivided lands into farms for individual families, the seven square-mile commons was a jointly held forest that yielded wood to supply sawmills and shipbuilders. Scituate managed its publicly held resources carefully. As a result of a democratic decision-making process, all Scituate inhabitants enjoyed the right to cut in the town forest and participate in the expanding market for lumber. This shrewd and sophisticated move secured labor for the town and its new industry.

Although making Scituate's pine and oak trees available to the shipbuilding industry was important, the primary purpose of the creation of the commons was to assure the creation of a bona fide town labor system that superseded a free-labor market or patriarchal family labor. In 1683 Scituate had plenty of forest on private land, and shipbuilders could purchase this lumber at market prices. The commons was really about creating a sustainable labor force for shipbuilding. Young adult men, whether single or married, had access to timber resources and did not have to depend on

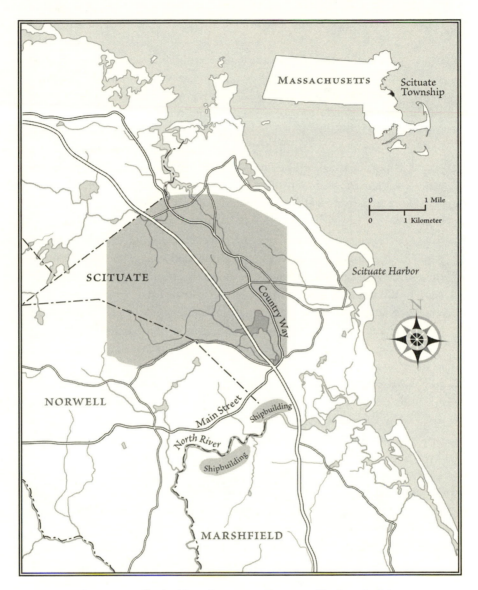

Map 2. The Scituate Shipbuilding Commons. From specifications in Scituate town meeting records. Adapted from Donald Sluter.

employment by large landholders or inheritance from their fathers in their pursuit of independence and a "competency"—the modest property that supporting a family required.[18] Even with the minimal wage of two shillings a day (and they could make far more if they had access to their own wood), they could maintain small families by working in the forest. The commons assured that the young men of Scituate would stay and marry in the town and provide a self-sustaining labor force for sawmill operators and shipbuilders. Town-born males now had real privileges irrespective of their fathers' whims or the date of their ancestors' arrival in town, and employers had a town labor force to rely on.

Those who formed the great common clearly had the position of local white laborers in mind. The town meeting passed bylaws that reserved the commons to town-born labor and protected the wages of town-born white men. "It shall not be lawful for any that is a settled inhabitant to employ any stranger either English or Indian, to work on the town's commons under any man on the forfeit of five shillings a day or part of a day for each person so employed," resolved the town meeting on April 5, 1683. When Humphrey Johnson attempted to dispute the commons and grab land for himself in cedar swamp, the town meeting replied in a petition that "out of our cedar swamps we are supplied with timber to fence our land and with clapboards and shingles to close and cover our houses with all and also poor men are forced to make shingles in winter time to procure clothing for their families."[19] The commons was clearly part of their policy of supporting and retaining labor by protecting laborers' ability to use town resources for themselves and their families.

At the same time, the town policed inhabitants' use of the commons so that it would serve local industries. In 1683, the town declared that tan bark and cordwood could not be transported out of town to avoid "destroying much timber." Inhabitants destroying oak trees would have their bark or cordwood confiscated and the informer would be rewarded with half the bark or cordwood. A year later, the town voted to prohibit anyone from selling or transporting timber from the commons outside of the town, or even moving it to the waterside for export. The timber was to be used only for local industries. In order to ensure that wood would be utilized for ship and house building but not for fuel, the town meeting in 1686 decreed that no inhabitant could cut logs that were shorter than five feet in length, suitable for fireplaces. In May 1697, upset by "the great damage that doth daily happen and accrue to the said town by reason of such great numbers of horses and horsekind as are daily running at large upon common lands," the town meeting decided to allow inhabitants to pasture only one tethered horse on the commons. The town's commitment to ensuring that timber cut from the common remain in town was reinforced in 1700 when the town meeting decided to make every inhabitant apply to one of five town officials, called timber agents, to get a license to cut wood upon the commons. Applicants had to spell out their plans to dispose of the timber in town in order to prevent the secretive cutting of wood for export.[20]

The commons soon became a source of Scituate inhabitants' sense of their separateness from people around them, of their distinct identity as a privileged and vigilant laboring people with their own turf and industry. Town timber had to be protected from outsiders. People from Hingham and Cohasset had previously been just people living in another place, but after 1683 they became redefined as predatory foreigners. On January 20, 1685, the town meeting appointed William Barrell, Joseph Sylvester, and Joseph Turner as agents to prosecute all strangers who dared cut and transport wood from the Scituate commons. In 1686, the town commended inhabitants near the Hingham border for taking "care to prevent the great strip and waste that was made of our wood and timber on Hingham side by stopping or blocking up a cart way on Hingham side wherein much of our wood and timber was transported out of our town and more like to be transported off from our town's common or undivided lands." The town meeting even gave advance permission to these inhabitants to block or destroy any roads that might be built "on the Hingham side" of the town boundary "provided they proceed in a civil and orderly way therein." In 1691, the town meeting gave inhabitants permission to "sue or attack [attach] any such trespassers" and promised them part of the stolen timber as a reward. In 1695, the town appointed Joseph Otis and Peter Collomare as agents to sue foreigners for taking Scituate trees, and ensured that town residents served on the Plymouth colony and county grand juries that heard these cases. In March 1692, for example, Anthony Callimore, Benjamin Stetson, Sr., and Jeremiah Hatch sued Joseph Greene of Weymouth for trespass, alleging that the defendant "hath cut or carried away a considerable quantity of timber off from the commons of Scituate sometimes within this two years." The jury found for Scituate and made Greene pay £3 12 shillings, a considerable sum. In the September court that same year, the Scituate team sued Nathanial Beals, junior, of Hingham, on the grounds that Beales "sometime or times since the 20th May 1691 trespassed upon the lands of the town of Scituate . . . by working on the reputed commons or undivided lands of said town by felling, cutting, or carrying away wood or timber from off said lands contrary to the order of said town." The jury again found for Scituate, extracting £1 in damages and nearly £2 in court costs. Outsiders could not invade and attack the political economy of Scituate without penalty.[21]

Inspired by their creation of a town labor system centered on its massive common lands, Scituate inhabitants developed many other town institutions. By 1694, they regularly chose nineteen officers annually, as did most Massachusetts towns. After 1670, the town began to warn out strangers regularly. In 1675, the two churches in Scituate reconciled their disagreements. They decided not to merge, since the town was large enough to warrant two churches, but each offered communion to the other's members. In 1700, the Scituate town meeting began a publicly supported school system. Hiring James Torrey to teach children to read and write, they agreed to pay five shillings per pupil and the child's parent or master had to pay another fifteen.[22] By 1700, Scituate had defined its borders, developed a strong town meeting, began public education, and formed a town labor system based on the huge and carefully defended timber commons that gave laborers access to timber to sell within the town. The seven-square-mile commons guaranteed the future of the Scituate shipbuilding industry and created a New England town labor system.

These changes reshaped the town's social structure. Accounts of the fundraising for a new meeting house in northern Scituate indicate that though farming was still important, many upriver residents were involved in the Atlantic market. The Congregational Church collected £54 in contributions from forty families. The accounts list the types of payment offered by thirty of them: twenty paid fully or partly in money, fourteen paid fully or partly in corn or meat, eight paid fully or partly in boards, and two paid fully or partly in shoes. The shipbuilding industry and its cash economy had spread quickly from the riverside. A petition to the General Court in 1726 reported that fifty-six families lived in Scituate west of the Third Herring Brook and were engaged "in considerable trade and traffick, having no less than five saw mills and three iron works." At least as many sawmills were located between these sites and Scituate harbor. By the 1770s, the old town of Scituate contained over twenty mills, while in 1781 Hanover—a new town carved out of western Scituate—had ten grist and sawmills, another mill (probably a fulling mill), and two iron works. All this labor, in addition to farming, occupied 211 adult males. Scituate itself had another fifteen sawmills. The town contained 419 male workers: farmers, shipbuilders, tanners, shoemakers, millwrights, sawyers, and carters.[23]

The distribution of land in Scituate was uneven, and few families tried to accumulate land to bequeath to sons. In the 1726 tax lists, the top 20 percent of rate-payers in regards to wealth (forty-seven men and women) owned 61 percent of the real estate, and the top 30 percent (seventy persons) owned no less than 76 percent of the real estate. On the other hand, the bottom 49 percent of the rate-payers in regards to wealth (117 persons) owned just 20 percent of the real estate. Such inequalities were not unusual in early modern societies; landownership and tenancy were far more restricted in England. What is curious, however, is that the top 30 percent of taxpayers, while owning three-quarters of the land, paid only half of the total tax bill, while the poorest half, who owned little or no real estate, paid a third. Massachusetts tax policy dictated that each male over sixteen years of age had to pay a six-shilling tax, called a "poll" (or head) tax, while the tax on land was proportionately lower. This system reflected the fact that in eighteenth-century Massachusetts, land had comparatively less value in relation to labor than historians are used to seeing in rural communities.[24]

Large landowners in Scituate failed to accumulate many male adult laborers in their households. The man with the most land had only two polls, nine men with the next greatest share of the land had an average of 1.8 polls, and fifty-three men with the next greatest share had 1.4 polls. On the other hand, 157 men with only small pieces of real estate had an average of 1.2 adult male laborers in their households. In short, rich men relied on the labor of people living outside their household but within the town, notwithstanding the contributions of family labor. Moreover, employers had to pay high wages in proportion to rents. Records of an elaborate state tax assessment done in 1771 exist for many Massachusetts towns, including the assessment of how much each rate-payer's real estate rented for annually. These lands were not necessarily rented; this amount was an estimate of what rent the land would bring, based on its specific size and quality and on standard rents in the town. In Marshfield, the town south of Scituate along the coast, land rented for 4.75 shillings an acre. At the minimum wage of 2 shillings per day, a laborer could rent twenty acres of land in Marshfield by working forty-eight days. In the agricultural town of Concord, land rented for only 3.26 shillings an acre, thus a man could rent twenty acres by working just thirty-three days. In eighteenth-century England, by contrast, farmland rented for about 8 shillings per acre and the common wage was only one shilling a day; a laborer would need work 160 days, or spend over half his annual income, to rent a twenty-acre farm. Today a minimum wage worker can barely rent a room for less than half of his or her salary in Concord or Scituate. The power of workers and the high wages they enjoyed in eighteenth-century Massachusetts towns is unimaginable to present-day Americans.[25]

Relatively high wages and low rents were not confined to Massachusetts. Indeed, how to produce value when labor was so costly and so hard to keep given the cheapness and availability of land was a central conundrum of the American colonies. Other colonial elites solved this problem by importing indentured servants who did not receive wages and could not buy land until they had worked out their terms. When bound labor proved too demanding and disorderly, they shifted to African slaves. Coercive forms of labor dominated most parts of America and shaped its destiny. Massachusetts provided value in a different way through the town labor system, a deliberately designed political economy based on Christian values that, by restricting the labor market, assured high wages for the town born and those allowed into the town. In Scituate, which developed this policy rather late, the town labor system also included access to a huge common, a vital resource workers could share that served the local industry. By following these policies, entrepreneurs developed a major shipbuilding industry based on privileged and skilled labor that dominated colonial production and rivaled even England in the production of ships.

This distinctive labor system did not rely solely or even primarily on family labor. A kin-based system would have bound sons to fathers who were unable to use their labor productively instead of allowing them to work for local entrepreneurs. It would have confined young adult men to toiling on farms while their wives took care of toddlers, bearing an excessive burden of dependency that would have rendered them unable to make optimal use of whatever land they had. Instead, young men in rural towns like Scituate could work for wages or on their own account, finding a market in rural industries with a global reach. The "little commonwealth" imagined by so many historians was not the primary labor system found in New England. Fortunately for the growth of a rough, and rare, version of economic equality and workers' power in America, the town labor system came to prevail in Massachusetts.

Working with Town Labor

Not all entrepreneurs understood the Massachusetts town labor system. These gents paid the price for their ignorant adherence to hierarchal or liberal orthodoxies. A prime example is Thomas Coram (later the founder of the Foundling Hospital in London), who attempted to establish a shipyard in rural Taunton, Massachusetts, but failed dramatically.[26] Coram was blind to the town's empowered work force, trying instead to deal only with individuals through contracts based purely on market prices.

Thomas Coram was born in 1668 in Lyme Regis, a port on the rugged south coast of Dorset in the west of England. The son of a sea captain, he became a mariner and a shipbuilder and developed the leadership capacities to succeed at both. Landing in Boston in 1693, he was impressed with the resources available to shipbuilders in the colony and with the political power and status they enjoyed in the town. In June 1700, he married Eunice Wait, daughter of John and Eunice Wait, neighbors to Judge Samuel Sewall. After working on several vessels in Boston, Coram drew on his connections to both English capital and Boston merchants to go into business for himself. In 1697 or 1698, he moved to Taunton, buying land on the Two Mile River. He described it as "in the most commodious place on the river, with so good a depth of water, that if need were a fourth-rate frigate might be launched there." Taunton had several advantages as a site for a shipyard. It was well settled, having a workforce capable of providing Coram with the wood he needed. It also had an iron forge, good forests nearby, and an excellent river system. Indeed, the name Taunton means "town on the River Tone"; the original English settlers, many of whom were from Somerset in the west of England, honored their shire town in choosing its name. These natural resources allowed Coram to build larger vessels for less cost in Taunton than in Boston. He soon had contracts from English merchants for a 130-ton ship and a great ship of 234 tons.[27]

Coram was poised for success in Taunton, and his London backers thought his success was assured. He had the bluff self-confidence of a gang leader on the waterfront. However, his stay in Taunton soon proved disastrous. Historians have ascribed his difficulties to his adherence to the Anglican faith in contrast to the Congregationalism of most Taunton residents.[28] Religion played a role, perhaps, but many of the leading citizens of Taunton were not religiously orthodox. Coram's problems stemmed mainly from his refusal to pay deference to the town's labor system. His beliefs about work, not about God, were the issue.

Taunton was well organized by the 1690s, as the Leonard family's approach to developing a major iron forge or bloomery in the town demonstrated. Skilled iron workers from Monmouth, Wales, the Leonard brothers had been employed at several Massachusetts forges. At first their manners brought them into conflict with towns' ways of doing business, but they soon learned how to deal with localist ethics. When Henry and James Leonard established a forge in Taunton to utilize the bog iron ore found there, they carefully planted the business deep in the town. The Leonards went directly to the town meeting to gain permission to build a bloomery and to get rights to cut wood on the commons. In return, they gave shares in the forge to at least twenty-eight town residents by 1653 and made the town itself a shareholder. The Taunton forge produced iron throughout the colonial period and even forged the anchor for the U.S.S. *Constitution*. Thomas Leonard, the clerk, became a judge and a captain of the militia. The economy of eighteenth-century Taunton was so centered on iron that bars even served as a medium of exchange.[29]

While the forge was a privately and publicly owned facility, Coram's yard was an entirely private enterprise, and Coram, though a manly and obstinate leader, lacked any interest in dealing with the people of Taunton as a collectivity. A practitioner of liberal, free market principles, he sought the best contract he could get for materials and labor, held the contractor to the letter of the agreement, and used the courts to discipline lazy workers. He presumed that like-minded gents of the propertied elite would support him. Unlike the Leonards, Coram raised his capital in England, not in Taunton. He promised his financial backers that his yard would turn out excellent ships at the lowest possible cost so he could deliver high returns on investment and attract more capital. He expected gratitude and cooperation from the other rich men of Taunton, and he expected laborers to show deference to those with more capital and skill who were providing good wages for the lowly. He assumed they would understand that he could bring more money into Taunton than they had ever seen. He failed to understand that by the time he arrived Taunton had developed a political economy that privileged town labor over individual capitalists and that, if he intended to do business, he had to respect the local labor system. Instead, he was surprised by the Taunton folk's willingness to use violence in defense of their perceived rights.

Coram bought land and built a house and shipyard in Taunton, where he housed his whole skilled workforce, largely imported from Boston and Charlestown. He would have been wiser to have asked for the hospitality of Taunton's people and mixed his shipwrights with the local population. He did not go to the town meeting or even to Justice Leonard to organize his purchase of the thousands of trees required to construct the two large ships he had contracted to build in Taunton. Instead, he sought out a marginal figure in town, Daniel Maclothling, an Irishman, who had land near the Two Mile River and lived in Daniel Walker's house in the winter. Coram got the best deal he could from Maclothling. As Timothy Weston, one of Coram's workers, later testified, "in the month of October 1698 . . . I heard Thomas Coram and an Irish man named Daniel MacClockthin . . . did agree with each other that the said Coram should have as many trees off said Daniel's land in Taunton as the said Coram had occasion for at 12 pence a tree." Weston remembered the deal well, because "Mr. Coram spoke to me to call John Millner one of Coram's servants to come in to that room to hear the bargain, Coram saying that Irish fellow had done basely before in denying something about timber and had us take particular notice of said bargain." The lowness and dishonesty of Taunton residents became a constant theme in Coram's discourse. Coram evidently thought this deal would be easily enforceable against a man who belonged to an ethno-religious group that was generally disliked in Protestant New England. Maclothling soon had second thoughts and wanted to renegotiate the contract. Coram sued. A number of Taunton residents testified to Maclothling's justifiable anger. In their testimony, they backed their adopted Irishman. Taunton residents testified to exactly the opposite of what Coram's servants said. For example, Thomas Eliot and Esther Holloway testified that "we heard Thomas Coram and Daniel Macloclathlin discoursing together sometime in the fall of the year 1698 and Thomas Coram asked Daniel Maclochling how many trees he said Daniel would let him have and he said Daniel told Coram he should have none, not so much as a twig to pick his teeth."[30]

To make matters worse, Coram arranged for the carting of the timber in the same way, negotiating a contract with Daniel Walker at the lowest possible price, leading to another confrontation and court case. Because the carting employed a large number of Taunton residents, Coram might have diplomatically asked for advice in regard to the price and work schedule required. These men were farmers who labored irregularly in their by-occupations. But Coram sued Walker for not behaving like an urban carter who fulfilled the contract to the precise letter of the agreement. The court records reveal a supercilious attitude on the part of Coram and his city-bred workers, a sense that the local carters were incompetent, lazy, and unworthy—a criminally idle group who wanted discipline. Significantly, in Boston carters were often black, and as slaves subjected to both strict discipline and social stigma. Eleazer Starr, a fifty-one-year-old Boston sawyer, testified that

Coram had hired him to saw ten thousand feet of plank and that he spent too many hours idle because the Taunton carters were inefficient. Walker and his men apparently brought thousands of logs to the shore but failed to take them into the yard as the contract stipulated. The skilled workers sat complaining as they waited for the logs to be moved several hundred feet. "The logs lay wasting in the river many days," testified Starr, "whilst he was forced to be idle for want of them and should have lost much more time had not Mr. Coram sometimes put other men to fetch them." Coram resented having to pay his skilled workers for "unskilled" labor or having to hire additional workers. Making things worse, a storm sent the wood on the shore into the river and it drifted miles away. Coram blamed Walker and the quirky Taunton labor force. "I have been at work in many places and on many ships," concluded Starr, "and never knew such damage for want of carting as Mr. Coram have received through the neglect of Peter Walker."[31] Starr had apparently never worked in a rural shipyard before.

The Boston workers expected efficiency, and the rural carters failed to satisfy them. Another Bostonian, Stephen Bolton, complained: "last week I saw great quantities of beams, knees, and plank logs, crooked timber lying in the reputed lands of Eliezer Walker which my self helped cut get and hew for building said ship." He resented being "forced to break off from the ship's work to help haul up plank logs with tackle and rollers from the river to the sawpit side." Skilled workers should not be made to do such menial labor. Bolton observed that "often times the sawyers stood still and lost their time for want of plank logs to be sawed for the ship and hindered the carpenters to go forward with planking said ship." The urban shipwrights had their own view of how the flow of work should be organized and distinguished themselves as skilled artisans from mere carters, but they never considered that Peter Walker and his rural carters had their own conception of time as farmers and could not achieve the same efficiencies as urban carters, especially enslaved Africans. Coram hoped to use the courtroom to bludgeon the rural crews into conforming to his definition of work.[32]

Instead of siding with Coram, the Bristol County courts and local elite sided with Walker and the rural workers. When the stubborn entrepreneur refused to relent in his drive to get the cheapest labor at the lowest cost, regardless of its indignity, they decided that Coram had to go back where he came from forever or pay serious consequences. Coram later argued that the conniving Taunton residents conspired against him. He was correct, but he failed to realize that the conspiracy was provoked by his own actions and attitudes. He regarded Taunton folk as stupid, backward, and lazy. He blamed Taunton farmers for the high mortality among cattle during the exceptionally cold and snowy winter of 1698. Coram confided to the Reverend Benjamin Colman of Boston that, "being Lords of their own soyle," the locals were too lazy to build barns to shelter their livestock. "Those lazy vermin would ly all night by one anothers firesides contriving how to hurt their industrious neighbours rather than take a little pains to preserve their own cattle."[33] Neither sea captains nor captains of shipyards were accustomed to accommodating a body of empowered workers; Coram's failure to develop this aptitude in Taunton cost him dearly.

Not only did Walker win the case, but the court decided to assess Coram damages and then refused to accept his bonds to cover his potential expenses, which provided a basis for court officers to seize his property to cover a £500 debt. The court appointed Abel Burt deputy sheriff for the purpose of going to Coram's shipyard and seizing the two ships and all his property in lieu of a bond. This was a plan to drive Coram out. In essence, the people of Taunton used the law to find a pretext for organizing a small army of rural toughs to force Coram to leave. Coram and the Boston workers housed at his shipyard became the hated outsiders, and the court case provided a method of legally applying coercion in order to destroy Coram's enterprise and send him away in disgrace.

After January 18, 1700, Abel Burt and a large troop of Taunton farmers invaded Coram's yard repeatedly, seized property, issued proclamations, intimidated workers, and disrupted production. Thomas Stephens, a Charlestown shipwright, was so disturbed by the frequent invasions of the yard that he decided to abandon the project: "although I came from Charlestown on purpose to work upon that ship and had agreed to work upon her until spring of the year," Stephens testified, "said Burt having been there so often making disturbance as deputy sheriff and so disturbed me and my family that I could not be satisfied to work there afterwards, although Mr. Coram offered me 50 pieces of 8 [a Spanish gold coin] over and above my wages." Stephen Phillips, another member of Coram's imported crew, described the frightful invasion. He saw "Abel Burt of Taunton, deputy sheriff as he saith with great company of men entered into Mr. Coram's house and he turned myself out of the house and the rest of Mr. Coram's work men and forbid me from working any more." Burt cleverly ordered "Joseph Tisdale to carry Mr. Coram's bed upon his horses out of the yard with the bedding belonging to it." Coram was so hated in Taunton that he could not find a place for himself and his wife to sleep among the towns' nearly two hundred dwellings; that night they had to retreat to Boston, abandoning his ship and his yard.[34]

Coram's failure to win the support of Taunton's farmers spelled his economic doom in town. Back in Boston, where capital was more respected, Coram got the General Court to reverse Burt's action and the Bristol court's rulings. The General Court even gave Coram additional property in Taunton in order to compensate for the damages he had suffered, including fifty-nine acres of Abel Burt's land. Coram boldly but foolishly attempted to enforce the order. Burt and others in Taunton refused to honor the act of the General Court, and the Bristol County magistrates backed the locals. Coram later noted that when "the High Sheriff and I came from said land into the highway (we) were fired upon out of some thick bushes near the roadside." Coram said he "could not see the man that shot but the bullets whistled very near us and I am morally assured it was this deputy sheriff whose name is Abel Burt." Coram had good reason for suspicion. "And some time afterward on the 26th of May 1702, this Burt threatened me if I ever should come upon the land which the sheriff had delivered me." Burt's threats were not mere rhetoric. On that very day, Coram testified, "the said Burt then laid violent hands on me and [I] believe he would have murdered me had not others rescued me." Coram went to Captain Leonard to get a court order to restrain Burt, but Leonard would not listen. He became the subject of a local boycott; nobody in Taunton would mow hay on the land Coram appropriated from Burt. Coram testified that he feared he would be killed if he set foot in Taunton again. Wisely, he never returned. Coram later said he believed that the people of Taunton were "some of the very worst of the creation."[35] He had reason for this belief; they destroyed his promising business and physically threatened him. But his inability or outright refusal to understand the Massachusetts labor system was the major cause of his failure.

The people of Taunton hated Coram and his arrogance; they did not hate economic development or Boston capital. These were not traditionalist farmers, but defensive workers. Shipbuilding continued to prosper after Coram left. Between 1698 and 1713, shipwrights built at least thirty-four vessels in Taunton, with an average size of nearly one hundred tons. The Two Mile River and Taunton's farmers, who cut and carted vast quantities of wood seasonally, allowed the construction of some of the largest ships built in New England. In 1712, the four-hundred-ton *Sea Nymph* and the six-hundred-ton *Thomas and Elizabeth* were both built in Taunton yards. During this period, capital from Boston and England continued to pour into the town; some ninety men invested in these vessels. Taunton developed a power-ful town labor system capable of supporting large-scale production. The new shipbuilders obviously understood the town better than Coram did. They respected the town's workers. By 1786, the towns that had composed old Taunton boasted seven iron works or furnaces and no less than thirty-four sawmills. Taunton was one of the most dynamic rural centers of shipbuilding and ironmaking in the British North American colonies.[36] The town labor system was protected and enforced by a defensive, even violent body of work-ers who would retaliate effectively when attacked by arrogant employers.

Exploiting Massachusetts Forests

The expansion of the shipbuilding industry transformed the landscape of Massachusetts. Although New Hampshire and Vermont later yielded much timber and Maine furnished the tall white pines used for masts, Massachu-setts itself was the prime supplier during the early years. Shipbuilding and its related industries equaled farming in economic importance, in part because their labor demands were complementary and their schedules compatible. Farmers made good wood men. They were physically strong, with as much sturdy endurance as muscular strength. They could command and drive the oxen used to pull logs out of the forest and draw loads of wood (tasks done today by tractors and mammoth trucks). They had time on their hands dur-ing the winter, the best season to cut trees and transport logs. The trees were drier and more easily cut. Badly rutted, pothole-filled, muddy roads became passable once they were frozen; so did ponds. When snow covered the New England tundra, out came the oxen, sledges, and axes.

Massachusetts and Connecticut diaries and memoirs from the eighteenth century show that men spent much of the winter time cutting firewood; timber for ship-, house-, and barn-building; barrel staves; and shingles. They had intimate knowledge of the mysterious ways of wood. In southern Con-necticut, Joshua Hempstead noted in his diary on January 10, 1712: "I was at home all day about oars. A bitter cold day. The post lead his horse over the ferry on ice. They sled wood over into town from Groton." Hempstead made oars to ship to the West Indies, where they were used to propel boats along the coast carrying slaves and sugar. He cut the wood for the oars near his house. Cutting trees was dangerous labor. On October 14, 1746, Hempstead recorded: "Clement Leech had both his legs broke in felling a tree yesterday."

Hempstead often assembled large crews from New London to cut trees for his shipbuilding and other projects. On March 4, 1730, he noted: "I had six hands Thursday felling timber besides my self and Adam [his slave] vizt Ed Fanning, Will Crouch, Gershom Holderige, St. Bent, John and William Cook." Hempstead was not only an expert in varieties of wood but also an aficionado of snow, particularly the optimal conditions for moving timber. January 16, 1747, was a nearly perfect day: "fair and warm, a moderate sw wind. It thawed the snow considerably. Some warm places run a little but the face of the earth is all covered with ice and snow on it that never was better sledding wood."[37]

In the inland town of Westborough, the minister Ebenezer Parkman was preoccupied with wood during the winter. His diary records chronic shortages of firewood, relieved by mustering his neighbors to cut wood on his property and sled it to his front door. When his children were young, sick, or lame, hired laborers also cut it. Parkman, whose father was a Boston shipbuilder, noticed the shipbuilding-related activities in the town. On January 31, 1739, he recorded that "Mr Aaron Forbush had my oxen to sled down a large stack of ship timbers to Marlborough." On March 10, 1739, Parkman loaned his oxen to his neighbors: "with Brother Hick's cattle and neighbor Aaron Hardy's joined to my own team, Ebenezer Maynard and John Kidney carried a large log to the sawmill." Little wonder that Westborough by 1786 retained only 18 percent of its land in wood and that 46 percent of its usable land had been cut over.[38]

Asa Sheldon spent his childhood in Lynnfield, originally a well-forested town between Boston and Salem. As a child, Sheldon became expert at leading oxen, making him a good plowman in the summer and an adept carter in the winter. In December 1796, Sheldon's father, a stonemason, bought "a lot of standing wood" in North Reading, hired a laborer to fell the trees, and set his nine-year-old son to "drive a team with a very large yoke of cattle in dragging off the wood." "Sometimes we turned our teams across the side of Putnam's millpond for the pleasure of driving on glare ice." It "attracted some attention to see so small a boy beside a loaded team." Schoolchildren would catch a ride while the load was moving: "the method was for one or two boys to take hold of the hind end of the load, then a girl took hold of his clothes, and other hold of hers, and so on, till a long string was made out, oftentimes two strings." The timber on the way to the shipyard and the children on the way to school—a perfect tableau of the hard-working New England town labor force in a moment of winter joy.[39]

CHAPTER SEVEN

Crews

NEW ENGLAND'S FIRST knight was William Phips, a mariner and ship-builder from the Kennebec River in what is now Maine. In 1687, with English and Boston financial backing, he discovered and retrieved a treasure of some £300,000 in gold and silver from the sunken Spanish galleon *Concepcion* in the shallows north of Hispaniola. Finding and retrieving the treasure was easy compared to returning it intact to England. As Cotton Mather described it, "But there was one extraordinary distress which Captain Phips himself plunged into: for his men were come out with him upon seamen's wages, at so much per month; and when they saw such vast litters of silver sows and pigs, as they call them, come on board them at the captain's call, they knew not how to bear it, that they should not share all among themselves, and be gone to lead a short life and a merry, in a climate where the arrest of those that had hired them should not reach them." Phips promised the crew that if they refrained from mutiny, which would have enabled them to divide the £300,000 among themselves and desert their duty and their families, but instead, obeyed his commands and returned home, he would make sure each of them got a sizeable bonus, even if it reduced his own share. He also swore that in the future he would work for the benefit of Boston, which he and some of his sailors called home. As Mather put it, he took a vow that he "would for ever devote himself unto the interests of the Lord Jesus Christ, and of his people, especially in the country which he did himself originally belong unto." Apparently impressed by these promises, the crew of the *James and Mary* sailed peaceably to England with their outrageous booty. Each of the seventy-some common sailors on the expedition got a bonus of £50, and

Phips got £11,000 and a knighthood.[1] England and its establishment reaped a bonanza—but Boston held his loyalty.

Why did Boston mean so much to Phips and his men? Was it some kind of mariners' paradise in whose name Phips could gain the allegiance of his crew? Promising to invest the money there seems an implausible way to avoid a mutiny, yet Phips fulfilled his vow. A native of coastal Maine, Phips had only lived in Boston for a year, working as a shipwright and marrying Mary Spencer Hull, a merchant's widow. He learned to read and write in Boston, though rather badly. After being knighted at court, Sir William Phips returned to Boston with his booty and built a "fair brick house in the green lane of north Boston," the rough waterfront neighborhood. He joined the Mather party in opposing the Dominion of New England under Governor Andros that suppressed the normal political economy of the city, and after it was overturned in revolution he supported the new charter that restored the town's autonomy. In 1690, at the age of thirty-nine, he was finally baptized, becoming a member of Mather's North Church and proclaiming publicly in his profession of faith "that if God had a people anywhere, it was 'here'; and I resolved to rise and fall with them; neglecting very great advantages for my worldly interest, that I might come and enjoy the ordinances of Lord Jesus here." He commanded and funded an unsuccessful expedition against the French in Montréal and was appointed royal governor of Massachusetts. His knighthood notwithstanding, Phips continued to represent, and feel most comfortable with, the sailors and shipwrights of Boston's North End.[2]

Mather wrote and published Phips's biography in 1697 and incorporated it in his *Magnalia Christi Americana* in 1702. Chief among its purposes, alongside documenting the role of divine providence in shaping New England's history, was to advertise Boston as the best city for poor sailors, a place where a humble man by hard work and honesty with the help of God could become rich—even a knight with a stately mansion in the North End. In truth, the relatively privileged position of mariner families in eighteenth-century Boston and its outports did attract able men, initially advancing and ultimately challenging the British Empire. Mariners had a stronger attachment to locality and more access to legitimate political power in New England than in other colonial ports because of the region's distinctive town labor system. The political economic order, including widespread property holding, public education, acceptance of suffering, and the democratic exercise of political power, raised Massachusetts-born men willing to go to sea and attracted foreign mariners happy to settle in Massachusetts. Marriage

and family life and local institutions and peer groups, not merely good commodities and location on the Atlantic, fostered mariners in New England,
saving this region from poverty and giving it a place in the commercial empire of the Atlantic. However, the lure of middling Massachusetts culture
and society to mariners also caused problems within the British Empire. English naval leaders thought too many of their seamen deserted in Boston.
When the navy tried to recover its men or impress substitutes, officers found
themselves kidnapped or threatened by the town's entire population. Riots,
murder, and eventually a revolution followed—as could be expected in a city
that treated its workers too well to make them obedient subjects.

Typically, British "Jack Tars" were poor, desperate men far from their
families. These illiterate seamen had little chance of upward mobility; they
remained common seamen well into adulthood. In wartime they were impressed into the English navy. Their voyages were endless, not the three- or
four-month forays to the West Indies and back that New England's sailors
enjoyed. They formed a distinctive blue-water culture cut off from landed
society, and they lacked all political power. Marcus Rediker has convincingly
argued that these men initiated the workers' rights movement in modern
society; they were the first to strike sail, to mutiny against captains, and to
turn pirate.[3] These isolated and alienated mariner communities also typified
the powerlessness of sailors based in the major colonial ports outside of New
England.

It is instructive to compare colonial New York City's maritime workforce
with that of Boston's. By the mid-eighteenth century, New York rivaled Boston as a port and had a marine workforce of comparable size. However, the
great majority of New York mariners were not well integrated into the city.
They were not recognized as citizens who had a voice in government or
whose rights the government needed to protect. In Boston and other New
England maritime towns, an elaborate infrastructure nurtured mariners, protected their interests, and guaranteed their citizenship. Boston mariners' political power had much to do not only with Sir William Phips's ability to
avoid a mutiny but also with mutinies of the city of Boston itself against the
empire.[4]

Raising and Making Mariners

Eighteenth-century Massachusetts, as noted, produced little that warranted
the arrival of merchant vessels from England. New England farmers chiefly

raised livestock. Their cows, sheep, pigs, and corn were good to eat, but found no market in Europe. New England seemed destined to be a pious backwater, akin to the Welsh and Scottish uplands where intelligent, good-hearted, but very poor farmers grazed livestock and made do without sophisticated consumer goods. The New Englanders' modest agricultural products and their timber harvest became economically valuable, however, when carried by ships of their own making manned by their own sailors to the tropics or southern Europe. In the Caribbean, British West Indian planters—the richest men in British America—used almost all their land and thousands of slaves to grow and process sugar cane. Instead of buying expensive foodstuffs from distant England, the planters were eager to buy cheaper New England produce. As the English agents of the British sugar islands described the situation to Parliament, the planters were eager for meat "and many other necessaries of life, having seldom a supply on their islands for more than two months." In order to export their sugar to Europe in wooden hogsheads (the only containers available), the West Indian planters also needed plenty of coopers and stacks of New England wood "for the purpose of making casks."[5] By servicing planters on the tropical islands of Barbados and Jamaica, exchanging their wood, pork, horses, fish, and corn for sugar and molasses, and ultimately by supplying the Empire with ocean-going vessels, New Englanders became central to the Atlantic economy.

In order to attain and hold this position, Massachusetts required hundreds of merchants and shipbuilders and thousands of mariners. The labor needs of the carrying economy were huge. Between 1697 and 1707, during the transport boom, the Boston fleet grew from a few hundred vessels to 1,057 vessels with a carrying capacity of 59,350 tons. If all were at sea simultaneously, these vessels employed some 8,500 seamen. Between 1714 and 1717, Boston alone shipped 20,927 tons, the majority to the West Indies, that required 3,000 crew berths and from 1,000 to 1,500 mariners annually. By 1772, the city shipped 42,506 tons that required 4,300 crew berths and employed between 1,500 and 3,000 men annually. Since Boston's total adult male population was then less than 4,000, supplying mariners put a heavy burden on the labor pools of Boston and nearby towns.[6]

Where did all the seamen come from? Historians have correctly identified maritime labor as miserable and dangerous; but they have assumed or implied that early eighteenth-century Boston had access to a large, powerless proletariat. Some suggest that mariners were drawn from both despised and indebted Indians and Africans as well as rural white youths demoralized by their families' loss of land; others argue that young men raised near the sea simply went to sea as they grew up. Nonwhite men in the underclass who shipped from Boston formed an important fraction of the labor force, but there were too few of them to do the job. New England Indians had been decimated by King Philip's War in 1675; few survivors wanted to live and work in Boston, especially when the Christians among them had been fatally incarcerated on a fortified island in the harbor. During the late eighteenth century, blacks made up as much as 20 percent of the mariners in Providence, Rhode Island, but only some 5 percent of those in Salem and Boston. As for English youths, not enough Massachusetts families had lost their land by 1680 or 1716 to generate the large pool of abject available labor required. Land scarcity had little meaning in towns where town-born labor was protected from outsiders. Finally, although most early Americans grew up near the sea, only New England produced a large and able maritime labor force. In 1839, no less than 75 percent of all American blue-water mariners lived in New England.[7]

Had New England generated a mass of impoverished youth desperate or rebellious enough to run away to sea, they could not have been hired or adequately trained. There was no free market in labor in colonial Massachusetts. Employers could not buy labor at the lowest possible cost whenever or wherever they pleased. The movement of labor between one New England town and the next—even between adjacent towns—was filtered by laws and selectmen who removed outsiders from the town within two weeks unless their employers or patrons posted substantial bonds. Wishing to avoid extra costs, employers of long-term labor preferred the town born. Lacking access to a large underclass or the ability to hire outsiders without extra costs, parents, guardians, and masters demanded their children's labor. In colonial Massachusetts, nearly all labor was town labor: workers either had been born in the town where they were hired, or they had been adopted financially by local employers.[8] This system distinguished New England from other places and distinguished New England mariners from mariners elsewhere, in places such as New York City.

Moreover, a critical mass of mariners had to have enough education to enable them to navigate, keep accounts, and write letters. During the eighteenth century, trading vessels were usually less than a hundred tons apiece and required crews consisting of no more than seven men. To move large amounts of cargo took many vessels, and each had to have at least two or preferably three men who could navigate and were literate and numerate. At the same time, seamen had to be taught to fight, yet remain disciplined. Learning to fight effectively under command was one purpose of the officially authorized gangs in Boston and other ports. A large educational infrastructure was required in which books, ferules, and brickbats were key accessories. Merely growing up near the sea did not guarantee that enough young men would become functional members of a large maritime labor force.

Boston, though the largest town in New England, empowered its workers and provided this infrastructure. Through the American Revolution, the Boston selectmen decided who could live in Boston for more than two weeks. If newcomers desired to stay longer, they needed £50 bonds per person placed in the city treasurer's office (or the equivalent in goods or real estate invested in Boston). The money covered the living and potential medical expenses of the newcomer and his or her family for five years. A sea captain, upon entering the mid-eighteenth-century city, had to post bond for every passenger who was not a resident of Boston. A special impost book was bought and maintained to collect the names of passengers and sea captains.[9] Given the realities of the Massachusetts political economy, the marine labor force had to be created and retained in Boston. Outsiders could be employed, but only if they were adopted as family by Boston merchants. Hiring a labor force entirely from the underclass was not an option. Nor was accumulating a large mariner population that was not included in the body politic. Such a group would cause public disorder, and worse, God would punish a city that harbored a large population who lacked access to the tools of salvation: literacy and discipline. Such neglect or blindness, however, was regarded as normal in other seaports.

Outsiders were certainly important in the New England mariner labor market. As Marblehead marriages demonstrate, although New England had a high birthrate and low rates of infant and childhood mortality, the town of Boston and families of mariners in other towns could not, by themselves, reproduce enough mariners to sail the fleets to the Caribbean, let alone man its fishing vessels, coasters, and whalers. The death rate among mariners was very high, surviving mariners retired at fifty or earlier, farmers' children were needed at home, shipbuilding and lumbering pervaded New England, and like other colonial New England industries, the sea trade and its labor needs grew steadily. When it came to mariners, Massachusetts seaports welcomed seafaring outsiders—although on their own terms.

In the eighteenth century, thanks in part to its sluggish economy but chiefly to restrictive policies, colonial Massachusetts attracted relatively few immigrants. Those who came tended to be seamen, and they often found acceptance. According to the Boston impost book, in March, May, June, July, and September 1716, 213 vessels entered Boston with 445 passengers. Half the vessels had no passengers; only twelve vessels (from London, Bristol, Scotland, Ireland, and Newfoundland) brought ten or more. Mariners were the largest occupational group among them: 166, or 37 percent of the total. The next largest occupational groups were eighty-five servants and seventy-five artisans. The mariner passengers were not crew members of the incoming vessels, but men who paid or worked their passage to America. A few were Boston residents returning after their ships had been sold abroad. Many were outsiders hoping to find a vessel and perhaps a home in Boston.[10]

From groups like these, Boston selected the mariners it wanted. Boston authorities treated foreign mariners better than some other strangers; they gave mariners immediate care if sick or hurt, and usually a longer probation period than other newcomers. Nonetheless, alien mariners too had to post bond, or find someone to post bond for them, to avoid being warned out and then ejected. For example, on October 6, 1737, "Elizabeth Ray widow living in Battery March" informed the selectmen "that Thomas Roach a sailor has been about fourteen days at their house, that he came from Virginia with Captain Cross, that he is now very sick of a fever and has no effects she knows of." The selectmen decided that if Roach stayed in town, Captain Cross was legally obligated to post bond for him, since he was Captain Cross's passenger. Judging the sailor worthy, William Cross and Thomas Hubbard did pay the bond, and on October 26, 1737, "Thomas Roach lately from Virginia mariner" was admitted as a Boston resident.[11]

Some mariners were rejected. On May 11, 1743, the Boston selectmen considered the case of John Bird, "who came over sailor in a schooner from Barbados Job Pinkum master." Bird was living at the house of Mary Foreland in Milk Street. Mrs. Foreland attended the selectmen's meeting in the upper rooms of Faneuil Hall and asked that "care might be taken of the said Bird he being poor, sick, and lazy." The last adjective destroyed his case. The selectmen "ordered that Mr. Savell be directed to see that the said Bird forthwith depart the town."[12]

The authorities of colonial Boston expected hard work from mariners. In return, they protected strangers' dignity from the debasement that the British Empire usually inflicted upon white men and women who did the worst and most dangerous jobs. Though they made distinctions when handing out rewards, Boston and other Massachusetts port authorities educated, humiliated, and flogged their own children and strangers with a similar mix of generosity, callousness, and restraint. This harsh, yet enveloping, town labor system maddened and destroyed some people, but it created an equitable and combustible society of loyal workers willing to do work that took courage and emotional disassociation. Such a combustible labor force could also turn on the empire in which it existed.

Painful Discipline for All

Boston society raised the outsider Hector McNeill into a useful and loyal seafarer by subjecting him to challenge and violence. The childhood of town-born Ashley Bowen shows how harsh Yankee love, or its excused absence, made a potential native swell into a hard-boiled mariner. Ashley Bowen was born in 1728 in the North Shore outport of Marblehead. His father, Nathan Bowen, was a lawyer and justice of the peace who styled himself "esquire," one of the wealthiest men in the town. Still, Ashley Bowen's childhood and passage to sea was as hard as any poor immigrant's child, certainly worse than McNeill's in Boston.

The judge and his wife were not protective, much less indulgent, parents. Nathan Bowen taught navigation, and his students convinced him to allow the eager eleven-year-old lad to make a year-long commercial voyage to Bilboa, Spain. Two years later, Bowen's mother died and his father soon "went a-suiting to Mistress Hannah Harris, a fine rich widow." The middle-aged lovers agreed to reduce their families by putting out children to apprenticeship. Mrs. Harris bound her son Nathaniel to a house carpenter, and Nathan Bowen bound Ashley, age thirteen, to Captain Peter Hall of Boston, commander of the *Hawke*. "We sailed about the first of May (1741) and before we got Halfway Rock astern, I had a smart rope's ending from my master," noted Ashley Bowen in his journal, exclaiming "O Dear my Mother!"[13]

Peter Hall caned, flogged, and physically abused the judge's son for the next five years, while Marblehead and Boston looked on and did virtually nothing. Hall's corrections were arguably educational. They usually followed an error made by Bowen, the cabin boy. Though administered with an aura of authority and self-control, the punishments were hideous and disgusting. After Bowen burned part of Hall's dinner by mistake, Hall calmly promised to flog him a thousand times the next day. Since Hall had flogged Bowen before and was a man of his word, the captain's threat was credible and terrible. The cabin boy hid in a cranny without food for several days. When Bowen carelessly soiled one of Hall's towels, Hall tied Bowen to the ship's rail by his wrists and lowered Bowen's trousers; "master would take his cat with 9 parts of log line and give me a dozen strokes on my back; then take his hand full of pickle [juice used to store meat in] and pat it on my back; then take his quadrant and look for the sun; then took a tiff of toddy, and so regularly he would do that office, one after another." Hall told a shipmate that the flogging would continue until Bowen broke into tears. Too emotionally disrupted to cry, Bowen licked his hands and applied false tears to his eyes, and the brutality stopped for the day. In order to punish Bowen for attempting to run away in Gibraltar, Hall ordered Bowen "to be lashed by my two thumbs and to hang across the rig rope of our awning without trousers or breeches." Captain Hall's genteel British dinner guests, who were not used to New England educations, "cried out: 'Captain Hall, for God sake let us go on shore again on a Christian land'!" Hall ordered Bowen to be cut down, "but the company would not stay to eat." In Port Mahon in 1744, Hall hit Bowen with a cane across the face, breaking the lad's nose.[14]

New Englanders saw the floggings, suspensions, and canings. Some were disturbed, but they recognized corporal punishment as part of a responsible effort to prepare a child for life at sea. In Philadelphia, a friend of the Bowen family deplored Hall's sadism and alerted Bowen's father. When the *Hawke* returned to Boston in 1742, Nathan Bowen visited Hall and begged him to limit his punishment. Yet, though quite wealthy and authoritative, Judge Bowen refused to pay the money "to get me clear of Hall," Ashley wrote. When Bowen and Hall got to sea, Hall beat Ashley with renewed ferocity. The *Hawke's* mate did shorten the span of at least one beating. While witnessing a severe flogging, the mate told Captain Hall that if Bowen "should die on the passage out he would be a witness against him." Fearing the noose, Hall stopped.[15] Although Hall's treatment of Bowen was considered on the borderline of criminal abuse, no New Englander was willing to intervene until Hall actually murdered Bowen. Hall was probably not a typical master, but he was an allowable one and Bowen's education was acceptably harsh.

Captain Hall took his responsibility as mentor to Bowen seriously and pridefully. When Bowen hid himself in the ship, Hall so visibly expressed his love for the boy that the crewmen pleaded, "Ashley, your master will die if you do not come out!" Hall was generally pleased with Bowen, in fact. In 1744, Hall decided to hold a Christmas Eve baptismal ceremony in Port Mahon for the lad (Bowen's father was a Baptist and therefore was awaiting

Bowen's adult conversion to baptize him.). Hall invited thirty-three guests, including merchants, an admiral, a general, and naval captains. Many attended the grand fete that Bowen summarized as "two large cases, a fine large English cheese with many sorts of wine, rack punch, rum ditto, and brandy ditto in a large upper room." Hall believed that his strict disciplinary regime had created a likely Christian sailor, and he wanted to show his educational prowess while honoring his student.[16]

Ashley Bowen saw Hall as the worst specimen among a violent group of New England nautical educators. At the age of nineteen, Bowen finally ran away. By that time, he believed Hall had committed so many crimes against him that he could prove in court Hall's violation of the original servant contract. In addition, Bowen knew that Hall was carrying on an extramarital affair in Port Mahon and could spill the beans if brought to court. Bowen eventually returned to Marblehead and reunited with his father, Nathan. Astonishingly, Bowen never criticized his father openly for making his youth miserable. Bowen's anger was buried in muted rebellion against his hometown; he remained a lifelong Anglican and was a passive Tory during the Revolution. His dryly humorous truth-telling was his only revenge.

On recommendation of his family and friends, Bowen soon shipped with Captain Richard James, but he immediately left the voyage in Boston because James proved to be still another violent New England educator, whom Bowen called "bloody Dick." In 1747, still not legally an adult, Bowen looked for a gentle captain and reasoned that he best seek a non–New Englander. As Bowen expressed it, "I finding my townsmen to prove so bad, I was determined to go abroad and try strangers, and in October I went to Boston and went up and down from North End to South to find the biggest rogue I could." As a good seaman, Bowen had many offers, "but none suited me as well as an Irishman which bore a name of the biggest rogue. His name was John Capinthorne, a Corkcolen." Bowen's idea of inverting his culture's definition of the good teacher and master by seeking out the hated "other"— the rogue—worked: "I found the best friendship in him as I ever found in an American or Englishman."[17] Bowen spent much of his adulthood as a mariner, rising to first mate on several voyages, serving with the famous Captain Cook at Quebec, quitting to become a rigger in Marblehead after he married. Several of his sons followed the sea and some died there. His early life shows how love, indifference, and dramatic brutality combined to transform a relatively privileged town-born youth, a son of a wealthy lawyer and justice of the peace, into a common mariner willing and able to face the harshest rigors of the Atlantic.

Well-meaning Massachusetts guardians taught a knight's son no differently. Sir Charles Hobby, a Massachusetts and Jamaican merchant, died in 1714. Hobby, whose father was a Boston merchant, became knighted for his service in the earthquake that in 1692 literally sank Port Royal, Jamaica. He accumulated enormous amounts of New England land, but died in debt. Massachusetts Governor Jonathan Belcher assigned the newly poor knight's son, John Hobby, to a nautical career with the governor's trusty brother-in-law, Captain John Foye, master of the Boston ship *Protestant Caesar*. By the time the knight's son sailed into London harbor in 1738, he was shaken. Someone advised him to see kindly Thomas Coram, friend of the family, former New Englander, shipbuilder, sea captain, London businessman, philanthropist, and correspondent with Boston clergyman Benjamin Colman— and himself an eyewitness victim of New England political culture. After interviewing the young man, Coram grew again outraged by Yankee callousness. He "found Captain Foye had not used him kindly or humanely, had messed him in the forecastle with a Negro during the voyage and had suffered everybody that pleased to beat and ill use the poor lad." At first Coram "could scarce believe" that even a Boston sea captain could so abuse and humiliate a knight's son. However, Coram "talked with Captain Foye about it who owned it all, and said he did not bring him to make a gentleman of him (which I thought was true enough) . . . and that he should do no better for him."[18] Whatever the denials of modern historians, eighteenth-century New Englanders were unapologetic about the harsh educational system they used to create mariners. Coram once again confronted the fierce ethos and rough equality of the New England town labor system.

Families for the Sea

Strangers were important to the Massachusetts ports, yet middling local families carried the main burden of labor. These families united maritime careers and political power in the towns. Among eighty-six Boston mariners whose probate records were filed in Suffolk County between 1770 and 1774, fifty-two, or 61 percent, came from middling families that had been in Massachusetts or Boston by the 1720s, usually earlier. The rest came from families that were relatively new to Boston and Massachusetts. These men were less likely to have married and were poorer than mariners from old Boston or Massachusetts families.[19] In nearby Salem, the organization of mariner labor and the relative contributions of town born and strangers were similar, as Daniel Vickers has shown. In both ports, no matter whether they came from established or new families, many mariners advanced economically, and socially, and politically.

A significant number of Boston mariners came from families that had long been dedicated to the sea, many since the seventeenth century. In 1679, for example, William Bryant was servant to Captain Hudson, owner of the Castle Tavern on Dock Square. In 1681, Bryant married Hannah Gillett, and in 1683 he was a sailor on the *Golden Rose*, commanded by William Phips. He retired from the sea and became a tavern keeper, dying in 1697 at the age of fifty-four. Among his two surviving sons, Benjamin was master of the sloop *Fraternity* by the age of twenty-seven. He owned a house in the South End of Boston, but had no children who survived him; he died at thirty-four. The other son was John Bryant, a mariner and tavern keeper who lived to be fifty. His one surviving son, John Bryant, was born in 1718 and lived to 1757, dying at the age of thirty-nine. He, too, was a mariner. During the American Revolution, the Royal Navy blockaded Boston harbor, so John's two sons were kept from the sea. One died in the war; the other lost an arm and became an executive at the national arsenal in Springfield, Massachusetts. After the Revolution, a number of Bryant children returned from Springfield to the sea and became master mariners. The most famous, John Bryant, trekked from Springfield to Boston at the age of sixteen. He became a supercargo on a voyage to Bordeaux, France, and in 1809 to China. He then helped establish the shipping firm of Bryant and Sturgis in Boston that carried almost half the trade to China between 1810 and 1841. John died a millionaire in 1865.[20]

Major Boston mariner families bore the surnames Allen, Atkins, Atwood, Barnard, Blake, Brown, Cunningham, Davis, Delano, Frazier, Freeman, Gardner, Giles, Harris, Jarvis, Johnson, Knox, Low, Magee, Newless, Nichols, Phillips, Prince, Scott, Skimmer, Smith, Thompson, Watts, and Wendell. Some of these families had roots or collateral branches in other port towns, particularly those on the Cape or in southern Massachusetts. Each of these seafaring families had from two to seven members among the some 1,200 Boston mariners who left Suffolk County probate records between 1750 and 1809, and several captains who became members of the Boston Marine Society.[21]

By their mid- to late twenties, most career Boston mariners were no longer wage earners but either mates or captains, who were usually active traders on their own accounts. Their median wealth was similar to that of Boston tradesmen of comparable age. Mariners who lasted into their forties did much better financially than such artisans as blacksmiths, braziers, and tallow chandlers of comparable age; the mariners had nearly twice their average wealth. If he died in his forties, a mariner usually left a house to his widow who could turn or remain shopkeeper or boarding-house keeper. If a sea captain survived into his fifties, he often retired from the sea, turned merchant or innkeeper, joined the Boston elite, and died without the title "mariner" attached to his name in the estate, though people called him "Captain." The small numbers of mariners dying in their fifties, sixties, and seventies and the relative poverty of those who remained ordinary seamen at that age reflects the upward mobility of mariners as well as their frequent premature deaths. Their abnormally young age at death partly explains why big city mariners have gained the reputation among colonial historians of being unusually downtrodden. Historians who have looked at Boston mariners' wealth at death from probate records have found it less than most other city men. They have never corrected for the relative youth of so many men designated as a mariner at death, however. Preindustrial urban life was very risky for most working men and women, but mariners died youngest.[22]

The old Boston families' domination of the forecastle and quarter-deck of local vessels was similar to that of old families in Salem, Massachusetts. Crew lists from 1803 to 1807 survive for this port. Daniel Vickers and Vince Walsh, who exhaustively studied these lists, found a society in which upward mobility was normal, but their findings are worth emphasizing and deserve reinterpretation in the light of New England's political economy. Young men from Salem and nearby towns composed the clear majority of men on the crew lists of ninety vessels with 803 crew positions that left Salem for Europe, Asia, and the West Indies in 1803. About 77 percent of these positions were held by men born in New England, 61 percent by men born in Salem and its adjacent towns. Collation of the 1803 crew lists with North Shore towns' death records show that, as in Boston, a majority of North Shore crew members (at least 214 of 415) were members of second- or third-generation mariner families in which the men got most of their income from going to sea. The Beverly death records show, for example, Ebenezer Woodberry lost at sea coming from Lisbon in 1759, Nicholas Woodberry lost at sea in 1760, and Captain Isaac Woodberry dying of natural causes in 1775. The 1803 Salem crew lists contain six sailors from the Woodberry family. The Manchester records note that in 1783 a Captain Amos Hilton had been lost at sea coming from the West Indies. He was most probably the father of Amos Hilton, a sixteen-year-old seaman from Manchester on the 1803 crew lists.[23]

As in Boston, seafarers' families were of the middling sort, and many had much wealth. At least 60 percent of the crew members native to Salem came from patrilineal clans that held urban real estate. For example, Joseph Archer sailed as an 18-year-old seaman in 1803. In 1798, the Archer family owned five houses in Salem worth $8,940. At age eighteen, Thomas Dean shipped in 1803 as an ordinary seaman. A third-generation mariner family, the Deans owned five houses in Salem at a combined worth of $6,055 and provided income from six tenants. William Felt, a mere cabin boy in 1803, came from a third-generation mariner family holding eight houses worth $8,310 in 1798.[24]

As the 1803 Salem crew lists show, most local men went to sea after leaving school. Their sea careers paralleled the apprenticeships of other urban youth. Almost three-quarters of seamen from Salem were twenty-four years old or younger, and nearly 30 percent were under twenty. The average age of mates was just twenty-seven; many were much younger. The youth of seamen suggests one reason why some men found the career attractive. At age twenty-five, most farm and lumbering lads were working for wages in their town. At the same age Massachusetts seamen were earning wages, making trades, and moving up the vessels' hierarchy. They could support wives. At age twenty-seven, most Salem sailors were mates in command of other men, and not a few were captains of brigs and ships. In the rural towns, young men of the same age were still near the bottom of a farm community's labor system. And while urban apprentices waited until twenty-one to free themselves from their masters and earn journeymen wages, seamen had by age twenty-one accumulated five years of wages, received their blows and hazing from masters and peers, and were established seamen. Many were officers.[25]

A career at sea had a lot to recommend it economically. After a few voyages, some men left the sea for other careers. Yet, thanks to good economic times and Salem's strong town labor system, including public schools, many North Shore men tended to make the sea their career. Among 338 native North Shore men who shipped in 1803 as cabin boys, seamen, or mates, 191, or 57 percent, died at sea or remained seamen for at least five years. Among the 147 men who cannot be traced as career seamen, about half most probably left the North Shore and may well have worked as mariners in other ports.[26] Upward mobility was common among native white North Shore mariners, especially those who persisted at sea. Almost half the common seamen who stayed at sea for five years became officers in the Beverly–Salem custom district, and almost a quarter became captains. Poverty and economic stagnation were hardly characteristic of New England mariners.

Premature death, not poverty, was the mariners' main problem, making the career a chilling choice. At least 12 percent of the North Shore boys, seamen, and mates died between 1803 and 1807 (about 2 percent annually), almost all from occupational causes. Whites native to Salem enjoyed a single-career ladder. Among local white men, family wealth rarely determined position aboard ship. The town born, to be sure, had an advantage over outsiders or blacks. Outsiders advanced more slowly, and blacks hardly at all. While in 1803 some 54 percent of the common seamen were North Shore natives, 83 percent of the officers or mates, from which the next crop of sea captains would come, were white North Shore natives. At the same time, seamen, mates, and boys came from Salem families with consistently differing amounts of property.

Virtually every Salem vessel reflected a labor system typical of rural towns in which the children of wealthy and poor locals were supplemented by the work of outsiders and blacks. For example, on August 8, 1803, the 120-ton brig *Rajah* cleared Salem harbor for a voyage to the Mediterranean with a crew of nine. The crew included seven Salem natives (five whites and two blacks), a white Bostonian, and a white Pennsylvanian. The master was twenty-two-year-old Gamaliel H. Ward, part-owner of the vessel. The Wards were a third-generation Salem mariner family that in 1798 owned no fewer than seven houses, together worth $17,340. Ward had been at sea for many years, but his youthful achievement of captain status was due largely to his wealth. The first mate was an upwardly mobile man, William Towser, a thirty-two-year-old first-generation mariner whose family in 1798 owned a modest Salem house worth $750. The other officer was an experienced seaman from Boston, thirty-year-old Thomas Whitney. Whitney did not like the Salem people; he deserted the vessel in Europe.

Class and money partly determined the rankings of the *Rajah*'s officers, but the crew before the mast was financially and socially jumbled. The oldest man in the forecastle was thirty-year-old James Smith, a black seaman from Pennsylvania. He sailed on the *Rajah* with two other blacks: twenty-seven-year-old William Jones, a seaman from Salem, and eighteen-year-old John Brooks, the cook. The status of seaman was the highest blacks attained on

Salem vessels because of the town folks' racism. In 1803, fifty-five blacks shipped on the Salem vessels. Only 15 percent were seamen; the rest were cooks, boys, and stewards—all service workers. Still, the black seamen did the same type of work and received the same pay as white men in the forecastle, many of them "privileged" youth from the town's prominent families.

The oldest white before the mast was twenty-four-year-old Isaac Knapp, a first- or second-generation Salem mariner whose family lacked Salem real estate in 1798. Though penniless, Knapp was upwardly mobile. According to the 1807 crew lists, he rose to become a mate five years later and in 1812, at the age of thirty-three, he became master of the brig *Argus*. At just sixteen, William Osgood was designated a "young seaman," receiving low wages. He came from an established Salem family that in 1798 owned four houses worth $8,100. Still at sea some twenty years later, he became master of the ship *Zephyr*. The youngest, shortest, most menial on board was thirteen-year-old Henry Ward, the ship's cabin boy—essentially the cook's assistant, captain's valet, and messenger boy—the position held by Ashley Bowen. Henry Ward was the captain's nephew. In 1807 he rose to become a full "seaman," but he then disappeared from the Salem marine record.[27]

Boston and New York City

Among the mariners dying between 1770 and 1774 in Suffolk County, Massachusetts, some were rootless drifters. In 1753, Susanna Gross of Boston married William Mills, mariner. He prospered sufficiently to buy a small house on Fish Street, where Susanna ran a boarding house. In 1759, the Boston selectmen noted that "Susannah Mills wife of William Mills mariner informs that she has let a room in her house on Fish Street to one Carrol who came from the Eastward, ten days since, with his wife and four children, is a cooper by trade, and Mrs. Mills believes he is in pretty low circumstances." This family of six crowded into a single room, though it was probably normal living space by mid-eighteenth-century standards. Yet, the Millses provided penniless strangers with kindness, or at least credit and a room—in exchange for being the full beneficiaries of their wills. It was a credit arrangement, for poor mariners could become suddenly rich at sea as privateers and could also simultaneously die. In the 1760s, four mariners left wills giving their whole estates either to William Mills, mariner, or his wife, Susannah Mills. In 1760, for example, Cornelius Haelstrom from Holland left his total estate to "my esteemed friend Mrs. Hannah Mills, wife of William Mills, aforesaid mariner, and to her heirs." His estate came to just £5. He probably had not known his "esteemed friend" very long, for he called Susannah Mills "Hannah" in his will. Occasionally, Susannah Mills made considerable money by wagering rent and nursing against death. She did provide genuine care for men whose families were far away. In 1761, Alexander Anderson left his whole estate to Mrs. Mills. It amounted to £42 5 s, a considerable amount. Susannah Mills's account shows that she provided Anderson with doctor's care (£3) and a respectable, if modest, funeral (£5).[28]

But isolation was not typical of most Boston mariners, even among the relative newcomers. The identity of estate administrators or executors of mariners tells much about these mariners' connections to Boston society. Among 1,158 Suffolk County mariners from 1750 to 1808, a majority were involved in local families: 640, or 55 percent, of these mariners chose relatives who lived in Boston. Most of the administrators were the mariners' wives (429, or 37 percent); many others were mothers, sisters, brothers, uncles, and children. Not all mariners were family men. Many dead mariners left a will that neither mentioned any local family members nor gained an administration in which the head was a family member (518 men, or 45 percent). Yet the majority of these men had ties to the Boston community that went deeper than the kindly or exploitative landlady.

Many mariners, probably those without relatives nearby, chose members of the Boston elite as their administrators and executors. These seamen had impressive estates. Many were sea captains before they arrived in Boston. The merchants and distillers were their patrons and creditors. A sizable group of mariners with modest estates had tradesmen friends as their administrators. Commercial ties drew mariners and tradesmen together. Before 1812, most common mariners received not just a wage but space (often a barrel or two) aboard ship for goods. Boston grocers cultivated Jack Tars in order to get steady supplies of lemons and other tropical goods. Grocers and victuallers sold tropical goods, rum, wine, and spices. Many mariners roomed with grocers and probably paid their rent with barrels of lemon or bottles of rum, and many mariners retired into the job of retailing West Indian goods. Additionally, many young mariners were related to the town's spinsters, whose brothers and fathers were or had been sailors. Mariners' families frequently intermarried. About 45 percent of the recent immigrant mariners who died between 1770 and 1774 were married. For example, Benjamin Franklin's niece, Jane Mecom, married the Guernsey Island sailor, John Collas.[29]

Finally, only thirteen percent of the total—most of whom were comparatively young and rather poor—had administrators who were nonrelated mariners or landladies like Susannah Mills.[30] In truth, most Boston mariners were members of established Massachusetts middling families, and Boston society rapidly integrated the outsiders into local society. Drifters mixed with kinsmen, whether by birth or adoption, in eighteenth-century Massachusetts ports. The Yankee way of life, with its odd mix of economic power, saintly women, and small homes, enticed the newcomers to settle down. Many mariners became family men, deserting the typical British sea life and sometimes the English navy itself. Boston offered them a place where their presence counted.

The figure of the mariner as powerless outsider can be found in ports in other regions, but not in Boston. It is instructive to compare colonial New York City's maritime workforce with that of Boston. By the mid-eighteenth century, the population of mariners in New York and Boston was nearly equal. However, the great majority of New York mariners were not integrated into local society. In fact, New Yorkers rarely recognized them as part of the body politic. New York and Boston were both incorporated towns, which means they both controlled who was recognized as a citizen with a voice in local politics—that is, they distinguished between mere residents and people who belonged and had a voice. In Boston, freeman status—which was open only to men—depended on sponsorship by residents and on acceptance by the selectmen and the town meeting. Anyone residing in Boston for two months, unless warned out, became an inhabitant and could vote and do business in the town. Boston selectmen often refused immigrants, though they were partial to mariners. In New York, by contrast, freemanship depended on being born in the city or paying a substantial fee. Anyone willing to pay could work and vote in New York, including nonresidents. Fees ranged from several pounds sterling for merchants to just over a pound sterling for laborers and mechanics.

Although they composed a large share of the adult male population of the city, mariners in New York were seldom freemen. Between 1750 and 1760, New York City's corporation enrolled 668 new freemen, among whom mariners composed just 26 men, or a paltry 4 percent. In comparison, 230 new freemen were laborers (34 percent), and forty-four were cordwainers (shoemakers) (7 percent). New York's leaders refused to recognize the seamen who worked in their port as their own. It is plausible that men who enrolled as laborers later became mariners, especially during the French and Indian

War, when many New Yorkers served on privateers. However, examination of the wills of 154 mariners probated between 1744 and 1764 in New York City shows that only seventeen, or just 11 percent, were freemen. Only three of them had initially registered as "laborer"; the others had registered as "mariner" or with such maritime occupations as "shipwright." Although they composed at least 20 percent of New York City's white laborers, mariners composed a tiny fraction of its citizens. Most were frozen out.[31]

Mariners sailing out of New York City were far more isolated than their counterparts in Boston. Among 156 New York City mariners whose wills were probated during this period, fifty-five men, or 35 percent, wrote wills leaving their estates entirely to other mariners, or to caregivers such as innkeepers, tavern-keepers, and widows.[32] For example, in 1745, Daniel Greedy, New York mariner, testified that on board the privateer *Clinton* he heard two mariners, "the said John Ward and Jams Fisher agree together, that as they had not any relations, and were intimate friends and messmates that the longest liver of them should have all the estate which the first deceasing person should leave." Here was an enclosed world of mariners cut off from the city. Many more New York mariners left their estates to an innkeeper who befriended them or to whom they owned money. In 1748, Peter Power, New York mariner, left "to my loving friend Henry O'Bryant of New York, innkeeper, one gold ring and all the rest of my estate, real and personal, it being for his good service done to me in my sickness." Power had no other friends in the city.[33]

New York magistrates demanded that all day laborers, especially carters and porters, become part of the body politic by enrolling as freemen. They hoped to earn their votes by restricting these positions and prerogatives to whites. Why did they exclude mariners from such privileges? In England, freemanship protected the designated citizen from the press gang. New York was the center of the English naval establishment, a rich source of revenue to merchants. If New York recognized mariners as citizens, the city would have had to protect them from the press gangs, which would have angered the English. New York City's leaders chose to exclude mariners from their protection, while encouraging them to frequent the city. In New York, press gangs operated with tacit city approval. The English navy executed a number of unchallenged presses in New York City. On May 20, 1757, for example, some three thousand soldiers surrounded the city, "whilst many different parties patrolled the streets, searched the taverns and other houses, where sailors usually resorted and impressed about 400, taking all kinds of tradesmen and

Negroes, near 800 were impressed on the whole, but not above 400 retained in the service." Some sailors tried to resist, but the city's elite did nothing.[34]

Mutiny of a Town

In Boston, the press always faced the united fury of the whole town. New England sailors had families and houses to come home to, the possibility of upward mobility, and political power in their towns. The average round-trip voyage between New England and the West Indies took three to four months. These absences from home, while severe, did not make family and civic life impossible. Rather, their strong local attachments fueled their resistance to oppression, especially by the Royal Navy. Accustomed to violence in child-hood and youth and with much to lose, they angered quickly and danger-ously. However, their resistance was not a matter of mariner or lower-class solidarity, as it was in New York. Yankee sailors had allies—tradesmen, mer-chants, innkeepers, and even kinswomen—who joined them on the streets to protect the town labor system from the insults of outsiders.[35] Through its local culture and political organization, Boston threatened the power of the British Empire.

Officers of the Royal Navy especially detested Boston. Commander James Scott, Admiral Charles Knowles, and Lieutenant Henry Panton all captured New Englanders to serve as seamen and sought to recover seamen who had deserted in New England ports. The locals responded badly. Men-aced by the ugliness and debasement of British sailors' lives, which could mean a nearly indefinite term, Bostonians defended the human rights of the city's workers and protected them from press gangs. They disliked Knowles, hated Scott, and even championed the Irish sailors who fatally harpooned Lieutenant Panton through the neck.[36]

Making special adjustments for the domestic ties of New England mari-ners was the official policy of the British government. In the eighteenth cen-tury, the Royal Navy fought frequently in the West Indies against the Spanish, Dutch, and French. The navy lost many men in the tropics to disease and desertion. Lacking sufficient volunteers to man the fleets, naval commanders sent out press gangs and press boats in order to replenish their crews. In response, New England sailors refused to embark for the British West Indies, where they stood a chance of being pressed. New England vessels went instead to the Danish and Dutch West Indies. The cost of provisions and wood in the British islands skyrocketed. Thanks to the power of the Boston maritime community, in 1708, West Indian merchants used their considerable interest in Parliament to pass "The Act for Encouragement of Trade to America," which prohibited the British Navy from pressing mariners employed on American ships or on shore in America. Edward Trelawny, governor of Jamaica, later described to Newcastle why New England seamen, unlike most British seamen, were nearly impossible to press successfully: "they have most of them small families and properties at home, and when they are pressed, their desire is so strong to return to their families and the life they were used to, that they desert the first opportunity they have or for the most part die soon if they can find no such opportunity." By refusing to put themselves in jeopardy, New England mariners earned all American mariners a valuable privilege.[37]

The renewal of war in 1739 placed enormous pressure on the Royal Navy to evade the 1708 act exempting American sailors from impressment. When they arrived in tropical waters in force, the navy suffered enormous losses from disease and desertion. In 1741, for example, among sixty-five ships with 19,805 in total crews, 3,499 men, or 18 percent, were "discharged by death," and another 760 men, or 4 percent, deserted. In a single year, Admiral Vernon lost 21 percent of his seamen. Conflict with New England arose when Vernon sent the storeship *Astrea* under Commander James Scott to Boston to obtain masts and provisions for his fleet. Vernon hoped to save money by using the skills, produce, and proximity of North America's premier port. However, while in New England, the *Astrea* lost 93.6 percent of her rated complement to desertion. As the historian Duncan Crew summed up the situation, "virtually everyone other than officers ran." While desertion was a chronic problem, mass escapes were unusual. None of the other vessels operating in the West Indies had a comparable desertion rate; the next highest were the *August* and the *Experiment*, with about 13 or 14 percent. The overall annual desertion rate was only 4 percent.[38] The attractions of a familial, respected, middling mariner society in Boston spelled disaster for the Royal Navy.

At first, Commander Scott adhered to the 1708 act when responding to the crippling manpower emergency aboard the *Astrea*. He persuaded Massachusetts Governor Jonathan Belcher to issue a press warrant demanding that the sheriff of Middlesex County seek fifty-nine deserters "and all other seamen who have deserted any other of his majesty's ships of war; and also to impress for his majesty's service such a number of seamen as to make up the number wanting, allowing for such deserters as they may take up." In defer-ence to the law, however, the warrant prohibited the sheriffs and authorities from pressing "inhabitants of this province, nor any persons belonging to any fishing vessels, wood vessels, and coasters." In New York, such a strategy worked because most mariners were not deemed citizens of the city. In New England, the strategy of selecting strangers and exempting inhabitants failed. Middlesex County sheriff Richard Foster stated in April 1741 that "I cannot find any sea men that are not inhabitants of this province," and by June he and others had found only one deserter and two strangers whom they im-pressed. Commander Scott could not lose nearly all his crew and expect to remain an officer of His Majesty's navy. Furious as well as desperate, he decided to do whatever was necessary to obtain a crew.[39]

Scott began sending out armed boats in Boston Harbor to stop, search, and detain men from fishing and coasting vessels. Looking for deserters, he was soon collecting hostages. New England mariners and coasters complained bitterly, often emphasizing the disastrous impact of press gangs upon New England families. Their protests depicted almost every Jack Tar taken as a hard-working family man, a pillar of local society. For example, Jeremiah Simpson, master of the sloop *Three Friends,* a coasting vessel from York (now Maine), complained that on March 17 "he had two hands taken from on board the said sloop namely Joseph Cole and David Adams by a boat manned with armed men belonging to his Majesty's Ship *Astrea* who forcible carried the said two men on board said ship and did detain them." Simpson stressed that "Joseph Cole has a wife and four small children who have no other dependence but the said Cole's industry to maintain them and was coming to Boston to buy provisions for the said family."[40]

Scott and his officers blundered badly. They stopped one man on a coaster wearing drab working clothes who appeared a hardened sailor. In Boston, however, artisans and gentlemen often had similar social positions, and even wealthy men wore work clothes. The man taken was not a mariner but William Pratt, "a housewright of more than fifty years of age who has a wife and large family of children and who has always lived in good repute among us, is a master workman." According to the petition for his release, Pratt held "real estate of two thousand pounds value in this town." The petitioners thought that Pratt's natural rights had been flagrantly violated. It was signed by eighty-six Boston freemen, including Thomas Hutchinson, a prominent merchant, head of the probate court, and future lieutenant gover-nor of the province.[41]

Meanwhile, unlike New York City (whose elite was busy with an alleged conspiracy of slaves and white workingmen to burn down the town), the town of Boston erupted into violence. On June 8 at about 9 o'clock in the evening, some three hundred men from all walks of life armed with cutlasses, sticks, and clubs besieged Scott's lodgings at Brown the shoemaker's house on King Street. According to Scott, the mob threatened to break into the house, drag him out, and kill him. Being told that Scott was not within, the men roamed through Boston looking for him and for Scott's officers. No local authorities tried to challenge the "mob" that represented the will of Bostonians.[42]

Six years later, a similar drama was reenacted on a grand scale. Thanks to the power of Boston mariner families and their deep connections to a city that acknowledged them, the conflicts between the demands of the British Empire and the principles of a city of politically empowered workers exploded. Around October 1, 1747, Admiral Charles Knowles brought his ship *Canterbury*, along with a squadron of ships, into Boston for rest and repairs. After a few days, Vice Admiral Charles Knowles, anchored on the Nantasket Road, discovered that forty to fifty of his men had overstayed their leaves in Boston. Knowles ordered Captain Blyhe to take the schooner *Achilles* into Boston Harbor and get the men with the promise that Knowles would forgive all if they returned to their duty.

Captain Blyhe stayed in Boston for many days. Upon his return, he told Knowles that all the deserters he met in Boston refused to come aboard the *Achilles*. They seemed emboldened by their new surroundings, which granted mariners dignity and protection. Some were signing up for voyages on the outward-bound merchant ships. They wanted to be Bostonians. Knowles sent Blyhe back to Boston with orders to take his boats around the harbor and board outbound merchant vessels and coasters to find the deserters or other strangers to take their place. Initially, the British press boats failed to discriminate in favor of Bostonians in their searches. But Knowles intended to abide by the 1708 act. Benjamin Hallowell, a Boston tradesman then repairing Knowles's vessels, saw the *Achilles* returning and, after seeing the forty-six pressed men, told Knowles that some of them were Boston inhabitants. Hallowell testified that Knowles "told me he would not keep a man that belonged to the town or the Colony, he wanted nothing but strangers." In fact, Knowles ordered an officer to go aboard the schooner "and bring him an account of every man's name, where they were born, and what their occupations were." Yet, before this culling took place, a messenger came telling the Admiral that Boston was in full rebellion. The whole town was ablaze with righteous fury. Governor Shirley had lost control of the town and sought refuge at Castle Island. At this news, Knowles decided to keep the New England men until the outcome of the rebellion was determined.[43]

The rebellion in Boston was manned chiefly by sailors, but not confined to Jack Tars. It was a well-organized insurrection against the British navy. Shirley's house was besieged; the undersheriffs were beaten, plundered, and put in stocks. When Shirley called on the Boston militia, the locals refused to come to his defense or to quiet the mob. Captain Erskine, a British naval commander of a man-of-war, was kidnapped and imprisoned in the home of a wealthy merchant, Colonel Brenley of Roxbury; other British officers were also held hostage.[44] The mob embodied the whole town of Boston.

Shirley and Knowles understood the gravity of the rebellion, which had nearly universal support in Boston. However, in 1747 the town had no allies in other colonies; it needed British capital and credit, and had embarked with England on the colonization of Halifax. So a cover story needed to be invented to excuse the town from treason, while defending its sailors and protecting its unusual political economy. The cover story was that the riot was an expression of the emotional and fickle lower orders. Such lower-class riots, the mobs, were common and often dismissed by the English elite as part of the normal course of politics in which the poor could not express their will in any other way. In his first letter about the rebellion, Governor Shirley told Josiah Willard that there was reason "to apprehend the insurrection was secretly countenanced and encouraged by some ill minded inhabitants and persons of influence in the town." However, he quickly changed his tune. In his second letter to the Lords of Trade, Shirley blamed the riot solely on the lower orders. The militia was merely tardy rather than rebellious, he said. Yet, even this letter included the view that Boston was run by the meaner sort. Shirley told the Lords of Trade that he thought that "the principal cause of the mobbish turn in this town is its constitution." The town meeting "may be called together at any time upon the petition of ten of the meanest inhabitants, who by their constant attendance there generally are the majority and outvote the gentlemen, merchants, substantial traders, and all the better part of the inhabitants; to whom it is irksome to attend at such meetings." As a consequence, argued Shirley, a major trading port was led from the bottom, by "working artificers, seafaring men, and low sort of people."[45] Shirley understood how crucial political economy was.

Admiral Knowles, too, realized that he was confronting empowered mariners embedded deeply in a culture of sovereign workers. A number of Boston tradesmen, on board the *Canterbury* doing repairs, argued with Knowles as he maneuvered his fleet with loaded guns into Boston harbor for a bloody reckoning. Joseph Ballard, a Boston locksmith, was putting a lock on the cabin door of the *Canterbury*. After discovering Knowles's design to bombard the city, he asked him, "Oh! How will that do Sir; the righteous will suffer with the wicked—how will you find out the rebels?" According to Ballard, Knowles answered: "the North End people were the rebels." Knowles saw himself fighting, not a mob of isolated mariners, as he might find in New York, but a politically empowered laboring community that had seduced and captivated his sailors and seemed determined to frustrate all his efforts to retrieve them. With his guns loaded, Knowles determined to give the renegade city a scare.[46]

Later, when devising an alternative to impressments for manning the British navy, Knowles referred implicitly to his experience in Boston. In his 1758 "proposal for the Encouragement of Seamen," he suggested that the government build a large number of small houses at all the English dockyards and let these seaside cottages to married mariners at a subsidized rent of fifty shillings a year. The rent money would be credited to the landlords directly from the navy as part of the mariner's wages. If a seaman deserted, however, his wife and children would be evicted from the house. Sick sailors would be lodged at the married mariners' cottages in order to give them a pleasant environment and to provide additional income to the sailors' families. The mariners' children would be employed "in the services of the navy so soon as capable thereof," and their households would be paid for their children's work. Knowles was in effect proposing that government subsidize the creation of communities of mariners that resembled the North End of Boston, a place of small families and small properties (as Trelawny described the Massachusetts mariner life). The idea was to encourage good morals and loyalty to the navy by assuring sailors that their families would be well taken care of in their absence at sea and by making good care dependent on the sailor's loyalty. As the author noted: "By the comfortable habitation here proposed for the seaman's wife and family during his absence, his mind will be relieved from those oppressions of domestic grief and care; he will then consider himself and family as becomes the concern of the state." Knowles did not refer to the Boston model, but to the model of the coastal cottage-holding communities of Scotland and Northern England involved in the coal trade, whose sailors were known "for robustness, cleanliness, and sobriety."

Knowles might have made the mariner family order of Boston his model, but the remembrance that some ten years earlier he had nearly destroyed the North End with cannon shot probably deterred him.[47] At the same time, he probably did not want to recommend developing a mariner society resembling Boston's, in which common sailors had the vote.

The British could never solve the problem of sailors' desertions in America, especially as New Englanders tended to expand their definition of a nautical inhabitant to nearly everyone. Early on the morning of April 22, 1769, off the coast of Marblehead, Massachusetts, H.M. frigate *Rose* intercepted and stopped the Marblehead brig *Pitt Packet* (Thomas Power, master), manned chiefly by Irishmen, homeward bound from Cadiz, Spain, with a cargo of salt. Henry Panton, the lieutenant (executive officer) of the *Rose*, came aboard with some sailors and marines. He asked for the vessel's papers and started a search for seamen to press. He told Power that he wanted two of his six-man crew, that the New England inhabitants were free from the press, and that he wished to take no married men. Panton and the navy were still honoring the 1708 act in letter and spirit. In the forepeak, a small space under the weather deck between the stem and the main hold, Panton discovered Irish-born crewmen Michael Corbet, Pierce Fenning, John Ryan, and William Conner hiding, variously armed with fish gig, musket, hatchet, and harpoon. Michael Corbet was the leader and spokesman; he threatened to kill Panton if the British sailors or marines broke down the bulwark and tried to invade the room. Panton scoffed at the threats, summoned reinforcements, and ordered the destruction of the wall separating the men from the press gang. When the bulwark had been breached, Corbet thrust at Panton with his harpoon, cutting across the carotid artery and jugular vein in Panton's neck. The English naval officer died in less than two hours. As Corbet thrust, an English officer shot his pistol, hitting one of the Irish crewmen in the shoulder. Corbet and the other men in the forepeak were put on trial for their lives in Boston in front of an Admiralty Court. John Adams defended the Irish Jack Tars.[48]

Why did Corbet and the other crewmen so vigorously resist the press gang and why were they so vigorously defended by one of Boston leading lawyers? Adams in effect identified them as New Englanders instead of Irishmen. During their repartee with the Lieutenant, the men talked abstractly about their determination to defend their liberty, picking up the rhetoric of the protests against the Stamp and Townshend acts in New England. Boston citizens, who filled and surrounded the court house, rallied to their cause partly because their arrest seemed another part of a conspiracy to destroy liberty and republicanism by a corrupt regime in England. However, the connections were also familial and therefore political. William Peacock, who broke down the bulwark, testified that he heard the prisoners declare "that all they had in the world was there and they were defending it." Corbet had probably not been long in New England before he shipped on the *Pitt Packet*. Yet he had fallen in love and had been accepted in a Massachusetts town. On March 25, 1769, about a month before the homicide, Michael Corbet and Abigail Chapman published their intentions to marry in Marblehead. Abigail Chapman was from a long-established Marblehead family. Like many a British seaman, Corbet had been adopted by a mariner-hungry New England town. Another prisoner, John Ryan, also fell in love with a Marblehead woman. After his acquittal, he married Margaret Mauney on July 16, 1769. The English navy had offered him a position as a cook for £30 a year, a good salary, but Ryan turned it down and sued the navy for the injuries he incurred in the fracas. He got £30 as a settlement. His first child was baptized in Salem in 1770.[49] What Ryan and Corbet had was less an alternative working-class culture than a hope for the small families and small properties that Edward Trelawny had declared was the passion and possession of New England mariners. It was all they had in the world. They risked their lives and killed others, not for a proletarian revolution or out of mariner solidarity, but to keep the simple dignity and humanity that New England society gave them.

In the Boston trial, Adams showed through witnesses that Lieutenant Panton boarded the *Pitt Packet* to impress men, that the 1708 act exempting Americans from the press was in force, that Panton had no valid press warrant, and therefore that he was acting essentially like a pirate. Corbet and the rest of the crew were plausibly New Englanders and thus fully in the right, argued John Adams, to defend themselves, even by striking a fatal blow with a harpoon, against Panton and his crew who were threatening their liberty, who had fired a pistol at them, and who were determined to imprison them as impressed sailors for an indeterminate term. The judges acquitted the four men who had successfully crossed the invisible border from powerless British Jack Tar to New England worker and citizen.[50]

Figure 9. *Landscape (View of a Town)*, after 1753, oil on Eastern white pine panel, by unknown artist. In this eighteenth-century portrait of a New England town, the artist emphasizes commerce and prosperity, ships and well-dressed town folk. Courtesy of the Worcester Art Museum, Worcester, Massachusetts, Gift of Dr. and Mrs. Roger Kinnicutt.

PART III

Town People

CHAPTER EIGHT

Orphans

What a privilege to parents it is, to be able to employ their children at home, and thus keep them around them.
        Asa Sheldon, 1862

THE PRESCRIPTIVE LITERATURE read in colonial Massachusetts demanded a well-ordered patriarchal household. Yet this normative ideal, coupled with Puritans' reforming zeal, often justified the intrusive intervention of public authorities into the family. Many town selectmen took the patriarchal ideal so seriously that they removed children from fathers who failed to discipline, educate, or employ them properly. Indeed, far from forming a society that required children to live with their parents, New Englanders adopted many policies that propelled the scattering of young children among households. Early modern English households had often sent their children out to service at age fourteen, but thousands of children in colonial New England left home much earlier, often during infancy, and seldom returned. By creating a supervised labor market for children, the fathers of the towns facilitated the movement of thousands of children from their homes of birth at early ages without arousing protest, or even much visible notice. The towns were patriarchal insofar as they were led by successful men, but many families in the town were often not so; by choice, coercion, and death they rarely retained all their living children very long.[1]

John Winthrop, John White, and other New England leaders did not base their Christian humanistic society on the illusion of staffing a majority of households with nearly immortal male Calvinist potentates. Devotees and witnesses of the impact of mankind's fall from grace into original sin, Puritan leaders anticipated widespread parental inadequacy.[2] For Yankee fathers, retaining their children was more an earned privilege than a right, and was often deemed a ruinous or inconvenient policy. In short, the conventional depiction of the relationship between fathers, labor, children, and land in early Massachusetts needs revision.

Disapproved and Distancing Parents

In each Massachusetts town, male inhabitants voted for selectmen who were given the power to regulate the labor market, including the labor within households. Given the need not only to produce goods but also to inculcate industriousness, selectmen tolerated no idle children, especially when the household had nothing productive for them to do. With the permission of one or two judges, selectmen moved children from households they deemed unproductive to households that had enough resources to employ them— that is, from lower-class to middling and elite households. For example, in Boston in 1672, a special meeting that included the governor, deputy governor, and town selectmen demanded that more than ten families "dispose of their several children (herein nominated or mentioned) abroad for servants, to serve by indentures for some term of years, according to their age and capacities; which if they refuse or neglect to do, the magistrates and selectmen will take their said children from them, and place them with such masters as they shall provide." Eleven girls and three boys, some as young as ten years of age, were removed from these families, most of them headed by males. The policy was of long standing, though it was usually applied one family at a time.[3]

In many years, explicit orders were unnecessary to accomplish this policy. The movements of children were achieved through advice and pressure. As Boston grew larger, regulation increased. In 1707, the town instituted an annual family visiting day on which selectmen, overseers of the poor, and judges inspected households one by one "in order to prevent and redress disorders." These visits menaced the poor. In January 1715, the Boston records noted, "the justices and selectmen do now agree to visit the families in the several parts of this town . . . to inspect disorderly persons, new-comers, and the circumstances of the poor and education of their children." Twenty-four inspectors and eight wards (watchmen) manned the sweep and child press. The annual event lasted well into the 1740s, and was responsible for the movement of hundreds of "idle" children from their parental households into employment.[4]

Other towns followed similar policies, forcing the movement of children at early ages from the unproductive households of their birth parents to productive households of kin and strangers. Poor households, which required relief or only an abatement of taxes, were visited by selectmen and stripped of excess children. In 1670, the Watertown selectmen explained these policies, noting in regard to the household of Edward Sanderson that even if the town could provision his household, "yet it would not tend to the good of the children for their good education and bringing up so as they may be useful in the commonweal or themselves to live comfortably and usefully in time to come . . . we have therefore agreed to put out two of his children." In Dedham, the town meeting entrusted the relief of Widow Dunckley's poverty to the selectmen with the proviso that they "dispose of such of those children as they shall judge meet, it being expected that the woman should attend the advice that may be given her." Resistance to these enforced separations was rare, and usually came from women, not from men. In Dorchester, when the selectmen advised Thomas Bale to "dispose of two of his children, his answer was that his wife was not willing. . . . The selectmen persuaded him to persuade his wife to it." Male participation in New England town government included the proviso that a male household head would oblige willingly, or be compelled if necessary, to shed some or all of his children if he could not employ them productively.[5]

Troubled or inadequate households were sometimes identified by testing children's literacy and learning. In Watertown in 1660, the selectmen took "a survey of the inhabitants of the town with reference to the answering of that law which requires the knowledge of God and exercising reading to the advancing of catechizing." The selectmen reported back the names of "divers poor families that must be in the first place relieved, and afterwards care to be taken" that the children be instructed. Several of the eighteen children in these four households were removed and placed elsewhere. In a few cases, the selectmen deemed that the holdings of a household were adequate to employ the children but the father was an inadequate manager. In these cases, the father was sent to the workhouse or subordinated for instruction and reform to an outside manager who ran the property, supervised the family labor force, and often disposed of children.[6]

The selectmen and the colony regarded many fathers and mothers as inadequate employers of their own children simply on the ground of their race. For example, masters regularly gave away the infants of their African American slaves, separating these children from their parents. Slavery was not the major source of labor in Massachusetts, but owners imposed a strict labor regime so that slaves would work for them, not spend time nursing their own children. Slave children, too, were expected to work at an early age to avoid idle habits. Especially in Boston, masters and mistresses did not have the ability to construct slave quarters, as Thomas Jefferson did at Monticello in Virginia, where proximity of slave households and careful management of slave families provided older children for the convenient nursing and supervision of the youngest slaves. In Boston, enslaved African American and Indian children were regularly offered for free, like excess kittens, to other households headed by whites. When slave children got to be seven years old, especially those who had survived smallpox, they were often sold for profit. Yet chattel babies, especially those who had not yet had smallpox, were simply given away to those who wanted to raise them, accept the risk of their loss, and make use of their labor or sell them when grown.

From the 1730s to the 1770s, Massachusetts masters and mistresses advertised slave children to be given away to others no less than fifty-five times in the *Boston Evening Post*. Doubtless many more slave infants were given away without the expense and trouble of newspaper advertising. The owners seemed somewhat embarrassed by broadcasting the free availability of slave infants, since they rarely identified themselves. A typical advertisement read: "A Negro child a few days old to be given away. Inquire of the publisher" (June 11, 1739); "a likely, healthy Negro child, a week old, to be given away. Inquire of the printer" (December 1, 1760). In contrast, when looking for runaways, the masters gave their names and addresses. Some masters were probably embarrassed about exposing their sexual looseness signified by giving away their own biological children. For example, a suspicious advertisement read: "two or three mulatto children to be given away. Inquire of the printers" (November 10, 1766). Fortunately, some slave owners, innocent or not of sexual relations with slaves, were willing to reveal their motives and names. Thomas Fleet, the publisher of the *Evening Post*, offered free slave children himself: "a fine Negro male child, about two months old, to be given away by the publisher of this paper." In 1772, Fleet revealed that he owned an industrious maidservant who was too fertile for his household needs. He offered her for sale: "to be sold for no fault (only that of breeding too fast) a healthy Negro woman that can do any household business. She is strictly honest, and can be well recommended. . . . N.B. a healthy Negro child to be given to the person who may buy her."[7]

Boston's residents included free people of color—mulattos, blacks, and Indians—who toiled as porters, domestic servants, artisans, stevedores, rope workers, and mariners. The prevailing racism, as well as the demands of the local labor market and the town fathers' compulsion to teach all children diligence, meant that the town required all households of color to give away their children in infancy. In 1723, the Boston town meeting codified the rules by which the free people of color were, and would be, treated. In addition to ensuring that free colored people would not bear arms or entertain slaves as visitors to their households, the proposed code stated "that every free Indian, Negro, or Mulatto shall bind out all their children at or before they arrive to the age of four years to some English master or upon neglect thereof the selectmen or overseers of the poor shall be empowered to bind out all such children till the age of twenty-one years."[8] The enforced removal of all children by age four from free families of color was an affliction only more severe in degree than in kind, for many white poor households were also required to give up their children, although they could keep them a little longer.

Surprisingly, the permanent removal of excess young children from their own fathers and mothers to surrogate parents was a highly recommended, frequently adopted, and well publicized policy among substantial middling households. Sarah Goodhue's *Valedictory and Monitory Writing* (1681) demonstrates that Massachusetts authorities endorsed the practice of giving away a portion of young children as a solution to family crises and underemployment even among the well-to-do. Sarah Goodhue was a goodwife from Ipswich, Massachusetts, who during her eighth pregnancy sensed that her death was approaching. She wrote an eloquent and heroic ten-page letter with requests, advice, and admonitions to her husband and children. She soon died in childbirth as she prophesied. Her grieving family found the letter, and authorities published it in Cambridge in 1681; it was reprinted in Salem in 1770, in Portland in 1805, and again in Cambridge in 1830 (and in 1905 as part of a town history of Ipswich). Goodhue articulated some ideas that well support the orthodox historical interpretation of New England families and their potent yet controlling child-centered patriarchs. For example, she expressed and demonstrated the vigor of Calvinistic parenting. From just beyond the grave, she told her children, "consider what you are by nature, miserable sinners, utterly lost and undone; and that there is no way and means whereby you can come out of this miserable estate but by the mediation of the Lord Jesus Christ." Goodhue's description of her husband, a man economically and emotionally devoted to his children, seems also to support prevailing views of New England patriarchy: "you that are grown up, cannot but see how careful your father is when he cometh home from his work to take the young ones up into his wearied arms by his loving carriage and care towards those, you may behold as in a glass, his tender care and love to you every one as you grow up." Yet, Goodhue hardly believed that her husband, if loving and hardworking, was a possessive father; indeed, she asked him to give away immediately almost half of their children.

The main purpose of the valedictory was precisely to tell her husband Joseph Goodhue, when understandably disarmed by her death, to give away three or four of his and her infants. "My desire is that if thou art so contented, to dispose of two or three of my children." She asked that the newborn (who turned out to be twins) be given to her father-in-law and mother-in-law, the elder Goodhues. "And also my desire is that my cousin Symond Stacy should have John if he please, I freely bequeath and give him to him for his own if thou art willing." Goodhue requested "that my cousin Catherine Whipple should have Susanna, which is an hearty girl, and will quickly be helpful to her, and she may be helpful to the child, to bring her up." Goodhue believed her husband would surrender the children since she suggested that he had done so before: "thou hast been willing to answer my request formerly and I hope now thou wilt, this being the last as far as I know." Goodhue's request that her husband give away almost half of their young children seems problematic in relation to current interpretations of New England's domestic patriarchy. In that context, Joseph might be construed unfairly as an inadequate Calvinist male. Yet the request not only came from the heart of seventeenth-century New England culture but also among privileged and able people. Sarah Goodhue's father, John Whipple, was an elder of the Ipswich church, a representative to the General Court for eight years, a prominent landowner in Ipswich (the Ipswich Historical Society occupies and owns his house). Sarah Goodhue's husband, Joseph, was a member of the Ipswich church and in 1697 elected a selectman. By printing and reprinting the valedictory, authorities endorsed the distribution of children at early ages. The subsequent reprinting of the work demonstrated that this policy was recommended for over a century.[9]

Many New England middling and wealthy fathers, usually when widowed, followed Sarah Goodhue's published advice. For example, David Perry was born in Rehobeth, Massachusetts, in 1741, the oldest child of Eliakim and Sarah Perry. His mother died in 1748, when he was seven years old. "In consequence of this event, my father broke up housekeeping and put out his children." All the children—babies, toddlers, and teens—were sent packing. Three of the children, including David Perry himself, went to live with David Joy, the brother of Perry's deceased mother. "I lived with my uncle, (who treated me very kindly) until my fifteenth year: when I was placed with Mr. David Walker, in Dighton, Massachusetts to learn the trade of tanner and shoemaker." Perry later became a soldier in the French and Indian War, an active fighter in the early stages of the revolution in Massachusetts, and a respected founder of towns in Vermont and Ohio (Perry, Ohio, bears his name). His father played little role in his life; indeed, Perry never mentioned his father again.[10]

Ashley Bowen's story was similar. Bowen, son of a wealthy Marblehead justice of the peace, was shipped out with an abusive sea captain, Peter Hall, following his father's remarriage. After his wife died in 1808, the Boston merchant Dudley Tyng also farmed out his eight children, including Charles Tyng, then seven years old, to live among relatives. When the merchant remarried a few years later, as his son Charles Tyng described it, he rationed access to his new household in Milk Street: "We boys were allowed to come home twice a year, once in the fall to get our winter clothes, and once in the spring to get our spring clothes." Charles Tyng never got to know his brothers and sisters well: "We were never allowed to be home at the same time, so that years passed without our seeing one another."[11]

Some wealthy parents thought that removing young orphans was good educational policy, not simply a convenience. When his father died in 1775, Josiah Quincy was arguably the wealthiest four-year-old in Massachusetts. His mother, Abigail Phillips Quincy, "was so scrupulously careful lest the passionate fondness of a young widow for her only son should overflow in a hurtful indulgence, that she refrained, as he used to tell, from the caresses and endearments which young mothers delight to lavish upon their children." In order to toughen him up in the absence of a demanding father, she daily "caused her son, when not more than three years old to be taken from his warm bed, in winter as well as summer, and carried down to a cellar-kitchen, and there dipped three times in a tub of water cold from the pump." When he reached the age of six, she sent her son off to Phillips Academy. She established a policy by which for the next twelve years she allowed him to visit her only three times. Her grandson thought her "maternal tenderness was the guiding principle of her life, and wisely directed her whole conduct towards her son, who returned it with more than filial affection." She thought detachment and absence a wise, though painful way to raise an orphan, not selfish and callous. Her son Josiah Quincy later became mayor of Boston.[12]

Some middling fathers also gave away their children with their children's worldly interests in mind. For example, William Bentley, the noted minister, diarist, and journalist of late eighteenth-century Salem, grew to prominence partly because he was neither raised nor financially supported by his father. Born in 1759 to Joshua Bentley, a Boston ship carpenter, and Elizabeth Paine, Bentley left home in infancy. Perhaps because he showed more a bookish than mechanical aptitude, Joshua Bentley generously gave his son William to his father-in-law, William Paine, a prominent Boston merchant. Paine adopted Bentley, sent him to Harvard, and supported him during his employment in the East Parish of Salem, Massachusetts. Bentley's father accepted the loss of his son manfully and rarely appeared in his son's four-volume diary except to ask his son to coax money for him from the tight-fisted Paine. In later life, when meeting his brothers at a funeral, William Bentley measured the social distance he had traveled by the donation and adoption from his household of birth. While he had become a major book collector, essayist, journalist, and minister, he realized that his home-raised, mechanical brothers could barely read.[13]

Absent by Death

Many children left home because their parents died before the children reached adulthood. The number who lost a father, mother, or both in childhood remained high throughout the colonial period. Massachusetts had unusually fertile families with long-living husbands and wives, but got its wealth primarily from dangerous overseas commerce.

I have reconstituted 2,309 households formed by marriage in thirteen Massachusetts towns between 1630 and 1799.[14] The sample of towns and families is deliberately biased by my selection of places where I expected dangerous occupations to swell the ranks of orphans. Four of the thirteen towns studied, and about half of all the families came from fishing towns or seaports where the loss of adult men to accidents and diseases related to their trades was common. In these towns, 46 percent of all children who survived

TABLE 3. THIRTEEN TOWNS RANKED BY PROPORTION OF ORPHANS, 1640–1800

	Town economic base	Orphaned percentage[a]	Percentage of orphans who lost		
			Both parents	Father	Mother
Deerfield	Western[b]	54	6	68	27
Gloucester	Fishing	49	7	70	23
Salem	Seaport	46	10	60	30
Malden	Farming	46	8	69	24
Marblehead	Fishing, seaport	46	7	69	24
Newton	Farming	46	11	57	32
Marlborough	Farming	43	11	59	30
Beverly	Seaport, farming	43	8	70	22
Rowley	Farming	42	11	60	29
Haverhill	Farming	42	10	71	19
Shrewsbury	Farming	37	13	55	32
Topsfield	Farming	30	12	56	32
Oxford	Farming	29	7	59	34

[a] Total number orphaned (meaning one or both parents died before child turned twenty-one) equals 11,832.

[b] "Western" economic base was frontier defense, lumbering, and/or farming.

Sources: Family reconstitution based on *Deerfield Vital Records, Marblehead Vital Records, Marlborough Vital Records, Beverly Vital Records, Haverhill Vital Records, Malden Vital Records, Newton Vital Records, Oxford Vital Records, Rowley Vital Records, Shrewsbury Vital Records, Salem Vital Records, Topsfield Vital Records, Gloucester Vital Records.*

to the age of fourteen years lost at least one parent by the time these children reached twenty-one. Nonetheless, six of the towns studied were eastern farming and artisan towns that included a large share of the Massachusetts population. In these towns, 43 percent of all surviving children lost at least one parent. Only two towns in central Massachusetts, Shrewsbury and Oxford, had a relatively small proportion of half-orphans (only one parent dead) and full orphans: just 33 percent of all children who survived to the age of fourteen years. Among all the children studied, 44 percent lost at least one parent before the age of twenty-one. Among those who survived to fourteen years of age, 4 percent (479) lost both parents, 11 percent (1,315) lost their mothers, and 29 percent (3,414) lost their fathers (Table 3).

A majority of the children in the sample were born after 1740, but orphanhood was not confined to the mid-eighteenth century. The earliest period of Massachusetts history does appear exceptionally stable. Less than 35 percent of the children born before 1660 lost a parent. But this unusual degree of family stability ended quickly. Among the children born between 1660 and 1679, over 47 percent lost a parent before these children reached twenty-one. This proportion remained above 40 percent until after 1800, with the exception of children born between 1760 and 1779. Only 37 percent of the surviving children born in this period lost a parent, despite the American Revolution. War-related deaths were not the major factor in the production of full- and half-orphans, as some historians have asserted. Seafaring was most dangerous. It was disrupted by the English blockade during the war, so there were fewer deaths in the ports.[15] For most of early Massachusetts history, families were precarious. When fathers were often absent, inadequate, or distancing, the movement and placement of so many orphaned children required a carefully designed political economy.

In Massachusetts, almost half the children became full- or half-orphans. Colonial Massachusetts enjoyed high fertility and relatively low childhood mortality, but these blessings meant that many children were vulnerable if either of their parents died in middle age. Logic dictates that large families of healthy children produce more orphans than small families reduced by childhood mortality. Additionally, many men remarried younger women and produced additional children with younger wives; these men often distributed the children of their first marriage to other households for their labor and nurturance, as Judge Bowen did. Massachusetts depended economically on its fisheries and merchant trade, and a substantial proportion of fathers were deep-water fishermen or mariners, the most dangerous occupations in the early modern world. Massachusetts participated in numerous wars against Frenchmen and their Indian allies, and was the battlefield for many of them. While war was not the main cause of orphanhood, it increased their number, especially in inland towns such as Deerfield.

Given the large number of children who became orphaned, orphans should be visible figures in the social history of Massachusetts. Yet they remain nearly invisible. Their absence from historical narratives is less due to historians' myopia than to the colonists' success at placing orphans in other local households. Orphaned children usually stayed in their home towns, or circulated within their kin groups, and only a minority was involved in the market for child labor between towns. In order to study their movement in society, I compared the fates of 2,454 orphans and half-orphans with those of 396 nonorphans.[16] When a parent died, the orphans and half-orphans were on average between eleven and twelve years old. Children who lost their fathers were somewhat younger than those who lost their mothers (their average ages were ten and fifteen). Some of this difference is explained by the sad fact that many children who lost their mothers in infancy themselves died before the age of fourteen. Nevertheless, there were no dramatic differences among the mortality rates of orphans, half-orphans, and nonorphans between the ages of fourteen and thirty-five. Among the nonorphans, 5.5 percent died within these years, compared to 6 percent of those whose fathers had died, 8 percent of those whose mothers had died, and 5.4 percent of those who lost both parents.

What happened to children after a parent died varied markedly. Aggregate statistics based on vital records give only a faint outline of their fates. Many saw their surviving parent remarry. Among 625 children whose mothers had died, at least 60 percent (391) acquired a stepmother. Widowed men were much more likely to remarry than widowed women were. Among 1,581 children whose fathers had died, only 19 percent of their mothers remarried in their hometown, and 40 percent died in their hometown without remarrying. Another 41 percent neither died nor remarried in their children's hometown; they probably moved elsewhere.

Another way to gauge the social and economic placement of orphans is by the frequency, location, and timing of their first marriages. The town records allow the historian to examine at what age children married, and whether or not they married within their hometowns. Orphans and half-orphans appear to have experienced somewhat more geographic mobility in childhood and youth than nonorphans. Among both nonorphans and children who lost their mothers, two-thirds married in their hometowns. The experiences of those who had lost their fathers, or both parents, during childhood differed: among children who lost a father, 54 percent married in their hometowns, and among children who lost both parents, 46 percent did so. Geographic mobility or the frequency of a single life varied directly with the age at which a child lost his or her father. Among children whose fathers died when these children were two years old or younger, 43 percent married in their hometowns, while 64 percent of those who were already eighteen years of age when their fathers died married in their hometowns—a situation almost identical to nonorphans.

Differences of age at first marriage visible among those who did marry in their hometowns confirm the expectation that the presence of a living father delayed the marriage of his children. A son who lost his father could gain his inheritance at twenty-one (for daughters, at eighteen) and take full advantage of the high wages paid in the town without the worry of family obligations. They could gain the means to marry and establish an independent household faster than children with long-living parents. Among those who married in their hometowns, 63 percent of the fatherless married before the age of twenty-five, compared to 47 percent of those with two living parents. Only 8 percent of the fatherless children married at the age of thirty-five or older, compared to 14 percent of nonorphans.

Despite these interesting differences of marriage and geographic mobility, what is most striking are the similarities in patterns of geographic mobility, mortality, and marriage among orphans, half-orphans, and nonorphans. The data provide proof positive that the key to the Massachusetts and Connecticut labor system was the town, not the household, labor system. Thanks to the coercive policies of the General Court, the political economy of towns, and the practices of their selectmen, the value of child labor was kept high. Towns were protected from young people moving too quickly into independence, from outsiders devaluing hometown labor, and from child labor accumulating in the households of inefficient and undemanding adults. Because of these policies, whatever the trauma that attended the loss of parents, orphaned and half-orphaned children grew up and became integrated into seventeenth- and eighteenth-century Massachusetts society. In a society in which many children with parents grew up in others' households, orphans who had lost their parents would not have felt so strange as in a society where it seems that everyone except them was living with parents. I suspect that the prevalence of the practice of moving children around "normalized" the situation of orphans to some degree. Ironically, historians have long been able to sustain a delusion that Massachusetts was dominated by demographically stable and continuous patriarchal households because people were so adept at using coercion and the town organization to create "mutual advantages" that handled household discontinuity quietly and relatively invisibly. Indeed, it is likely that the town labor system allowed Massachusetts couples to produce so many children without fear that they would become marginalized if something happened to their parents.[17]

Work for Orphans

The political economy of towns ensured that thousands of children found a niche in the labor market and grew successfully into adulthood outside the households of their parents. The system did not always appear pleasant. To mangle Dr. Samuel Johnson's famous question about slavery and the American Revolution in order to suit the mostly nonslaveholding rebels in Massachusetts: how is it that we hear the loudest yelps for liberty from the drivers of orphans? On April 12, 1772, Samuel Adams wrote to James Warren: "I am much obligd for your Care in procuring for me a Boy." Adams continued, "I shall be ready to receive him about the middle of next month, and shall take the best care of him that shall be in my Power till he is 14 years old, perfecting him in his reading and teaching him to write and cypher if capable of it under my own Tuition for I cannot spare him the time to attend School."[18] Samuel Adams and his contemporaries were interested in young boys and girls primarily for their labor, which was seen as a form of education and was accompanied by instruction. The fact that the lad would have no time to attend school suggests that this boy would work hard and long for the great republican.

The labor performed by poor and orphaned children in Massachusetts society is illuminated by an earlier case involving the Reverend Ebenezer Parkman and a Boston half-orphan, John Storey. In 1726, when Parkman met Captain Storey in Boston, Parkman was recently married and was setting up house and farm in Westborough. His children were infants, his wife was pregnant, and he had little time to work in or for his household because he was the town minister. He was frantic for labor. On January 20, 1726, he consented to a widowed sea captain's request that Parkman take his son as a servant. Parkman wrote down the oral agreement verbatim in his diary: "His words were these about the conditions of our discourse. 'Take the lad, Sir, till about May, when I expect to return from sea, but if it please God to prevent me, if you like the Boy keep him till he is 15 or 16 years old, when I would have him put to apprentice. All I desire is that you keep him warm, and feed him suitably. Instruct him Christianity. My main expectation and hope is that you'll give him education proper to such an one. Let him serve you as he is able, impose not on him those heavy burthens that will either cripple him or spoil his growth. But in all regards I am willing he should serve you to his utmost'."[19]

Although Parkman soon hired a variety of female and male workers and was the recipient of enormous amounts of town labor, he did not mention "the boy" until two months later when on April 8 and 9, "neighbour Clark with my boy went to . . . in ploughing and sowing of wheat and rye and barley." Parkman then hired Robert Henry, an expensive adult worker. The boy was not mentioned again for another two months, when his name is noted for the first time: "I sent John Storey to Marlboro for Silence Bartlett" (a domestic worker). In late June the "boy" assisted in the haying, and in mid-August he was working for Parkman's wife as a personal servant: "my wife rode away from us for Cambridge (the lad John before her)." Parkman did not speak of John again until early December, when he sent him to Marlborough to fetch a stray heifer. Parkman never commented on the boy's leaving or dying, but John Storey is not mentioned again. Certainly he was gone by July 30, 1726, when Parkman noted: "now we are entirely alone having no servant nor any one in the House."[20] John Storey made a modest labor contribution to the Parkmans' household. He helped do farm work, assisted with domestic chores, and carried messages. Samuel Adams probably needed a gofer too; the usefulness of having someone to run errands should not be underestimated in an age without telephones.

In Hardwick, Massachusetts, an ardent patriot, Paul Mandell, made more intensive use of orphans and poor children. Mandell was a selectman, militia captain, delegate to the first and second provincial congresses, and the father of a number of Harvard graduates. From 1760 to 1778, he signed into his household no less than ten poor Boston children between the ages of five and eleven. He enrolled all of them until they reached adulthood and received a total of 123 child-years of labor.

Paul Mandell and his wife, Susannah Ruggles, daughter of the grand-living Tory Timothy Ruggles, had five surviving children of their own. The first Boston orphans arrived in 1760 when the Mandells' oldest daughter, Hannah, was thirteen years old and their oldest son, Moses, was just nine. The poor children, Susannah Holmes and Arthur Keeve, were both five years of age at the time. Moses and Paul, Jr., needed to avoid the plow in favor of study, for they would attend Harvard College. The Mandell daughters became refined young ladies who married well between the ages of eighteen and twenty-two, relatively young by contemporary Massachusetts standards. There was plenty of work to do in the Mandell household. The 1771 Massachusetts tax valuation shows real estate worth £24 annually, twenty-four sheep and goats, pasturage for twenty-five cows, and twelve acres of tillage. Mandell also had a tavern. Apparently Mandell used the orphans' inexpensive labor to make possible his own children's leisure.[21]

Squire Mandell's household resembled Robert Carter's Virginia plantation insofar as the biological children studied and played elegantly, while drudges did the work. In the Carter household the drudges were African American slaves, and in that of Squire Mandell they were white but poor children; the 1771 valuation shows that the liberty-loving Mandell held no slaves. This kind of arrangement, using orphans in lieu of slaves or more expensive town labor in order to provide leisure for biological children, spread among the Mandells' relatives and neighbors in Hardwick. One of Squire Mandell's neighbors was Jonathan Warner, a selectman, minuteman captain, later a brigadier general, and Massachusetts state senator. On February 5, 1766, Jonathan Warner married Hannah Mandell, the eldest daughter of Paul Mandell. Their first child, Susanna, was born in 1767, and three years later the Warners took in their first Boston poor child, Margaret Burton, age eight years. They later took in two more poor children from Boston. Although the Warners' eleven children probably worked, there was plenty of work for everyone: Jonathan Warner owned a farm, a store, and a tavern.[22]

Despite the ingenuity of the scheme, these cases were exceptional. In my analysis of over a hundred host families of Boston poor children between 1740 and 1790, I found that the great majority of the poor children did not tumble into the hands of well-established and long-married elite hosts like the Warners or the Mandells.[23] In most cases, the host families were newlyweds of modest means with no children or only very young ones, and they probably expected their own children to work as they matured. These couples rarely took in more than one orphan. In most cases, orphans were not substitutes for slaves in service to aspiring gentry households. Rather, Boston orphans usually supplemented the labor of modest families that were just starting out and whose fathers probably worked away from home much of the time. They performed the routine chores of children their ages: gathering and chopping wood, carrying water, tending livestock, spinning wool and flax, and weeding the garden. Equally important was running errands, which parents often delegated to their own children or orphans they had taken in. The local economy was built on a myriad of exchanges of goods, services, and labor between households, and it was customary to send less productive, and sometimes restless, young persons on errands.

In Dedham, orphans and poor children provided a major source of out-of-town labor to supplement that of town-born youth. At the town's founding, the Dedham town meeting made renting land to outsiders or hiring outsiders as workers subject to the approval of the selectmen. Any avoidance of the selectmen's authority brought a stiff fine. Yet by 1681, despite sporadic enforcement, many households had smuggled in strangers. Troubled by the extent of noncompliance, the selectmen "proposed whether the town would prosecute the order concerning inmates and servants or repeal it—to which the town answer that they will have it prosecuted." Invigorated by renewed authority, the selectmen gave notice that on February 11, 1681, "the inhabitants as have such servants and inmates to come to them this day, which accordingly diverse persons did, and we have attended them and heard each of their answers and allegations." What resulted from the parade of town people confessing to harboring outsiders in their households was not only an impressive display of the selectmen's intrusive authority but also a detailed census of persons from outside the town and the Dedham households that had them. One-fifth of all households in Dedham (22 of 112) had outsiders; these twenty-two households held a total of twenty-eight inmates who did not belong to the town. Significantly, twenty-four of the twenty-eight outsiders (86 percent) were preadolescent children, and twenty of the twenty-four children were white. They were called "boys" and "girls," poor children less than fourteen years of age. Faced with these confessions, the selectmen displayed their power in deciding who could keep their stranger children and on exactly what terms. For example, "Michill Metcalfe informeing that he have a boy from Boston he is allowed to keep the said boy provided he clear the town of him within four years unless he have further order." "Boys" and "girls" were distinguished from young men and women by the price of the bonds needed to secure them. Puberty was the dividing line. For example, "Edward Richards informing that he have a man servant an apprentice it is agreed that he shall give twenty pound bond unless he make it appear that he gave notice to one or more of the selectmen according to town order." An apprentice, usually an adolescent, was designated a "man." The bonds for "boys" and "girls" were usually five pounds; adult men and women had to be secured with bonds four times that amount. The difference arose from the risks that harboring adolescents entailed; these youths could get pregnant or impregnate, reproducing other children whom the town would be obligated to support.[24]

In the language used by the town meeting records, these outside workers included: 8 girls, 1 English girl, 2 maids, 10 boys, 1 lad, 1 apprentice man, 1 Negro man, 2 Negro boys, and 2 Indian boys. Why did white boys and girls predominate? One explanation is the destructive impact of King Philip's War, which had occurred only five years previously and left many young orphans, white as well as Indian. Dedham had real estate ties to Deerfield. Charity played some role in the presence of so many outside children in town. On the other hand, the presence of "a boy from Boston" and an "English girl" (her high bond implied that she had been born in England) suggests that other factors were at work, especially the selectmen's policies with regard to labor.

The Dedham selectmen were unabashedly dictatorial. Although they allowed most of the twenty-two householders to keep their servants for at least a year, they told each householder exactly on what terms he or she could keep the young laborers. For example, when Doctor Jonathan Avery gave "notice that he have a Negro in his family," the selectmen said he could keep him if Avery "shall give ten pound bond." As "for his maid, he hath liberty to keep her provided he clear the town of her within a year unless he have further order." And so it went. Robert Avery reported that he had "a lad Tho Boilson by name," but the selectmen "allows it not at present but shall further consider of it and if there be cause he may repair to the select men for their approbation." Josiah Fisher had two boys; the selectmen let him keep one for just four years and the other indefinitely, provided that he secure him with a £5 bond. The selectmen were not obligated to explain on what calculations or criteria they made these fine distinctions.[25]

The selectmen's policies made children a comparatively affordable form of outside labor. In 1681, the selectmen demanded just £5 bonds for white New England-born girls and boys and from £10 to £20 bonds for adolescents, adults, English children, African American children, and Indian children. If a man or woman promised to adopt the children "as his own," there was no need to post any bond whatsoever. "Robert Fuller having two grandchildren with him saith that the boy is to be put out to a trade, when he attain to the age of 15 years and the girl is to be with him during the natural life of himself and wife and that he intends to give them that portion which their mother should have had if she had lived, whereupon they are allowed."[26] Orally adopting a child constituted a legal pledge to pay all damages the child might cause.

White New England orphans were cheaper than outside adult workers because they would most likely leave town to return to their families of origin and because they were preadolescents and incapable of getting pregnant or impregnating others. Indeed, families that promised to dispose of their orphans before they reached puberty could often keep them without charge. Indian and African American children were usually slaves or lifelong servants. They would remain in town after adolescence, lacking a family to return to and being, as Orlando Patterson described it, socially dead.[27] Thus, they cost more. Of course, the prices for child servants, whatever their origins and irrespective of selectmen's policies, were much lower than for adults of similar status. Only the wealthiest households could afford to post bond for adult servants. Thanks to the enormous power given by the town meeting to the selectmen to protect town-born labor, poor children became the major remedy for labor shortages in Dedham. Orphans taken in as servants and laborers were found in many other towns as well. In some places they became visible. In Salem, overworked orphans who had been moved there to escape Indian battles on the Maine frontier helped spark the witchcraft craze.[28] By 1700, while orphans continued to be a source of labor in Dedham, their representation among outside laborers declined. At the same time, the selectmen warned out orphans at a significantly lower rate than other strangers.[29]

The Circulation of Orphans

While most orphans stayed in their hometowns, a regional labor market in orphans remained robust. Most poor children moved through informal networks involving kin and friends. Parkman got John Storey by such informal means, and Samuel Adams hoped to get his "boy" through James Warren's connections. Joshua Hempstead of New London moved his motherless children to his extended family on Long Island.[30] While the study of informal transactions would be difficult, if worthwhile, the records of Boston overseers of the poor provide many formal transactions that allow easier study of the Massachusetts market for orphaned and homeless child labor during the second half of the eighteenth century. Between 1734 and 1806, the Boston overseers carefully put out for service 1,134 poor children. They supervised the process closely, demanding that all potential host families submit letters of recommendation from their town selectmen.[31] They placed some of the children in Boston. However, since Boston was groaning under poor rates and provincial taxes, the overseers frequently looked outside the town. The overseers placed 838 children (74 percent) outside of Boston.

Surprisingly, the host families were young and of modest means. Some of the men taking children affected honorific titles. A few, such as Paul Mandell, who took ten orphans, and Thomas Hopkins, who took eight, were building their households' labor regime around orphans. Nonetheless, the Boston orphans rarely went to families like theirs. Among the 1,134 children placed out, 908 (80 percent) were the only Boston orphans taken into the household. The 940 families who took in poor children from Boston were dispersed among some 220 towns, chiefly in Massachusetts but also in New

Hampshire, and Connecticut. The harboring and employment of orphans was widespread in New England.

In order to study the kind of New England families that took in needy children for terms of service that averaged ten years, I decided to scrutinize a sample of host families genealogically and economically. I reconstituted 124 families in ten Massachusetts towns.[32] I expected that host families would be economically advantaged, well-established couples who perhaps had fewer children than average and took on orphans well into their marriages, when their own children were beginning to leave home. Some cases fit this pattern. In general, however, the host families were middling but modest. More surprisingly, they took orphans at or soon after marriage, when their economic stability was quite uncertain. Among the 124 orphans, ninety-four (76 percent) arrived during the first fourteen years after a couple's marriage. A clear majority (seventy-nine, or 64 percent) arrived within nine years of the couple's marriage. Virtually all of these families had plenty of children of their own. Among the 110 orphans whose host families' demographic facts could be known, only five lived with childless couples. Fully 72 percent of the orphans lived in families with four or more surviving children. Typically, a Boston orphan or poor child arrived into a family that had some young children and more on the way. By the time the Boston orphan's time was up, the host families' many children would be approaching their productive years.

Each town displayed slightly different patterns of employing orphans. In Hardwick, Massachusetts, wealthy families apparently replaced their own children's labor with that of Boston orphans. Daniel Billings, a merchant, took one child; Joseph Blake, who owned a forge and a sawmill and sent two sons to Harvard, took two children; Luke Brown, a lawyer and Harvard graduate, took one child; Daniel Oliver, son of Governor Andrew Oliver, took one child; Timothy Ruggles, Jr., owner of two houses and three tanneries, took two children; and Paul Mandell and Jonathan Warner together took thirteen Boston orphans. Twenty-six orphans accumulated in Hardwick. The girls were all to learn housewifery, and most of the boys farming. On average, they arrived fifteen years after the host family was formed.[33]

More typical were situations in Bridgewater, Massachusetts, an inland town in Plymouth County, where eighteen families contracted for nineteen Boston orphans: ten girls, whose average age was ten, and nine boys, whose average age was just seven. The girls typically served for eight years and the boys for fourteen years. Five of the girls were to learn housewifery and five were to be "spinsters" in domestic textile production. Among the boys, five were to work as farmers, one as a blacksmith, and three as weavers. The orphans came to couples who had been married between four and five years and eventually had many children, an average of six surviving children per couple. Jonathan and Susanna Bass were the only couple in Bridgewater who took more than one Boston orphan. In early October 1741, Jonathan was in Boston signing for William Negars, a seven-year-old who would serve them for fourteen years, and Elizabeth Mathews, a three-year-old who would serve them for fifteen years. Jonathan Bass was betrothed, and just a month later, on November 11, 1741, he married Susanna Byram. William Negars was to work as a weaver and Elizabeth Mathews as a house servant. Since the Boston overseers of the poor were some thirty miles away, the Bass household probably had a degree of flexibility in these children's work assignments. The Basses eventually had three surviving children of their own.

In 1759, Susanna Peraway, a six-year-old Boston orphan, was taken in for twelve years of domestic service by Robert Haward, Jr., and his wife Abigail. The Hawards had been married for two years, and Abigail was pregnant with her first child. Eventually, the Hawards had five surviving children, four of them girls. By 1771, they had amassed modest wealth: real estate worth £11 annually and a small share in a mill.[34] Perraway left service in 1771 and apparently stayed in Bridgewater, for she married Paul Smith there on April 6, 1775. Robert Haward might have been kind to his orphan maid, for a probable relative of his in Bridgewater, James Hayward, Jr., had married Sarah Harris, a Boston orphan, in 1751. This Sarah Harris, then fifteen years of age, came to serve for three years as a spinner to the household of Ebenezer and Mary Keith in 1748, whose oldest child was five and their youngest just one. Sarah probably met James Hayward, Jr., while she was a servant; she married him in Bridgewater just four months after leaving service.

Farnel Chamberlane arrived in Bridgewater in 1750 at the tender age of four. He was to serve the troubled household of Daniel and Susannah Alger for a full seventeen years as a farm laborer. Daniel Alger had married Susannah Forbes of Easton two years earlier (December 1, 1749), but the couple had already lost two children. The first (who might have been premature) was stillborn on July 24, 1749; the second, born in mid-June 1750, lived only a day. Farnel Chamberlane started in September, just three months later. Perhaps he was a replacement for the children that Susannah seemed unable to produce. Perhaps the Alger family anticipated the need for labor and was eager to have a child who had already survived four years. When Farnel arrived, Susannah Alger had just conceived her first surviving child, Daniel, born nine months later. By the time his contract was completed, Farnel Chamberlane was surrounded by ten surviving children, all legitimate heirs.[35]

The nineteen Boston orphans who entered Marblehead, a fishing and commercial seaport, had a different experience, though, like those in Bridge-water, they tended to enter young families. Marblehead's mariners and fish-ermen died prematurely and left many orphans themselves. Apparently, the demand for seafaring labor was so great that Marblehead had an insatiable appetite for boys' labor and was willing to import poor children. Seventeen of the nineteen orphans who entered Marblehead from Boston were male, and eight were apprenticed as mariners. Many of the Marblehead host fami-lies were led by mariners. The eighteen host families had the fewest number of their own surviving children, just under four on average. Nonetheless, the host families were young, only eight years after marriage on average when they took a Boston orphan.

Michael Wormsted, the only Marblehead man to take two Boston or-phans, married Mary Bull in December 1752. By the time Wormsted went to Boston to enroll the two Fessenden brothers, Joseph at age five and Parker at age seven, Wormsted already had three children of his own; the oldest, Sarah, was five. Eventually he had two surviving daughters and two surviving sons of his own. Wormsted was a ship's captain and in 1758, six years after his marriage, he signed the young boys on to become mariners for fourteen- and sixteen-year stints, respectively. Michael Wormstead was then thirty-one. Unfortunately, the Fessenden brothers relived the original trauma of their orphaning. The older orphan, Joseph, got out of service in April 1774. In November of that year, Michael Wormsted died at the age of forty-five. His younger brother, Parker, had almost two more years to serve.

Not all the young boys who came from Boston to Marblehead were trained as mariners. In late 1754, Joseph Stricker, a maker of sails, married Hannah Griffin. Four years later his sickly wife died at the age of twenty-five. In 1760, the childless widower traveled to Boston and signed on William Shirley, a nine-year-old, as a servant to learn and practice the art of sail making. Joseph Stricker was still a young man with a valued skill, so it was no surprise that he got married again, to Joanna Burchstead at Lynn in 1762. Eventually Stricker and Joanna produced two children of their own. Unlike many of the Boston orphans, William Shirley stayed on in the town. He got out of service in 1772 and married Abigail Vickery about a year later. He eventually had three children of his own and died in Marblehead in 1807 at the age of fifty-six. At his death he was designated a sail maker.[36]

Twenty-five Boston orphans went to nearby Roxbury, which adjoined the peninsula on which Boston was built. Many hosts eventually became well-to-do, but most couples were relatively young when they took these children. Four Roxbury families took two orphans, a boy to work on the farm and a girl to work in the house. Fifteen of the Roxbury-bound orphans were girls designated to work as spinsters or as servants in housewifery; seven of the ten boys were designated servants in husbandry. On average, these Boston children arrived just eight years after the marriages of the host couples and they eventually had six surviving children of their own.

Some elite families in Roxbury took orphans many years into marriage. Nathaniel Ruggles, a lawyer, chief justice of Massachusetts, and Congressional representative, married in 1786. He and his wife, Sally Fairfield, experienced much tragic loss early in their marriage. Their firstborn, Sally, survived until 1805, when she died at the age of eighteen. However, Joseph, born in 1790, died in 1795; John Fairfield died the year of his birth, 1792; and Martha Fairfield died at age one in 1796. Ruggles went to Boston to enroll five-year-old Dublin Badger as a servant that year. Three years later they enrolled a five-year-old African American Boston orphan, Mary Smith, as a domestic servant. In 1800, they were living with a nine-year-old Boston boy, a six-year-old Boston girl, and their thirteen-year-old daughter. Given their wealth and the ten-year gap between their marriage and their first signing on Boston children, charity was a more likely motive than among some other elite families. They seemed to be replacing their departed children with charity children. Still, they needed children to work and they chose an African American girl, whom they could probably not easily identify as a surrogate biological child.

Other Roxbury families fit the dominant pattern of taking poor Boston orphans soon after marriage. On November 14, 1745, Joseph Mayo married Ester Kendrick of Newton. Less than a year later, during his wife's pregnancy, he went to Boston and signed on sixteen-year-old Jonathan Smally to help with his farm work, and eight-year-old Elizabeth Pearce to do spinning and domestic tasks. The Mayos eventually had eleven surviving children. They prospered economically as well. The 1771 tax evaluation shows that the Mayos had two houses and a shop in Roxbury, real estate worth £17 annually, merchandise worth £30, and a farm with 29 acres of pasture and two acres of salt marsh, four horses, and two oxen. Joseph Mayo was a major in the Roxbury militia and a frequent officeholder who held the title of Esquire. The orphans came early to the Mayos' marriage and gave their household a running start.[37]

Family labor had a glaring weakness: it took a child at least fourteen years to become a productive worker. Newly married couples were in an unenviable situation. The woman would spend the next twelve to twenty years in various stages of pregnancy and nursing. Infants and toddlers would be swarming underfoot, making daily chores numerous and exhausting. Most couples, coming from families with many children and little capital, lacked the funds necessary to hire local laborers. Indeed, the man was probably one of those hired workers. These families, rather than more established families with adult children, found it both an act of charity and a financial advantage to take what they could afford: a young boy or girl from Boston's overseers of the poor. They might not get much work from these children immediately, but a five-year-old girl could help a pregnant woman with toddlers. Most child laborers grew bigger and stronger, though most got sick and a few died. When the orphan's term of service was ending, the couple's own children were becoming productive and capable workers.

The arrival of an orphan or two early in marriage had psychological advantages as well. Beginning a marriage with a real act of charity should not be overlooked. The orphan provided the young couple with practice for one of their most demanding responsibilities, the transformation of their own children into a productive household and town labor force. The economy of Massachusetts relied chiefly on couples' own children who worked primarily in their hometown. For colonial Americans, it was no simple matter to find the correct blend of loving endearments, threats, rewards, and corporal punishments to get children to work efficiently. If the poor children were emotionally or physically scarred by their treatment, the parents would not have to see the scars as long as they would those of their own children. Taking on orphans early in marriage also eased their eventual departure. The child came at a time when his or her work was truly needed. Being the most able and valued—or even the only—child in a household could give a needed boost in self-esteem to a child traumatized by poverty and the death or desertion of parents. Gradually, the orphan was eased out from his or her central place as the host couple's own children matured. They would displace the servant to the margins of the household and prepare him and her for departure. When of age to leave, the family would be ready to let the orphan go. The world outside looked far more enticing than the host family full of their progeny. The orphans left just when the host family realized the enormous wealth it would take to help their own growing children get established in life.

Indeed, most poor children not only left their host families but also their host towns. Among the 124 servants whose host families have been studied, only twenty-five (20 percent) left a record in their host towns. This proportion was substantially lower than the 65 percent of nonorphans married within their home towns and the 46 percent of full orphans who married in their hometowns. Perhaps orphans found new towns in Maine and Worcester County attractive places to begin adulthood.

The system seems to have worked reasonably well for males. Orphaned girls who were placed out as servants had even higher rates of unmarried pregnancy than other servant girls; their vulnerability was a concern of William Bentley, and later generations founded asylums for their protection. Relationships between couples and orphan servants were unsentimental and open to severe abuse. Rufus Putnam, George Washington's major military engineer, was orphaned in central Massachusetts at the age of seven, lived with his maternal grandfather for two years, and then in 1747 went to live with his stepfather, Captain John Sadler. Putnam later complained bitterly that Sadler exploited him by not paying any attention to his education. His material grandfather had ensured "I was keept at School as much as Children usually were at that day, and could read pritty well in the bible." While living with his stepfather, however, "I never saw the inside of a school house, except about three weeks." Putnam tried to teach himself, but "I was made a ridecule of, and otherwise abused for my attention to books, and attempting to write, and learn arethmatic." In 1754, Putnam was bound apprentice to Daniel Mathews of Brookfield, a millwright. "By him my education was as much neglected, as by Capt. Sadler, except that he did not deny me the use of a light for study in the winter evenings." Nonetheless, Putnam learned a trade that he made good use of by enlisting in the provincial corps of the British army during the Seven Years War. In his memoirs, Putnam blamed his grammatical inelegance on his former masters. Yet, he had enough self-esteem, education, and mechanical skills to become a general.[38]

Successful Boston orphans included the father of Paul Revere. Isaiah Thomas, the famous newspaper editor and founder of the American Antiquarian Society, was a poor orphan of eight in 1756, when he was put out for thirteen years to Zachariah Fowle to be an apprentice printer. Thomas was not only a client of the system but also a provider. In July 1771, Isaiah Thomas took Anthony Haswell, a fifteen-year-old, to be an apprentice printer for six years. The act was based solidly on mutual advantage. When Thomas took Haswell, Thomas was not yet a famous editor. Only two years out of his service himself, he was just setting up his business.[39] Taking Haswell was not only an act of charity but also the cheapest labor he could get.

The success of Massachusetts's system of placing out orphans, insofar it was a success, was based on this combination of charity and self-interest. The mutual advantage between orphan and host family was neither accidental nor simply natural. Massachusetts authorities created both the town system of labor and the supplementary labor market in orphans self-consciously and with ample application of coercion, both inside and outside the household. The system allowed Massachusetts fathers to have more children than they could ever portion.[40]

The public distribution of young, impoverished and orphaned children was halted in the 1840s, when Massachusetts policy makers adopted the belief that children's continuing connections with their parents was crucial to their upbringing and lifelong achievement. They demonstrated this shift with the greatest flurry of name changing in English or American history. In 1885, the secretary of the Commonwealth of Massachusetts published a four-hundred-page *List of Persons Whose Names Have been Changed in Massachusetts, 1780–1883*, which included five thousand persons who changed their names by a private legislative act. (Women who changed their name at marriage were excluded.) The only counterpart covers all of Great Britain, extends from 1760 to 1901, and includes newspaper announcements as well as legal name changes, yet the British volume was smaller. In 1847, for example, twenty-three Britons changed their names; while in Massachusetts 167 people did so. In the mid-nineteenth century, thousands of Massachusetts residents modified or abandoned the names their fathers had given them. A few were Jews and Irish who wanted to fit into Protestant society. Others had embarrassing names. Chiefly, their name changing exposed the replacement of the past pattern of spreading children widely among households by a norm favoring adoption. Massachusetts residents took the names of the people who had actually raised them, and guardians renamed the orphans in their household as their own birth children. For example, in 1855, two hard-working children in Northampton had their surnames changed: George Stowell became George Temple, and Eliza Gorman became Eliza Tower.[41]

In her 1869 novel *Oldtown Folks,* Harriet Beecher Stowe condemned her ancestors' system for the care of orphans. Stowe highlighted the cruelty toward the orphan seven-year-old Tina by her assigned guardian, Miss Asphyxia, a middle-aged rural spinster intent on extracting work. "In taking a child, she had had her eyes open only to one patent fact,—that a child was an animal who would always be wanting to play, and that she must make all her plans and calculations to keep her from playing." "Miss Asphyxia did not hate the child, nor did she love her. She regarded her exactly as she did her broom and her rolling-pin and her spinning-wheel—as an implement or instrument which she was to fashion to her uses." Predictably, Asphyxia afflicts Tina with endless work; the girl calls Asphyxia a "witch." Asphyxia whips Tina, and Tina runs away.[42] An eager advocate of domesticity, Stowe offers insights about all these events that would satisfy a trauma therapist and a modern historian, but also ignores the fact that her ancestors lacked the immigrant Irish work force of her day that made the work of white middle-class children superfluous and the leisure and expressive playfulness of adopted orphans possible. In recent times, historians have not only continued to champion gentle domesticity but have made the New England colonists more easily reached within this scheme by reimagining them as the builders of a world of patriarchal domesticity and household labor in which orphans were extraordinary, not, as they were in truth, nearly half the population. Eighteenth-century New England town folk relied heavily on the resilience of children and on Christian humanistic politics to answer the riddle of love, loss, and labor.

CHAPTER NINE

Prodigals or Milquetoasts?

THOMAS SHEPARD, THE minister of Cambridge, Massachusetts, complained in 1672 that "there are divers children who . . . grow to that pride,
and unnaturalness, and stubbornness, that they will not serve their parents
except they be hired to it." Shepard's concern about the premature autonomy
of youth and the inversion of proper parent-child relationships arose from
the distinctive organization of labor in the colony, which centered not on the
family but on the town. Not only did Massachusetts farmers lack the ample
supply of labor available to property holders in Shepard's native England, but
the colony and its towns carefully controlled the influx of workers, ensuring
that labor remained in short supply. Farmers often hired town-born youth
and found that their own sons drifted off to nearby farms to work. For a
godly society with a patriarchal ethos, the economic emancipation of rural
youth posed a moral problem. Shepard saw Massachusetts as filled with sin-
fully empowered sons, who "are ready to say as the Prodigal, *Luke 15:12, Give
me the portion of goods that falleth to me.*" He concluded sadly, "I wish there
might be seasonable redress thereof."[1] Yet, except for threatening youth with
divine judgment and inflicting physical punishment, no solution was ever
found. The early autonomy of young men was built into the political economy of New England towns.

Despite Shepard's lament, historians have envisioned rural Massachusetts
entirely differently, as having from its founding until the late eighteenth
century a social order based on the patriarchal family rather than the town.
Powerful fathers awed their children, controlled their labor, and withheld
property until their sons were full adults. Instead of economically weak

fathers facing prodigal sons, they see dictatorial fathers facing milquetoasts. This argument is made by the most influential study of relationships in an early New England town, Philip Greven, Jr.'s *Four Generations: Population, Land, and Family in Colonial Andover, Massachusetts* (1970). For this innovative and still exemplary work, Greven reconstituted hundreds of Andover families, linking their births, deaths, and marriages from vital records and genealogies to produce some of the first demographic facts about colonial New England, revealing the longevity of first- and second-generation farmers and their wives. He painstakingly studied 273 estates, including those of 30 first-generation colonists, 57 second-generation sons, 103 third-generation grandsons, and 83 fourth-generation great-grandsons, organizing his analysis within a generational rather than chronological frame. From wills and deeds, he examined the transfer of property from fathers to sons and how these transactions intersected with marriages, births, and deaths.

Greven portrayed Andover as a society of strong fathers and spineless sons. Despite being surrounded by ample land, second-generation sons waited to marry until their mid- to late twenties, much as they would have done in old England where hardly any land was available for middling folk. They stayed in Andover and spurned new towns. They waited even longer to become landowners, which Greven saw as the key to autonomy. The source of their timorous behavior was their fathers. Their fathers grabbed all the land and held onto it with an iron grip, Greven argued. Many sons married and lived on their fathers' land for years without having legal title to it. "Although the great majority of second-generation sons were settled upon their fathers' lands while their fathers were still alive," Greven observed, "only about one-quarter of them actually owned the land which they lived upon until after their fathers' deaths." In his view, fathers used land to control their sons' marriages, their lives, and their labor, creating clannish extended families confined to the town. Sons seemed to wait sheepishly for their fathers to die and, unluckily for them, the autocrats lived a long time. Nor did the strength of fathers and the weakness of nearly middle-aged sons change much during the eighteenth century, according to Greven. "The sustained control of the land by the older generation and the delayed maturity of many third-generation sons who waited not only to marry but also to gain their full economic independence continued to be prominent characteristics of family life in Andover."[2] Historians such as Daniel Vickers and Allan Kulikoff endorsed and elaborated on this picture of powerful fathers and covertly enraged milquetoast sons. "Paternal attempts to control adult sons, especially in New England, led to intergenerational strife," remarks Kulikoff, "and propelled sons to migrate to frontier lands to establish their independence as adults."[3]

There are grave conceptual and evidentiary problems with this picture. First, it is based on a dyadic analysis of fathers and sons, leaving out the town's political economy, which was crucial to all human relations, particularly those revolving around land and labor. Second, though account books can be read to support this vision, all major New England diaries, which reveal what was actually happening, show the predominance of town labor over family labor in the development of farms and rural industries.[4] For most of their lives, diary-keeping fathers relied on the labor of neighbors and other town folk, not on the work of their own children.

Consider the Westborough minister Ebenezer Parkman, who maintained a farm as well as his ministry and wrote a wonderful diary. As Richard Dunn has shown, Parkman employed many laborers, especially for day work, during some eighteen years while his children grew up. Every New England family went through a protracted period after marriage when the children were too young to work productively. "In 1738," observed Dunn, Parkman "mentions fifty-five different Westborough men and boys who put in a day or two apiece on his place and five women and girls who similarly aided his wife." When the minister's eldest son, Ebenezer, Jr., was seventeen years of age, he began working steadily on the family farm and continued to toil there for eight years. During this period, however, Parkman hired Thomas Winchester, Joseph Bowker, Joseph Bruce, and Daniel Hastings as live-in workers for several weeks apiece during the summer, and he employed many town residents by the day, especially during haying, harvesting, and the winter getting of wood, when ten or more local men commonly appeared with axes and oxen for a day or two. Parkman never tried to confine his growing sons to toiling at home. He sent his second son, Thomas, to learn the saddler's trade. When he completed his apprenticeship, Parkman largely excused him from farm work and allowed him to ply his trade in a shop on the farm, as his elder brother worked alongside hired laborers in the fields. Realizing that Ebenezer was too puny for farm work, the minister tried to apprentice his first-born son to a gunsmith in Harvard, Massachusetts.[5]

Contrary to the conventional view, the minister exercised no control over Ebenezer's marriage. In 1751, at the age of twenty-four, Ebenezer, Jr., told his father of his desire to marry. About five months later, Parkman recorded, "Ebenezer brought Mrs. Eliza Harrington to dinner here. . . . 'Tis thought he courts her. I earnestly pray that God may be guardian and director of my dear son in this important matter before him!" Parkman's surrendering guardianship to God was not mere rhetoric. By this time Ebenezer was working a portion of the minister's land independently, though it had not been deeded to him. A month later, the minister heard that his son had brought a boy to work and live with him. Three months after that, the minister recorded, "My son Ebenezer came up from Watertown last night and brought his bride, Mrs. Elizabeth Harrington, the daughter of Mr. Joseph Harrington of Watertown, with him, for they were marry'd yesterday p.m. and Mr. John Rogers came with the team loaded with her goods. May God please to make 'em an happy pair!" Perhaps the couple had neglected to invite the groom's father to the wedding because he had been ill. On the day of his son's marriage, Parkman was at home interviewing the Reverend Mr. Price of Hopkinton about books. More impressive than his absence from the wedding was the absence of any evidence that he knew when, or even if, it would occur. Far from being upset, the minister happily joined the just-arrived newlyweds for dinner at Ebenezer, Jr.'s house.[6]

The minister seemed to feel indebted to his eldest son, who had worked for him for eight years without the compensation he paid to local laborers. Indeed Ebenezer, Jr., sometimes subtly dunned his father. Perhaps nudged by his new bride, in November 1752 "in the eve, Ebenezer was here," noted the minister, "and we had some talk of our settling our affairs—his labor on the place as taking it to the halves, etc. I have him two . . . pigs of last spring, over and above, but we defer the exact settling." Ebenezer, Jr., apparently wanted half the profits of the farm from the time he reached adulthood, but the minister was reluctant to agree to that arrangement because he had many more children to portion (he eventually had twelve). Ebenezer, Jr., hardly seemed awed, just expectant. Thereafter, the minister rarely asked for, or got, his eldest son's labor, but relied chiefly on hired hands. Between April and October 1755, although he had sons aged sixteen and fourteen years, Parkman had local laborers do over 80 percent of his farm work.[7]

The diary of Abner Sanger tells a similar story from a worker's perspective. Sanger was born in Hardwick, Massachusetts, in 1739. The Sanger family moved to Keene, New Hampshire, in 1752, where Abner inherited land after his father died in 1765. However, Abner Sanger sold this land for £350 and lived with his sister, brother, and other families in Keene for decades while working for others and developing land he rented for a season, as his lively diary shows. For example, from January to June 1779 Abner Sanger worked for sixty-two different Keene residents, often for two in a day, chopping wood, making wheels, planting, and so on. He never mentions being without work, and he almost always returned home at the end of the day.[8] Sanger's diary shows the predominance of hired labor within the town over family labor. In short, when the town is considered, the world of work revolves around localities rather than families.

Family labor played only a secondary role in farm economies, but father-son relations, especially regarding property, were still important. We cannot assume that the few extant diaries are representative. And the issue of whether sons were prodigals or milquetoasts matters to more than family history. The neoliberal construction of American history depends on the trope of the overbearing father and the spineless son awaiting land. This narrative tells us that male individualism did not emerge in New England until the fathers were weakened, humiliated, and rendered impotent at the time of the Revolution.[9] It tells us that sons only slowly learned to adjust to autonomy after the town fathers lost their land and power. Not only does such a narrative provide a fiercely oedipal reading of New England history, but it sees the town, its fathers, and their English inheritance as oppressive; only with their destruction on the American frontier could freedom emerge. This book offers an antidote to this confusing myth, demonstrating that the political economy of New England towns, while inflicting much suffering on the indigenous inhabitants and even its participants, enabled productivity, some equity, and even individualism among middling people despite the labor shortages endemic to the colonies. The absence of this sort of political economy elsewhere often led not only to the subjugation of Indians but also to the exploitation of millions of Africans in slave societies. In New England, the town's political economies and local labor system allowed fathers and sons to face one another with a modicum of freedom and dignity.

Labor and Property Relations in Dedham

Demographic information and land records are useful for elucidating inter-generational relations, but town sources, particularly about property taxes, must be added to reconstruct a complete picture of land and labor. In Dedham, Massachusetts, a rural town twenty miles southwest of Boston and thirty-eight miles south of Andover, many fathers gave land to their married sons in old age, long after the sons had reached adulthood. Many sons lived next to their fathers, and some married sons lived on their father's land. Married sons even shared the same roof with their fathers on occasion. Kenneth Lockridge observed these father-son relationships in his pioneering study of Dedham, though he made less of them than Greven did for Andover.[10] But a more complete study of Dedham shows that the prevailing notion of New England as a land of controlling, aging patriarchs and dutiful adult sons is inaccurate. Sons were already economically autonomous when they got land from their fathers by will or deed. Fathers and sons depended to a degree on one another, but both depended chiefly on the political economy of the town for their well-being. When fathers gave their sons land, sons already had land, or at least enough substance to buy it. Fathers had access to other adult labor in the town. Exchanges of land and labor between fathers and sons were more chosen than codependent.

Analyzing tax lists is essential in order to trace the fortunes of young men. A full study of taxes in colonial New England is long overdue, but even a town-level study reveals a society and economy of powerful workers. In 1647, the Massachusetts General Court ordered the selectmen of the towns to raise taxes by listing and taxing all the able-bodied men sixteen years and older, and stipulated that "for such servants and children as take not wages, their parents and masters shall pay for them, but such as take wages shall pay for themselves." The tax lists show when sons became free laborers who earned wages for themselves and, alternatively, how long they remained submerged within their father's household economies as servants or workers whose payment was being deferred.[11] In Dedham, the assessors began to list polls in their tax summaries in 1705; before that time they folded the polls into the general assessment of each man's wealth. A study of sixty-six men born in Dedham between 1690 and 1724 shows that more than three-quarters were earning their own money by the age of twenty-five and less than a quarter were still working entirely for their fathers beyond that age. Many men worked for their fathers a few years beyond the age of twenty-one, but few did so for more than a year or two.

The eighteenth century saw only minor liberalization of rules limiting young men's and women's freedom to live independently. In the 1650s and 1660s, the Puritan colonies passed laws insisting that all unmarried men, no matter their age, be placed in a household under the control of an approved patriarch or matriarch. The law was aimed to counter the economic power that laborers could wield in a labor-hungry, high-wage colony and reflected officials' fear of a culture of overly empowered youth. Young men's economic power and authorities' fears remained strong. A law of 1710 showed only a slight increase of trust in youths' discretion. It decreed in Massachusetts that "no single person of either sex under the age of twenty-one years shall be suffered to live at their own hand, but under some orderly family government." Once they attained the age of majority, however, men and women could live where they wanted, in their own household or any other household deemed orderly by the selectmen.[12]

Focusing on all the polls in Dedham, we see that the town's households, including those headed by fathers, rarely fully retained their sons' labor beyond the age of twenty-five—at least as unpaid workers.[13] By 1710 and probably before, the town was composed of free laborers who sold their labor in the restricted town labor marketplace. It was not a town of isolated households or plantations, each monopolizing or trading the labor of adult sons until they were released for marriage and land ownership by their fathers. From the stories Greven told of controlling fathers, we might expect that many households contained two or more polls, for such powerful fathers should have the muscle to retain one or more sons from the age of sixteen to the mid- or late twenties. Doubtless such fathers would add even more adult male laborers by accumulating indentured servants and apprentices (the tax law said that slaves were included in personal estate, but all male servants above fifteen years of age, whatever their race, were counted as polls).[14] Greven's portrait suggests that lacking an alternative labor force, it was crucial for fathers to accumulate household workers to develop their assets and that they held sons in place as long as possible.

That was not the case in Dedham. A study of polls in thirteen Dedham tax lists between 1710 and 1748 shows that in this rural town at least 75 percent of the people listed commanded only one adult male worker, including themselves. The average household lacked even a single male laborer under control of the household head. Only between a quarter and a fifth of all men listed on the tax lists commanded more than a single poll, and a tiny percentage had three or more polls or controlled more than themselves and another single male over fifteen years of age.[15] People did not accumulate labor in their households. They bought it by paying wages to the workers in the local labor market. Most married men and landowners often sold their own labor to others. Dedham was a town of workers with land.

Many wage-earning adult sons lived with their fathers. Even more lived near their fathers, if the order in which households are listed reflects neighborhood configurations. These sons were not unpaid servants of their fathers, however, but independent laborers who worked for wages. They might work for their fathers by moral obligation a few days a week in haying time, but they were otherwise free. It is mistaken to treat the household as defining and controlling the organization of labor in Dedham. Dedham was not composed of plantations with large reserves of labor. The local labor force could be used by anyone in the town who needed workers and could pay for them. After men were married and had land, they still worked for others as their children grew into usefulness.[16] They could hardly turn into plantation owners with a small plot of ground worked by a gang of toddlers.

The detailed 1771 assessment of taxes in Dedham, which includes individual holdings, provides a snapshot of the relations of labor and land resources in Dedham on the eve of the Revolution. In 1771 there were 436 taxpayers in Dedham, of whom 77 percent were taxed no more than one poll. No one was taxed on more than three polls. Well into the second half of the eighteenth century, then, Dedham was a town composed of workers with land, not of laborers under the control of a group of privileged patriarchs or matriarchs.[17] It cannot be assumed, however, that every taxpayer had land or a house. Many taxpayers were young laborers. The 1771 tax list assesses houses, allowing historians to differentiate taxpayers who owned a house in Dedham from those who did not. A slight majority, 58 percent, owned a house. Among these householders, 63 percent had no more than one poll, 37 percent had two or three polls, and none had more than three. Even the people who owned a house generally had a single male laborer at home under their constant control, virtually always the household head himself. The householders averaged only 1.4 polls per house. Their agricultural assets were equally modest. The house owners had on average nine acres of pasture, three acres of plow land, four acres of upland meadow, and five acres of marsh or fresh meadow, amounting to twenty-one acres of productive land. Many had additional trades. These small amounts of land were consistent with the amount of labor they had available to them in the town, the quality of the land, and the seasonal demands for labor in farming and other occupations.

A substantial minority (184 people, 42 percent of all taxpayers) did not own a house. Nearly half of them (47 percent) paid no poll tax. A few of these people were from other towns but owned land in Dedham; more were landowning women residents in others' households; and many were children who had inherited land but were too young to pay poll taxes or head households. Among these nonhouseholders, just over half (54 percent) paid polls and held almost no land; most were young workers. The 1771 assessment list, like the earlier tax lists, paints a picture of smallholders who worked for one another; few owned enough land or controlled enough labor to monopolize the time and energies of many adult males. Seeing colonial society as a composite of separate farm families, each chiefly devoted to the development of its own resources, distorts reality. Dedham was a working people's town in which labor was protected by the democratically elected town meeting, and consequently was well paid and in constant demand. Most men owned land that they spent only a portion of their work time developing.

The variety, seasonality, diversity, and commercial sophistication of Dedham workers are clear in account books. Deacon John Aldis kept an account of his efforts to finance the Dedham Church between 1671 and 1694. Each year he helped decide the proportion of the minister's salary assigned to each householder and laborer in his parish and noted how he collected it. Householders paid the reverend's salary according to their occupations and resources. In 1682, Deacon Aldis recorded that Sargeant Pond paid £1 10 shillings in "worck," while Thomas Herring gave as part of his payment "a load of wood," and Samuel Colburn got five shillings' credit for "mowing of Inglish grase." The deacon's account shows that by 1680 Dedham was connected to the Atlantic economy. Men and women sold goods, crops, lumber, and services to merchants for money and used that money to pay their civic obligations as well as to buy land. In 1681–1682, Aldis collected £60 for Reverend Adams in money from over a hundred parishioners. He collected nearly £45 (74 percent) in silver, about £10 (16 percent) in labor, £4 (7 percent) in crops, and £1.5 (3 percent) in other goods (such as shoes). Many men paid their tax in several different forms. Deacon Aldis himself paid his share of the Reverend's salary in silver, "in fencing stuff, and repairing of fence by myself."[18]

Although most Massachusetts men were independent wage-earners by the time they reached twenty-five, it is possible that they may have simply lacked the earning capacity to save enough money to buy land and therefore may have been as dependent on their fathers as Greven believed. Laborers made some 1 to 3 shillings a day and land cost from £1 to £5 per acre, though land prices and labor values fluctuated over time and place. For unimproved land at £1 an acre, a young man would need to work at least ten days per acre, assuming he had room and board. Purchasing land through their own labor was possible enough that sons were not forced to work for and obey fathers in order to obtain property. But idle speculation is unnecessary when solid information is available.

By looking at a series of tax lists, along with deeds and wills, we can ascertain not only when a young man became an independent worker but also how well young men did in Dedham with and without their father's gifts. We can see what the land that fathers contributed, or held back, actually meant. This analysis shows clearly that fathers usually gave land to autonomous sons, not to dependent, landless ones. Their gifts were meaningful and often helpful, but their sons did not absolutely need them. They needed the town more. The neoliberal picture of relations between Massachusetts fathers and sons is a grave distortion.

Among ninety-four men born in Dedham between 1677 and 1724, thirty-one (33 percent) had lost their fathers before they reached the age of twenty-six and inherited land at relatively young ages; I call these the orphans. Another twenty-nine (31 percent) got land by deed on or before the age of thirty; I call these the gifted. Another twenty-two (23 percent) got land past the age of thirty either by deed or by will from their fathers; I call these "the dependent," since they seem to fit the story told by Greven and others. Finally, twelve men left their father's household and got land entirely on their own. This analysis shows that sons gained autonomy thanks chiefly to their own labor and the town's political economy. Labor, more than inheritance, determined their lifelong success. Parental gifts helped, of course, as they do today. The similarity in the levels of wealth at middle age attained by men who were orphans, recipients of deeds, or so-called dependents is equally remarkable.

The Orphans

Thirty-one sons inherited land or money while they were in their twenties because their fathers had died. Many had guardians during their childhood. Study of these Dedham orphans shows how important labor was; land ownership meant less than expected. Many orphans had land when they arrived at adulthood, but simply having land in a town of sharp dealers and high labor costs was not a guaranteed ticket to prosperity. The stories of unsuccessful orphans were probably used by the elders to tell the youth of their town about the importance of diligence and the folly of indulgence.

Thomas Aldridge (1685–1759) was an orphan who got property early but whose economic performance was so lackluster that his sister effectively challenged his right to control the family land. Thomas's parents, Thomas and Hannah Aldridge, had four children, but only Thomas and his sister

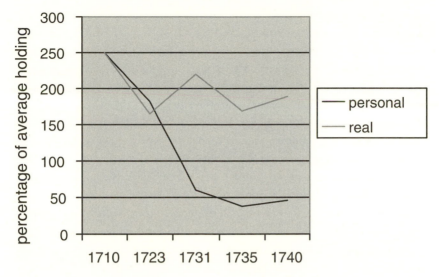

Figure 10. Thomas Aldridge's Progress: real and personal estate holdings, 1710–1740.
Source: *Dedham Records*, vols. 6, 7.

Mary survived childhood. Their father Thomas died October 23, 1694, leaving Thomas and Mary orphans at the ages of nine and eleven. As the eldest son, Thomas got the real property when he turned twenty-one. He appeared on the Dedham tax lists in 1710 with two and a half times the average amounts of both personal and real property. At just twenty-five years of age, he was one of the wealthiest men in town.

Yet, as Figure 10 shows, the neophyte soon spiraled downward. Thomas Aldridge managed his affairs poorly. He did not sell his real estate, but had a difficult time maintaining its productivity. His personal wealth dropped steadily to only 40 percent of the average holding by the time he was fifty-five. The downward trend was alarming.[19]

Thomas Aldridge appeared to be healthy and free of major vices. Yet, there was something wrong. Despite his early wealth, he never married nor held a single town office. There is no indication that he was simply a lazy dunce. In 1709, 1710, and 1721, the town paid him for helping with the building of the cart bridge from the mainland to Great Island in the Charles River. The town never complained about his idleness. He seemed good natured. Nonetheless, his widowed sister who lived in Roxbury grew disgusted with her privileged brother's baffling and unsuccessful management of the family wealth. The Dedham town meeting noted on March 26, 1733, "upon

complaint of Widow Mary Lion of Roxbury that her brother Thomas Aldridge of Dedham is non compos and by foolish bargains and other negligence embezzles his estate, ye selectmen desire John Metcalfe to acquaint the
honorable judge of probate for the county of Suffolk with it in order to
redress." Thomas Aldridge was then forty-seven years old, near the bottom
of a prolonged and steep economic decline, and his sister, who had children
of her own to provide for, was not amused. A few months later, on May 15,
1733, the selectmen reported that "also having received a warrant from ye
honorable judge of probate for the county of Suffolk to inspect and inquire
into the circumstances of ye above named Thomas Aldridge, ye selectmen
desire Michael Metcalfe and Ephraim Wilson to attend yt affair and make
report thereof as soon as may be." They judged him incompetent. Neither
the probate court records nor the county court records indicate a formal judgment of incapacity and a formal takeover of Aldridge's affairs. Most likely he
was cooperative and some informal arrangement was made for counseling and
financial planning. At least Aldridge's decline slowed. When he died in 1759,
he left an estate worth £831 for his sister and other relations to share.[20]

Historians insist that the inheritance of land was the key to wealth in the
colonial economy. Thomas Aldridge's financial failure shows that in conditions in which the labor market was controlled to make labor expensive and
many young men and women, not to mention the crafty old, were on the
make, a young man who had wealth handed to him could easily squander it
among these Yankee traders, workers, and crooks. Land should have gotten
him a wife, but it did not. When his sister asked the town to intervene to
stop his decline, they partly succeeded.

Sadder was the case of Gill Belcher (1711–1752), the son of Reverend
Joseph Belcher, who died in 1723. Some said that the behavior of Gill and his
other brothers hastened their father's death. Gill was beyond redemption, at
least economically. Gill inherited considerable property in Dorchester and
Dedham at the age of twelve. His guardian was Oxbridge Thatcher of Boston. As a child Gill at least owned a fifth part of a paper mill in Milton and
a fifth of one hundred acres in the same town. Upon adulthood, Gill quickly
squandered his early inheritance, probably because he had a drinking problem and lacked self-control. In 1738, at the age of twenty-seven, he got Mary
Finney of Swansey pregnant and married her. He soon sought an annulment
on the grounds that he was too drunk on his wedding day to know what he
was doing, creating a large file of court papers devoted to the question how
much Gill Belcher drank on his wedding day and how little he knew about

what he was doing. The court records contain no verdict. He might have gotten the marriage annulled by making a financial settlement with his bride's family, the Finneys. Deeds show him selling property rapidly, and no marriage record exists for him and Finney in Swansey or Dedham. He soon returned to Dedham penniless and alone. He appeared as a laborer on the tax list in 1740 at the age of twenty-nine, paying a poll but having no personal or real estate (as he did again in 1744). In a deed in 1732, he was described as Gill Belcher of Dedham, laborer. He might have been battling an addiction to alcohol. By 1750, he was living in Dedham at the house of Timothy Baker at town expense. The town declared in 1751 that he had to "provide for himself in the future." However, in 1752, the Dedham Meeting noted "that Gill Belcher is dangerously sick of a fever, and that he has no means of his own whereby to provide for his subsistence." Work and rum did not agree with him. The selectmen asked Benjamin Fairbanks "to see to it that he is nursed and provided for." Gill Belcher died at the age of forty-one, a rich orphan gone very sour in a workers' town.[21]

Early inheritance need not be a curse. Many orphans learned to work well, despite their early accession to property. Samuel Chickering (1690–1778) was one of the younger sons of Nathaniel Chickering, who died in 1699 with a small estate in Dedham. Trained as a cordwainer (shoemaker), Samuel made steady progress on his own with his small inheritance. He appeared first on the tax lists in 1710 at age twenty paying a poll but having no real estate or personal estate. He first paid real estate taxes in 1716 at the age of twenty-six. The source of his small real estate holding is unclear; perhaps it was part of an estate settlement, but perhaps the young man had purchased land. Samuel married around 1720 at the age of thirty. By thirty-seven, he reached the average level of wealth in the town. His rise was slow and steady, more a matter of work than of windfall inheritance. The dip in the real estate in 1723 was due to an exchange he made of thirty-six acres for land and money from Amos Fisher.[22] By the time he reached the age of forty-eight, Chickering held more than the average real and personal estate and, unlike the better-endowed Belcher, he was married and esteemed (Figure 11).

Chickering often served the town as a sealer of leather. As a shoemaker, he knew leather. In 1731, at the age of forty-one, he was elected constable.[23] An orphan, Samuel was not dependent on his father for his success, though his portion helped him some. He was dependent chiefly on the institutions of the town of Dedham that assured him an education, the ability to work, and good wages for his skilled labor by controlling the influx of shoemakers.

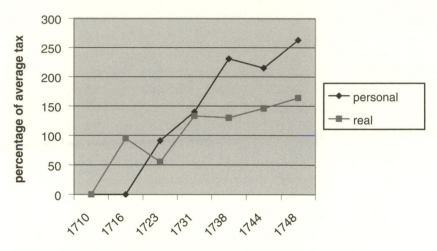

Figure 11. Samuel Chickering's Progress: real and personal estate holdings, 1710–1748. Source: *Dedham Records*, vols. 6, 7.

Although most orphans in the sample stayed in Dedham, a few left. Faxon Dean (1718–1807) was an adventurous lad who decided to depart at a relatively early age with some money. This strategy failed to work well in the long run, at least financially. Faxon lost his mother when he was only a year old, and his father Joseph Dean, clothier, died when Faxon was two. Joseph Dean left an estate of £405, including land and a house in Dedham and ten acres in Dorchester. In 1731, the court decided that it would be best to give the eldest son, Thomas Dean, all the real estate and to give £45 to each of the other five children, including Faxon. Thomas Dean, the eldest son, became Faxon's guardian. In 1740, after he turned twenty-one, Faxon appeared on the tax list as a poll payer but without personal or real estate. He was due £45 and 6 percent interest on it annually from 1732, a total of about £67. He apparently spent it elsewhere, disappearing from Dedham until 1806, when he suddenly was heard from again. Faxon was then sixty-six years of age. In 1806, Dedham got word from Sheffield in western Massachusetts that "Faxon Dean come into . . . town in the month of June last and soon after was taken lame and became chargeable . . . and continues to be so." He claimed legal settlement in Dedham. The town clerk wanted no part of lame old Faxon, so he searched property records in order to establish Faxon's residency in some other town. The clerk noted:

I could not find all the deeds of Mr. Dean's lands . . . I found one
deed from Samuel Lawrence of Brimfield . . . to Faxon Dean . . .
one acre of land lying in Brimfield, dated 8/21/1761. . . . I found on
record at Springfield a deed from Elisha Cleveland to Faxon Dean
of one third part of the mill yard, stream, and dam, lying in West-
field on the Great River at a place called the half mile falls . . . dated
March 10, 1783, which, it is supposed, will give him a settlement in
that town. . . . I found on the Court Records at Northampton that
Dean was warned to depart the town of Hadley on the 26 February
1765, but could not find any records of his being warned to depart
the town of Brimfield, which being the fact undoubtedly gives him
settlement in that town.

Faxon Dean had clearly invested some of his patrimony in 1761 in lands and
mills in western Massachusetts. He apparently had no supportive children.
He came to a sad end, limping back in late middle age to a hostile hometown.
No wonder many young men stayed in their own towns and cultivated family
land.[24]

Other orphaned members of the Dean family, despite hard work and a
handsome inheritance, failed to attain economic heights because of their family responsibilities. The orphan's fate was not always as shiny as it looked
financially. Thomas Dean (1709–1745) was the eldest son of Joseph Dean,
clothier, who died in 1721 when Thomas was twelve years old. His mother
died in 1720 and stepmother in 1722. In 1731, when Thomas was twenty-two,
the selectmen (John Metcalfe, Richard Everett, and William Avery) decided
it was a mistake to divide the land of Joseph Dean among all his children, so
the court gave "the housing and homestead together being about ten acres of
land" and an additional "wood lot containing ten acres" all worth some £320
to Thomas Dean. The inheritance seemed a bonanza for the young man.
However, the court required that Thomas Dean pay "£45–14s-3p apiece before 29 October 1732" to each of his five siblings. If Thomas did not have
enough money for the other heirs, he had to pay interest at six percent a year
to each of his younger siblings on the unpaid amount, a burden that totaled
at least £225. His siblings included Mary Smith, Joseph Dean, Sarah Dean,
Elizabeth Dean, and our Faxon Dean. Thomas Dean married Grace Wads-
worth and they had several children, adding to his responsibilities. Thomas,
like his father, was a clothier. In 1737, he took in Joseph Corey, probably as

an apprentice. There is no indication that Thomas was a poor worker, but he was apparently overburdened and never reached even average wealth. His personal estate, including his house and livestock, never kept pace with his ample real estate holdings. (It is possible that he held his wealth mostly in cloth, so the personal estate understates his real wealth.) When he died prematurely in 1746 at the age of thirty-seven, he had £69 worth of clothier's tools but only one cow and two hogs. His land and buildings were still a major asset. His widow was awarded £60 (old tenor) for herself and the children. It was not always easy to be the eldest son; inheritance and early landownership could backfire when burdened with responsibility for younger siblings.[25]

The Gifted

Roughly an equal number of Dedham sons got deeds from their fathers before reaching the age of thirty. In this group, 78 percent got the land as a gift, and only 15 percent clearly had to pay for it. The deeds reflected the reality that sons and their new brides were favored workers in the eyes of their fathers and the town.

In March 1707, Nathaniel Richards gave his son James Richards a small farm in Dedham: "Know ye, that the said Nathaniel Richards for and in consideration of my son James Richards of Dedham aforesaid husbandman his living with me well nigh these twenty-four years last past in which time he has not only carried himself dutifully but also hath been very helpful to me in carrying on my husbandry affairs and for and in consideration of the natural love, good will, and affection which I have and bear unto him."[26] Nathaniel generously started counting his son's years of dutiful service when James was born, not when he became old enough to work on the family farm. James was exactly twenty-four years old when he got the land and had probably worked on the farm for eight years. His father gave him the land, retaining only the option of using one-third of the meadow during his natural life. James married Hannah that same year. Nathaniel's gift, or repayment for his son's services, was probably connected to his marriage. The size of the gift was typical: a twenty- to thirty-acre farm without a house, a starter kit for family life. Dedham fathers differed from wealthy Delaware Valley Quaker farmers who also gave their sons land at early ages; Quakers gave their sons a house and much more land, often two hundred acres. These sons immediately became proprietors who had unfettered access to slaves and indentured servants, without having to worry about a nosy and controlling town meeting. The Quaker prophet John Woolman later claimed that these men should have worked harder themselves.[27]

In Dedham, men lacked easy access to outside labor. The town privileged local labor instead. Young married men continued to work for others and earn wages while their families grew. They worked on their own farms only seasonally. The tax sample starts in 1710, when James Richards was twenty-seven. His father's early gift got him off to a good, though modest start. The deed paved the way for a strong relationship between generations. Recently married and the father of a toddler and an infant, James had only about half the average holding in land, but as he and his family matured his land holdings grew. In 1710, he had less than 50 percent of the average land holdings but over 100 percent of the average personal holdings. By 1735, at the age of forty-seven, he had achieved almost 150 percent of the average real estate holdings and more than that in personal estate. He gained more from his own labor in the context of the town economy than he got from his father.[28]

Timothy Draper, born in 1711, was somewhat an exception to the rule of gradual enrichment by labor. In 1734, Daniel Draper deeded half his farm to Timothy, who was just twenty-three. The generous deed was granted, the father said, from "love," and it stated that land was given "without any manner of condition, reckoning, accompt, payment of any sum or sums of money or answer therefore to me or any in my name to be rendered given or done in time to come."[29] The father wanted to announce that he was relinquishing all control over the property. Timothy Draper started and remained consistently wealthier than the average Dedham inhabitant. He married at twenty-one and three years later, thanks to his father, he had more than the average real and personal estate. He never dramatically increased his holdings, but maintained himself among the town's average farmers. By 1748, he had achieved the average personal estate and some 150 percent of the average real estate holding.[30]

Some early gifts were part of intergenerational partnerships. John Fuller deeded his son Hezekiah sixty acres of land in 1709, when Hezekiah was just twenty-two years old. Hezekiah continued to work with his father, who in his will in 1719 called him a "loving" son, made him the sole executor among the four sons, and gave him the largest part of the estate. Hezekiah's voluntary immersion in his father's household may have caused the Dedham constables not to tax Hezekiah as an individual until 1723, at the age of thirty-five. Yet Hezekiah was a well-to-do property owner before that date. This loyal son took in many tenants during his lifetime and served as constable, fence viewer, and surveyor. He seemed to be on good terms with the selectmen, for he usually got his tenants accepted. His financial acumen was respected, for he was on the committee to inspect the treasurer's accounts and the committee that ran the line from Dedham to Needham.[31] Despite his wealth and town responsibilities, he never became a selectman. The fluctuations in his personal estate might be tied to his luck with tenants on his ample lands. By 1731, he obtained twice the average real estate holding and his personal estate holdings reached as high as four times the average. The Fullers trusted each other, and it is hard to see this as a relationship between a dominant and a submissive family member.

Isaac Bullard (1709–1770) also had a close business relationship with his father William Bullard, with whom he lived until William died in 1747. Yet, there was nothing arbitrary or sentimental about their finances. Both men were shoemakers, and they expected production. In 1731, when Isaac was just twenty-two, his father made an eccentric deed in which he sold his house and large farm near the meeting house to his son for £2,000 current money. Isaac did not complete the deal until 1742, at the age of thirty-three, when he paid his father and cleared the title. Father and son continued to live together. In 1742, father William suddenly had a lot of money and no land, while Isaac had little money left and lots of land and shops. Isaac did not marry until 1747, at the age of thirty-eight. He may have been tyrannized by his father, for whom he worked for eleven years. Yet, if Isaac could have amassed £2,000 in eleven years by cobbling shoes, he obviously could have made a life without his father. He could have bought his own land, but he chose to work for his father's benefit and the promise of land. His father also had a free choice. They did well together financially. The Bullards had consistently twice the average personal estate and twice the real estate. From their strange relationship rose a prominent Dedham shoemaking family. Nobody in town regarded Isaac as a wimp. He first served the town consistently as sealer of leather. He became an ensign in the militia (his father was a lieutenant) and served on the committee to procure ammunition for the town. In October 8, 1765, Ensign Isaac Bullard was named to the committee from Dedham to prepare a draft of instructions for the town representative to the General Court protesting the Stamp Act. These are not the public acts of a weakling under his father's thumb.[32]

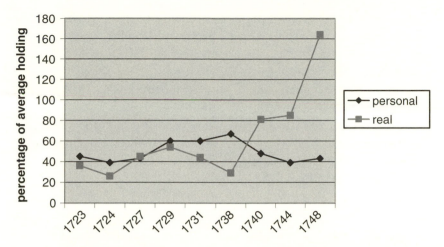

Figure 12. William Ellis's Progress: real and personal estate holdings, 1723–1748. Source: *Dedham Town Records*, vols. 6, 7.

The "Dependents"

Another twenty-two sons got land from their fathers by will or deed after these men had passed the age of thirty. Many of these cases seem to be Dedham versions of Greven's classic stories about dependent sons and controlling fathers who governed a patriarchal family by tightfistedness. For example, William Ellis, born in Dedham in 1694, was thirty-eight years old before he received twenty-four acres in Dedham by will from his father; the plot included ten acres "on which his dwelling house stands."[33] William Ellis had married Elizabeth Barnard at the age of thirty-two. He and his wife lived on his father's land for the next six years, and it took his father's death to end this patriarchal extended family. Here was an apparently clear case of a middle-aged son dependent on a stern patriarch, living in what Greven called a modified, extended family. The households were separate, but the father held the land and the purse strings.

The whole story is quite different. While living on his father's land, William Ellis had ample property that he had earned himself. In the sample of tax lists, William appears for the first time in 1723 at the age of twenty-nine. He owned about 50 percent of the average individual holding in both real and personal estate. He was not rich, but he was an independent landholder in his own right (Figure 12).

Ellis later accepted the land his father gave by will in 1732, but—contrary to the conventional story—it did little to make him. His real wealth came later, not through the inheritance from his father but rather through his own skill in town politics. In 1744, Ellis got £55 from the town for allowing a large road to run through his property. The road ruined his farm operation, yet Ellis used the compensatory sum to buy not more land, but rum. At least he got fined the next year for selling drink to the strangers who were traveling along this new road to Boston. He acknowledged his miscarriage and paid his fine to the poor, and that very year secured approval from the county court, with the support of the selectman, to be a tavern and innkeeper. He flourished, eventually becoming one of the largest landowners in Dedham. His lack of livestock was reflected in relatively low personal estate assessments, but tavern owners did not need large herds of sheep. In the 1750s, he frequently entertained the selectmen. In 1765, at the age of seventy-one, he became weary of tavern keeping and told the court he wanted to turn the business over to his son William Ellis, Jr., "a person of sober conversation." His political magic failed him for once; the court turned him down.[34]

William Ellis was more dependent on the town's labor arrangements, his own work and shrewdness, and his participation in town politics than he ever was on his father. The story Philip Greven told about dependent sons and tyrannical patriarchs fits the limited evidence Greven examined. However, when all the relevant evidence, including the tax lists, is taken into account, the story changes dramatically. The accumulation of property depended more on the political economy of the town than on relationships within families.

Virtually every apparent dependency story undergoes the same transformation once the tax lists are examined carefully. In 1749, John Draper, Sr., died and left a will that gave his son John Draper, Jr., "that land where he is now settled and built his house." He also got a proportion of his father's household movables and a share of the Cedar swamp holdings in Walpole.[35] John Draper, Jr., was then fifty-seven years old. He had never received a gift of land from his father before. In 1724, at the age of thirty-two, he married Mariah Hall. They apparently lived and developed their own household on his father's land for the next twenty-five years. This arrangement, Greven has argued, typified the powerful fathers and meek sons of Puritan Massachusetts. Fathers retained ownership of the land even after their sons had married, and thereby maintained control over their sons until death ended their dominion. But the Dedham tax lists show that John Draper, Jr., held plenty land of his own earlier and was not economically dependent on his father. He began paying taxes on his labor in 1714 at the age of twenty-two. He first had real estate and personal estate of his own at the age of thirty-two. By the age of thirty-seven, he owned about the average amount of personal estate and about 60 percent of the average real estate, all without any gift from his father. It did take him a long time to earn his way into independence. By protecting the value of his labor from outsiders, his town institutions—not his father—made his progress possible. John Draper's decision to build and live on his father's land may have saved him rent and been a sign of loyalty and love, but it was not a sign of abject economic dependence. At any time, John Draper, Jr., could have left his father. He did well on his own. His father's gift was not essential to his autonomy.[36]

The Metcalfes had an extended family. Nathaniel Metcalfe's father, Deacon Jonathan Metcalfe, wrote his will in 1724 and died three years later at the age of seventy-seven. Nathaniel was then thirty-eight years old. He had married Mary Gay in 1713 at the age of twenty-four, and they lived with his father, who owned all the land. In the will, Jonathan wrote, "and further my son Nathaniel having lived with me and been helpful to me and done for me in work and in repairing buildings and fences and the like, in consideration thereof and what he may further do for me, I do in particular give and bequeath to him and his heirs forever, my dwelling house and barn and my lot containing twelve acres." He also gave Nathaniel two-thirds of the estate. Jonathan Metcalfe had three other sons (Jonathan, Ebenezer, and John), to whom the deacon had already given land. In the will, which took these earlier property transfers into account, he left them between £35 and £40 apiece. The deacon also had daughters, Hannah and Mary, long married; they got money, as did grandchildren from a deceased son, Joseph Metcalfe.[37]

The Metcalfe story appears to be about a son's dependency on his father: the young man and his wife lived on his father's land and in his very house until they were well into their late thirties and worked for the father in order to get land that the old man stingily withheld in order to control them and to protect him in his old age from destitution and loneliness. Here, apparently, is the extended family that Greven posited, without even the separate households that modified dependence and authority. Once again, analysis of the tax lists shifts the story line dramatically. Although Jonathan Metcalfe may have dominated his youngest son emotionally, he did not do so economically. Their material relationship was more symbiotic. At the age of twenty-five, Nathaniel was economically autonomous thanks to his skill and vigor as a shoemaker and leather worker. The value of his work was protected by the policies and political structure of his town, which prevented the free entrance

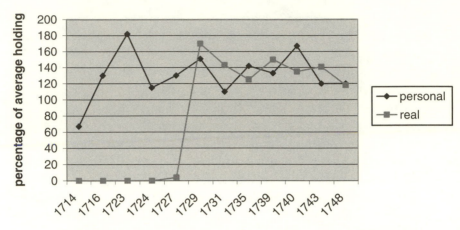

Figure 13. Nathaniel Metcalfe's Progress: real and personal estate holdings, 1714–1748. Source: *Dedham Town Records*, vols. 6, 7.

of shoemakers and tanners into Dedham. Nathaniel had already amassed 67 percent of the average holding in personal wealth by the age of twenty-five, and by twenty-seven he had more personal wealth than the average Dedham taxpayer. By the age of thirty-four, Metcalfe had almost twice the average personal estate as the average taxpayer (his wife's contribution deserves study). Today this would be considered doing very well indeed. He had enough money to buy land in Dedham, and he could have become a large land owner in a newer town. He could have lived and worked elsewhere, as his brothers had done. Yet he chose to remain landless, to live with his parents and wait for his inheritance (Figure 13).

Perhaps he was motivated by the duty often incumbent on youngest sons to support their parents in old age in return for the family farmstead after their fathers' death. But Nathaniel had economic freedom and power. When Deacon Jonathan died, Nathaniel immediately became a landowner with more real estate than average. Earlier the town's institutions helped Nathaniel to amass goods by working independently from his father. While fulfilling his filial duties, he had ample time to earn money by practicing his trade. Deacon Jonathan's ownership of land may have compensated psychologically for his flagging prowess and energy at the age of seventy-seven. Nathaniel voluntarily devoted his labor power to his father, perhaps as an act of love. He could have simply left the old man to his decline without much economic penalty.

The inequality of his bequests to his children worried the old deacon. He left much more to Nathaniel than to the other sons. In his will, he explained Nathaniel's unique contribution to his welfare as a justification for the unequal division. He spoke of Christian love: "and now to all my children I do in the name of God, and with the compassion and authority of a father exhort and charge you that you be contented and satisfied, and with this my disposal and carry it on towards another with the affections and correspondence of Christians and brothers and sisters and live in love and peace, and the God of love and peace shall be with you." Tellingly, Jonathan Metcalfe placed a father's compassion before his authority. He also placed faith and grace above possessions: "I recommend you all to God and the Word of his grace which is able to build you up and to give you inheritance among them that are sanctified. Amen."[38] Thanks to the town privileging of labor, his words were plausible to his children, though modern historians have not attended to such testaments. Nathaniel served not only his father but also the town, being elected surveyor, leather sealer, hog reeve, fence viewer, tithing man, and constable. The town voters hardly saw him as a meek dependent. Both father and town had cared for him and valued his labor, and he returned the favor.[39]

Some seeming patriarchs did not wait until they died to leave their sons land, but gave their sons deeds when they were relatively old, suggesting their desire to control their sons by withholding land as long as possible. Josiah Richards, born in 1713, married Hannah Whiting in 1737. Josiah's father, Edward Richards, waited nine years, until 1746, to deed Josiah thirty acres at Strawberry Hill in Dedham "in consideration of love, good will, and affection." The tax lists and deed books show that Josiah had not been waiting in poverty and powerlessness for his father's gift. A year after his marriage, at the age of twenty-five, Josiah bought thirteen acres from the Dedham innkeeper Benjamin Gay for £130 (old tenor). His father's later gift, while doubtlessly welcome and meaningful, was not essential to his well-being or standing in town. In 1749, Josiah bought an additional thirty acres from Benjamin Gay for £800 (old tenor). Analysis of the tax lists shows that Josiah Richards was a good earner who in his mid-twenties approached the average holding of personal estate in Dedham and could afford to buy land for himself.[40] Josiah served the town as field driver and surveyor of highways.[41] He died in 1771 at eighty-nine. When his father Edward gave him land in 1746, Josiah was already autonomous.

Consider a final case. In 1706, twenty-four-year-old Samuel Fuller married Sarah Fisher, both from Dedham. The groom's father, Jonathan Fuller, waited until 1717 to deed a 34-acre lot and several other parcels to Samuel, who was then thirty-five years of age.[42] By that time Samuel and Sarah Fuller had many children. This case appears to be an authentic instance of a powerful and stingy patriarch creating an extended family to protect him in his old age, whatever his powerless and cringing son might desire. When only wills and deeds are read, it appears that Samuel and his wife lived for eleven years under the thumb of his father, who only reluctantly gave them any land. However, tax lists and assessments show that Samuel and Sarah had ample personal and real estate in Dedham by 1710, when Samuel was thirty. Indeed, Samuel Fuller had then more personal and real estate than the average taxpayer. His father's gift in 1717 only made him richer. In Dedham, thanks to the town's political economy, young men and women could earn enough through their own labor in order to accumulate property before inheriting it.[43]

Excluding Strangers

A local economy offering good wages and constant employment allowed sons to grow into autonomy. This pattern of intergenerational relations was no accident, but a political achievement. New England towns kept unwanted people out of their labor markets. Towns were walled only figuratively, and even then the barriers to entry were not impermeable. Nonetheless, they excluded strangers who would have depreciated the value of town-born workers' labor. According to the Dedham town records, people reported taking into their homes 573 individuals, couples, and families between 1690 and 1795; the law required that they report these people to the selectmen or get fined.[44] A significant proportion of the newcomers (52 percent) was warned out: and only a relatively small proportion of them (39 percent) stayed in Dedham long.[45] These numbers are underestimates, as the selectmen did not bother to warn out people they knew would leave, such as apprentices with homes in other towns. Men often reported the settling of a fiancée, and she was seldom warned out; as soon as she married a town-born man, she became a legal inhabitant. Dedham grew more hospitable, or more attractive to outsiders, over the years, for increasing numbers of newcomers arrived and the town allowed a higher proportion to remain. Nonetheless, the town accepted only about half of the reported strangers.

It is difficult to find a clear pattern in the Dedham selectmen's decisions. The selectmen helped well-heeled town residents with good connections to selectmen (and some selectmen themselves) to retain tenants for their lands. For example, between 1736 and 1756, Hezekiah Fuller reported taking five families as tenants. The selectmen warned out only one of these families; two remained in the town. The town also accepted many poor visitors, as the law suggested they do. The colony of Massachusetts did not want to develop a large population of itinerant people, so they wrote the settlement law intentionally to create tension and suspicion between newcomers and established townspeople.[46]

The town showed charity when in 1771, "Daniel Fisher Jr. informed . . . that he received into his family a lad named Richard Ward, November 8; he came from on board a man of war, was stolen from his friends in London, and is very ragged." Perhaps excited by the concurrent debate with the English ministry, the town never warned out Richard Ward, or even demanded security from Fisher. Not every charity case was handled so gracefully. On July 5, 1701, "upon information that a lame girl is come lately into our town whose name is Wadkins, entertained at the house of Edward Cooke," the Dedham selectmen gave "notice to said lame girl that she do depart forthwith out of this town of Dedham and also . . . notice to said Edward Cooke that he is disallowed to entertain her in our said town." A few newcomers successfully challenged the town's edict. Miriam Dean came to town in 1766 and got word from the selectmen "to depart this town in fourteen days." She ignored it. About a month later Benjamin Herring, a Dedham native, announced his intention to marry Miriam, and they were wed in May 1767. Miriam stayed in Dedham and mothered a large family. The selectmen rejected other visitors. On July 11, 1726, "the selectmen desired Capt. Avery to warn Elizabeth Waits to depart out of this town for they do not allow her to continue here as an inhabitant." She ignored them, but the next month, on August 10, 1726, "the selectmen desired Captain Avery to go to a justice and endeavor to get a warrant . . . for the conveying Elizabeth Wait out of this town, she neglecting to depart according as she hath been warned." The selectmen called Wait's bluff; she is never mentioned again in any town records. Anyone who remained after being warned out could, by law, be treated as a vagrant.[47]

New Englanders were woefully xenophobic, but they deserve a share of dignity in the historical record. People submitted their applications and took their chances in Dedham, and some one in two got it. Dedham-born folk had the value of their labor protected, and family members could relate to one another as adults from positions of personal autonomy and economic strength, given their power in the local labor market. This situation added some grace and equality to family relations. Family disputes that could not be resolved informally, by their intervention of relatives and neighbors, were few. Only three Dedham families erupted into fights over property in over a century, and each case was relatively minor.[48] Robert Frost's neighbor suggested that "Good fences make good neighbors."[49] In New England, good walls around town labor markets improved family relations. Valuing work made families less tense and conflictual than many historians have dared to imagine, though the beating and traumatizing of children in the local school must have taken its toll.

Epilogue

IN 1727, THE selectmen of Middleborough, Massachusetts, petitioned the General Court for an abatement of their provincial taxes on the ground "that their husbandry has been neglected and the people greatly impoverished" because of "a very grievous sickness by which great numbers among them have been carried off, and most of the survivors visited therewith." The town received a £40 abatement. Other towns sent similar petitions. In 1693, Deerfield asked for an abatement because of "their distressed and hazardous condition being the most utmost frontier town in the county of west Hampshire and much impoverished by keeping and maintaining of garrison men." After being attacked by French and Indians in the so-called Deerfield Massacre in 1704, the selectmen came back, asking for an abatement of half their assessment of £68, pleading "that at least one half of the inhabitants that should have paid it were killed and taken captive and their estates destroyed and burnt up." The General Court gave the devastated town an abatement of only £17, not the £34 they requested.[1]

What is surprising here is not that Massachusetts people and their towns groaned under the twin burdens of death and taxes but that the General Court took as their units of apportionment, assessment, and collection not individuals or even households, as the Internal Revenue Service does today, but rather towns. Massachusetts legislators understood that the household was not a meaningful economic entity in isolation from the local labor force and the town economy. The legislators understood that a pig, an acre, or a horse did not mean the same thing in a remote hamlet like Deerfield as it did in Boston; they evaluated all property, and sometimes labor, in town context. In 1726, for example, when the General Court decided it needed to raise £20,000, it divided the amount into 117 town assessments based on each town's evaluated wealth. Boston had to pay £3,368 16s 8d, and Dedham only £145 15s 0d. At the town level, all men sixteen years or older who were inhabitants (or their masters or mistresses) were assessed 100 pence, or a little more than eight shillings. These polls composed about 30 percent of a town's assessment. The rest was assessed on town residents according to their property holdings and other assets. The larger the town assessment per person, the more each property holder had to pay.[2]

This scheme heightened individuals' sense of their intimate connection with their town's labor system, economy, and politics, while helping make the Massachusetts "town state" into a powerful revenue generator. The General Court decided on assessments, reevaluations, and apportionments almost annually, forcing distant towns to stay alert to provincial politics. Towns and their inhabitants needed to send able representatives to the legislature, despite the expense. Otherwise, the General Court not only fined neglectful towns financially but almost willy-nilly imposed unfair tax burdens on them. Aggrieved towns frequently petitioned the General Court. In 1736, having neglected to send a representative the year before, a committee of the town of Abington complained "of the largeness of their province tax and that it has been lately raised above their proportion in former years, and much above their ability." In 1748, Mr. Thomas Pratt, representative of Chelsea, complained "in behalf of the said town that in the last general valuation their estate was set considerably too high (as they apprehend) by reason of their not having any person to represent them in the General Court and they have been accordingly overtaxed ever since." The overwhelming majority of towns sent representatives to the provincial legislature.[3]

Towns studied their local economies carefully, not only by having frequently to assess all their wealth but also to defend the economic realities they faced against the envy and overestimation of others. Boston citizens often complained to the General Court that the city was overtaxed. The Boston town meeting submitted major petitions in 1736, 1745, and 1753. Some historians misread these detailed and sophisticated arguments as descriptions of the woeful decline of Boston.[4] In truth, the petitioners argued chiefly that Boston declined proportionately to the other towns, which they saw as prospering newcomers. "We need only name the Countys of Essex, Middlesex and Worcester to shew the increase of inhabitants and husbandry," noted the Boston Town Meeting petition of 1753, "and the towns of Plymouth, Salem, Marblehead, Newbury, Gloucester, Nantucket, York, and Falmouth in Casco Bay, to evidence the great and flourishing foreign trade carried on, which formerly wholly cordered in Boston, but is now gone from it, to these several growing and flourishing towns; if a fifth or a sixth part of the tax was Boston's proportion formerly, a tenth or a twelfth part is much more than their proportion now." The petitioners argued that Boston's suffering was due primarily to provincial politics itself: the unfairly high tax burden on the town was persuading as many as a thousand solid property holders and high ratepayers to flee and become inhabitants of surrounding towns. "It must be a strong temptation to be able to sleep quietly a few miles out of Boston, and escape paying five hundred or a thousand pounds a year." Such cogent arguments brought some tax relief to the town.[5]

The political process of taxing in Massachusetts was complicated. Towns and their representatives constantly fought over rates, assessments, and valuations, while maintaining an emphasis on consensus on the town and provincial levels. Without developing a sizeable and expensive bureaucracy, the town state of Massachusetts allowed the province to collect at least £1,196,478 old tenor between 1692 and 1756. These revenues permitted the province to launch several amphibious assaults on Port Royal and Louisburg, and to invent and maintain its own currency. The costs of local government might have been even higher: they included paying ministers, building and maintaining roads, building schools and paying schoolmasters, and supporting the poor. In the late 1740s, Boston paid some £13,000 annually in province taxes, and some £15,000 annually in poor rates and town taxes. Outlying towns might have had proportionately lower poor rates, but more landowners.[6] The fiscal muscle of the Massachusetts town state, thanks to its concentration on town economies rather than household economies, was powerful, indeed.

The strength and success of the town state well into the eighteenth century raises the question of how and when Massachusetts's political economy was transformed into a capitalist order with a free market in labor. The studies presented in this book reveal no radical change in the political economy through the Revolution. The colonists were well aware and appreciative of markets and actively promoted economic growth, but also determined to control the economy to create a just social and equitable order pleasing to a potentially destructive God. With the exception of the Dominion of New England, which they overthrew, they remained politically active Christian humanists.[7] They used the town government to provide an arena in which economic growth and the dignity of labor might flourish together. They used violence to turn their own children into productive workers who often did the work that other early American societies assigned to a permanent and distinct caste of enslaved Africans. They nourished a religion that encouraged parents to awaken their children with hard work and what we would now call traumatic experiences. They hired teachers to ferule their children daily before the eyes of other children. They used their democratic town governments, whatever the inconvenience to entrepreneurs, to control local labor markets to guarantee the privileges of the town born and those whom the town adopted by general consent.

The forces of change were mitigated, though not entirely absent. Even today, many of Massachusetts's peculiarities remain. As of 2007, some towns still retain the town meeting system and others hold large, representative town meetings, now with full participation by women. The state is commonly regarded as having a relatively intrusive government dedicated to economic equality, dubbed "the People's Republic of Massachusetts." Public subsidies are offered to attract major employers to the state. Universities are powerful engines of technological innovation and economic growth, while the state's public schools lead the nation on many standardized achievement tests. Every member of its Congressional delegation belongs to the Democratic Party, suggesting a continuing belief that the government can encourage economic growth and equity simultaneously. (Vermont has a Socialist senator, though in New Hampshire refugees from "Taxachusetts" elect some Republicans.) At the same time, towns no longer control their boundaries. Massachusetts workers are free to live and work anywhere they can rent or buy a home. Public-school teachers cannot use corporal punishment to control their students. The children of the middle class no longer do the hardest jobs; instead, low-paid physical labor is reserved for immigrants and the underprivileged. The state's professionals inveigh against exposing children to traumatic experiences with the same zealous conviction the colonial Massachusetts ministers denounced indulging children and sheltering them from dangerous work and the presence of death.[8]

Massachusetts's political economy changed significantly after the American Revolution because of a potent combination of external challenges and internal problems. One of the most severe attacks on its political economy, which the province and then state survived without much structural change, came from the British Empire. In the 1760s and early 1770s, imperial officials designated Massachusetts, and especially Boston, as a dangerous center of social leveling and targeted it for destruction. Massachusetts folk lost faith in the Empire as well. As Fred Anderson has shown, Massachusetts soldiers meeting regular English army soldiers in the French and Indian War in the late 1750s were astonished at the illiteracy and lack of self-discipline displayed by working-class English men and appalled at the ways they were flogged and otherwise mistreated by their arrogant upper-class officers. Massachusetts workers realized that what separated them from degrading treatment and degradation was only their town political economies. The men fully supported and often savagely defended their town-born way of life. In 1775, they provided en masse the initial bridgehead and shock troops against the world's greatest empire.[9]

Ironically, it was Massachusetts's subsequent involvement in the formation of the United States that encouraged profound political and economic change. In order to accommodate Southern slave owners, Massachusetts accepted the federal Constitution, including the three-fifths compromise that gave white Southern men almost two votes to their one in presidential elections. After 1800, New Englanders faced a long and seemingly never-ending string of slave-holding southern presidents and administrations. These political realities encouraged the reorganization of the Massachusetts economy. As Dinah Mayo-Bobee has shown, Jefferson and his successors designed a foreign policy based on using the federal government to impose embargo after embargo. These embargos and the War of 1812 ruined the commercial and shipping economy that had bolstered colonial New England. New Englanders decided that Southerners hated the promiscuous freedom of trade. The wealthiest New England merchants decided to transfer their capital from commerce and shipping into manufacturing, especially cotton production, which would be safer from the slavocracy's interference. New England was full of literate and mechanical people. However, reliance on manufacturing demanded a drastic reorganization of the relationship between the owners of property and the sellers of labor. To compete on the national and world market, New England manufacturers had to amass cheaper labor without regard to local politics and town privileges.[10]

To enable such fundamental changes, the political economy of Massachusetts had to be transformed. The Massachusetts legislature made gradual changes in basic legal and political structures. First, they made it more difficult to secure a legal settlement, allowing the town born to feel that newcomers could be removed more easily if necessary. At the same time, the state decided in 1793 that it would reimburse any town for the support of the poor who had no lawful inhabitancy in that or any other town and who had no kin in the state. From then on, towns could and did charge the state for their care of the poor who were not legally settled. In 1811, during Jefferson's embargo, Boston was reimbursed $8,549.74 "for boarding and clothing sundry paupers to 1st June, 1811." More routinely, it was reimbursed $3,601.63 in 1825 "for the support of sundry paupers." Even small towns could care for strangers without cost. In 1811, the state gave Colrain in western Massachusetts $30.95 "for boarding and nursing Sally Lamonier to 25th May, 1811."[11] State support of strangers pulled the teeth from local resistance to strangers and allowed the development of a geographically mobile but socially immobile proletariat whose welfare was not the financial responsibility of the towns through which they passed.

Factory owners, seeking to lower the cost of labor, recruited tens of thousands of Irish workers in the 1840s and 1850s. By 1850, Catholic Irish immigrants composed over a quarter of Boston residents, 82 percent of the city's laborers, and 72 percent of its domestic workers.[12] For the first time, Massachusetts's prosperity relied on an out-group to do its dirtiest, most onerous, and most dangerous work. Instead of misery being centered on middling residents' children who might graduate from their educational ordeal, if they survived, to a more privileged adulthood, work was concentrated among an immigrant population whose progress from miserable poverty into privilege or even a competency was doubtful or nonexistent by design.

The construction of an out-group to do the bulk of the hard work freed middling Massachusetts folk to correct some of their oddities. Fewer native-born white parents and children had to suffer through their sons' and fathers' deaths at sea. No longer preparing their sons for seafaring and their daughters to bear and raise eight or ten children apiece, middling parents stopped hiring men to beat their children so savagely in school. Town meetings deemphasized corporal punishment or altogether denounced it, and gentler mistresses replaced masters in district schools. Looking back from the 1870s to the days before the reign of the domestic ideal and the romanticization of childhood, Edward Jarvis described the daily beatings with ferule and whip that went on in Concord classrooms between 1790 and 1830. Jarvis explained that he spent so much space describing school brutality because "in these days of ameliorated ideas and manner . . . it would hardly be believed that such scenes and events as I have described could have existed in any of our schools except from the evidence of an eye witness." Today, many historians still do not believe it. The movement toward gentle, Quaker-like domestic life for the middle classes was one of the most radical changes stimulated by the alteration of the political economies of the towns.[13]

Even as their state became flooded with immigrants, a new proletariat formed, and wages decreased, New Englanders attempted to retain their hold on economic equity. As Richard Abbot, William Hartford, Bruce Laurie, and Carl Siracusa have shown, between 1820 and 1860 Massachusetts citizens advocated and instituted a wide variety of social reforms, from a renewed public school system to nativist, anti-immigration laws and antislavery in order to restore economic equity, expressions of their continued conviction that economic growth should benefit everyone. Most dramatically, as Bruce Laurie has shown, Massachusetts people provided the impetus for a strong antislavery movement, not only as the holy monomania of William Lloyd Garrison and John Brown, but as part of a complex and far-reaching attempt to maintain or restore the dignity of labor. The Whig Party split as insurgents identified some leaders as "Cotton Whigs," textile factory owners who brought immigrants into the state and who allied with slaveholding Southern planters. Cotton factory owners and cotton producers, reformers argued, gave priority to profits and degraded labor in an unholy alliance; Charles Sumner dubbed them "the Lords of the Loom and the Lords of the Lash." The Cotton Whigs, the argument went, betrayed the commonwealth principles of the state and its Puritan heritage. They hoped that the commonwealth might be saved by initiating real reform: controlling immigration, improving education, limiting the work day, and opening federally controlled lands in the West for free labor instead of slavery. In the 1860s, Massachusetts legions went off to war against the Southern advocates of slavery to save "free labor" with the same violent fervor they had previously used to defend their equitable economic system and the dignity of workers against the British Empire. They lionized their Puritan ancestors and the town, despite its recent legal emasculation.[14]

Today, inequity and inequality are in command in the United States, producing a new Gilded Age of wealth and misery, and it is unlikely that the town will be a rallying point, much less a blueprint, for renewed efforts at reform leading to a democratic commonwealth supporting economic equity. Dividing America into ten square-mile enclaves in which the labor supply can be controlled by resident landowners and workers in public meetings seems implausible, to say the least. Only in allowing urban schools and neighborhoods to traumatize youth with daily gang violence does contemporary society resemble the colonial past, but these youth are not even being prepared for gainful employment. The otherness of New England colonists and their descendants must be respected, not revered. As Nathaniel Hawthorne remarked, "Let us thank God for having given us such ancestors; and let each successive generation thank Him, not less fervently, for being one step further from them in the march of ages."[15]

Nonetheless, this study shows that if equity is to be achieved, or if it unravels fully, the cause will be political, not simply economic. It is a consolation to interrupt the triumphant and smug, if fallacious, neoliberal narrative of American history to begin to understand how and why how Christian humanists by political means provided a harsh but effective way of balancing equity, economic growth, and democracy in the colonies, where labor shortages usually led to the introduction of slavery and other forms of brutal exploitation. America was always a cruel place to live. Yet, by dignifying labor and workers, by empowering Yankee Doodle in the towns, early New Englanders for two hundred years amazed and unsettled the world.

NOTES

INTRODUCTION

1. John Adams, November 25, 1760, *Diary and Autobiography of John Adams*, ed. Lyman H. Butterfield (Cambridge, Mass.: Harvard University Press, 1962), vol. 1: *Diary 1755–1770*, 172–73.

2. Allan Kulikoff, *From British Peasants to Colonial American Farmers* (Chapel Hill: University of North Carolina Press, 2000).

3. David Eltis, *The Rise of African Slavery in the Americas* (Cambridge: Cambridge University Press, 2000); David Brion Davis, *Inhuman Bondage: The Rise and Fall of Slavery in the New World* (Oxford: Oxford University Press, 2006).

4. Jack Marietta and G. S. Rowe, *Troubled Experiment: Crime and Justice in Pennsylvania, 1682–1800* (Philadelphia: University of Pennsylvania Press, 2006); Sharon Salinger, *To Serve Well and Faithfully: Indentured Servants in Pennsylvania 1682–1800* (Cambridge: Cambridge University Press, 1987); Simon P. Newman, *Embodied History: The Lives of the Poor in Early Philadelphia* (Philadelphia: University of Pennsylvania Press, 2003); Billy G. Smith, *The "Lower Sort": Philadelphia's Laboring People, 1750–1800* (Ithaca, N.Y.: Cornell University Press, 1990).

5. John J. McCusker and Russell Menard, *The Economy of British North America, 1607–1789* (Chapel Hill: University of North Carolina Press, 1991), 80–101, 189–229; Timothy H. Breen, *The Marketplace of Revolution: How Consumer Politics Shaped American Independence* (Oxford: Oxford University Press, 2004), 180–95.

6. Edmund S. Morgan, *American Slavery, American Freedom: The Ordeal of Colonial Virginia* (New York: Norton, 1975).

7. A notable exception is Elizabeth Mancke, *The Fault Lines of Empire: Political Differentiation in Massachusetts and Nova Scotia, ca. 1760–1830* (New York: Routledge, 2005).

8. Edward M. Cook, *The Fathers of the Towns: Leadership and Community Structure in Eighteenth-Century New England* (Baltimore: John Hopkins University Press, 1976); Kenneth A. Lockridge, *A New England Town: The First Hundred Years: Dedham, Massachusetts, 1636–1736* (New York: Norton, 1970); Michael W. Zuckerman, *Peaceable Kingdoms: New England Towns in the Eighteenth Century* (New York: Knopf, 1970). The classic

work in this vein is Robert E. Brown, *Middle-Class Democracy and the Revolution in Massachusetts, 1691–1780* (Ithaca, N.Y.: Cornell University Press, 1955). The classic homage is Alexis de Tocqueville, *Democracy in America*, trans. Henry Reeve (New York: Colonial Press, 1899), vol. 1, 59–68.

9. John P. Demos, *A Little Commonwealth: Family Life in Plymouth Colony* (Oxford: Oxford University Press, 1970); Philip J. Greven, Jr., *Four Generations: Population, Land, and Family in Colonial Andover* (Ithaca, N.Y.: Cornell University Press, 1970); Mary Beth Norton, *Founding Mothers and Fathers: Gendered Power and the Forming of American Society* (New York: Knopf, 1996).

10. Bernard Bailyn, *The New England Merchants in the Seventeenth Century* (Cambridge, Mass.: Harvard University Press, 1955). See also Phyllis Whitman Hunter, *Purchasing Identity in the Atlantic World: Massachusetts Merchants, 1670–1780* (Ithaca, N.Y.: Cornell University Press, 2001).

11. Daniel Vickers, *Farmers and Fishermen: Two Centuries of Work in Essex County, Massachusetts, 1630–1830* (Chapel Hill: University of North Carolina Press, 1994); Kulikoff, *From British Peasants to Colonial American Farmers*; Margaret Ellen Newell, *From Dependency to Independence: Economic Revolution in Colonial New England* (Ithaca, N.Y.: Cornell University Press, 1998); Stephen Innes, *Creating the Commonwealth: The Economic Culture of Puritan New England* (New York: Norton, 1995).

12. Patrick Collinson, "*De Republica Anglorum*: Or, History with the Politics Put Back," in *Elizabethans* (London: Hambledon, 2003), 1–29. See also R. B. Goheen, "Did Peasants Have Politics? Village Communities and the Crown in Fifteenth-Century England," *American Historical Review* 96 (1991): 42–62. An exceptional book that recognizes and contributes to this trend in American historiography is Francis J. Bremer and Lynn A. Bothelo, eds., *The World of John Winthrop: Essays on England and New England, 1588–1649* (Boston: Massachusetts Historical Society, 2005).

13. Bernard Bailyn, *Voyagers to the West: A Passage in the Peopling of America on the Eve of the Revolution* (New York: Knopf, 1986), 26.

14. Ibid., 209.

15. Ibid., 225–28.

16. John Hutchins, *The American Maritime Industries and Public Policy, 1789–1914: An Economic History* (Cambridge, Mass.: Harvard University Press, 1941); David Macpherson, *Annals of Commerce, Manufactures, Fisheries, and Navigation* (London, 1805), iii, 570, as quoted in James F. Shepherd and Gary M. Walton, *Shipping, Maritime Trade, and the Economic Development of Colonial North America* (Cambridge: Cambridge University Press, 1972), 243; Shepherd and Walton, *Shipping*, 242–45.

17. See Chris Tilly and Charles Tilly, *Work Under Capitalism* (Boulder, Colo.: Westview Press, 1998), 5–16. This book's conceptualization has been heavily influenced by the Tillys' work.

18. The chief works establishing a rich typology of towns are Bruce C. Daniels, *The Connecticut Town: Growth and Development 1635–1790* (Middletown, Conn.: Wesleyan University Press, 1979), and Stephen Innes, *Labor in a New Land: Economy and Society in Seventeenth-Century Springfield* (Princeton, N.J.: Princeton University Press, 1983).

19. This position is well stated by Virginia DeJohn Anderson in her review of Roger Thompson, *Divided We Stand: Watertown, Massachusetts 1630–1680* (Amherst: University of Massachusetts Press, 2003), *William and Mary Quarterly*, 3rd ser., 60, no. 1 (January 2003): 216–18. See also Richard Archer, *Fissures in the Rock: New England in the Seventeenth Century* (Hanover, N.H.: University Press of New England, 2001).

20. For example, compare David Hackett Fischer, *Paul Revere's Ride* (Oxford: Oxford University Press, 1994), to Frank Ketchum, *Divided Loyalties: How the Revolution Came to New York* (New York: Henry Holt, 2002). See also Gary B. Nash, *The Urban Crucible: Social Change, Political Consciousness, and the Origins of the American Revolution* (Cambridge, Mass.: Harvard University Press, 1979).

21. G. B. Warden, *Boston 1689–1776* (Boston: Little, Brown, 1970), 82.

22. Benjamin Colman, *The Blessing of Zebulun and Issachar: A Sermon Preached before the Great and General Court or Assembly in Boston: November 19, 1719* (Boston: B. Green, 1719).

23. Taxes were allocated by town on polls and estates. See *Acts and Resolves of Massachusetts Bay*, vol. 2, *Acts, 1719* (Boston: Wright and Potter, 1874), 113–17.

CHAPTER I. POLITICAL ECONOMY

1. Steve Hindle, "Hierarchy and Community in the Elizabethan Parish: The Swallowfield Articles of 1596," *The Historical Journal* 42, no. 3 (Sept. 1999): 835–51.

2. Kenneth Lockridge, *A New England Town: The First Hundred Years. Dedham, Massachusetts, 1636–1736* (New York: Norton, 1970), 3–7.

3. Patrick Collinson, "*De Republica Anglorum*: Or, History with the Politics Put Back," in *Elizabethans* (London: Hambledon, 2003), 24.

4. In discussing early New England towns, historians have largely confined their debate to the timing of the shift from "community" to "society," the governing trope in this field: Bernard Bailyn, *The New England Merchants in the Seventeenth Century* (Cambridge, Mass.: Harvard University Press, 1964); Timothy H. Breen and Stephen Foster, "The Puritans' Greatest Achievement: A Study of Social Cohesion in Seventeenth-Century Massachusetts," *Journal of American History*, 60, no. 1 (June 1973): 5–22; Richard D. Brown, *Modernization: The Transformation of American Life, 1600–1865* (New York: Hill and Wang, 1976); Robert E. Brown, *Middle-Class Democracy and the Revolution in Massachusetts, 1691–1780* (Ithaca, N.Y.: Cornell University Press, 1955); Richard L. Bushman, *From Puritan to Yankee: Character and the Social Order in Connecticut, 1690–1765* (Cambridge, Mass.: Harvard University Press, 1967); David Hackett Fischer, *Albion's Seed: Four British Folkways in America* (New York: Oxford University Press, 1989); Richard P. Gildrie, *Salem, Massachusetts, 1626–1683: A Covenant Community* (Charlottesville: University of Virginia Press, 1975); Charles S. Grant, *Democracy in the Connecticut Frontier Town of Kent* (New York: Columbia University Press, 1961); Philip S. Greven, Jr., *Four Generations: Population, Land, and Family in Colonial Andover, Massachusetts* (Ithaca, N.Y.: Cornell University Press, 1970); Phyllis Whitman Hunter, *Purchasing Identity in the Atlantic*

World: Massachusetts Merchants, 1670–1750 (Ithaca, N.Y.: Cornell University Press, 2001); Kenneth A. Lockridge, *A New England Town: The First Hundred Years: Dedham, Massachusetts, 1636–1736*; Darrett Rutman, *Winthrop's Boston: A Portrait of a Puritan Town* (Chapel Hill: University of North Carolina Press, 1965); Helena M. Wall, *Fierce Communion: Family and Community in Early America* (Cambridge, Mass.: Harvard University Press, 1990); Joseph S. Wood, *The New England Village* (Baltimore: Johns Hopkins University Press, 1997); Michael W. Zuckerman, *Peaceable Kingdoms: New England Towns in the Eighteenth Century* (New York: Knopf, 1970). Recently historians have been more skeptical, though a new model of development has not emerged: Francis J. Bremer and Lynn A. Botelho, eds., *The World of John Winthrop: England and New England, 1599–1649* (Charlottesville: University Press of Virginia, 2005); Bruce C. Daniels, *The Connecticut Town: Growth and Development, 1635–1790* (Middletown, Conn.: Wesleyan University Press, 1979); Stephen Innes, *Labor in a New Land: Economy and Society in Seventeenth-Century Springfield* (Princeton, N.J.: Princeton University Press, 1983); Stephen Innes, *Creating the Commonwealth: The Economic Culture of Puritan New England* (New York: Norton, 1995); Margaret Ellen Newell, *From Dependency to Independence: Economic Revolution in Colonial New England* (Ithaca, N.Y.: Cornell University Press, 1999); Roger Thompson, *Divided We Stand: Watertown, Massachusetts, 1630–1680* (Amherst: University of Massachusetts Press, 2001); Daniel Vickers, *Farmers and Fishermen: Two Centuries of Work in Essex County, Massachusetts, 1630–1850* (Chapel Hill: University of North Carolina Press, 1994).

5. Steve Hindle, *The State and Social Change in Early Modern England, 1550–1640* (New York: Palgrave, 2002); Michael J. Braddick, *State Formation in Early Modern England, 1550–1700* (Cambridge: Cambridge University Press, 2000); Keith Wrightson and David Levine, *Poverty and Piety in an English Village: Terling, 1525–1700*, 2nd ed. (New York: Academic Press, 1979), 176. The term "state" encompasses all forms of political authority, from local governments and county courts to parliamentary and royal rule. During this period, the locality was the most pervasive and salient level of state power, and its authority was buttressed by late sixteenth-century and early seventeenth-century reforms.

6. This conception of the intimate interconnections between politics, the law, property, and labor signified by "political economy" developed in seventeenth-century England, although the phrase was first used systematically by eighteenth-century thinkers such as Adam Smith. Historically, political economists include both liberals and radicals, e.g., Smith, Ricardo, Marx, and Malthus. In the sixteenth and seventeenth centuries, English authors called these arrangements a "commonwealth"; see Whitney R. D. Jones, *The Tudor Commonwealth, 1529–1559: A Study of the Impact of the Social and Economic Developments of Mid-Tudor England Upon Contemporary Concepts of the Nature and Duties of the Commonwealth* (London: Athlone Press, 1970).

7. Virginia DeJohn Anderson, *New England's Generation: The Great Migration and the Formation of Society and Culture in the Seventeenth Century* (Cambridge: Cambridge University Press, 1991), 28–29; Timothy H. Breen and Stephen Foster, "Moving to the

New World: The Character of Early Massachusetts Immigration," *William and Mary Quarterly*, 3rd ser., 30 (1973): 189–222, quotation on 199; Roger Thompson, *Mobility and Migration: East Anglian Founders of New England, 1629–1640* (Amherst: University of Massachusetts Press, 1994), 26, 98; David Cressy, *Coming Over: Migration and Communication Between England and New England in the Seventeenth Century* (Cambridge: Cambridge University Press, 1987), 66. The sample was assembled from all the entries in Robert Charles Anderson, *The Great Migration Begins: Immigrants to New England, 1620–1635*, 3 vols. (Boston: New England Historic Genealogical Society, 1995). Francis J. Bremer, *John Winthrop: America's Forgotten Founding Father* (Oxford: Oxford University Press, 2003), 5–20.

8. Paul Seaver, *The Puritan Lectureships: The Politics of Religious Dissent 1560–1662* (Stanford, Calif.: Stanford University Press, 1970), 88; Thompson, *Mobility and Migration*, 46–49, Table 7.

9. Fischer, *Albion's Seed*, 14–49; Cressy, *Coming Over*; Breen and Foster, "Moving to the New World"; Anderson, *New England's Generation*; Alison Games, *Migration and the Origins of the English Atlantic World* (Cambridge, Mass.: Harvard University Press, 1999); Thompson, *Mobility and Migration*.

10. Katherine L. French, *The People of the Parish: Community Life in a Late Medieval Diocese* (Philadelphia: University of Pennsylvania Press, 2001); Beat Kümin, *The Shaping of a Community: The Rise and Reformation of the English Parish, c. 1400–1560* (Aldershot, UK: Ashgate, 1996); Eamon Duffy, *The Voices of Morebath: Reformation and Rebellion in an English Village* (New Haven: Yale University Press, 2001); Katherine L. French, Gary G. Gibbs, and Beat A. Kümin, eds., *The Parish in English Life, 1400–1600* (Manchester: Manchester University Press, 1997).

11. Christopher Haigh, *English Reformations: Religion, Politics, and Society Under the Tudors* (Oxford: Oxford University Press, 1993), 105–68; Duffy, *The Voices of Morebath*; Eamon Duffy, *Stripping the Altars: Traditional Religion in England, 1400–1580*, 2nd ed. (New Haven: Yale University Press, 2005), 377–504; Ronald Hutton, *The Rise and Fall of Merry England: The Ritual Year, 1400–1700* (Oxford: Oxford University Press, 1994). On popular rebellions, see R. W. Hoyle, *The Pilgrimage of Grace and the Politics of the 1530s* (Oxford: Oxford University Press, 2003); Anthony Fletcher and Diarmaid MacCulloch, *Tudor Rebellions*, 5th ed. (London: Longman, 2004), 26–64; Haigh, *English Reformations*, 174–76. Sir William Petty, *Political Arithmetic, a Discourse Concerning the Extent and Value of Lands, People, Buildings, Husbandry, Manufacture, Commerce, Fishery, Artizans, Seamen, Soldiers; Publick Revenues, Interest, Taxes . . . &c. as the same relates . . . particularly to the Territories of His Majesty of Great Britain* (London, 1690). E. A. Wrigley and R. S. Schofield, with Ronald Lee and Jim Oeppen, *The Population History of England, 1541–1871: A Reconstruction* (1981; repr. Cambridge: Cambridge University Press, 2002), 15. Duffy, *Morebath*, 182.

12. Paul Slack, *Poverty and Policy in Tudor and Stuart England* (London: Longman, 1988), 125–29.

13. Slack, *Poverty and Policy*; Wrigley and Schofield, *Population of England*, 217–19,

443, 449, 528; Slack, *Poverty and Policy*, 47; E. H. Phelps-Brown and S. V. Hopkins, "Seven Centuries of the Prices of Consumables Compared with Builders' Wage Rates," in *Essays in Economic History*, ed. E. M. Carus-Wilson, vol. 2 (London: Arnold, 1962), 179–96; A. L. Beier, *Masterless Men: The Vagrancy Problem in England, 1560–1640* (London: Methuen, 1985); William Hunt, *The Puritan Moment: The Coming of Revolution in an English County* (Cambridge, Mass.: Harvard University Press, 1963), 235–44; Thompson, *Mobility and Migration*, 99.

14. G. R. Elton, *Reform and Renewal: Thomas Cromwell and the Common Weal* (Cambridge: Cambridge University Press, 1973); James Kelsey McConica, *English Humanists and Reformation Politics Under Henry VIII and Edward VI* (Oxford: Oxford University Press, 1965); Robert Tittler, *Townspeople and Nation: English Urban Experiences, 1540–1640* (Stanford, Calif.: Stanford University Press, 2001); Robert Tittler, *The Reformation and the Towns in England: Politics and Political Culture, c. 1540–1640* (Oxford: Oxford University Press, 1998); Patrick Collinson, *The Birthpangs of Protestant England: Religious and Cultural Change in the Sixteenth and Seventeenth Centuries* (London: Macmillan, 1988); Paul Slack, *From Reformation to Improvement: Public Welfare in Early Modern England* (Oxford: Oxford University Press, 1999), 29–52; Vanessa Harding, "Reformation and Culture 1540–1700," in *The Cambridge Urban History of Britain*, ed. Peter Clark, vol. 2, *1540–1840* (Cambridge: Cambridge University Press, 2000), 263–88. Margo Todd, *Christian Humanism and the Puritan Social Order* (Cambridge: Cambridge University Press, 1987); see also Markku Peltonen, *Classical Humanism and Republicanism in English Political Thought, 1570–1640* (Cambridge: Cambridge University Press, 2004); Avihu Zakai, *Exile and Kingdom: History and Apocalypse in the Puritan Migration to America* (Cambridge: Cambridge University Press, 1992), 216–19.

15. Robert Jenison, quoted in Slack, *From Reformation to Improvement*, 29; see also Robert Jenison, *The Cities Safetie* (London: John Haviland, 1630). Thomas Hooker, *The Danger of Desertion* (1631), in *Thomas Hooker: Writings in England and Holland, 1626–1633*, ed. George Williams et al. (Cambridge, Mass.: Harvard University Press, 1975), 221–52.

16. On Samuel Ward, see Patrick Collinson, *The Religion of Protestants: The Church in English Society, 1559–1625* (Oxford: Oxford University Press, 1982), ch. 4, esp. 175–78. *Thomas Hooker: Writings in England and Holland*, ed. Williams; Sargent Bush, *The Writings of Thomas Hooker: Spiritual Adventure in Two Worlds* (Madison: University of Wisconsin Press, 1979). Slack, *Poverty and Policy*, 150. For Salisbury, see John Patten, *English Towns 1500–1700* (Folkestone, Kent, UK: Dawson Achron, 1978), 106; Paul Slack, "Poverty and Politics in Salisbury, 1597–1666," in *Crisis and Order in English Towns, 1500–1700*, ed. Peter Clark and Paul Slack (London: Routledge and Kegan Paul, 1972), 164–203. Isabel Calder, *New Haven Colony* (New Haven: Yale University Press, 1934). Slack, *Poverty*, 150. Larzer Ziff, *The Career of John Cotton: Puritanism and the American Experience* (Princeton, N.J.: Princeton University Press, 1962). Samuel Eliot Morison, *Builders of the Bay Colony: A Gallery of Our Intellectual Ancestors*, ed. Sentry (Boston: Houghton Mifflin, 1958), 21–50. David Underdown, *Fire from Heaven: Life in an English Town in the Seventeenth Century* (New Haven: Yale University Press, 1992).

17. *Norwich Mayorlty Court Minutes*, vol. 15, 212.

18. John T. Evans, *Seventeenth-Century Norwich: Politics, Religion, and Government 1620–1690* (Oxford: Oxford University Press, 1979), 26–62. *Norwich Mayorlty Court Minutes*, November 1631, January 20, 1631. Five people were whipped in December; Dennys Powle, a repeat offender, was whipped several times. The archaic term "michery" comes from the Middle English verb *meech*, to skulk or hide, and denoted sneaking about, playing truant, cringing, and whining; only later did the verb *mooch* come to mean begging rather than absenting and concealing oneself.

19. Paul Griffiths, "Masterless Young People in Norwich, 1560–1645," in *The Experience of Authority in Early Modern England*, ed. Paul Griffiths, Adam Fox, and Steve Hindle (London: Macmillan, 1996), 146–86. *Norwich Mayorlty Court Minutes*, April 16, 1631, v. 15, 146. In June 1631: "William Cobbold heretofore committed to Bridewell for begging is willing to serve the King in his wars and therefore sent to the captain, and so for the present is discharged out of Bridewell." *Norwich Mayorlty Court Minutes*, v. 15, 169.

20. *Norwich Mayorlty Court Minutes*, June 9, 1631, v. 15, 170.

21. J. F. Pound, "An Elizabethan Census of the Poor," *University of Birmingham Historical Journal* 8 (1962): 135–61; J. F. Pound, ed., *The Norwich Census of the Poor, 1570*, vol. 11 (Norfolk, UK: Norfolk Record Society, 1971); Slack, *Poverty and Policy*, 149–50; *Norwich Mayorlty Court Minutes*, October 18, 1630, January 15, 1631, v. 15, 92, 172, 178, 180.

22. *Norwich Mayorlty Court Minutes*, October 18, 1630, v. 15, 92.

23. Ibid., June 1, 1631, 160.

24. Ibid., February, 1632; December 17, 1631, 209, 227.

25. Ibid., August 7, 1630; May 14, 1631, 75, 155.

26. Wrightson and Levine, *Poverty and Piety in an English Village*, 64.

27. Ibid., 179, 183, 222.

28. Ibid., 154; Hindle, *The State and Social Change*, 221.

29. Hindle, *The State and Social Change*, 221.

30. Slack, *Poverty and Policy*, 170; David Underdown, *Revel, Riot, and Rebellion: Popular Politics and Culture in England, 1603–1660* (Oxford: Oxford University Press, 1987).

31. Underdown, *Revel, Riot, and Rebellion*, 9–32; Todd, *Christian Humanism*, 176–205; Peltonen, *Classical Humanism and Republicanism*, 12–13, 240–41, 56; Paul A. Fideler, "Poverty, Policy and Providence," in *Political Thought and the Tudor Commonwealth: Deep Structure, Discourse, and Disguise*, ed. Paul A. Fideler and T. F. Mayer (New York: Routledge, 1992), 194–222; Paul A. Fideler, *Social Welfare in Pre-Industrial England: The Old Poor Law Tradition* (London: Palgrave Macmillan, 2006); Timothy H. Breen, "The Non-Existent Controversy: Puritan and Anglican Attitudes on Work and Wealth, 1600–1640," *Church History* 35 (1966): 273–87.

32. Paul Slack, Paul Fideler, and Margo Todd point out that Puritans and reformers were not a single, synonymous group. John White quoted in Todd, *Christian Humanism*, 149. See also J. C. Davis, *Utopia and the Ideal Society: A Study of English Utopian Writing*

1516–1700 (Cambridge: Cambridge University Press, 1981), 299–367; Charles Webster, *The Great Instauration: Science, Medicine, and Reform 1626–1660* (London: Duckworth, 1975).

33. Slack, *Poverty and Policy*, 151–52.

34. The problem of labor is ably elucidated in Vickers, *Farmers and Fishermen*, 44–60. On Indians, see Jean M. O'Brien, *Dispossession by Degrees: Indian Land and Identity in Natick, Massachusetts, 1650–1790* (New York: Cambridge University Press, 1997); Neal Salisbury, "Red Puritans: The 'Praying Indians' of Massachusetts Bay and John Eliot," *William and Mary Quarterly*, 3rd ser., 32 (1975): 27–54. Slave-owning societies are skillfully differentiated from slave societies in Phillip D. Morgan, "British Encounters with Africans and African-Americans Circa 1600–1780," in *Strangers Within the Realm: Cultural Margins of the First British Empire*, ed. Bernard Bailyn and Phillip D. Morgan (Chapel Hill: University of North Carolina Press, 1991), 157–219. For a portrait of the problems of a slave society, see Richard S. Dunn, *Sugar and Slaves: The Rise of the Planter Class in the English West Indies, 1624–1713* (Chapel Hill: University of North Carolina Press, 1973).

35. *Boston Records*, vol. 13, 183; vol. 13, 13; vol. 11, 197.

36. *Boston Records*, vol. 8, 57–58; vol. 15, 140–41, 117, 121–22.

37. *Watertown Records*, vol. 1, 95, 98, 104–7, 24–25; *Dedham Records*, vol. 4, 132, 146–47.

38. *Dedham Records*, vol. 3, 29, 134; vol. 4, 92, 93–94, 118; vol. 3, 133–34, 148.

39. *Dedham Records*, vol. 3, 2.

40. *Boston Records*, vol. 2, 5; *Dedham Records*, vol. 3, 24; *Boston Records*, vol. 2, 9–12; *Dedham Records*, vol. 4, 194.

41. *Boston Records*, vol. 2, 10, 90; vol. 7, 7; *Dedham Records*, vol. 5, 118; vol. 6, 177; *Watertown Records*, vol. 2, 16; *Boston Records*, vol. 2, 152–53; vol. 8, 104.

42. *Boston Records*, vol. 15, 12.

43. *Boston Records*, vol. 11, 227, 218. See *Dedham Records*, vol. 5, 62, when town leaders were looking for a tanner.

44. *Boston Records*, vol. 7, 22; vol. 8, 177.

45. Peter Clark, ed., *The Cambridge Urban History of Britain*, vol. 2: *1530–1840* (Cambridge: Cambridge University Press, 2000), 170, 283, 284, 372, 546.

46. *Boston Records*, vol. 7, 7, 35; *Watertown Records*, vol. 2, 24–25; *Dedham Records*, vol. 5, 232. Between 1630 and 1739, selectmen in Boston, Dedham, and Watertown intervened in labor issues in some 689 cases, usually involving the hiring of outside laborers. All cases involving taverns and inns were excluded. *Boston Records*; *Dedham Records*; *Watertown Records*.

47. *Watertown Records*, vol. 2, 51; *Dedham Records*, vol. 5, 287; *Dorchester Records*, vol. 4, 224.

48. *Watertown Records*, vol. 2, 50, 66, 156.

49. *Watertown Records*, vol. 2, 44–45.

50. *Boston Records*, vol. 13, 31; vol. 7, 27.

51. Many studies assume the sanctity of the family and parent-children relations in New England and fail to consider the effects of the political economic emergency on the

minds of the colonists; see, for example, Judith Graham, *Puritan Family Life: The Diary of Samuel Sewall* (Boston: Northeastern University Press, 2000).

52. *Boston Records*, vol. 11, 221; vol. 15, 159–61. In 1739, the inspection team included 56 men.

53. *Acts and Resolves of Massachusetts Bay*, vol. 1, 67, 528, 654.

54. *Watertown Records*, vol. 1, 49; *Boston Records*, vol. 2, 132–33; *Watertown Records*, vol. 2, 192.

55. *Watertown Records*, vol. 2, 341; vol. 3, 7–8. Similar policies were followed in Connecticut; see Nancy H. Steenburg, "Not of Full Age: Minors and Connecticut Legal Culture, 1635–1780," *Connecticut History* 37, no. 2 (1996–97): 71–99.

56. *Watertown Records*, vol. 2, 341.

57. *Records of Massachusetts Bay*, vol. 1, 186.

58. Griffiths, "Masterless Young People in Norwich." Griffiths demonstrates that in Norfolk the law against living alone was chiefly enforced against women.

59. *Watertown Records*, vol. 1, 52.

60. *Dedham Records*, vol. 5, 53–54.

61. David Eltis, *The Rise of African Slavery in the Americas* (Cambridge: Cambridge University Press, 1999).

62. In Massachusetts, slavery could have developed as a significant form of organizing labor, lacking political interference. By 1690, Massachusetts had a number of industries such as lumbering and coopering in which entrepreneurs might well have used slave gangs; slaves were used in the forest industries of North and South Carolina. But Massachusetts inhabitants could not afford to accumulate slaves, given the bonds required by the towns.

CHAPTER 2. STRIPES

1. John Winthrop, *Winthrop Papers, 1498–1654* (Boston: Massachusetts Historical Society, 1929–92), vol. 2, 244, 255; John Winthrop, *The Journal of John Winthrop, 1630–1649*, ed. Richard S. Dunn, James Savage, and Laetitia Yeandle (Cambridge, Mass.: Harvard University Press, 1996), 276, 375, 556–58.

2. The term is taken from the major biography of John Winthrop by Francis J. Bremer, *John Winthrop: America's Forgotten Founding Father* (New York: Oxford University Press, 2003).

3. For an overview of Anglo-American labor systems which argues that New England's was most egalitarian, see Richard S. Dunn, "Servants and Slaves: The Recruitment and Employment of Labor," in *Colonial British America: Essays in the New History of the Early Modern Era*, ed. Jack Greene and J. R. Pole (Baltimore: Johns Hopkins University Press, 1984), 184.

4. Susan Dwyer Amussen, "Punishment, Discipline, and Power: The Social Meanings of Violence in Early Modern England," *Journal of British Studies* 34, no. 1 (Jan. 1995): 1–34.

5. Richard S. Dunn, *The Age of Religious Wars, 1559–1715*, 2nd ed. (New York: Norton, 1979), 103–51; J. D. Chambers, *Population, Economy and Society in Pre-Industrial England* (Oxford: Oxford University Press, 1972); Peter Clark, *English Provincial Society from the Reformation to the Revolution: Religion, Politics and Society in Kent, 1500–1640* (Hassocks: Harvester Press, 1977); Peter Clark and Paul Slack, *English Towns in Transition, 1500–1700* (Oxford: Oxford University Press, 1976); Keith Wrightson and David Levine, *Poverty and Piety in an English Village, Terling, 1525–1700*, 2nd ed. (Oxford: Oxford University Press, 1997).

6. *Winthrop Papers*, vol. 2, 139.

7. Karen Ordahl Kupperman, *Providence Island, 1630–1641: The Other Puritan Colony* (Cambridge: Cambridge University Press, 1993), 149–51.

8. Russell R. Menard, "From Servants to Slaves: The Transformation of the Chesapeake Labor System," *Southern Studies* 16 (1977): 355–90; Russell R. Menard, "Five Maryland Censuses, 1700–1712: A Note on the Quality of the Quantities," *William and Mary Quarterly*, 3rd ser., 37, no. 4 (Oct. 1980): 616–26; Allan Kulikoff, *Tobacco and Slaves: The Development of Southern Cultures in the Chesapeake, 1680–1800* (Chapel Hill: University of North Carolina Press, 1986), 54–76; Darrett B. Rutman and Anita H. Rutman, *A Place in Time: Middlesex County, Virginia, 1650–1750* (New York: Norton, 1984), chap. 6; and Edmund S. Morgan, *American Slavery, American Freedom: The Ordeal of Colonial Virginia* (New York: Norton, 1975), chap. 15.

9. Anthony S. Parent, *Foul Means: The Formation of a Slave Society in Virginia, 1660–1740* (Chapel Hill: University of North Carolina Press, 2003), 124, 131.

10. Jack D. Marietta and G. S. Rowe, *Troubled Experiment: Crime and Justice in Pennsylvania, 1682–1800* (Philadelphia: University of Pennsylvania Press, 2006), 107, 210.

11. Richard Saltonstall to Emmanuel Downing, February 4, 1632, in *Letters from New England: The Massachusetts Bay Colony, 1629–1638*, ed. Everett Emerson (Amherst: University of Massachusetts Press, 1976), 92. *Winthrop Papers*, vol. 3, 423; see also 422–26, 463–76.

12. Based on the ship lists to Massachusetts 1635 and 1637 in Peter Wilson Coldham, *The Complete Book of Emigrants, 1607–1660*, 4th ed. (Baltimore: Genealogical Publishing Company, 1993). See also Richard Archer, *Fissures in the Rock: New England in the Seventeenth Century* (Hanover, N.H.: University Press of New England, 2001), 109.

13. For innumerable laws to regulate livestock devastations, see *Records of Massachusetts Bay*. The problem is discussed in Daniel Vickers, *Farmers and Fishermen: Two Centuries of Work in Essex County, Massachusetts, 1630–1830* (Chapel Hill: University of North Carolina Press, 1994), 44–47; Virginia DeJohn Anderson, *Creatures of Empire: How Domestic Animals Transformed Early America* (Oxford: Oxford University Press, 2004), 141–71. For evidence of greater productivity in the Chesapeake in these years, see Menard, "From Servants to Slaves"; Gloria L. Main, *Tobacco Colony: Life in Early Maryland, 1650–1720* (Princeton, N.J.: Princeton University Press, 1983). *Winthrop Papers*, vol. 4, 232–33.

14. Morgan, *American Slavery, American Freedom*. For a more optimistic view, see James Horn, *Adapting to a New World: English Society in the Seventeenth-Century Chesapeake* (Chapel Hill: University of North Carolina Press, 1994).

15. Keith Wrightson, *English Society, 1580–1680* (London: Hutchinson, 1982); Ann Kussmaul, *Servants in Husbandry in Early Modern England* (Cambridge: Cambridge University Press, 1981).

16. Virginia DeJohn Anderson, *New England's Generation: The Great Migration and the Formation of Society and Culture in the Seventeenth Century* (Cambridge: Cambridge University Press, 1991). For an illustrative autobiography, see John Dane, "A Declaration of Remarkable Providences in the Course of My Life," *New England Historical and Genealogical Register* 8 (1854): 149–56.

17. The minister had not yet seen the children work, or even eyed the cleared land, but knew it was nearby: "I am told that about three miles from us a man may stand on a little hilly place and see divers thousands of acres of ground as good as need to be, and not a tree in the same." Francis Higginson, *New England's Plantation, Written by a Reverend Divine Now There Resident* (London, 1630); "Francis Higginson to His Friends at Leicester, July 1629," in *Letters from New England*, ed. Emerson, 25, 31. William Wood, *New England's Prospect*, ed. Alden Vaughan (Amherst: University of Massachusetts Press, 1977), 68.

18. Winthrop, *Journal*, 102. The issue is discussed in Richard B. Morris, *Government and Labor in Early America* (New York: Columbia University Press, 1946), 44–79.

19. For wage rates see Joan Thirsk, ed., *The Agrarian History of England and Wales, 1500–1640, Volume 4* (Cambridge: Cambridge University Press, 1967), 864; E. H. Phelps-Brown and Sheila V. Hopkins, "Seven Centuries of Building Wages," *Economica* 23 (1955): 200, 205.

20. Hilary Beckles, *White Servitude and Black Slavery in Barbados, 1627–1715* (Knoxville: University of Tennessee Press, 1989), 122.

21. Wood, *New England's Prospect*, 73. Francis J. Bremer, *John Winthrop: America's Forgotten Founding Father* (Oxford: Oxford University Press, 2003), 300, 317. Winthrop was over £2,600 in debt. The malpractice of his steward caused some of the problem, but much was caused by the high cost of wages.

22. Peter Wilson Coldham, *The Complete Book of Emigrants, 1607–1660*, 3 vols. (Baltimore: Genealogical Publishing Company, 1987), vol. 1, 134–36.

23. Lucy Downing to John Winthrop, July 1636, *Winthrop Papers*, vol. 3, 279.

24. Winthrop, *Journal*, 430, 200.

25. Nathaniel Ward to John Winthrop, Jr., December 24, 1635, *Winthrop Papers*, vol. 3, 215–17. Coldham, *Emigrants*, vol. 1, 320–25.

26. Emmanuel Downing to John Winthrop, ca. August 1645, *Winthrop Papers*, vol. 5, 38.

27. John White to John Winthrop, c. 1637, *Winthrop Papers*, vol. 3, 335–36.

28. Winthrop, *Journal*, 175–76.

29. See comparison with Virginia and New Netherlands, below.

30. *Records of Plymouth Colony*, vol. 1, 121–22, 139–40.

31. Winthrop, *Journal*, 171; Mary Dudley to Margaret Winthrop, January 1636, *Winthrop Papers*, vol. 3, 221.

32. John Eliot to Sir Simonds d'Ewes, September 18, 1633, in *Letters from New England*, ed. Emerson, 107–8. D'Ewes did not emigrate to Massachusetts. Winthrop, *Journal*, 93.

33. *Records of Massachusetts Bay*, vol. 1, 76, 127, 186, 267. In Connecticut, a 1644 law authorized punishment of servants for working for others besides their masters, "whereas many stubborn, refractory, and discontented servants and apprentices withdraw themselves from their masters service to improve their time to their own advantage. . ."; *Records of Connecticut*, vol. 1, 105.

34. *County Court Records of Accomack-Northampton, Virginia, 1640–1645*, ed. Susie M. Ames (Charlottesville: University Press of Virginia, 1973); *Archives of Maryland*, ed. William Hand Browne et al. (Baltimore, 1883–), vols. 1–2.

35. *Essex County Quarterly Court Records*. Internal evidence shows that at least half (148) were children and servants, and the number who were underage is likely to be much higher. Edgar J. McManus, *Law and Liberty in Early New England: Criminal Justice and Due Process, 1620–1692* (Amherst: University of Massachusetts Press, 1993), 201–10, confirms this count.

36. On sexual offenses, Else L. Hambleton, *Daughters of Eve: Pregnant Brides and Unwed Mothers in Seventeenth-Century Essex County, Massachusetts* (New York: Routledge, 2004). *Records of Connecticut*, vol. 1, 124. *Essex County Quarterly Court Records*, vol. 1, 34. Although confirming the more frequent use of whipping to control servants in New England than in the Chesapeake, Mary Beth Norton argues misguidedly that New Englanders espoused the ideas of Sir Robert Filmer when it came to conceptualizing the family and the state; Mary Beth Norton, *Founding Mothers and Fathers: Gendered Power and the Forming of American Society* (New York: Vintage, 1997), 133, 409.

37. *Records of Plymouth Colony*, vol. 1, 127; vol. 2, 105; *Records of New Haven Colony*, vol. 1, 245; *Essex County Quarterly Court Records*, vol. 1, 424.

38. Dennis Sullivan, *The Punishment of Crime in Colonial New York: The Dutch Experience in Albany During the Seventeenth Century* (New York: Lang, 1997), 30–35; Paul Griffiths, "Bodies and Souls in Norwich: Punishing Petty Crime, 1540–1700," in *Penal Practice and Culture, 1500–1900: Punishing the English*, ed. Simon Devereaux and Paul Griffiths (Basingstoke: Palgrave Macmillan, 2004), 90. *Essex County Quarterly Court Records*, vol. 1, 35. Anderson, *Great Migration*, vol. 1, 298–301; Sullivan, *Punishment of Crime*, 124.

39. Essex County Quarterly Court Records, vol. 1, 19; vol. 2, 39; *Records of Massachusetts Bay*, vol. 2, 179, 39; vol. 1, 155. Winthrop, *Journal*, 425.

40. One consequence of the rationalization of violence was that New England colonies almost alone made wife-beating illegal; see Elizabeth H. Pleck, *Domestic Tyranny: The Making of American Social Policy Against Family Violence from Colonial Times to the Present* (1987; New York: Oxford University Press, 2004). On the legal acceptability of wife-beating in Dutch New York, see Sullivan, *Punishment of Crime*, 104.

41. Winthrop, *Journal*, 302–5; *Records of Massachusetts Bay*, vol. 1, 275. See also Norton, *Founding Mothers and Fathers*, 117–18.

42. Winthrop, *Journal*, 310–11.

43. Ibid., 528–30.

44. *Laws of Connecticut and New Haven*, 263. Translation and interpretation from *The Pentateuch and Haftorahs: Hebrew Text, English Translation, and Commentary*, ed. J. H. Hertz, 2nd ed. (London: Soncino, 1990), 853–54.

45. *Essex County Quarterly Court Records*, vol. 8, 302–3; vol. 5, 232–33.

46. Ibid., vol. 8, 222–25.

47. Ibid., vol. 8, 315–16.

48. Ibid., vol. 3, 224–25.

49. Winthrop, *Journal*, 111–12.

50. Mary Downing to Emmanuel Downing, Nov. 27, 1635, in *Letters from New England*, ed. Emerson, 179–80.

51. *Records of Massachusetts Bay*, vol. 3, 355.

52. John Fiske, *The Notebook of the Reverend John Fiske, 1644–1675*, Publications of the Colonial Society of Massachusetts 47 (1977): 120–21; *Essex County Quarterly Court Records*, vol. 8, 22–25.

53. *Essex County Quarterly Court Records*, vol. 6, 93–98; Asa Sheldon, *Yankee Drover, Being the Unpretending Life of Asa Sheldon, 1788–1870* (Hanover, N.H.: University Press of New England, 1988), 13.

54. *Essex County Quarterly Court Records*, vol. 8, 22–25.

55. *Records of Massachusetts Bay*, vol. 5, 60–61; *Watertown Records*, vol. 1, 98.

56. Lucy Larcom, *A New England Girlhood: Outlined from Memory* (1889; rep. Boston: Northeastern University Press, 1986), 49.

57. *Essex Country Quarterly Court Records*, vol. 1, 404; *Ancient Town Records of New Haven*, vol. 1, 12–14.

58. Amussen, "Punishment, Discipline, and Power," 27–33.

59. Cotton Mather, *Memorable Providences, Relating to Witchcrafts and Possessions* (Boston, 1689); reprinted in *The Narratives of the Witchcraft Cases*, ed. George Lincoln Burr (New York: Charles Scribner's Sons, 1914), 99–128.

60. Ibid., 100.

61. Ibid., 109.

62. Ibid., 110.

63. Ibid., 123.

64. Ibid., 113.

65. D. W. Winnicott, *Playing and Reality* (London: Penguin, 1971), 38–53.

66. Mather, *Memorable Providences*, 124n.

67. John Putnam Demos, *Entertaining Satan: Witchcraft and the Culture of Early New England* (New York: Oxford University Press, 1983), chap. 4; Carol F. Karlsen, *The Devil in the Shape of a Woman: Witchcraft in Colonial New England* (New York: Norton, 1987), chap. 7; David Hall, ed., *Witch-Hunting in Seventeenth-Century New England*, 2nd ed. (Durham, N.C.: Duke University Press, 2005), 197–98.

68. Hall, *Witch-Hunting*, 198–211.

69. Ibid.

70. Ibid.

71. Bernard Rosenthal, *Salem Story: Reading the Witch Trials of 1692* (Cambridge: Cambridge University Press, 1993), 32–50; Mary Beth Norton, *In the Devil's Snare: The Salem Witchcraft Crisis of 1692* (New York: Knopf, 2002). The first to describe witchcraft accusations in terms of labor was Kenneth Silverman, *The Life and Times of Cotton Mather* (New York: Harper & Row, 1984).

CHAPTER 3. SETTLEMENT

1. Nathaniel Hawthorne, *The Scarlet Letter*, 2nd ed. (Boston: Bedford/St. Martin's, 2006), 26–30.

2. This and the following analysis of surnames are based on *Essex County, Massachusetts, Probate Index, 1638–1840*, ed. W. P. Upham, 16 vols. Latter-Day Saints Genealogical Library, accessible at Ancestry.com and Genealogy.com.

3. K. D. M. Snell, "The Culture of Local Xenophobia," *Social History* 28, no. 1 (Jan. 2003): 1–30.

4. Jules Zanger, "A Note on Skipper Ireson's Ride," *New England Quarterly* 29, no. 2 (June 1956): 236–38; Eston Everett Ericson, "'John Hort' and 'Skipper Ireson'," *New England Quarterly* 10, no. 3 (Sept. 1937): 531–32. The tale must be interpreted with caution. In the late nineteenth and early twentieth centuries, there was considerable controversy about whether Ireson or his men had refused to help the distressed ship *Active*; the sailors may have blamed the captain to exculpate themselves.

5. William Bentley, *The Diary of William Bentley, Pastor of the East Church, Salem Massachusetts* (Salem: Essex Institute, 1905–1914), vol. 4, 118. According to the *Oxford English Dictionary*, the term "stocky," which derives from sturdy tree trunks, had positive connotations when applied to men through the mid-seventeenth century, but thereafter was applied mostly to animals and lower-class men and women.

6. Alison Games, *Migration and the Origins of the English Atlantic World* (Cambridge, Mass.: Harvard University Press, 1999), 189. The same phenomenon is described in Virginia DeJohn Anderson, *New England's Generation: The Great Migration and the Formation of Society and Culture in the Seventeenth Century* (New York: Cambridge University Press, 1991).

7. Philip Greven, Jr., *Four Generations: Population, Land, and Family in Colonial Andover, Massachusetts* (Ithaca, N.Y.: Cornell University Press, 1970); Allan Kulikoff, *From British Peasants to Colonial American Farmers* (Chapel Hill: University of North Carolina Press, 2000).

8. The minimum number per surname was three.

9. Its *Marblehead Magazine* still exudes local patriotism. See, for example, the essay "Twenty Things a True Marbleheader Knows," including pejorative terms for strangers— people who recently moved to town; available at http://www.legendinc.com/Pages/MarbleheadNet/MM/MarbleheadMagazine.html.

10. Edwin Haviland Miller, *Salem Is My Dwelling Place: A Life of Nathaniel Hawthorne* (Iowa City: University of Iowa Press, 1991).

11. For a good overview, see Lynn Hollen Lees, *The Solidarities of Strangers: The English Poor Laws and the People, 1700–1948* (Cambridge: Cambridge University Press, 1998); Paul Slack, *The English Poor Law, 1531–1782* (Cambridge: Cambridge University Press, 1990); K. D. M. Snell, "Pauper Settlement and the Right to Poor Relief in England and Wales," *Continuity and Change* 6, no. 3 (1991): 398; K. D. M. Snell, *Parish and Belonging: Community, Identity, and Welfare in England and Wales, 1700–1950* (Cambridge: Cambridge University Press, 2006).

12. *General Lawes of Massachusetts; Acts and Resolves of Massachusetts Bay.*

13. K. D. M. Snell, *Annals of the Labouring Poor: Social Change and Agrarian England, 1660–1900* (Cambridge: Cambridge University Press, 1987); Sidney Webb and Beatrice Webb, *English Local Government From the Revolution to the Municipal Corporation Acts*, vol. 7, part 2: *The Old Poor Law* (London: Longmans, 1927); Dorothy Marshall, *The English Poor in the Eighteenth Century* (London: Routledge, 1926).

14. The sources or parish registers studied are detailed in the tables and bibliography. For England, I studied 764 people married in Askham, Cumbria, between 1650 and 1790; 440 people in Hollesley, Suffolk, between 1682 and 1790; 666 people married in Horringer, Suffolk, between 1653 and 1790; and 1,002 people married in Walton-le-Dale, Lancashire, between 1654 and 1790. The English sample was 2,872 people, not counting their children. For Massachusetts, I studied 1,002 people married in Malden, Middlesex, between 1650 and 1790; 1,002 people married in Marblehead, Essex, between 1676 and 1793; 1,000 people married in Scituate, Plymouth, between 1643 and 1790; and 1,620 people married in Watertown, Middlesex, between 1695 and 1789. The Massachusetts sample was 4,624 people, not counting their children. I determined whether each person getting married was town born, a stranger, or a person born elsewhere but settled in the parish or town. In order to decide whether a person was born in the parish or town, I examined the birth records of the town or parish from forty to fifteen years before the marriage. I decided a person was town born when his or her name was mentioned or when one or more couples with the same surname were having children in that time span. This method might overestimate the number of town born. As noted below in the text, I also studied whether or not the couples in these towns or parishes had children there and how many. The geographic and social-political aspects of these towns and parishes are discussed in the text. Other historians might well use this method, or improve upon it, to see whether similar patterns are found in other towns and parishes across the Atlantic world.

15. Because of the importance of settlement, record keepers in England and New England virtually always specified where each member of a marrying couple resided and/ or had legal settlement. For example, the minister of Great Whelnetham in Suffolk, England, noted in the parish register that September 15, 1704, he married "William Wilder of Cockfield day laborer and Ann Wilden of Bradfield Combast." Unless the couple settled without challenge in Great Whelnetham and bought or rented land there, they and their children had no right of settlement in the parish, though they could reside there.

From these records, historians have been able to study marriage horizons—how far people went to find spouses or marry—which suggests not only how far they traveled to find employment but also how significant their ties to particular communities were to their futures. These patterns suggest the contours of local culture and political economies.

Many historical demographers have used the marriage registers alone to gauge how many people married within the town where they resided, but there are problems with this method for the study of migration. The English registers reliably recorded whether a bride or groom was "of the parish" or "of the town" or came from another town or parish, usually specifying his or her current residence. In England the registers recorded residence, not legal settlement. A man was described as "of the parish" if he resided there for as little as a month before marriage, even if his "home parish" or legal settlement—where he and his wife and children might obtain support—lay elsewhere. In contrast, in Massachusetts, where the settlement laws differed, many towns' marriage records distinguished between those resident and those legally settled. A man was described as "resident in Marblehead," implying legal settlement elsewhere, or simply "of Marblehead," denoting legal settlement in Marblehead. The ambiguity of marriage records and the differences in practice between England and Massachusetts creates confusion when they are used in isolation from other sources to study migration.

16. Ronald Sands, *Portrait of Wordsworth Country* (London: R. Hale, 1984); Richard Ferguson, *A History of Westmoreland* (London: E. Stock, 1894); John Housman, *A Topographical Description of Cumberland, Westmoreland, Lancashire, and a Part of West Riding of Yorkshire* (Carlisle, UK: F. Jolbe, 1800); J. Bailey, *General View of the Agriculture of Northumberland, Cumberland, and Westmorland*, 3rd ed. (Newcastle upon Tyne: Graham, 1972); Llewellyn Frederick William Jewett, *The Stately Homes of England* (Philadelphia: Gebbie and Barrie, 1873), chap. 16. For upland English social structure and agricultural practices, see also David Hey, *An English Rural Community: Myddle Under the Tudors and Stuarts* (Leicester: Leicester University Press, 1974).

17. "Joseph Livesey," in *Dictionary of National Biography* (London: Macmillan, 1893), ed. Sidney Lee, vol. 33, 380–81; William Farrer and J. Brownbill, eds., *The Victoria History of the County of Lancaster* (London: Constable, 1908), vol. 2, 337.

18. Arthur Young, "A Five Days Tour to Woodbridge," in *Tours in England and Wales, selected from the Annals of Agriculture* (1784; repr. London: London School of Economics, 1930).

19. John Hervey, Baron, *Lord Hervey and His Friends, 1726–1738* (London: Murray, 1950).

20. Arthur Young, *General View of the Agriculture of the County of Suffolk* (1784; repr. New York: Augustus M. Kelley, 1969), 11–12.

21. E. J. Buckatzsch, "The Constancy of Local Populations and Migration in England Before 1800," *Population Studies* 5, no. 1 (July 1951): 62–69.

22. For an example of this point of view, see Richard D. Brown, *Modernization: The Transformation of American Life, 1600–1865* (New York: Hill and Wang, 1976).

23. Bernard Bailyn, *Massachusetts Shipping, 1697–1714* (Cambridge, Mass.: Harvard University Press, 1959); *1784 Tax Valuations*.

24. William Page, ed., *The Victoria History of the County of Suffolk* (London: Institute of Historical Research, 1975), 2 vols. Richard Wilkie and Jack Tager, *Historical Atlas of Massachusetts* (Amherst: University of Massachusetts Press, 1991).

25. Snell, *Annals of the Labouring Poor.*

26. See Daniel Vickers, with Vince Walsh, *Young Men and the Sea: Yankee Seafarers in the Age of Sail* (New Haven: Yale University Press, 2005).

27. See Douglas L. Jones, *Village and Seaport: Migration and Society in Eighteenth-Century Massachusetts* (Hanover, N.H.: Tufts University Press, 1981); Ruth Herndon, *Unwelcome Americans: Living on the Margin in Early New England* (Philadelphia: University of Pennsylvania Press, 2001).

28. *Watertown's Early Settlers*, vol. 1, 302; *Watertown Records*, vol. 3, 142–43.

29. *Watertown's Early Settlers*, vol. 1, 151; *Watertown Records*, vol. 2, 132; *Watertown's Early Settlers*, vol. 1, 414–15; *Watertown Records*, vol. 5, 232.

30. *Watertown's Early Settlers*, vol. 1, 193–96; *Watertown Records*, vol. 3, 175.

31. *Watertown's Early Settlers*, vol. 1, 619, 960.

32. *Watertown's Early Settlers*, vol. 1, 163–64; *Watertown Records*, vol. 5, 319–20; *Watertown's Early Settlers*, vol. 1, 240–49.

33. *Watertown's Early Settlers*, vol. 1, 381.

34. *Watertown's Early Settlers*, vol. 1, 124.

35. *Watertown Records*, vol. 3, 302.

36. *Watertown Records*, vol. 5, 62.

37. This pattern, of a poor but able-bodied woman having the town pay her house rent and taking care of other poor folks in exchange for payment from the Overseers of the Poor was common in late eighteenth- and early nineteenth-century Massachusetts. Some married men did the same, but they were more often regarded as unscrupulous profiteers, and abuses of this system, coupled with demands for efficiency, helped to fuel the call for poor farms.

38. *Watertown Records*, vol. 5, 267.

39. *Watertown Records*, vol. 6, 24, 121, 147, 164; *Watertown's Early Settlers*, vol. 1, 355, 855.

40. *Watertown Records*, vol. 5, 247; *Watertown's Early Settlers*, vol. 1, 651.

41. Bentley, *Diary*, vol. 1, 214; vol. 2, 455.

42. Pamela Horn, *The Rural World, 1780–1850: Social Change in the English Countryside* (New York: St. Martin's Press, 1980), 14. Charles Phythian-Adams, ed., *Societies, Cultures, and Kinship, 1580–1850* (Leicester: Leicester University Press, 1993). As Phythian-Adams characterizes his new thinking: "The major conceptual advance has increasingly involved the discarding of single, and putatively 'bounded,' entities as central objects of study, and their replacement by a qualitative understanding of variously definable patterns of social *linkage*—between individuals, between social entities, and between those entities and yet higher orders of social and cultural reality" (xiii).

43. David Jaffee, *People of the Wachusett: Greater New England in History and Memory, 1630–1860* (Ithaca, N.Y.: Cornell University Press, 1999).

44. Bernard Bailyn, *Voyagers to the West: A Passage in the Peopling of America on the Eve of the Revolution* (New York: Vintage Books, 1986), 10, 209.

45. See the website of David Pane-Joyce, a genealogist at Clark University: http://alepho.clarku.edu/~djoyce/gen/report/. William Hutchinson Rowe, *Ancient North Yarmouth and Yarmouth, Maine, 1636–1936* (1937; repr. Somersworth, Me.: New England Press, 1980), 75, 78–79.

46. Maine was originally settled by the Plymouth Company, was sold to Massachusetts Bay in 1677, and remained a district of Massachusetts until 1820, when it was admitted to the Union as an independent state.

47. *Watertown's Early Settlers*, vol. 1, 45–76. See also introduction to Henry Bond, *Genealogies of the Families and Descendants of the Early Families of Watertown*, CD-ROM (Boston: New England Historic and Genealogical Society, 2007).

48. Bentley, *Diary*, vol. 2, 293; Charles E. Clark, *The Eastern Frontier: The Settlement of Northern New England, 1610–1763* (New York: Knopf, 1970), 182, 203.

49. Clark, *Eastern Frontier*, 228; George Augustus Wheeler, *History of Castine, Penobscot, and Brooksville, Maine* (Bangor, Me.: Burr and Robinson, 1875), 312.

50. As quoted in David E. Van Deventer, *The Emergence of Provincial New Hampshire, 1623–1741* (Baltimore: Johns Hopkins University Press, 1976), 36.

51. The best study of mobility in New England is Jaffee, *People of the Wachusett*. However, Jaffee overemphasizes the role of patriarchy and kinship and underemphasizes the role of the political economy of the town itself as a motive for and sustainer of expansion.

52. The laws make clear that ratable polls were all able-bodied men aged sixteen or older; unratable polls supported by the town were infirm adult men and others who were inhabitants of the town but exempt by reason of their vocations from being counted as workers (such as schoolmasters), while unratable polls unsupported by the town were men aged sixteen years or older working in the town who were not accepted as inhabitants because they were settled inhabitants of other towns.

53. This is based on a sample of towns from the 1784 Tax Valuations, which are included in the Massachusetts Archives (see below). The lists for each town were aggregated or summarized, making this count possible.

54. *1784 Tax Valuations*, vol. 162, 205; *1786 Tax Valuations*, vol. 163, 2.

55. Miller, *Salem Is My Dwelling Place*, 501.

CHAPTER 4. POLITICAL FABRIC

1. This chapter is co-authored with Susan Ouellette, Saint Michaels College. Additional details on her views of Massachusetts textiles are Susan Ouellettte, "Divine Providence and Collective Endeavor: Sheep Production in Early Massachusetts," *New England Quarterly* 69, no. 3 (September 1996): 355–80 and *U.S. Textile Production in Historical Perspective: A Cast Study from Massachusetts* (New York: Routledge, 2006). Edward John-

son, *Wonder-Working Providence of Sions Savior in New England* (1654; repr., Delmar, N.Y.: Scholars Facsimiles and Reprints, 1974), 130.

2. See, for example, Phyllis Whitman Hunter, *Purchasing Identity in the Atlantic World: Massachusetts Merchants, 1670–1789* (Ithaca, N.Y.: Cornell University Press, 2001).

3. Virginia DeJohn Anderson, *New England's Generation: The Great Migration and the Formation of Society and Culture in the Seventeenth Century* (New York: Cambridge University Press, 1991), 134. See also Roger Thompson, *Mobility and Migration: East Anglican Founders of New England, 1629–1640* (Amherst: University of Massachusetts Press, 1994).

4. David Shi, *The Simple Life: Plain Living and High Thinking in American Culture* (New York: Oxford University Press, 1985), 14–15.

5. Lucy Downing to John Winthrop, July 1636, in *Winthrop Papers*, vol. 3, 279.

6. John White to John Winthrop, Nov. 16, 1636, in *Winthrop Papers*, vol. 3, 321.

7. Eric Kerridge, *Textile Manufactures in Early Modern England* (Manchester, UK: Manchester University Press, 1985); Herbert Heaton, *The Yorkshire Woolen and Worsted Industries from the Earliest Times Up to the Industrial Revolution,* 2nd ed. (Oxford: Oxford University Press, 1965).

8. Hugh Peter to John Winthrop, ca. April 10, 1639, in *Winthrop Papers*, vol. 4, 113.

9. *The Journal of John Winthrop, 1630–1649*, ed. Richard S. Dunn, James Savage, and Laetitia Yeandle (Cambridge, Mass.: Belknap Press, 1996), 353.

10. Letter from Edward Brown to Nehemiah Wallington, quoted in Peter Wilson Coldham, *The Complete Book of Emigrants, 1607–1666*, vol. 1 (Baltimore: Genealogical Publishing Company, 1987), 228.

11. *Files and Records of the Essex Quarterly Court*, November 1652, vol. 1, 274.

12. Joseph Lancaster testified that "on a very cold day" he observed Goodman Elsly's servant "very destitute of clothes and without stockings." *Files and Records of the Essex Quarterly Court*, October 1666, vol. 3, 365–66.

13. *Records of the Governor and Massachusetts Bay Company in New England*, ed. Nathaniel Shurtleff (Boston: William White, 1853–1854), vol. 2, 105 (May 4, 1645).

14. *The Journal of John Winthrop, 1630–1649*, 353.

15. Plymouth Colony laws reprinted in Edmund Whitman, *Flax Culture: An Outline of the History and Present Condition of the Flax Industry in the United States* (Boston: Rand Avery Company, 1888), 79; *Records of the Colony of New Plymouth in New England*, ed. David Pulsiver (Boston: William White, 1861; repr., New York: AMS, 1968), vol. 12: *Laws: 1623–1682*, 32, 36; for execution of laws see vol. 2, 17, 23.

16. Order of the Massachusetts General Court, May 13, 1640, *Records of Massachusetts Bay*, vol. 1, 294.

17. February 10, 1640, Ipswich Town Records, 1634–1662, Manuscript #21, Peabody Essex Museum, Phillips Library, Salem, Massachusetts (hereafter PEM).

18. Florence M. Montgomery, with Linda Eaton, *Textiles in America 1650–1870* (New York: Norton, 2007), 244–45.

19. Ibid., 218–22.

20. Inventory of Mahalaleel Munnings, Town of Boston, *Suffolk County Probate Records*, vol. 3, 229.

21. Account Book of George Curwin, vols. 1–3, 1652–1662, Mss 45, PEM; Estate Inventory of George Curwin, Box 9, Folder 5, Mss 45, PEM. See also Francis Ellis Letterbook and Samuel Ingerson Account Book, 1685–1695, PEM. See also the interesting and important discussion of Curwin and Massachusetts's economics in James E. McWilliams, *Building the Bay Colony: Local Economy and Culture in Early Massachusetts* (Charlottesville: University Press of Virginia, 2007), 75–83. However, he as usual sees New Englander political and economic innovators as folk, "hidebound by traditional habits," 78.

22. Joshua Buffum Account Book, 1674–1704, Buffum Family Manuscripts, FMS B9293, PEM.

23. Order of Massachusetts Bay General Court, May 14, 1645, *Records of Massachusetts Bay*, vol. 2, 105–6. Also reproduced in William Bagnall, *The Textile Industries of the United States Including Sketches of Cotton, Woolen, Silk, and Linen Manufactures in the Colonial Period, vol. 1, 1639–1810* (Cambridge, Mass.: Harvard University Press, 1893), 6.

24. Order of Massachusetts Bay General Court, August 22, 1654, *Records of Massachusetts Bay*, vol. 3, 355–56.

25. Account Book of Samuel Ingersol, 1685–1695, Mss 21, PEM. Ingersol recorded several sales of sheep while he was engaging in a regular Barbados-Newfoundland trade. The values recorded were substantially higher than the averages in most probates at the time.

26. *Records of Massachusetts Bay*, vol. 2, 252 (October 18, 1648).

27. For a survey of early Massachusetts laws and General Court orders relating to cloth production, see Bagnall, *Textile Industries of the United States*, vol. 1, *1639–1810*, 4–10.

28. April 25, 1657, Ipswich Town Records, 1634–1662, Manuscript #21, leaf 1, PEM.

29. January 5, 1639, Ipswich Town Records, 1634–1662, Manuscript #21, leaf 1, PEM. Will of William Fellows, March 27, 1677, *Essex County Probate Records*, vol. 3, 128–30.

30. December 12, 1658, Ipswich Town Records, 1634–1662, Manuscript #21, PEM. The "fold" was an enclosure made with high, solid wooden fences to keep the flock safe for the night. Sometimes the enclosure would be partly roofed over to provide shelter from rain as well. Shepherds would make a temporary residence for themselves right up against the fold's walls to be readily available if anything threatened the safety of the flock, especially the lambs.

31. April 25, 1657, Ipswich Town Records, 1634–1662, Manuscript #21, leaf 1, PEM.

32. For early modern England, see Thomas Tusser, *Five Hundred Points of Good Husbandry, 1580 edition reproduced* (London: Lackington, Allen, and Company, 1812), 149; for seventeenth-century Massachusetts, see Marblehead Town Records, *Essex Institute Papers* 69, nos. 3–4 (July–Oct. 1933): 207–329.

33. A "gate" was another form of measure for the common pastures. In Rowley, a gate was equivalent to one acre by order of the town selectmen; February 25, 1662, *Rowley Town Records* (Rowley, Mass., 1894), 129.

34. Will of Francis Lambert, *Essex County Probate Records*, vol. 1, 94.

35. Guardianship of Abigail Lambert, *Essex County Probate Records*, vol. 3, 426.

36. Will of Reverend Ezekiel Rogers, *Essex County Probate Records*, vol. 1, 331–36.

37. Will of William Stickney, *Essex County Probate Records*, vol. 2, 5–8.

38. *Salem Town Records*, vols. 1–3, 1634–1691, reproduced in Library of American Civilizations, microfiche # LAC20507.

39. Salem Quarterly Court Records, vol. 6, leaves 6, 13; February 5, 1650, Ipswich Town Records, 1634–1662, Manuscript #21, PEM.

40. *Marblehead Town Records*, vol. 1, 1648–1683 (Salem, Mass.: Essex Institute, 1933).

41. Salem Town Records, vols. 1–3, 1634–1691, microfiche #LAC20507.

42. Jared Eliot, *Essays Upon Field Husbandry in New England, As It is or May be Ordered* (Boston: Edes and Gill, 1762), 8.

43. Sarah Knight, *The Journal of Madame Knight* (repr. New York: Peter Smith, 1935), 62.

44. November 17, 1659, Ipswich Town Records, 1634–1662, Manuscript #21, PEM.

45. Order of October 7, 1640, *Records of Massachusetts Bay*, vol. 1, 303.

46. June 2, 1641, *Records of Massachusetts Bay*, vol. 1, 320.

47. Bagnall, *Textile Industries of the United States*, vol. 1, 5.

48. Heaton, *The Yorkshire Woolen and Worsted Industries*, 64–65.

49. June 14, 1642, *Records of Massachusetts Bay*, vol. 2, 7.

50. May 1656, *Records of Massachusetts Bay*, vol. 3, 396.

51. William Titcomb case, Records and Files of Quarterly Courts of Essex County, Massachusetts, WPA transcripts, vol. 3, 116–17.

52. December 10, 1656, Ipswich Town Records, vol. 1, 198.

53. October 15, 1656, *The Records of the Town of Cambridge, Formerly NewTown, Massachusetts, 1630–1703* (Cambridge, Mass.: 1901), 115.

54. Quoted in Roger Thompson, *Divided We Stand: Watertown, Massachusetts 1630–1680* (Amherst: University of Massachusetts Press, 2001), 95–96.

55. Bagnall, *Textile Industries of the United States*, vol. 1, 8.

56. December 22, 1671, Ipswich Town Records, vol. 2, 332.

57. Ipswich Town Records, vol. 1, 328, 348; vol. 3, 39, 60, 87, 162, 210, 329, 330.

58. For an effort to gain an estimate from inventories that takes these problems into consideration see Susan Ouellette, *U.S. Textile Production in Historical Perspective: A Case Study from Massachusetts* (New York: Routledge, 2006).

59. Thomas Banister, *A letter to the Right Honourable Lord Commissioners of Trade and Plantations, or, A Short Essay on the Principal Branches of Trade of New England; with the Difficulties they Labor under and Some Methods of Improvement: Printed in London, 1715* (facsimile edition, Boston, 1941).

60. Mr. Cummings to the Council of Trade and Plantations, July 15, 1718, *Calendar of State Papers—Colonial*, vol. 30, 312, item no. 620

61. Mr. Cummings to the Council of Trade and Plantations, May 23, 1719, ibid., vol. 31, 91, item no. 195.

62. Mr. Bridger to Mr. Popple, Boston, June 26, 1719, ibid., vol. 31, 139, item no. 270.

63. The custom officers wanted Admiralty courts to handle wool seizures. See Mr. Armstrong to the Council of Trade and Plantations, New Hampshire, New England, July 19, 1720, ibid., vol. 32, 68–69, item no. 153.

64. Mr. Cummings to the Council of Trade and Plantations, July 15, 1718, ibid., vol. 30, 312, item no. 620.

65. Governor Joseph Dudley to the Council of Trade and Plantations, March 1, 1709, ibid., vol. 24, 236, item no. 391. Joseph Dudley (1647–1720) knew Massachusetts well; he was born in Roxbury.

66. Mr. Bridger, Boston, to Mr. Popple, June 26, 1719, ibid., vol. 31, 139, item no. 270.

67. Mr. Armstrong, New Hampshire, to the Council of Trade and Plantations, July 19, 1720, ibid., vol. 32, 68–69, item no. 153.

68. Heaton, *The Yorkshire Woollen and Worsted Industries*, 282–312.

69. Christopher Leffingwell Account Book, 1698–1714, Connecticut Historical Society, West Hartford, Conn.

70. Christopher Leffingwell Account Book, 1698–1714, 27–28.

71. *Suffolk County Deeds*, 14 vols. (Boston, 1880–1906).

72. Roger Thompson, *Divided We Stand*, 96; *Ipswich Town Records*, vol. 1, 3, 7, 9, 11, 207; *Suffolk Deeds*, vol. 11, 80.

73. Pearson Family Papers: Byfield Mills, Box 1, folder 1, item 1, Phillips Library, PEM.

74. The Pearson ledgers were described in detail in George Brainard Blodgett, *Early Settlers of Rowley, Massachusetts* (Rowley, Mass.: Amos Everett Jewett, 1933), 272–73. Consider that the 65,000 yards of wool cloth was just a portion of the overall production of fabric. In nearly every probate reporting cloth goods, linen outweighed wool cloth by nearly three yards to one. If linen, linen/cotton, and linen/wool cloth were manufactured in the Rowley area in the same proportion that they appear in the probates, nearly 200,000 years of linen-based cloth would have been produced over the same period. See Susan M. Ouellette, "All Hands Are Enjoined to Spin: Textile Production in Seventeenth-Century Massachusetts" (Ph.D. diss., University of Massachusetts, Amherst, 1996), 167.

75. See *Proceedings and Debates of the British Parliaments Respecting North America*, ed. Leo Francis Stock (repr. New York: Kraus, 1966–1970), vol. 3, 5, 254; vol. 4, 91, 99.

76. *Diary of Cotton Mather,* vol. 2, 4.

77. Dudley to Council of Trade and Plantations, March 1, 1709, *Calendar of State Papers: Colonial*, vol. 24, 236, item 391.

78. John Jekyll to Council of Trade and Plantations, August 16, 1720, ibid., vol. 32, 100, item 190.

79. Governor Shute to Council of Trade, August 19, 1720, ibid., vol. 32, 105, item 200.

80. Governor Belcher to Council of Trade, December 4, 1731, ibid., vol. 38, 359–60, item 528.

81. "Representation of the Commissioners for Trade and Plantations to the House of Commons, 15 February, 1732," *Calendar of State Papers: Colonial Series: American and West Indies, 1732* (Kraus Reprint edition, Vaduz, 1946), vol. 39, 58, item 87.

82. Ibid, 62; John Smith, ed., *Chronicon Rusticus-Commericale; or Memoirs of Wool* (London: Smith, 1797), vol. 2, 264–65.

83. The issue remains debatable about how much the textile industry was in reality reduced. Further research is needed. In 1784, for example, Ipswich still had a flock of 3,482 sheep, and many other towns held huge flocks. Speaking of Massachusetts as late as 1757, William Burke noted, "They are almost the only one of our colonies which have much of the woolen and linen manufactures. Of the former, they have nearly as much as suffices for their own clouthing. It is close and strong, but a coarse stubborn sort of cloth." William Burke, *An Account of the English Settlements in America, In Two Volumes* (London: R. and J. Dodsley, 1757), vol. 2, 168.

84. Reverend John Wise, "A World of Comfort to a Melancholy Country" (Boston, 1721) in *Colonial Currency Reprints, 1682–1751*, vol. 2, 162.

85. Thomas Prince, "A Discourse Shewing that the Real First Cause of the Straits and Difficulties of This Province of the Massachusetts Bay is its Extravagancy" (Boston, 1721), in *Colonial Currency Reprints, 1682–1751*, vol. 2, 283–85.

86. John Colman, "The Distressed State of the Town of Boston Once More Considered" (Boston, 1720), in *Colonial Currency Reprints, 1682–1751*, vol. 2, 75.

87. See the brilliant discussion of the relationship between contemporary medical ideas of health and sickness and the language in the currency debates in Martha Yoder, "Violation and Immunity: The Languages of Politics and Health in Pre-Revolutionary Massachusetts" (Ph.D. diss., University of Massachusetts, Amherst, 2004), 209–76. See also T. H. Breen, *The Marketplace of Revolution: How Consumer Politics Shaped American Independence* (New York: Oxford University Press, 2004).

88. Anonymous, "A Letter to an Eminent Clergy-man in the Massachusetts Bay" (Boston, 1720), in *Colonial Currency Reprints, 1682–1751*, vol. 2, 235.

89. Anonymous, "New News from Robinson Cruso's Island" (Boston, 1720), in *Colonial Currency Reprints, 1682–1751*, vol. 2, 125, 133. Dudley's provocative quotation was published in "A Vindication of the Bank of Credit," ibid., vol. 1, 3–9, and again in "Reflections upon Reflections," ibid., vol. 2, 120.

90. Bailyn, *New England Merchants in the Seventeenth Century*, 71–74. Margaret Ellen Newell, *From Dependency to Independence*, nearly challenges Bailyn's position; so does Ulrich. Laurel Thatcher Ulrich, *The Age of Homespun: Objects and Stories in the Creation of an American Myth* (New York: Knopf/Random House, 2001).

91. Anderson, *New England's Generation*, 136–37.

92. Laurel Thatcher Ulrich, "Wheels, Looms, and the Gender Division of Labor in Eighteenth-Century New England," *William and Mary Quarterly*, 3rd ser., 55, no. 1 (January 1998): 3–38.

93. Adrienne Hood, *The Weaver's Craft: Cloth, Commerce, and Industry in Early Pennsylvania* (Philadelphia: University of Pennsylvania Press, 2003).

94. Ulrich, "Wheels, Looms, and the Gender Division of Labor," 6, 10, 12.

95. Marla R. Miller, *The Needle's Eye: Women and Work in the Age of Revolution* (Amherst: University of Massachusetts Press, 2006).

96. Anderson, *New England's Generation*, 136–37.

CHAPTER 5. OF WHARVES AND MEN

1. Benjamin Franklin, *The Autobiography* (Paris, 1791; London, 1793; repr. New York: Modern Library, 1950), 13.

2. *Boston Records*, 2nd Commissioners Report, Feb. 22, 1641, 59; Nov. 25, 1640, 58; John Winthrop, *The Journal of John Winthrop, 1630–1649*, ed. Richard S. Dunn, James Savage, and Laetitia Yeandle (Cambridge, Mass.: Harvard University Press, 1996), 402.

3. Joseph Cullon, "Colonial Shipwrights and Their World: Men, Women, and Markets in Early New England" (Ph.D. diss., University of Wisconsin, 2003), 28. Cullon argues that it took a thousand trees. However, 200 trees may be closer to the mark.

4. William L. Sachse, "The Migration of New Englanders to England, 1640–1660," *American Historical Review* 53, no. 2 (Jan. 1948), 251–78; Karen Ordahl Kupperman, *Providence Island, 1630–1641: The Other Puritan Colony* (Cambridge: Cambridge University Press, 1993).

5. Winthrop, *Journal*, 345, 417.

6. *Boston Records*, 2nd Commissioners Report, Sept. 29, 1641, 63; Sept. 27, 1641, 76–77; March 29, 1643, 73; May 31, 1643, 74–75.

7. *Suffolk County Deeds*, vol. 6, 329; Aug. 8, 1672, deposition.

8. *Boston Records*, 2nd Commissioners Report, Sept. 23, 1652, 112.

9. *Boston Records*, 2nd Commissioners Report, May 26, 1647, 91.

10. *Boston Records*, 2nd Commissioners Report, Feb. 26, 1652, 110.

11. *Boston Records*, 2nd Commissioners Report, May 30, 1660, 156; May 29, 1644, 80.

12. Josselyn quoted in Walter Muir Whitehill and Lawrence W. Kennedy, *Boston: A Topographical History*, 3rd ed. (Cambridge, Mass.: Harvard University Press, 2000), 15; Bonner map, 45.

13. This statement is based on inspection of several maps and pictures. As noted, the Bonner map of Boston in 1722 had seventy-one wharves. The historians Edwin G. Burrows and Mike Wallace's map of New York City from 1730 to 1770 shows just thirty-six wharves, a fact confirmed by Bernard Ratzer's plan of New York in 1767. George Heap's "An East Prospect of the City of Philadelphia, 1754" shows twenty-four wharves in the Quaker city. This city did build more wharves as it grew, reaching sixty-two in 1775, while Boston then had seventy-six. Additionally, neither New York nor Philadelphia's shoreline contained an engineering marvel like Boston's Long Wharf, built between 1711 and 1715. It intruded just over 1,562 feet into the harbor or about one-third of a mile, contained warehouses and additional wharves projecting from it, and allowed the largest ships of the time to connect to the city. Martin P. Snyder, *Views of Philadelphia Before 1800* (New York: Praeger, 1975), 30–31; Alex Krieger and David Cobb, eds., *Mapping Boston* (Cam-

bridge, Mass.: MIT Press, 2001), 175, 177, 179, 183; Gary Nash, *The Urban Crucible: The Northern Seaports and the Origins of the American Revolution* (Cambridge, Mass.: Harvard University Press, abridged edition, 1986), 190; Edwin G. Burrows and Mike Wallace, *Gotham: A History of New York City to 1898* (New York: Oxford University Press, 1999), 206; Nancy S. Seaholes, *Gaining Ground: A History of Land Making in Boston* (Cambridge, Mass.: MIT Press, 2003), 29–32.

14. Joshua Gee to the Council of Trade and Plantations, Oct. 26, 1721, *Calendar of State Papers—Colonial, America and West Indies,* March 1720 to December 1721, vol. 32, 474. John Colman, "The Distressed State of the Town of Boston" (Boston, 1720), in *Colonial Currency Reprints, 1682–1751,* ed. Andrew McFarland Davis (New York: Augustus M. Kelley, 1964), vol. 1, 403. Benjamin Franklin, "A Modest Enquiry into the Nature and Necessity of a Paper Currency" (Philadelphia, 1729), in *Colonial Currency Reprints, 1682–1751,* ed. Andrew McFarland Davis (New York: Augustus M. Kelley, 1964), vol. 2, 338–39. Joseph Goldenberg, *Shipbuilding in Colonial America* (Charlottesville: University Press of Virginia, 1976), 246–47.

15. In England, the skimmington ride was used against those who had violated community norms, but it did not always drive them away. See E. P. Thompson, *Customs in Common: Studies in Traditional Popular Culture* (New York: New Press, 1991), 467–531; Martin Ingram, "Ridings, Rough Music, and the Reform of Popular Culture," *Past and Present* 105 (1984): 79–103. For America, see William Pencak, Matthew Dennis, and Simon Peter Newton, eds., *Riot and Revelry in Early America* (University Park: Pennsylvania State University Press, 2002), 41–124.

16. *Suffolk County Court Records,* April 27, 1675, vol. 2, 602.

17. It is interesting to note that there is strong evidence that young men who accepted public physical correction after legal processes did not suffer ostracism. It was Langworthy's allowing himself to suffer an extralegal indignity that ruined him.

18. Most English shipwright apprenticeships involved several years at sea for this reason; see Philip Banbury, *Shipbuilders of the Thames and Medway* (London: Newton Abbot, 1971).

19. Robert Blair St. George, *Conversing by Signs: Poetics of Implication in Colonial New England Culture* (Chapel Hill: University of North Carolina Press, 1998), 220–21.

20. "The 1677 Petition of the Handycrafts-men of Boston," facsimile reprint, *Bulletin of the Public Library of the City of Boston,* whole ser. 12, no. 95 (Jan. 1894): 305–60. This petition was recently uncovered and analyzed by Robert Blair St. George. My interpretation differs from his, for I see it as a normal part of the continual tension in Boston between growth and control, a sign of the workers' attentiveness to their ideology of work and skill over the reckless use of money to debase skill. In my view, the petition shows the artisans' political power in Boston. St. George regards this as a real crisis of workers' power and mistakenly sees a large gap between the elite and the artisans. But the artisans participated in the elite, especially the shipwrights. The petitioners felt empowered, especially about their selectmen, over whom they wielded political control. St. George did an excellent analysis of the trades of the 126 signers. St. George, *Conversing by Signs,* 222–23.

21. *Suffolk County Deeds*, vol. 10, 132, Deed, July 4, 1677; *Suffolk County Probate Records*, Inventory, February 2, 1677, File #940; *Suffolk County Deeds*, Deed of Partition, December 4, 1684, vol. 13, 222.

22. *Suffolk County Court Records*, Files, #4609, April 5, 1699; #3950, September 12, 1699; #9093, July 7, 1713; #11142, September 21, 1716.

23. *Suffolk County Court Records*, Files, #2851, January 29, 1694. In his deposition, Sears says he is thirty-nine years old, which means he was born in 1655, so he was twenty in 1675 during Langworthy's ride. Great Britain, Public Record Office, *Naval Office Shipping Lists for Massachusetts, 1686–1765* (Microform, East Ardsley, UK: Micro Methods, 1968). *Suffolk County Deeds*, vol. 17, 118, James Barton and Margaret Barton to James Updick. *Suffolk County Court Records*, Files, #2630, September 6, 1691.

24. Interestingly, this is also the theme of Nathaniel Hawthorne's fictional story "My Kinsman, Major Molineux" in *The Complete Works of Nathaniel Hawthorne* (Boston, 1883), 3:641. A relevant interpretation of the story is Bertram Wyatt-Brown, *Southern Honor: Ethics and Behavior in the Old South* (New York: Oxford University Press, 1982), 4–14. Wyatt-Brown ignores the democratic and political economic implications of the story.

25. "Autobiography of Capt. Hector McNeill," *Proceedings of the Massachusetts Historical Society*, November 1921, 59.

26. Ibid., 59–61.

27. Ibid., 61–67.

28. For the suppression of billiards, see *Selectmen Minutes, 1764–1768*, in *A Report of the Record Commissioners of Boston, 1890* (Boston: Rockwell and Churchill, 1889), 147, 262. For an insightful examination of the suppression of the theater in Boston by the town meeting, see Jacqueline Barbara Carr, *After the Siege: A Social History of Boston, 1775–1800* (Boston: Northeastern University Press, 2005), 191–228.

29. Links between masculinity and violence are also discussed in Ann Little, *Abraham in Arms: War and Gender in Colonial New England* (Philadelphia: University of Pennsylvania Press, 2007).

30. Robert S. Rantoul, "Rantoul Genealogy and etc.," *Historical Collections of the Essex Institute* 5, no. 4 (Aug. 1863): 149–50.

31. This Browne may well have been related to the Samuel Browne who rode Langworthy through the streets of Boston.

32. Rantoul, "Rantoul Genealogy and etc.," 149–50.

33. Ibid., 149.

34. Ibid., 149.

35. Ibid., 152.

36. Benjamin Browne, "Some Notes upon Mr. Rantoul's Reminiscences," *Historical Collections of the Essex Institute* 5, no. 5 (October 1863), 201.

37. I disagree that Massachusetts's communities were prototypically "familiar," but recommend Brendon McConville, "Pope's Day Revisited, 'Popular' Culture Reconsidered," in *Explorations in Early American History* 4 (December 2000), 267, 268.

38. See Edmund S. Morgan and Helen Morgan, *The Stamp Act Crisis: Prologue to Revolution* (Chapel Hill: University of North Carolina Press, 1953); Hiller Zobel, *The Boston Massacre* (New York: Norton, 1970); Pauline Maier, *From Resistance to Revolution: Colonial Radicals and the Development of American Opposition to Britain, 1765–1776* (New York: Knopf, 1972); Dirk Hoerder, *Crowd Action in Revolutionary Massachusetts, 1765–1780* (New York: Academic Press, 1977); Jack Tager, *Boston Riots: Three Centuries of Social Violence* (Boston: Northeastern University Press, 2001); Pencak, *Riot and Revelry*, 125–54.

39. Edmund S. Morgan and Helen M. Morgan, *The Stamp Act Crisis: Prologue to Revolution,* revised edition (Chapel Hill: University of North Carolina Press, 1995), 128–35.

40. *Boston Advertiser,* November 9, 1821, and *Columbian Centinel,* November 10, 1821, quoted in Peter Benes, "Night Processions: Celebrating the Gunpowder Plot in England and New England," in *New England Celebrates: Spectacle, Commemoration, and Festivity,* ed. Peter Benes (Boston: Dublin Seminar, 2002), 26, 27; also Benes, "Night Processions," 23.

41. Dr. Edward Reynolds (1793–1881), *Reminiscences and Letters* (Boston, 1931), 36, quoted in Whitehill and Kennedy, *Boston: A Topographical History,* 29. *Columbian Centinel,* November 10, 1821, quoted in Benes, "Night Processions," 28.

42. John Barnard, "Autobiography of the Rev. John Barnard," in *Remarkable Providences 1600–1760,* ed. John P. Demos (New York: George Braziller, 1972), 90–91.

43. Barnard, "Autobiography," 112–18. Kenneth Silverman, *The Life and Times of Cotton Mather* (New York: Harper and Row, 1984), 226.

44. Daniel Vickers and Vince Walsh, *Young Men and the Sea: Yankee Seafarers in the Age of Sail* (New Haven: Yale University Press, 2005), 108–11, 161, 198, 262–63.

45. Cotton Mather, *Diary of Cotton Mather* (New York: F. Ungar, 1957), vol. 1, 323; vol. 2, 58, 73, 120, 209, 446, 447; Cotton Mather, *Magnalia Christi Americana, Books I and II,* ed. Kenneth Murdock (Cambridge, Mass.: Harvard University Press, 1977), 196. Increase (Creasy) did not become a minister, as his father hoped, but aimed to be a merchant. He died at sea as a supercargo between Barbados and Newfoundland. Silverman, *Life and Times of Cotton Mather,* 386–90.

46. Cotton Mather, *Diary,* vol. 2, 631, July 15, 1721: "widows multiply. Marahs to be spoken to."

47. Cotton Mather, "The Boston Ebenezer," in *Magnalia,* ed. Murdock, 180–96; Mather, *Diary,* vol. 1, 256–57. People asked for the lecture's publication.

48. *Calendar of State Papers—Colonial,* vol. 34, 242, 302, 316–17. Cullon, "Colonial Shipwrights," 19–20. Joseph Goldenberg, "An Analysis of Shipbuilding Sites in Lloyd's Register of 1776," *Mariner's Mirror* 59 (1973): 434; Joseph Goldenberg, "Shipbuilding in Colonial America" (Newport News: Mariners' Museum; and Charlottesville: University Press of Virginia, 1976).

CHAPTER 6. RURAL SHIPBUILDING

1. Bernard Bailyn, *Massachusetts Shipping, 1697–1714* (Cambridge, Mass.: Harvard University Press, 1959).

2. Charles F. Carroll, *The Timber Economy of Puritan New England* (Providence, R.I.: Brown University Press, 1975), 137–42; Joseph A. Goldenberg, *Shipbuilding in Colonial America* (Newport News: Mariners Museum; and Charlottesville: University Press of Virginia, 1979), 16; William A. Baker, *Colonial Vessels: Some Seventeenth-Century Sailing Craft* (Barre, Mass.: Barre Publishing Company, 1962), 33; Ian Friel, *The Good Ship: Ships, Shipbuilding and Technology in England, 1200–1520* (Baltimore: Johns Hopkins University Press, 1995), 46–47.

3. *Scituate Town Records*, vol. 3, 125–53. In his introduction, Jeremy Bangs shows how Scituate failed to follow patterns previously thought common to New England.

4. In 1898, a great nor'easter reconfigured the mouth of the river, turning the old outlet into sand dunes and creating a new, shallower opening two and a half miles to the south.

5. Joseph F. Cullon, "Colonial Shipwrights and Their World: Men, Women, and Markets in Early New England" (Ph.D. diss., University of Wisconsin, Madison, 2003), 42–99. Israel Hobart arrived from Hingham in the 1660s, Edward Wanton arrived from Boston about the same time, William Barstow came from Dedham, John Kent came from Charlestown around 1698, and Nathaniel Church settled in 1666. The rest were children of settlers who lived in Scituate before 1650. See L. Vernon Briggs, *History of Shipbuilding on North River, Plymouth County, Massachusetts, 1640–1872* (Boston: Coburn Brothers, 1889). Statistics based on analysis of "The Ship Register, 1697–1714," *Massachusetts Archives*, vol. 7.

6. George D. Langdon, Jr., *Pilgrim Colony: A History of New Plymouth, 1620–1679* (New Haven, Conn.: Yale University Press, 1966), 39–42; Samuel Deane, *History of Scituate, Massachusetts, from its First Settlement to 1831* (Boston: James Loring, 1831), 59–60; *Scituate Town Records*, vol. 3, 349–52.

7. "Secret Workes of a Cruel People Made Manifest" (London, 1659), in *Scituate Town Records*, vol. 3, 417–18.

8. Briggs, *History of Shipbuilding on North River*, 214–19; Deane, *History of Scituate*, 371–77; *Scituate Town Records*, vol. 3, 134–35, 99; Deane, *History of Scituate*, 329; *Scituate Town Records*, vol. 3, 97, 283.

9. *Scituate Town Records*, vol. 3, 159–60.

10. *Scituate Town Records*, vol. 3, 160.

11. *Scituate Town Records*, vol. 3, 191.

12. *Scituate Town Records*, vol. 2, 1–28; vol. 1, 59–63.

13. *Scituate Town Records*, vol. 3, 426–29.

14. *Scituate Town Records*, vol. 3, 430–31.

15. Deane, *History of Scituate*, 119–30; *Scituate Town Records*, vol. 3, 195–97.

16. *Scituate Town Records*, vol. 3, 195; "Journal of the Massachusetts House of Representatives," November 24, 1724, 114.

17. *Scituate Town Records*, vol. 1, 63.

18. For a definition of a "competency," see Daniel Vickers, *Farmers and Fishermen: Two Centuries of Work in Essex County, Massachusetts, 1630–1830* (Chapel Hill: University of North Carolina Press, 1994), 14–21.

19. *Scituate Town Records*, vol. 3, 197.

20. *Scituate Town Records*, vol. 3, 197, 207–8, 245.

21. *Scituate Town Records*, vol. 3, 207–8, 219, 501, 503.

22. *Scituate Town Records*, vol. 3, 227; Deane, *History of Scituate*, 88; *Scituate Town Records*, 387.

23. *Scituate Town Records*, vol. 3, 453; petition of western Scituate families, *Massachusetts Archives*, reel 113, 682.

24. *Suffolk County Court Records*, File #19809, 1726.

25. For current ratios of rents to wages, see Barbara Ehrenreich, *Nickel and Dimed: On (Not) Getting by in America* (New York: Henry Holt, 2001).

26. Gillian Wagner, *Thomas Coram, Gent., 1668–1751* (Woodbridge, UK: Boydell Press, 2004).

27. As quoted in Hamilton Andrews Hill, "Thomas Coram in Boston and Taunton," *Collections of the American Antiquarian Society* 8 (April 1892), 133–34; Wagner, *Thomas Coram*, 19–29.

28. This is the view of Gillian Wagner and Hamilton Hill.

29. They had first worked at Lynn/Saugus; James later moved to New Jersey, and Henry set up elsewhere in Massachusetts. Samuel Hopkins Emery, *History of Taunton, Massachusetts* (Syracuse, N.Y.: Mason, 1893), 613–21.

30. *Suffolk County Court Records*, File #5474.

31. *Suffolk County Court Records*, File #6183; see also #5471.

32. *Suffolk County Court Records*, Files #5471, #5474, #5475, #6183.

33. Thomas Coram to Benjamin Colman, London, July 9, 1737, in "Letters of Thomas Coram," *Proceedings of the Massachusetts Historical Society* (October 1922), 36–37.

34. *Suffolk County Court Records*, File #24739; #5475; #6183.

35. Hill, 141–42, 135. "Thomas Coram of London to the Reverend Benjamin Colman, July 9, 1737," in "Letters of Thomas Coram," *Proceedings of the Massachusetts Historical Society* (October 1922), 36–37.

36. "The Ship Register, 1697–1714," Massachusetts Archives, vol. 7; Bailyn, *Massachusetts Shipping*; *1786 Tax Valuations*, Massachusetts Archives, vols. 162, 163.

37. Joshua Hempstead, *Diary of Joshua Hempstead of New London, Connecticut* (New London: New London County Historical Society, 1901), 6, 468, 218, 474.

38. Ebenezer Parkman, *The Diary of Ebenezer Parkman, 1703–1782: First Part: 1719–1755*, ed. Francis Walett (Worcester, Mass.: American Antiquarian Society, 1974), 60, 61; *1786 Tax Valuations*.

39. Asa G. Sheldon, *Yankee Drover, Being the Unpretending Life of Asa Sheldon, 1788–1870* (Hanover, N.H.: University Press of New England, 1988), 11–12.

CHAPTER 7. CREWS

1. Peter Earle, *The Treasure of the Concepcion* (New York: Viking, 1980); Cotton Mather, *The Life of Sir William Phips* (Boston, 1697; repr. New York: Covici-Friede, 1929), 31–32.

2. Mather, *Life of Sir William Phips*, 60; Emerson W. Baker and John G. Reid, *The New England Knight: Sir William Phips, 1651–1695* (Toronto: University of Toronto Press, 1998), 178–201.

3. Marcus Rediker, *Between the Devil and the Deep Blue Sea: Merchant Seamen, Pirates, and the Anglo-American Maritime World* (Cambridge, Mass.: Cambridge University Press, 1993).

4. The best portrait of New England's mariner work force is Daniel Vickers with Vince Walsh, *Young Men and the Sea: Yankee Seafarers in the Age of Sail* (New Haven, Conn.: Yale University Press, 2005). However, Vickers and Walsh ignore political economy. Aside from Rediker, works that see sailors as political beings include Jesse Lemisch, *Jack Tar vs. John Bull: The Role of New York's Seamen in Precipitating the Revolution* (New York: Routledge, 1997).

5. "Petition of the Agents for the British Sugar Colonies in America," April 9, 1746, *Journals of the House of Commons* (London: House of Commons, 1803), vol. 25 (Oct. 17, 1745 to Nov. 21, 1750), 117.

6. Bernard Bailyn and Lotte Bailyn, *Massachusetts Shipping, 1697–1714: A Statistical Study* (Cambridge, Mass.: Harvard University Press, 1959), 42–45, 94–97. In 1716, there were seven tons to each crew member on most vessels, increasing to some ten tons per crew member by 1770; see James T. Shepherd and Gary M. Walton, *Shipping, Maritime Trade, and the Economic Development of Colonial North America* (Cambridge: Cambridge University Press, 1972), 196–97. My own estimates are conservative; Boston was not the only New England port, and the coasting trade has not been counted. *Historical Statistics of the United States: Colonial Times to 1970* (Washington, D.C.: U.S. Bureau of the Census, 1975), vol. 2, 1179.

7. W. Jeffrey Bolster, *Black Jacks: African American Seamen in the Age of Sail* (Cambridge, Mass.: Harvard University Press, 1977), 27, 235–38; Daniel Vickers, "The First Whalemen of Nantucket," in *After King Philip's War: Presence and Persistence in Indian New England*, ed. Colin G. Calloway (Hanover, N.H.: Dartmouth College and University Press of New England, 1997), 90–113. I agree that Indians and the poor were exploited and coerced into maritime labor, but the major contribution came from the sons of middling white families. The 1840 census, the first to list some occupations, recorded that some 75 percent of all citizen blue-water mariners lived in New England. See *Compendium of the Enumeration of the Inhabitants and Statistics of the United States . . . from the Returns of the Sixth Census* (Washington, D.C.: Blair and Rives, 1841), 99. For a different view, see Paul A. Gilje, *Liberty on the Waterfront: American Maritime Culture in the Age of Revolution* (Philadelphia: University of Pennsylvania Press, 2004), 26. However, the dominance of New England sailors even in New York City by 1820 is demonstrated also in Robert Greenhalgh Albion, *Square-Riggers on Schedule: The New York Sailing Packets to England, France, and the Cotton Ports* (Princeton, 1938; repr. New York: Archon, 1965), esp. 331–44.

8. See Barry Levy, "Girls and Boys: Poor Children and the Labor Market in Colonial Massachusetts," *Pennsylvania History* 64, Special Supplemental Issue (Summer 1997): 287–305.

9. *Report of the Record Commissioners*, vol. 29, 230–70.

10. Bernard Bailyn, *Voyagers to the West: A Passage in the Peopling of America on the Eve of the Revolution* (New York: Knopf, 1986), 213. *Report of the Record Commissioners*, vol. 29, 230–70.

11. *Report of the Record Commissioners*, vol. 15, 96–100.

12. Ibid., vol. 17, 17.

13. "The Journals of Ashley Bowen," *Publications of the Massachusetts Historical Society* (Boston: Colonial Society of Massachusetts, 1973) vol. 1, 5, 7, 8, 9.

14. Ibid., 14–19.

15. Ibid., 13, 16.

16. Ibid., 15, 21.

17. Ibid., 29.

18. "Letters of Thomas Coram," *Proceedings of the Massachusetts Historical Society* 56, (1922): 15–56.

19. The period 1770–1774 was chosen in order to collate the probate records with the well-indexed 1771 Massachusetts assessment of wealth. If a mariner's surname was shared by ten individuals in that assessment and was not Smith or Jones, I judged the family to be an older Massachusetts family. I also checked the names against the birth and marriage records in Boston as well as the immigrant list for the port of Boston and Boston selectmen records. The probate records are also helpful. Some newcomers gave part of their estates to people in Ireland or other American colonies. I was able to compile three or four items of information about every individual.

20. George Walter Chamberlain, "The Bryant Family," *New England Historical and Genealogical Register* 96 (October 1942): 321–27; 97 (January 1943): 43–51.

21. *Suffolk County Probate Records*; William A. Baker, *A History of the Boston Marine Society, 1742–1981*, 2nd ed. (Boston: The Society, 1982).

22. I compared 128 married laborers and tradesmen and seventy-three married mariners who left estates between 1759 and 1772. At the ages from twenty-one years to thirty-nine years, forty married tradesmen estates averaged £184 with the median being £28.5, while at the same ages forty-nine married mariners averaged £106 with the median being £29. Men with inventories and those without were included. Among men who died between the ages of forty and fifty, the tradesmen estates averaged £189 with the median being £60, while the mariners' estates averaged twice the wealth £308 with the median £60. The tradesmen included twenty-five housewrights, fourteen cordwainers, twelve laborers, twelve tailors, eleven shipwrights, eleven blacksmiths, ten coopers, eight braziers, seven sailmakers, five tallow chandlers, five glaziers, five ropemakers, five caulkers, and five bakers. Clearly, the wages of mariners should be considered in relation to their age. Most mariners, especially town-born or Massachusetts-born mariners, were common mariners only in their early twenties and became mates and captains in their mid-twenties. These men got much of their income from their trading privileges and received higher wages. Death, not poverty, was the main problem these men faced, though poverty was an issue for their widows. *Suffolk County Probate Records; Boston Records:* Marriages, vol.

28, 30. Gary B. Nash, *The Urban Crucible: Social Change, Political Consciousness, and the Origins of the American Revolution* (Cambridge, Mass.: Harvard University Press, 1979), 64.

23. *Beverly Vital Records, Manchester Vital Records*; "Salem Custom District Crew Lists," 1803, 1807.

24. *Massachusetts and Maine Direct Tax Census of 1798*, microfilm edition (Boston: New England Historic Genealogical Society, 1979), vol. 7, 2–82.

25. In 1803 and 1807 there were at least forty-two mates, a third of all the mates studied, who were between the ages of twenty and twenty-four years. "Salem Custom District Crew Lists," 1803, 1807, National Archives, Waltham, Mass.

26. My findings agree significantly with Vickers and Walsh, *Young Men and the Sea.*

27. "Salem Custom District Crew Lists," 1803, 1807; *Vital Records of Salem; Beverly; Ipswich; Manchester; Danvers*; "Ship Registers of the District of Salem and Beverly, 1789–1900," ed. A. Frank Hitchins, *Historical Collections of the Essex Institute* 39 (1903): 185–208; 40 (1904): 49–72, 177–200, 217–40, 321–36; 41 (1905): 141–64, 309–32, 357–80; 42 (1906): 89–110; "Entry Book, Import Book, Registers, Port of Marblehead, Massachusetts," ed. Francis B. C. Bradlee, *Historical Collections of the Essex Institute* 64 (1928): 82–96, 161–76, 365–80, 273–88; 65 (1929): 73–88, 193–208, 387–402, 563–78.

28. *Boston Selectmen Records*, vol. 19, 101. Cornelius Halstrom, probate, March 21, 1760, File #12300; Alexander Anderson, Boston, mariner, probate, January 23, 1761, File #12567; both *Suffolk County Probate Records.*

29. Carl Van Doren, ed., *The Letters of Benjamin Franklin and Jane Mecom* (Princeton, N.J.: Princeton University Press, 1950), 140.

30. Analysis based on the study of 1,158 deceased Boston mariners and their administrators, executors, executrixes, and their estates between 1750–1809, *Suffolk County Probate Records*. Rediker, *Between the Devil and the Deep Blue Sea.*

31. *The Burghers of New Amsterdam and the Freeman of New York, 1675–1866*, in *Collections of the New York Historical Society for the Year 1885* (New York: New-York Historical Society, 1886); the New York City probate records are discussed below.

32. *Abstract of Wills on File in the Surrogate Office of New York*, vols. 4–6: 1740–1766, *Collections of the New York Historical Society* 1895–1897 (New York: New-York Historical Society, 1896–1898).

33. Ibid., vol. 4, 52, 195.

34. Graham Russell Hodges, *New York City Cartmen, 1667–1850* (New York: New York University Press, 1988); Lemisch, *Jack Tar v. John Bull*, 23–25.

35. Lemisch, *Jack Tar vs. John Bull.*

36. Nathaniel A. M. Rodger, *The Wooden World: Anatomy of the Georgian Navy*, 2nd ed. (London: Collins, 1986).

37. Trelawny to Newcastle, July 29, 1742, Colonial Office, 137/37, as quoted in R. Pares, "The Manning of the Navy in the West Indies, 1702–1763," *Transactions of the Royal Historical Society*, 4th ser., 20 (1937): 45. Trelawny is a believable witness. Educated at Westminster School from 1713 to 1717, he matriculated at Christ Church, Oxford, and

served two terms in Parliament. At the age of sixty, he left England and became Governor of Jamaica, where he quieted the Maroon Wars and served longer than any other colonial governor. Frank Cundall, *Governors of Jamaica in the Eighteenth Century* (London: West India Committee, 1937), 171–73. Dora Mae Clark, "The Impressment of Seamen in the American Colonies," *Essays in Colonial History Presented to Charles McLean Andrews by His Students* (1931; repr. Freeport, N.Y.: Books for Libraries Press, 1966), 198–224.

38. Duncan Crewe, *Yellow Jack and the Worm: British Naval Administration in the West Indies, 1739–1748* (Liverpool: Liverpool University Press, 1993), 72–77.

39. Warrant of Jonathan Belcher, March 1741, 94; Memorandum of Richard Foster, Middlesex County, Sheriff, April 3, 1741, 163; both in *Massachusetts Archives*, vol. 64 (Maritime).

40. "The Humble Petition of Jeremiah Simpson, Master of the sloop, Three Friends, a coasting vessel to his Excellency William Shirley, Esq.," March 19, 1741, *Massachusetts Archives*, vol. 64 (Maritime): 168–69.

41. "The Humble Petition of Sundry Inhabitants of the Town of Boston, March, 1741," *Massachusetts Archives*, vol. 64 (Maritime): 177–79.

42. Jill Lepore, *New York Burning: Liberty, Slavery, and Conspiracy in Eighteenth-Century Manhattan* (New York: Knopf, 2005); "The Memorial of James Scott, Commander of His Majestys Ship, The *Astrea*," June 1741, *Massachusetts Archives*, vol. 64 (Maritime): 98.

43. "Deposition of Benjamin Hallowell, Boston, April 20, 1749," *Suffolk County Court Records*, File #65550.

44. "William Shirley to Josiah Willard, November 19, 1747," *Correspondence of William Shirley, Governor of Massachusetts and Military Commander in America, 1731–1760*, ed. Charles Henry Lincoln (New York: Macmillan, 1912), vol. 1, 406–9. See also John Lax and William Pancak, "The Knowles Riot and the Crisis of the 1740s in Massachusetts," *Perspectives in American History* 10 (1976): 163–216; Nash, *The Urban Crucible*, 222–23; Denver Alexander Brunsman, "The Knowles Atlantic Impressment Riots of the 1740s," *Early American Studies* 5, no. 2 (Fall 2007): 324–66.

45. Pauline Maier, "Popular Uprisings and Civil Authority in Eighteenth-Century America," *William and Mary Quarterly,* 3rd ser., 27, no. 1 (January 1970): 3–35; William Shirley to the Lords of Trade, December 1, 1747, *Correspondence*, vol. 1, 418.

46. "Deposition of Joseph Ballard, August, 1749," *Suffolk County Court Records*, File #65550.

47. Philo Nauticus (Vice-Admiral Charles Knowles), "A Proposal for the Encouragement of Seamen (1758)," in *The Manning of the Royal Navy: Selected Public Pamphlets 1693–1873*, ed. J. S. Bromley (London: Navy Records Society, 1974), 104–13.

48. *Rex v. Corbet* 1769, in L. Kinvin Wroth and Hiller B. Zobel, eds., *The Legal Papers of John Adams* (Cambridge, Mass.: Harvard University Press, 1965), vol. 2, 276–83.

49. Ibid., 305–6; 276–83. *Marblehead Vital Records; Salem Vital Records*.

50. The English ministry's intense and special hatred for Massachusetts and New England, whom they sometimes described as "levellers," is described in Julie Flavell, "Brit-

ish Perceptions of New England and the Decision for a Coercive Colonial Policy, 1774–1775," in Julie Flavell and Stephen Conway, eds., *Britain and America Go to War: The Impact of War and Warfare in Anglo-America, 1754–1815* (Gainesville: University Press of Florida, 2004), 95–115.

CHAPTER 8. ORPHANS

Note to epigraph: Asa Sheldon, *Yankee Drover: Being the Unpretending Life of Asa Sheldon, Farmer, Trader, and Working Man, 1788–1870,* foreword by John Seelye (Woburn, Mass.: E. T. Moody, 1862; repr. Hanover, N.H.: University Press of New England, 1988), 13.

1. Studies of New England's patriarchal households include Philip J. Greven, Jr., *Four Generations: Population, Land, and Family in Colonial Andover, Massachusetts* (Ithaca, N.Y.: Cornell University Press, 1970); Kenneth Lockridge, *A New England Town: The First Hundred Years* (New York: Norton, 1970); John Demos, *A Little Commonwealth: Family Life in Plymouth Colony* (New York: Oxford University Press, 1970). The classic work on prescriptive ideas about domestic relationships is Edmund S. Morgan, *The Puritan Family: Religion and Domestic Relations in Seventeenth-Century New England* (Boston: Boston Public Library, 1944; repr. New York: Harper Torchbooks, 1966). Among dissenters in regard to patriarchy are Roger Thompson, *Sex in Middlesex: Popular Mores in a Massachusetts County, 1649–1699* (Amherst: University of Massachusetts Press, 1986); Roger Thompson, *Divided We Stand: Watertown, Massachusetts, 1630–1680* (Amherst: University of Massachusetts Press, 2001); Toby L. Ditz, *Property and Kinship: Inheritance in Early Connecticut, 1750–1820* (Princeton, N.J.: Princeton University Press, 1986).

2. Perry Miller, *The New England Mind: The Seventeenth Century* (Cambridge, Mass.: Harvard University Press, 1939).

3. *Boston Records,* vol. 7, 67.

4. Ibid., vol. 11, 62, 221.

5. *Watertown Records,* vol. 1, 104–5; *Dedham Records,* vol. 4, 197; *Dorchester Records,* vol. 4, 236.

6. *Watertown Records,* vol. 1, 71. In 1665, "the selectmen agreed that they would go two and two together to go throw the town to examine how children are taught to read and instructed in the grounds of religion and the capital laws"; in 1679, "also the selectmen agreed to go two by two through the whole town to see that all children and youth under family government be in all respects brought up as the law doth require"; *Watertown Records,* vol. 1, 86, 145. See also vol. 1, 114.

7. *Boston Evening Post,* American Antiquarian Society series.

8. *Boston Records,* vol. 8, 173–74.

9. Sarah Goodhue, "Valedictory and Monitory Writing (1681)," in *Ipswich in the Massachusetts Bay Colony,* ed. Thomas Franklin Waters (Ipswich, Mass.: Ipswich Historical Society, 1905–17), appendix F, vol. 1, 519–24. For Goodhue and Whipple genealogy and

record, see Joseph B. Felt, *History of Ipswich, Essex, and Hamilton* (Cambridge, Mass., 1834).

10. David Perry, "Recollections of an Old Soldier," *Magazine of History* 137 (1928): 1–10.

11. Ashley Bowen, *The Journals of Ashley Bowen (1728–1813) of Marblehead*, ed. Philip Foster Smith (Boston: Colonial Society of Massachusetts, 1973), vol. 1; Charles Tyng, *Before the Wind: The Memoir of an American Sea Captain*, ed. Susan Fels (New York: Penguin, 1999), 4.

12. Edmund Quincy, *Life of Josiah Quincy of Massachusetts* (Boston: Ticknor and Fields, 1868), 19–27; Matthew Crocker, *The Magic of the Many: Josiah Quincy and the Rise of Mass Politics in Boston, 1800–1830* (Amherst: University of Massachusetts Press, 1999).

13. William Bentley, *The Diary of William Bentley, Pastor of the East Church, Salem, Massachusetts* (Salem: Essex Institute, 1905–14), vol. 1, 29; vol. 4, 295–96.

14. *Deerfield Vital Records; Marblehead Vital Records; Marlborough Vital Records; Beverly Vital Records; Haverhill Vital Records; Malden Vital Records; Newton Vital Records; Oxford Vital Records; Rowley Vital Records; Shrewsbury; Salem Vital Records; Topsfield Vital Records; Gloucester Vital Records.* All of these volumes alphabetize births, marriages, and deaths, facilitating family reconstitution. I included men who were recorded as having married, had children, and died in the town. This method underestimates the number of orphans and half-orphans, for it focuses on the stable part of the population. Men who married and moved to another town are not included. Presumably this category includes poorer men, who were more likely to die young. This method also underestimates the number of children who lost both a father and mother in childhood. Consider, for example, a man who married and died in a town and left a child, but the child's widowed mother moved to another town (as many did) and then died herself. The orphan is still a minor, and now has lost both parents. This method fails to catch this woman's death and counts this orphan erroneously as a half-orphan, a fatherless child. The conservative bias is this method ensures that the statistics indicate the minimum, not a maximum, number of orphans.

15. This misconception is repeated in Gary Nash, *The Urban Crucible: Social Change, Political Consciousness, and the Origins of the American Revolution* (Cambridge, Mass.: Harvard University Press, 1979), 22, 58–60, 65–66, 72, 74, 166, and corrected in Richard Buel, *In Irons: Britain's Naval Supremacy and the American Revolutionary Economy* (New Haven: Yale University Press, 1998).

16. For another study of orphans' fortunes, see Jackson Turner Main, *Society and Economy in Colonial Connecticut* (Princeton, N.J.: Princeton University Press, 1985), 190–92.

17. This finding is confirmed by Jackson T. Main. See also Gloria L. Main and Jackson T. Main, "The Red Queen in New England?" *William and Mary Quarterly*, 3rd ser., 56, no. 1 (January 1999): 121–50. Quakers in the Delaware Valley began limiting the size of their families in the eighteenth century. Robert Wells, *Revolutions in American's Lives: A Demographic Perspective on the History of Americans, Their Families, and Their*

Society (Westport, Conn.: Greenwood Press, 1982); Gloria L. Main, *Peoples of a Spacious Land: Families and Cultures in Colonial New England* (Cambridge, Mass.: Harvard University Press, 2001).

18. Samuel Adams to James Warren, Boston, April 13, 1772, *Warren-Adams Letters*, vol. 1, *1743–1777* (Boston: Massachusetts Historical Society, 1917), 10–11.

19. Ebenezer Parkman, *The Diary of Ebenezer Parkman, 1703–1783*, ed. Francis G. Walett (Worcester, Mass.: American Antiquarian Society, 1974), part 1, 8–9.

20. Ibid., 8–32.

21. Lawrence W. Towner, "The Indentures of Boston's Poor Apprentices, 1734–1805," *Publications of the Colonial Society of Massachusetts*, vol. 43, *Transactions: 1956–1963* (Boston, 1966): 417–68. The genealogical information was gathered from Lucius A. Page, *History of Hardwick, Massachusetts* (Boston: Houghton Mifflin, 1883), and *Hardwick Vital Records. 1771 Tax Valuation List, Massachusetts*, 309–10; David W. Conroy, *In Public Houses: Drink and the Revolution of Authority in Colonial Massachusetts* (Chapel Hill: University of North Carolina Press, 1996), 286.

22. Page, *History of Hardwick*; *1771 Tax Valuation List, Massachusetts*, 308–10; *Hardwick Vital Records*.

23. The sources and analysis are described below in note 32.

24. *Dedham Records*, vol. 5, 118, 120–22.

25. Ibid.

26. Ibid., 122–24.

27. Orlando Patterson, *Slavery and Social Death* (Cambridge, Mass.: Harvard University Press, 1982).

28. James Kences, "Some Unexplored Relationships of Essex County Witchcraft to the Indian Wars of 1675 and 1689," *Essex Institute Historical Collections* 120, no. 3 (1984): 179–212; Mary Beth Norton, *In the Devil's Snare: The Salem Witchcraft Crisis of 1692* (New York: Knopf, 2002).

29. Barry Levy, "Girls and Boys: Poor Children and the Labor Market in Colonial Massachusetts," *Pennsylvania History* 64, Special Supplemental Issue (Summer 1997): 287–307. This article contains additional analysis of Massachusetts orphans.

30. Joshua Hempstead, *Diary of Joshua Hempstead*, 59, 61.

31. John Murray and Ruth Wallis Herndon, "Markets for Children in Early America: A Political Economy of Pauper Apprenticeship," *Journal of Economic History* 62, no. 2 (June 2002): 365–67. This important article reveals great differences in the regimes in various colonies; Massachusetts had the largest and best supervised market in poor child laborers.

32. Based on Lawrence Towner's compilation, I reconstituted 124 families in six diverse Massachusetts towns. Selection was based on the existence of good vital records that would allow the host family, designated in Towner's list, to be fully described: marriage, other children, deaths. The towns included West Bridgewater, East Bridgewater, Bridgewater, Marblehead, Hardwick, Roxbury. *West Bridgewater Vital Records; East Bridgewater Vital Records; Marblehead Vital Records; Hardwick Vital Records; Roxbury Vital*

Records; Lawrence W. Towner, "The Indentures of Boston's Poor Apprentices, 1734–1805," *Publications of the Colonial Society of Massachusetts*, vol. 43, *Transactions: 1956–1963* (Boston, 1966), 417–68.

33. *Hardwick Vital Records*; Towner, "Indentures of Boston's Poor Apprentices."

34. *1771 Tax Valuation List.*

35. *West Bridgewater Vital Records*; *East Bridgewater Vital Records*; *Bridgewater Vital Records.*

36. Towner, "Indentures of Boston's Poor Apprentices"; *1771 Tax Valuation List*; *Marblehead Vital Records.*

37. *1771 Tax Valuation List*; *Roxbury Vital Records.* Joseph Mayo served as foreman of the jury that tried the soldiers in the Boston Massacre. A veteran of the French and Indian War, he was also an ardent Patriot and died while serving in the Continental Army.

38. Rufus Putnam, *The Memoirs of Rufus Putnam* (Boston: Houghton Mifflin, 1903), 9–11.

39. He actually ran away in 1766 and returned, but renegotiated his service contract with Fowle. Fowle later helped finance Thomas.

40. In addition to death, town institutions were vital toward handling sickness, a topic whose social implications are well discussed in Ben Mutschler, "The Province of Affliction: Illness in New England, 1690–1820" (Ph.D. diss., Columbia University, 2000). He shows that households alone could not handle the problem.

41. *List of Persons Whose Names Have Been Changed in Massachusetts, 1780–1883* (Boston, 1885), 144. *An Index to Changes of Name Under Authority of Act of Parliament or Royal License and Including Irregular Changes from 1 George III to 64 Victoria, 1760–1901*, ed. W. Phillimore and E. A. Fry (Baltimore: Genealogical Publishing Company, 1968). For the legal foundation, see Jamil Zainaldin, "The Emergence of a Modern American Family Law: Child Custody, Adoption, and the Courts," *Northwestern University School of Law* 73 (1979): 1033–89; Michael Grossberg, *Governing the Hearth: Law and the Family in Nineteenth-Century America* (Chapel Hill: University of North Carolina Press, 1985), chapter 7.

42. Harriet Beecher Stowe, *Oldtown Folks*, ed. Henry May (Cambridge, Mass.: Harvard University Press, 1966), 145, 160.

CHAPTER 9. PRODIGALS OR MILQUETOASTS?

1. Thomas Shepard, "Eye-salve, or, A watch-word from our Lord Jesus Christ unto his churches, especially those within the colony of the Massachusetts in New-England" (Cambridge, Mass.: Printed by Samuel Green, 1672).

2. Philip J. Greven, Jr., *Four Generations: Population, Land, and Family in Colonial Andover, Massachusetts* (Ithaca, N.Y.: Cornell University Press, 1970), 83–84, 126.

3. Allan Kulikoff, *From British Peasants to Colonial Farmers* (Chapel Hill: University of North Carolina Press, 2000), 239. See also Daniel Vickers, *Farmers and Fishermen: Two*

Centuries of Work in Essex County, Massachusetts, 1630–1850 (Chapel Hill: University of North Carolina Press, 1994), 64–77.

4. For the dominance of family labor, see Vickers, *Farmers and Fishermen*, 237–59. Winifred Barr Rothenberg's analysis of account books contains ample evidence showing the importance of hired labor on Massachusetts farms. She found that hired labor was almost always confined to town inhabitants: "Out of 1,810 names of men doing farm work, there are many who appeared in more than one farmer's book, but only four who appeared in the books of farmers in different towns." Winifred Barr Rothenberg, *From Market-Places to a Market Economy: The Transformation of Rural Massachusetts, 1750–1850* (Chicago: University of Chicago Press, 1992), 164.

5. Richard S. Dunn, "Servants and Slaves: The Recruitment and Employment of Labor," in *Colonial British America: Essays in the New History of the Early Modern Era*, ed. Jack P. Greene and J. R. Pole (Baltimore: Johns Hopkins University Press, 1984), 187. Ebenezer Parkman, *The Diary of Ebenezer Parkman, 1703–1783*, ed. Francis Walett (Worcester, Mass.: American Antiquarian Society, 1974), vol. 1, 187–88.

6. Ebenezer Parkman, *Diary*, vol. 1, 248, 256, 261, 248.

7. Ibid., 264, 290–310. Parkman hired some town-born farm workers who lived in.

8. Abner Sanger, *Very Poor and of a Lo Make, The Journal of Abner Sanger*, ed. Lois K. Stabler (Portsmouth, N.H.: Historical Society of Cheshire County, 1986). A similar pattern of town over family labor is seen in Matthew Patten, *The Diary of Matthew Patten of Bedford, N.H., from 1754 to 1788* (Rockport, Me.: Picton Press, 1993), and especially in Joshua Hempstead, *Diary of Joshua Hempstead of New London, Connecticut, 1711–1758* (New London, Conn.: New London County Historical Society, 1901). Hempstead rarely worked with his sons, compared to town labor, and knew little about their upcoming marriages, which he graciously accepted.

9. The quintessential work is Jay Fliegelman, *Prodigals and Pilgrims: The American Revolution Against Patriarchal Authority, 1750–1800* (New York: Cambridge University Press, 1982).

10. Kenneth A. Lockridge, *A New England Town: The First Hundred Years: Dedham, Massachusetts, 1636–1736* (New York: Norton, 1970).

11. My impression is that households paid a surprisingly large part of their annual income to their towns and province, but this matter needs further study. An innovative use of tax lists is Paul Clemens and Lucy Simler, "Rural Labor and the Farm Household in Chester County Pennsylvania, 1750–1820," in *Work and Labor in Early America*, ed. Stephen Innes (Chapel Hill: University of North Carolina Press, Chapel Hill, 1988), 144–88. *General Laws of Massachusetts*, 85.

12. *Acts and Resolves of Massachusetts Bay: Acts 1710–1711*, 634. Analyses of Watertown, Boston, and Dedham town records, including selectmen's minutes, show that this act was rarely, if ever, enforced; it is not clear whether young folk simply complied, or the law was ignored.

13. In a study of sixty-six Dedham men between 1710 and 1748, six men (9 percent) appeared on the tax lists for the first time at between the ages of nineteen and twenty

years; forty-five men (68 percent) appeared on the tax lists for the first time at between the ages of twenty-one to twenty-five years; and fifteen men (23 percent) appeared at age twenty-six years and older. No man appeared at an age older than thirty-five years. *Dedham Town Records* for 1710, 1711, 1714, 1716, 1723, 1724, 1727, 1729, 1731, 1735, 1738, 1740, 1744, and 1748.

14. *Acts and Resolves: Acts 1718* (Boston, 1893), 84. The annual bill usually exempted schoolmasters from all taxes.

15. A total of 3,195 Dedham people were studied between 1710 and 1748. See note 13 above for sources, and note 19 below.

16. This is clearly illustrated in the *Diary* of Joshua Hempstead, who worked for many town folk while his family was young. The period was for about twenty years after marriage. See Joshua Hempstead, *The Diary of Joshua Hempstead.*

17. *1771 Tax Valuations*, 122–25. The following discussion is based on an analysis of the Dedham list.

18. Robert Brand Hanson, ed., *The Deacon's Book: Records of the First Church, Dedham, Massachusetts, 1677–1737* (Bowie, Md.: Heritage Books, 1990).

19. I studied the tax lists from the Dedham town records in 1710, 1711, 1714, 1716, 1723, 1724, 1727, 1729, 1731, 1735, 1738, 1740, 1744, and 1748, entering all names in a relational database with their provincial tax, including polls, tax of personal wealth, and tax on real estate. Since the basis for evaluating taxes changed each year, I collated the lists by getting the average tax paid on each item in that year, then finding whether an individual paid the tax and discerning his exact position in reference to that average. This method allows a relatively accurate way of tracing the relative fortunes of individuals over time. *Dedham Records*, vol. 6, 19–23, 55–59, 78–83, 89–92, 128–32, 134–56, 166–70, 180–85, 224–29, 247–52, 275–79, 287–92, 324–29, 336–41, 360–65; vol. 7, 31–38, 88–96, 121–28, 134–38, 159–66.

20. *Dedham Town Records*, vol. 6, 346–47; Thomas Aldridge's Inventory, October 24, 1760, *Suffolk County Probate Records*, File #11947.

21. "When the elder Joseph Belcher died in 1723, it was said that 'twas the miscarriages of his family that killed that man of singular worth'." Quoted in Clifford Shipton, *Biographical Sketches of Those who Attended Harvard College*, vol. 4, *Class of 1690* (Boston: Massachusetts Historical Society, 1942), 165. *Suffolk County Probate Records*, 1726, File #5188; *Suffolk County Court Records*, Files #49305, #49182, #49344. Settlement Deed, May 5, 1732, *Suffolk County Deeds*, Book 58, 273. *Dedham Vital Records*, 495. Gill Belcher the laborer should not be confused with Gill Belcher the sea captain, who lived at the same time and retained more property.

22. *Suffolk County Court Records*, File #67839, contains a deed of exchange of June 12, 1723, between Amos Fisher, Dedham and Samuel Chickering, in which Chickering gave land and got land and money in return.

23. *Dedham Town Records*, vol. 6, 331.

24. Joseph Dean's administration and inventory, 1722, *Suffolk County Probate Records*, File #4558; Settlement, April 29, 1731, *Suffolk County Probate Records*, vol. 29, 3;

Suffolk County Court Records, File #6128; *Dedham Vital Records*, 570. I am indebted to Marla Miller for pointing out Faxon Dean's career as a clothier in Hadley, Massachusetts, from her study of the Porter-Phelps Papers.

25. *Dedham Vital Records*, 505; Will and Inventory of Thomas Dean, November 2, 1745, *Suffolk County Probate Records*, File #8412.

26. *Suffolk County Deeds*, Book 72, 174.

27. Barry Levy, *Quakers and the American Family: British Settlement in the Delaware Valley, 1650–1790* (New York: Oxford University Press, 1988).

28. See note 18 for methods and sources.

29. Daniel Draper to Timothy Draper, *Suffolk County Deeds*, vol. 56, 108.

30. *Dedham Town Records*, vol. 7, 159–166.

31. John Fuller, yeoman, to Hezekiah Fuller, October 7, 1709, *Suffolk County Deeds*, vol. 24, 238; *Dedham Town Records*, vol. 6, 261, 184, 346, 382, 206; vol. 7, 219.

32. William Bullard to Isaac Bullard, April 7, 1731, *Suffolk County Deeds*, vol. 65, 197; *Dedham Town Records*, vol. 7, 335.

33. Will of Ebenezer Ellis, November 27, 1732, *Suffolk County Probate Records*, File #6321.

34. *Dedham Town Records*, vol. 7, 115, 117, 333.

35. Will of John Draper, 1749, *Suffolk County Probate Records*, File #9250.

36. For sources and methods, see note 19 above.

37. Will of Jonathan Metcalfe, 1727, *Suffolk County Probate Records*, File #5453.

38. Ibid.

39. *Dedham Town Records*, vol. 6, 367, 369, 371, 380, 232, 241, 140, 355, 357.

40. Edward Richards to Josiah Richards, March 16, 1746, *Suffolk County Deeds*, vol. 78, 152. Benjamin Gay, innholder, to Josiah Richards, December 12, 1745, and September 28, 1749, *Suffolk County Deeds*, vol. 78, 152. It is easy to document many sons buying land during their twenties and thirties.

41. *Dedham Town Records*, vol. 7, 98, 117.

42. Jonathan Fuller to Samuel Fuller, March 3, 1717, *Suffolk County Deeds*, vol. 49, 226.

43. See note 19 for sources and methods.

44. *Dedham Vital Records*, 489–567.

45. The numbers are as follows: between 1690 and 1719, there were twenty-eight announced visitors, of whom twenty-six were warned out, and of those only two later left any record; between 1720 and 1749, there were seventy-seven announced visitors, of whom forty were warned out and nine later left a record; between 1750 and 1779 there were 287 visitors, of whom 124 were warned out, and of these sixty-four later left a record in the town; and between 1780 and 1795 there were 181 announced visitors, of whom 107 were warned out, and of these forty-two later left a record. Dedham became more open, yet chances of being warned out remained above 50 percent even in the last quarter of the eighteenth century. *Dedham Town Records; Dedham Vital Records*.

46. *Dedham Vital Records*. The stayers and leavers were determined by collating them with vital records, church records, and tax lists. *General Laws of Massachusetts*, 134.

47. *Dedham Vital Records*, 556, 279, 508, 613, 556.

48. *Suffolk County Court Files.*

49. Robert Frost, "Mending Wall," in *North of Boston*, 2nd ed. (New York, 1915).

EPILOGUE

1. *Acts and Resolves of Massachusetts Bay*, vol. 11, *1726–1734: Resolves*, 149; vol. 7, *1692–1702: Resolves*, 415.

2. *Acts and Resolves of Massachusetts Bay*, vol. 2, *Province Laws: 1725–1727*, 353–57. Robin L. Einhorn, *American Taxation, American Slavery* (Chicago: University of Chicago Press, 2006), 53–78.

3. Richard R. Johnson, *Adjustment to Empire: The New England Colonies 1675–1715* (New Brunswick, N.J.: Rutgers University Press, 1981), 72–77. *Acts and Resolves of Massachusetts Bay*, vol. 8, *Resolves: 1730–1736*, 223; vol. 9, *1747–1752*, 130.

4. An example of this problem in an otherwise important argument is Robert Blair St. George, *Conversing by Signs: Poetics of Implication in Colonial New England Culture* (Chapel Hill: University of North Carolina Press, 1998), 239–40.

5. *Boston Records*, vol. 14, *Boston Town Meeting Records 1742–1757*, 240. Using the tax apportions reported in *Acts and Resolves*, I compared Boston tax apportionment with five other towns in the 1720s, 1730s, 1740s, 1750s, and 1760s. Boston went from paying 75 percent of what these other towns did to 69 percent after 1760.

6. Michael W. Zuckerman, *Peaceable Kingdoms: New England Towns in the Eighteenth Century* (New York: Knopf, 1970). For an insightful case study of Boston's struggles to fund its poor in the eighteenth century, see Nian-Sheng Huang, "Financing Poor Relief in Colonial Boston," *Massachusetts Historical Review* 8 (2006): 73–103.

7. Johnson, *Adjustment to Empire*, 1–140.

8. Judith Herman, *Trauma and Recovery: The Aftermath of Violence—From Domestic Abuse to Political Terror* (New York: Basic Books, 1997).

9. Fred Anderson, *A People's Army: Massachusetts Soldiers and Society in the Seven Years' War* (Chapel Hill: University of North Carolina Press, 1984), 111–41. See also Robert Middlekauff, *The Glorious Cause: The American Revolution, 1763–1789* (1982; repr. Oxford: Oxford University Press, 2007).

10. Leonard Richards, *Slave Power: The Free North and Southern Domination, 1780–1860* (Baton Rouge: Louisiana State University Press, 2000). Dinah Mayo-Bobee, "'Something Energetic and Spirited': Massachusetts Federalists, Rational Politics, and Political Economy in the Age of Jefferson, 1805–1815" (Ph.D. diss., University of Massachusetts, Amherst, 2007). Christopher Clark, *The Roots of Rural Capitalism: Western Massachusetts, 1780–1860* (Ithaca, N.Y.: Cornell University Press, 1980); Robert Dalzell, *Enterprising Elite: The Boston Associates and the World They Made* (Cambridge, Mass.: Harvard University Press, 1987); Thomas Dublin, *Women at Work: The Transformation of Work and Community in Lowell, Massachusetts, 1826–1860* (New York: Columbia University Press, 1976); Jonathan Prude, *The Coming of Industrial Order: Town and Factory Life in Rural Massachu-*

setts, 1810–1860 (Amherst: University of Massachusetts Press, 1999); Carl Siracusa, *A Mechanical People: Perceptions of the Industrial Order in Massachusetts, 1815–1880* (Middletown, Conn.: Wesleyan University Press, 1979); Janet Siskind, *Rum and Axes: The Rise of a Connecticut Merchant Family, 1795–1850* (Ithaca, N.Y.: Cornell University Press, 2006).

11. Morton J. Horwitz, *The Transformation of Law, 1780–1860* (Cambridge, Mass.: Harvard University Press, 1977); J. M. Opal, *Beyond the Farm: National Ambitions in Rural New England* (Philadelphia: University of Pennsylvania Press, 2008). For a twenty-one-year-old male to gain legal residence in the town, the rule was: before 1701, three months without warning; 1701–67, a year without warning; 1767–89, by approval of town meeting only; from 1789 forward, two years for property holders and ten years for others with five years of taxes paid. Jonathan Leavitt, *A Summary of the Law of Massachusetts Relative to the Settlement, Support, Employment, and Removal of Paupers* (Greenfield, Mass.: John Denio, 1810). *General Laws of Massachusetts*, vol. 1, 447; *Resolves of Massachusetts* (1811), 258, 259; *Resolves of Massachusetts* (1828), 228.

12. Oscar Handlin, *Boston's Immigrants, 1790–1880*, revised ed. (New York: Atheneum, 1969), 246, 253.

13. Edward Jarvis, *Traditions and Reminiscences of Concord, Massachusetts, 1779–1878*, ed. Sarah Chapin (Amherst: University of Massachusetts Press, 1993), 108–18. This shift is denied in Gloria Main, *People of a Spacious Land: Families and Cultures in Colonial New England* (Cambridge, Mass.: Harvard University Press, 2001), but is asserted in Philip Greven, Jr., *Spare the Child: The Religious Roots of Punishment and the Psychological Impact of Physical Abuse* (New York: Vintage, 1992), and Barbara Finkelstein, *Governing the Young: Teacher Behavior in Popular Primary Schools in the Nineteenth-Century United States* (New York: Falmer Press, 1989). See Barry Levy, *Quakers and the American Family: British Settlement in the Delaware Valley, 1650–1780* (New York: Oxford University Press, 1988); Kathryn Kish Sklar, *Catharine Beecher: A Study in American Domesticity* (New York: Norton, 1976); Ann Douglas, *The Feminization of American Culture* (New York: Knopf, 1977).

14. Richard H. Abbot, *Cotton and Capital: Boston Businessmen and Anti-Slavery Reform, 1854–1868* (Amherst: University of Massachusetts Press, 1991); William Hartford, *Money, Morals, and Politics: Massachusetts in the Age of the Boston Associates* (Boston: Northeastern University Press, 2001); Bruce Laurie, *Beyond Garrison: Antislavery and Social Reform* (New York: Cambridge University Press, 2005), especially 102–5; Joseph Conforti, *Imagining New England: Explorations of Regional Identity From the Pilgrims to the Mid-Twentieth Century* (Chapel Hill: University of North Carolina Press, 2001).

15. Nathaniel Hawthorne, "Main Street," in *The Snow Image and Other Twice Told Tales* (Boston: Ticknor, Reed, and Fields, 1852), 85.

SELECTED PRIMARY SOURCES

All primary sources are cited in full in the notes. Arranged geographically, this listing includes primary sources referring to and/or originating from governmental records on all levels in England and North America, 1600–1800.

GREAT BRITAIN

Calendar of State Papers, Colonial Series. London: Public Record Office, 1933; repr. London: Kraus, 1964.

Journals of the House of Commons. London: House of Commons, 1803.

An Index to Changes of Name Under Authority of Act of Parliament or Royal Licence and Including Irregular Changes from 1 George III to 64 Victoria, 1760–1901. Ed. W. Phillimore and E. A. Fry. Baltimore: Genealogical Publishing Company, 1968.

Great Britain, Public Record Office. *Naval Office Shipping Lists for Massachusetts, 1686–1765.* Microform edition. East Ardsley: Micro Methods, 1968.

Proceedings and Debates of the British Parliaments Respecting North America. Ed. Leo Francis Stock. 5 vols. Washington, D.C.: Carnegie Institution, 1924–41; repr. New York: Kraus, 1966–1970.

Town Records

Registers of Askham in the County of Westmoreland from 1566 to 1812. Ed. Mary E. Noble. London: Bemrose, 1904.

Parish Records of Hollesley, Suffolk. Accessible at Ancestry.com.

Horringer Parish Records: Baptisms, Marriages, and Burials, 1558–1850. Woodbridge, Mass.: George Booth, 1900.

Minutes of the Mayoralty Court of Norwich, vol. 15: *1630–1631.* Ed. William Sachse. Norwich: Norfolk Record Society, 1942.

The Register of the Parish of Walton-le-Dale in the County of Lancaster: Baptisms, Burials, and Marriages 1609–1812. Transcribed by Gerald E. C. Clayton. Wigan, UK: Lancashire Parish Register Society, 1910.

NORTH AMERICA

Connecticut

Public Records of the Colony of Connecticut, 1636–1776. Ed. J. Hammond Trumbull and
    Charles J. Hoadly. 15 vols. Hartford, Conn.: Lockwood and Brainard, 1850–1890.
*The True-Blue Laws of Connecticut and New Haven, and the False Blue Laws Forged by
    Peters.* Ed. J. Hammond Trumbull. Hartford, Conn.: American Publishing Com-
    pany, 1876.
The Earliest Laws of the New Haven and Connecticut Colonies, 1639–1673. Wilmington,
    Del.: M. Glazier, 1977.
Records of the Colony and Plantation of New Haven, 1638–1649. Ed. Charles J. Hoadly.
    Hartford, Conn.: Case, Tiffany, 1857.
Ancient Town Records of New Haven, 1649–1769. 3 vols. New Haven: New Haven Colony
    Historical Society, 1917–62.

Maryland

Archives of Maryland. Ed. William Hand Browne et al. Baltimore, 1883–97.

Massachusetts Bay Colony, Plymouth Colony, Massachusetts

Records of the Governor and Company of Massachusetts Bay in New England. Ed. Nathaniel
    Bradstreet Shurtleff. 5 vols. Boston: W. W. White, 1853.
Records of the Court of Assistants of The Colony of the Massachusetts Bay, 1630–1692. 3 vols.
    New York: AMS Press, 1973.
The Book of The General Lawes and Libertys Concerning the Inhabitants of Massachusetts.
    Cambridge, 1660. Facsimile edited by John D. Cushing. Wilmington, Del.: Schol-
    arly Resources, 1976.
The Acts and Resolves, Public and Private, of the Province of the Massachusetts Bay. 21 vols.
    Boston: Wright and Potter, 1869–1922.
Resolves of the General Court of the Commonwealth of Massachusetts. Boston: Adams,
    Rhoades and Co., 1811; repr. Boston: Dutton and Wentworth, 1828.
Massachusetts Archives. Microfilm edition. 327 vols. Boston: Commonwealth of Massachu-
    setts, Archives Edition; Stoughton, Mass.: Graphic Microfilm, 1973.
"The Ship Register, 1697–1714," vol. 7.
List of Persons Whose Names Have Been Changed in Massachusetts, 1780–1883. Boston, 1885.
The Massachusetts Tax Valuation Lists of 1771. Ed. Bettye Hobbs Pruitt. Boston: G. K.
    Hall, 1978.
Grand Summaries, Commonwealth of Massachusetts. Massachusetts Archives.

Valuation of Towns, 1784. Massachusetts Archives. Microfilm edition. Boston: Commonwealth of Massachusetts, Archives Edition, reel #162.

Valuation of Towns, 1786. Massachusetts Archives. Microfilm edition. Boston: Commonwealth of Massachusetts, Archives Edition, reel #163.

Massachusetts and Maine Direct Tax Census of 1798. Microfilm edition. Boston: New England Historic Genealogical Society, 1979.

Records of the Colony of New Plymouth in New England, 1620–1692. Ed. Nathaniel B. Shurtleff and David Pulsifer. 12 vols. Boston: White, 1855–61.

COUNTY RECORDS

Records and Files of the Quarterly Courts of Essex County, Massachusetts. Ed. George F. Dow. 8 vols. Salem, Mass.: Essex Institute, 1911–21.

WPA transcripts. Phillips Library, Peabody Essex Museum, Salem, Mass.

Essex County, Massachusetts, Probate Index, 1638–1840. Ed. W. P. Upham. 16 vols. Latter-Day Saints Genealogical Library, accessible at www.ancestry.com and www.genealogy.com.

Records of the Suffolk County Court, 1671–1680. 2 vols. Boston: Colonial Society of Massachusetts [*Collections*, vols. 29–30], 1933.

Suffolk County Court Files, 1629–1799. Microfilm edition. 1671 reels, 1,289 vols. Salt Lake City: Genealogical Society, 1972–73.

Suffolk County Deeds, 1629–1697. 14 vols. Boston, 1880–1906.

Suffolk County Deeds, 1629–1886. Boston, 1880–1919. Microfilm edition. 828 reels, 1,706 vols. Salt Lake City: Genealogical Society, 1969.

Suffolk Country Probate Records, 1641–1899. Microfilm edition. 380 reels, 769 volumes. Salt Lake City: Genealogical Society, 1969.

TOWN RECORDS

Beverly

Vital Records of Beverly, Massachusetts, to the End of the Year 1849. Topsfield, Mass.: Topsfield Historical Society, 1906–7.

Boston

Reports of the Commissioners. 25 vols. Boston, 1815–1900.

A Report of the Record Commissioners of the City of Boston, Containing the Records of the Boston Selectmen, 1736–1742. Boston, 1886.

A Report of the Record Commissioners of the City of Boston, Containing the Records of the Boston Selectmen, 1764–1768. Boston, 1889.

Report of the Record Commissioners: A Volume of Records Relating to the Early History of Boston Containing Miscellaneous Papers. Boston, 1900.

Record Commissioners, Marriages Recorded in the Town Records of Boston from 1700 to 1751, vol. 28. Boston, Municipal Printing Office, 1898.

Records Relating to the Early History of Boston Containing Marriages from 1752 to 1809, vol. 30. Boston: Municipal Printing Office, 1903.

"The 1677 Petition of the Handycrafts-men of Boston." Facsimile reprint, *Bulletin of the Public Library of the City of Boston*, whole ser. 12, no. 95 (Jan. 1894): 305–60.

Bridgewater

Vital Records of Bridgewater, Massachusetts, to the Year 1850. Boston: New England Historic Genealogical Society, 1916.

Vital Records of East Bridgewater, Massachusetts, to the Year 1850. Boston: New England Historical Genealogical Society, 1917.

Vital Records of West Bridgewater, Massachusetts, to the Year 1850. Boston: New England Historical Genealogical Society, 1911.

Cambridge

The Records of the Town of Cambridge, Formerly New Town, Massachusetts, 1630–1703. Cambridge, Mass., 1901.

Dedham

Early Records of the Town of Dedham, Massachusetts. 5 vols. Dedham, Mass.: Dedham Transcript Press, 1886–1968.

Early Records of the Town of Dedham, Massachusetts, vol. 3, *1672–1706*. Ed. Don Gleason Hill. Dedham, Mass.: Dedham Transcript Press, 1899.

Early Records of Dedham, Massachusetts, vol. 6, *1706–1736*. Ed. Julius Tuttle. Dedham, Mass.: Dedham Transcript Press, 1936.

Early Records of Dedham, Massachusetts, vol. 7, *1737–1766*. Ed. Benjamin Fisher. Dedham, Mass.: Norwood Publishing Company, 1968.

Vital Records of Dedham, Massachusetts 1635–1845. Ed. Robert Brand Hanson. Rockport, Maine: Picton Press, 1997.

The Deacon's Book: Records of the First Church, Dedham, Massachusetts, 1677–1737. Ed. Robert Brand Hanson. Bowie, Md.: Heritage Books, 1990.

Deerfield

Vital Records of Deerfield, Massachusetts, to the Year 1850. Boston, 1920.

Dorchester

Fourth Report of the Record Commissioners of the City of Boston: Dorchester Town Records. Boston: Rockwell and Churchill, 1883.

Gloucester

Vital Records of Gloucester, Massachusetts, to the End of the Year 1849. Salem, Mass., 1923.

Hardwick

Vital Records of Hardwick, Massachusetts, to the Year 1850. Ed. Thomas W. Baldwin. Boston, 1917.

Haverhill

Vital Records of Haverhill, Massachusetts, to the End of the Year 1849. Topsfield, Mass.,
1910–1911.

Ipswich

Ipswich Town Records, 1634–1662. Manuscript #21. Peabody Essex Museum, Salem,
Mass.

Malden

Births, Marriages, and Deaths in the Town of Malden, Massachusetts, 1649–1850. Compiled
by Deloraine P. Corey. Cambridge, Mass.: Harvard University Press, 1903.

Manchester

Vital Records of Manchester, Massachusetts, to the End of the Year 1849. Salem, Mass.: Essex
Institute, 1903.

Marblehead

Marblehead Town Records, *Essex Institute Papers* 69, nos. 3–4 (July–Oct. 1933): 207–329.
Vital Records of Marblehead, Massachusetts, to the End of the Year 1849. 3 vols. Salem, Mass.:
Essex Institute, 1903–1908.

Marlborough

Vital Records of Marlborough, Massachusetts, to the End of the Year 1849. Worcester, Mass.,
1908.

Newton

Vital Records of Newton, Massachusetts, to the Year 1850. Boston, 1905.

Oxford

Vital Records of Oxford, Massachusetts, to the End of the Year 1849. Worcester, Mass., 1905.

Rowley

Rowley Town Records. Rowley, Mass., 1894.
Vital Records of Rowley, Massachusetts, to the End of the Year 1849. Salem, Mass., 1928–1931.

Roxbury

Vital Records of Roxbury, Massachusetts, to the End of the Year 1849. Salem, Mass., 1925.

Salem

Salem Custom District Crew Lists. National Archives, Waltham, Mass.
Salem Quarterly Court Records. Phillips Library, Peabody Essex Museum, Salem, Mass.

Salem Town Records, 1634–1691. 3 vols. Library of American Civilizations, microfiche LAC20507.

Vital Records of Salem, Massachusetts, to the End of the Year 1849. Salem, Mass., 1916–1925.

Scituate

The Seventeenth-Century Town Records of Scituate, Massachusetts. 3 vols. Ed. Jeremy Dupertuius Bangs. Boston: New England Historic Genealogical Society, 1999–2001.

Vital Records of Scituate, Massachusetts, to the Year 1850. 2 vols. Boston: New England Genealogical Society, 1909.

Shrewsbury

Vital Records of Shrewsbury, Massachusetts, to the End of the Year 1849. Worcester, Mass., 1904.

Topsfield

Vital Records of Topsfield, Massachusetts. Topsfield, Mass., 1903–1916.

Watertown

Watertown Records. 8 vols. Watertown, Mass.: Watertown Historical Society, 1894–1939.

Henry Bond, compiler. *Family Memorials: Genealogies of the Families and Descendants of the Early Settlers of Watertown, Massachusetts.* 2 vols. Boston: Little, Brown, 1855; repr. Boston: New England Historic and Genealogical Society, CD-ROM.

New York

Abstract of Wills on File in the Surrogates Office, City of New York. 17 vols. New York: New York Historical Society, 1893–1913 [*Collections*, vols. 25–41].

The Burghers of New Amsterdam and the Freemen of New York, 1675–1866, in *Collections of the New York Historical Society For the Year 1885.* New York: New-York Historical Society, 1886.

Virginia

County Court Records of Accomack–Northampton, Virginia, 1640–1645. Ed. Susie M. Ames. Charlottesville: University Press of Virginia, 1973.

INDEX

ACKNOWLEDGMENTS

Chapter 4, "Political Fabric," is coauthored with Susan Ouellette of St. Michael's College. I thank her for permission to use the chapter in this book. I also thank her for her advice on agricultural matters and the advice of Emile Ouellette on carpentry and shipbuilding.

This project has taken some twenty years, so I can hardly remember all the people whom I should thank. In 1988 the American Council of Learned Societies provided me with a fellowship to study at the Institute for Advanced Study, Princeton, and it is there that I discovered that colonial New England contained more orphans than a household-led society could possibly accommodate. Subsequently, a Charles Warren Fellowship at Harvard University gave me the time to think about alternative models for colonial New England's social and economic organization while in contact with scholars like Bernard Bailyn, and Fred and Virginia Anderson. More recently, a year-long American Antiquarian Society (AAS) Endowment for the Humanities fellowship provided the time and access to the AAS's collections needed to develop a new paradigm. There I also benefited from access to an unusual scholarly community, led by John Hench and Caroline Sloat, that sponsored fruitful and often electric exchanges between literary scholars and social historians.

My colleagues at the University of Massachusetts have provided direction, especially Jack Tager's work on social protest, Marla Miller's work on female tailors and artisanship, and Bruce Laurie's work on Massachusetts labor systems and antislavery thought. All have read chapters of this project and provided insights. Gerald McFarland and David Glassberg advised me on why a book was needed to develop my ideas; John Higginson shared his insights on youth, labor, and violence, while being nothing but encouraging. My students at the university have provided a demanding, honest, and expressive audience for my arguments. The supporters and staff of the Du Bois

Library, University of Massachusetts, have offered me and other scholars a collection I believe is unparalleled for its size and accessibility on early Massachusetts. I thank Hugh Bell for helping to amass it. I want to thank Beth Campbell and James Kelly for helping me use the collections.

I also owe much to my friends at the University of Pennsylvania. Richard Dunn gave not only encouragement but also the emphasis and formulations on early American labor systems that inform this book. Michael Zuckerman gave faith, criticism, and encouragement for decades. Richard Beeman told me to take politics seriously, and I finally listened. The McNeil Center for Early American Studies under the leadership of Daniel Richter provided an informed audience for the project at its beginning and toward its finish.

I also owe much to the larger world of scholarship. In particular, I want to thank Lois Carr, Neal Salisbury, and especially Bertram Wyatt-Brown for telling me at crucial points that I was on the right track. I benefited from criticism of the manuscript at various stages. Richard D. Brown, of the University of Connecticut, gave the manuscript a helpful reading, as did many anonymous readers. I have hardly answered all their objections, but the book is far better for my wrestling with them. Daniel Richter also read the manuscript and provided valuable advice.

At the University of Pennsylvania Press, Robert Lockhart nurtured the last stages of this project with intelligence and care. He introduced me to Grey Osterud, a fine historian and editor, who improved the rhetoric and the substance. I cannot imagine a better developmental editor to give this book the best shape possible.

My family not only lived patiently with this project for almost two decades but followed their own projects with gusto and success, educating me in life itself and much else. Thanks and love to my stepmother, Maisie Levy, and sister, Susan Worth, and especially to my sons, Amos and Aaron. Jackie Wolf gave so much in so many ways that I can only dedicate the book to her to express in a small way my gratitude and love.